THE YOGIC DEEDS
OF BODHISATTVAS

THE YOGIC DEEDS OF BODHISATTVAS

Gyel-tsap
on
Āryadeva's *Four Hundred*

Commentary
by Geshe Sonam Rinchen

Translated and Edited
by Ruth Sonam

Snow Lion Publications
Ithaca, New York

Snow Lion Publications
Post Office Box 6483
Ithaca, New York 14851 USA

Copyright © 1994 Ruth Sonam

First Edition USA 1994

Composed by Gigantic Computing

Printed in the United States of America

ISBN 1-55939-019-0 (paper)
ISBN 1-55939-014-X (cloth)

*Textual Studies and Translations in
Indo-Tibetan Buddhism Series* ISBN 1-55939-000-X

Library of Congress Cataloging-in-Publication Data

Rgyal-tshab Dar-ma-rin-chen, 1364-1432
    [Bzi brgya pa'i rnam bśad legś bśad sñiṅ po. English]
    The yogic deeds of Bodhisattvas : Gyeltsap on Aryadeva's Four
Hundred / commentary by Geshe Sonam Rinchen ; translated and
edited by Ruth Sonam. -- 1st ed.
    p.   cm. -- (Textual studies and translations in Indo-Tibetan
Buddhism)
    Includes bibliographical references and index.
    ISBN 1-55939-019-0 (pbk.) -- ISBN 1-55939-014-X (cloth)
    1. Āryadeva, 3rd cent. Catuḥśataka. I. Sonam, Rinchen, 1937-.
II. Sonam, Ruth, 1943-   . III. Āryadeva, 3rd. Catuḥśataka. IV.
Title. V. Series.
BQ2765.R4813 1993
294.3'85--dc20   93-23972
                                                CIP

Contents

GYEL-TSAP'S COMMENTARY ON
THE FOUR HUNDRED STANZAS

Introduction

MĀDHYAMIKA AND ITS IMPLICATIONS

Mādhyamika philosophy, based on the Buddha's Perfection of Wisdom Sūtras, was expounded by the great Indian master Nāgārjuna and by Āryadeva, Buddhapālita, Bhāvaviveka and Candrakīrti who followed him. It calls into question the very basis of our perceptions and conceptual framework and challenges us to become listeners and observers in the truest sense. To examine reality and what underlies it demands openness, which the great Mādhyamika masters stress as an indispensable prerequisite for successful development. Because the principles of Mādhyamika contradict our normal conceptions, we need courage to engage in the honest and rigorous investigation of reality that it advocates and to integrate the far-reaching implications of what is discovered into our lives.

Mādhyamika is a philosophy of the middle way between two impossible extremes, that of reified existence and that of total non-existence, neither of which describes the true status of phenomena. Though the term "reified existence" is used to refer to a whole range of impossible modes of existence that preclude dependence, in general it implies objective existence independent of the observer's participation. "Non-existence" refers to the lack of any kind of valid status that can be ascertained. Statements, made by the Buddha and frequently repeated by the great Buddhist masters, that things are "like dreams and illusions" are often misinterpreted and taken to mean that things do not exist. Mādhyamika philosophy demonstrates through the use of reasoning that though things do not exist independently and concretely as they seem to do, they nevertheless exist: their mode of existence is a dependent one. Mādhyamika philosophy extensively investigates the nature of this dependence.

The purpose of Mādhyamika is not to outwit opponents nor to enhance intellectual agility in what at times might seem like a philosophical balancing act. Its true and only purpose is to help us gain happiness and freedom.

The Buddha taught that ignorance lies at the root of our difficulties and suffering. This ignorance is not merely a lack of understanding but a misconception of how things exist and, most importantly, of how the self exists. Although the self is merely attributed to the combination of body and mind, our misconception fabricates a self which is an exaggeration of what actually exists. We cling to this and seek the kind of friends, possessions and surroundings that we imagine will ensure the happiness of this fabricated self. Anything that acts as an obstacle becomes a source of frustration. We suffer because we are buffeted by desire and anger and experience the effects of the actions we perform under the influence of these turbulent emotions. We fail to find the peace, success and security we seek and instead encounter difficulties and disappointments. This pattern keeps repeating. Through a correct understanding of reality we can eventually gain freedom from this suffering by ridding ourselves of the misconception which lies at its root.

The quest for this understanding involves us in an enquiry to determine the criteria for existence and in an investigation of how we perceive reality. These two are connected since, from a Buddhist point of view, something can be said to exist only if it is validated or certified by cognition. What we see depends on how we look. Conventional and ultimate truths are thus established in relation to the kind of awareness which investigates them.

Following the guidelines provided by the Mādhyamika masters we come to recognize that our apprehension of objects as isolated and independent does not accord with how things actually are. An underlying network of interdependence connects phenomena. This does not mean that all phenomena are mutually dependent parts of a greater whole, such as is posited in the current "Gaia hypothesis," for instance, which views that whole as a living conscious organism. In Mādhyamika, interdependence refers to the fact that everything existent depends on its parts, on imputation by thought, and in the case of impermanent things, also on causes and conditions. Recognition of this extends and alters our understanding, and can eventually lead to a fundamental transformation of perception and experience.

Contemporary literature reflecting the discoveries made in new physics expresses and examines the need for a world-view based on a radically different paradigm. Responsibility for the present dilemmas which face the world is often attributed to the fragmented and reductive world-view fostered by what is now commonly referred to as the Cartesian-Newtonian paradigm. From that perspective the root of our problems would only be a few centuries old. From a Buddhist standpoint, however, the misconception that things exist in and of themselves is not just an intellectual habit acquired through education and social conditioning but has been present throughout all our rebirths. Things appear to exist from their own side and we instinctively assent to this deceptive appearance. All living beings who have not understood the nature of reality respond in this way. The misconception is thus an unconscious habit of which we can rid ourselves only by first becoming aware of how it operates. It is so deeply engrained that even when it itself has been eradicated, the imprints it leaves cause the false appearance of objective existence to persist until one becomes completely enlightened.

Reality is multilayered and multifaceted in that everything existent has a complex conventional nature as well as a fundamental nature. At present we not only distort and are unaware of this fundamental nature but also distort conventional reality. To understand the fundamental or ultimate nature of things it is first necessary to gain a correct understanding of their conventional nature. The extent to which we habitually distort this can be measured by our discomfort when confronted by a description of the conventional, denuded of all unrealistic expectations and fantasies. We react with resistance because our attitudes and life-style seem threatened, since much that we do is based on mistaken assumptions: that we will live long, that our bodies are clean and innately pleasurable and that there is a very real and independent self which must be protected and satisfied.

Even though in daily life we can of course practise altruism and restraint from harmful activity, which are the essence of the Buddha's teaching, his recommendations stand in sharp contrast to the generally accepted values and norms of most societies. While the prevalent economic stance fosters continual growth, greed and consumption, the way of life advocated by the Buddha, which is both conducive to and a natural outcome of spiritual growth, is opposed to materialism, inequity and exploitation of all kinds. In fact the Buddha's teaching addresses the very issues which are essential to the survival of our world and its inhabitants—the need for non-violent and sustainable life-styles based on respect and concern for life and on the cultivation of contentment.

The ultimate and conventional are intimately connected, since from a philosophical point of view the two truths are considered to be one entity and different aspects of reality. A correct understanding of both conventional and ultimate reality will have profound practical and ethical implications. Our misconception of the self lies at the root of our selfishness, the main obstacle which prevents us from developing genuine altruism. Understanding the true nature of the self and recognizing how much others suffer because of their misconception of it can enhance our compassion toward them. This then inevitably finds expression in our physical and verbal activities. A genuine concern for the happiness of other living beings will naturally include concern for the well-being of the environment in which they live. In Buddhist teaching these two are referred to as the "contents and the container," thereby stressing their close connection. Recognition that events depend on a constellation of causes and conditions, that our perception of events is not necessarily reliable and that our own and others' negative behavior is underlain by confusion and disturbing emotions can help us to become more flexible and more capable of resolving conflict.

The Mādhyamika point of view that nothing whatsoever has true or independent existence has an extremely optimistic dimension. The disturbing attitudes and emotions which at present dominate our mind and behavior are entirely dependent on causes and conditions of which the internal are most influential. This means we can transform our attitudes and emotional responses by learning to create the specific causes and conditions from which positive and beneficial states of mind and feelings arise. We can therefore enhance the quality of life on our planet in as far as we, the individuals who inhabit it, each accept our role in creating such a change and are willing to undertake a personal transformation which can only come about through conscious effort.

ĀRYADEVA'S LIFE

The following account is based on the traditional biographies of Āryadeva found in Bu-dön's (*bu ston*) and Tāranātha's histories of Buddhism in India[1] and on other written sources[2] as well as the current oral tradition.

Āryadeva is said to have been born on the island of Sinhala, today identified as Śrī Laṅkā. Legend has it that there was a fine lotus pool in the royal gardens of Sinhala. During the day the lotuses opened to the sun and at night they closed and bowed their heads. The royal gardener noticed that one of them had stayed closed for many days and reported this to the king, who came to take a look. Intuition told him that something extraordinary was about to happen, and he instructed the gardener to take good care of the lotus. Every day the king and his court went down to the lotus pool, but the mysterious flower remained closed for seven days. On the eighth day, while everyone was watching, the lotus began to open. Its thousands of petals slowly unfolded and they saw at its center a bright-eyed eight-year-old boy whose body was covered with dew. The king was amazed and delighted, and at once decided to adopt the boy.

Tāranātha dismisses this story as too fanciful and bases his account on, among other sources, the brief statement concerning Āryadeva's life which Candrakīrti makes at the beginning of his commentary[3] and which Gyel-tsap cites in his preface.[4] According to this, Āryadeva was the son and heir of King Pañcaśṛṅga. Acting on his strong wish to be ordained, he abdicated the throne and received monastic vows from the abbot Hemadeva. He completed a thorough study of the three sets of teaching (*tripiṭaka*) before leaving his native land to visit the temples and reliquary monuments of south India.

He met Nāgārjuna while the latter was still in King Udayana's country, and when Nāgārjuna went to Śrī Parvata, Āryadeva accompanied him, became his disciple and remained there to study with him. Some accounts say that his qualities were as great, if not greater than, his teacher's. Before they came face to face, Nāgārjuna is said to have sent an attendant to Āryadeva with a bowl of water representing the depth of his knowledge. Āryadeva responded by placing a sharp needle in the water to indicate that he could penetrate all that Nāgārjuna knew. In histories of the eighty greatly accomplished yogis[5] he is identified with Karṇaripā who surpassed Nāgārjuna in the practice of living off vital essences compounded into pills. While Nāgārjuna's compound could bring a withered tree back to life, Āryadeva's urine alone was so potent that when he mixed it with a little water and sprinkled it on a dry tree, the tree burst into leaf. During the time he remained with Nāgārjuna, Āryadeva gained many powerful attainments and proficiency in both orthodox and heterodox philosophical systems.

A Brahmin called Durdharṣakāla, whom Tāranātha identifies with Mātṛceṭa,[6] and who according to the Tibetan tradition was in fact Aśvaghoṣa before he became a Buddhist, had been going from place to place for twelve years challenging Buddhists in philosophical debate and contests of magical feats. Wherever he went, he defeated them and seemed invincible. He forced the monks to pay homage to Śiva, deprived them of their power and humiliated them, thereby causing discouragement and chaos in the spiritual community. His invincibility had been gained by propitiating Śiva, who had appeared to him in a vision. When Śiva asked him what boon he could grant, Mātṛceṭa answered, "Give me victory in debate." Śiva promised that no one born from the womb should ever defeat him.

When Mātṛceṭa came to Nālandā, the Buddhist monks feared they could not defeat such a daunting opponent and decided to request Nāgārjuna for help. They performed a rite of offering to the protector Mahākāla. During this ritual a crow emerged from the heart of a naturally formed stone image of the protector. A letter was tied to the crow's neck and it carried their plea for help to the south. When he heard of the request, Āryadeva offered to go in his teacher's place. Before allowing him to leave, however, Nāgārjuna stringently tested his prowess in debate by holding the opponent's position. Their debate continued for seven days during which Āryadeva demonstrated his expertise. Finally in his elation, he got carried away and triumphantly declared Nāgārjuna's defeat. This was inauspicious. Although satisfied that his student could hold his own, Nāgārjuna warned him that he would have to make a sacrifice on the way. He also added that if he did so without regret, what he sacrificed would later be restored to him.

Āryadeva travelled north with miraculous swift-footedness. As he was passing through a forest, he came upon a woman who was trying to accomplish certain powers and needed the eye of a learned monk to do so. He pulled out his eye in response to her entreaty, but felt regret when he looked back and saw her grinding it with a stone. He therefore remained one-eyed for the rest of his life.

On arriving at Nālandā, he found that Mātṛceṭa and his followers had, with the king's consent, taken charge and were keeping watch on all coming and going to and from the monastery. He secretly sent in a message to tell the monks he had arrived. Some accounts say he entered the monastery accompanied by a water carrier, while another version recounts that he took off his robes and put them in his alms bowl which he hid in a load of wood. Having daubed his body with ashes, he shouldered his load and entered the monastery as a woodcutter in the company of a cowherd.

There were several skirmishes before the real contest began. As the monks entered and left the temple each day, Mātṛceṭa had been counting their shaven heads. On the day after Āryadeva's arrival Mātṛceṭa was counting the monks and was just about to touch Āryadeva's head with the counting stick, when Āryadeva took hold of his hand.

"Where has this round head come from?" demanded Mātṛceṭa.

"It has come from my neck!" replied Āryadeva.

Mātṛceṭa then said, "There's a one-eyed man here who wasn't here before," and thought, "So this is the one who is to debate with me!"

Āryadeva then exclaimed:

> The Fierce One[7] has three eyes but does not see reality;
> Indra has a thousand but does not see reality.
> But Āryadeva with his one eye
> Sees the reality of all three realms.[8]

That was their first encounter. After some days Mātṛceṭa and his followers were performing ritual ablutions in the Ganges for the purpose of purification. Āryadeva came down to the river carrying a golden pot and ostentatiously began to wash the outside of it. Mātṛceṭa asked him why he was washing the outside when the inside was full of excrement. Āryadeva replied, "What is the use of washing your body with water from the Ganges, when you are full of defilements?"

On another occasion, Mātṛceṭa challenged Āryadeva as he had unsuccessfully challenged other monks in Nālandā, for none of them were willing to face him in debate. Standing in a doorway with one foot on either side of the threshold, he demanded, "Am I going out or coming in?" Āryadeva answered, "That depends on your intention." Another day Mātṛceṭa held up a bird and asked, "Am I going to kill this bird or not?" Āryadeva answered, "That depends on your compassion."

One night Āryadeva entered a temple and made his bed there. At dawn he went into the room where the *ghanti*[9] was kept and began to strike the wooden gong used for summoning the monks. The monks who lived in the temple tried to stop him, but he continued to strike it and also beat a great drum used for the same purpose. The king, hearing the gong and the drum, enquired what was going on. When he found out, he ordered the debate between the Buddhists and non-Buddhists to begin. The Buddhist scholars were seated on one side of the hall, the non-Buddhist scholars on the other. Two seats piled high with cushions were placed in the center for the contestants, while the king sat in the place of honor. One cushion was to be removed from the opponent's seat each time a contestant won a point.

Mātṛceṭa began by challenging Āryadeva to debate with a magic slate on which the correct answers appeared of their own accord. Āryadeva promptly dealt with this by spreading oil on it, which prevented the answers from appearing. Next Mātṛceṭa produced a debating parrot also capable of giving the right answers, but Āryadeva at once emanated a cat which killed the parrot. When Mātṛceṭa accused him of having done an ill deed, Āryadeva told him that he had left a meditator in Śrī Parvata whose task was to purify him of ill deeds. Mātṛceṭa demanded to know how one person could purify another's ill deeds. Āryadeva replied by asking how, in that case, the cat's action of killing the parrot could be his ill deed.

Mātṛceṭa began to feel that he had met his match. He then introduced another emanation, Sister Pandita,[10] the queen of debate. In no time Āryadeva had emanated a shameless holder of layman's vows who exposed his private parts to her. She withdrew at once, flabbergasted by such outrageous behavior.

Having been outwitted three times by his opponent, Mātṛceṭa now hoped that Śiva would come to the rescue and enter him. However Āryadeva had already secured the whole place with spells, surrounded it with dirty rags and placed some excrement[11] on the canopy which was over their seats in order to keep Śiva away. The debate then started in earnest. At the beginning the king and all who were present found it quite easy to follow, and there was agreement on whose cushion should be removed, as first the one and then the other scored points. Gradually, however, only the most learned scholars could follow what was going on, and eventually even they could no longer understand the subtle matters under discussion. No one was in a position to adjudicate nor was anyone aware that Āryadeva had actually succeeded in defeating his opponent.

Suddenly Mātṛceṭa transformed himself into a thousand-eyed Indra. Āryadeva outdid him by immediately transforming into a thousand-armed Avalokiteśvara. Next Mātṛceṭa spewed flames, but Āryadeva extinguished them by releasing a jet of water from his mouth. Then there was no longer any doubt about who had won. In the hope of escaping, Mātṛceṭa flew up into the sky. Āryadeva followed him, and as they flew higher and higher, he called to Mātṛceṭa that he would die if he left the atmosphere. Mātṛceṭa thought this was a ploy to prevent his escape. To convince him Āryadeva told him to unwind one tress of his matted hair and allow it to stream up ahead of him. It was instantly destroyed.

Āryadeva brought Mātṛceta back to earth and shut him in a temple. He went berserk there and began throwing the scriptures around. Suddenly he noticed a page sticking up in a strange way and stopped to read it. To his amazement he found it contained a prediction concerning him made by the Buddha[12] and felt enormous contrition for what he had done in the past. He gathered up the books and began to read them. The more he read, the more his faith grew, till finally he decided to take monastic vows. He studied with Āryadeva, became a great master of the three sets of teachings and was famed for his eloquent and mellifluous praises of the Buddha. Āryadeva remained in Nālandā for a long time but eventually decided to return to the south.

Before Nāgārjuna passed away, he entrusted the quintessential teaching to Āryadeva who continued to work extensively for the good of living beings, studying and teaching with his students in the areas around Śrī Parvata. Having received building materials from the mountain and forest deities, he built twenty-four monasteries which became centers for the Mahāyāna teaching. In Raṅganātha near Kāñcī, Āryadeva entrusted Rāhulabhadra with the teaching and passed away.

In his preface, Gyel-tsap mentions that Bodhibhadra's *Explanation of the Compendium of Quintessential Wisdom*, a commentary on Āryadeva's *Compendium of Quintessential Wisdom*, speaks of Āryadeva as having attained the eighth Bodhisattva ground.[13] This is also stated in other accounts. Nevertheless the passage in the *Fundamental Tantra of Mañjuśrī*, said to predict Āryadeva, states:

> Further a holy ordained one
> Will live in the town of Siṅhala.
> Though not an *ārya*, his name will be "ārya,"
> And he will live on the isle of Siṅhala.
> Refuting outsider opponents,
> He will vanquish the Forders' spells.[14]

It is probable that Āryadeva lived between the middle of the second and third centuries C.E. and that his literary activity can be placed between the years 225 and 250 C.E.[15]

ĀRYADEVA'S WORKS

The Tibetan canon contains many works on both sūtra and tantra attributed to Āryadeva (*'phags pa lha*). The catalogue of the *Tibetan Tripiṭaka*,[16] listing the contents of the Peking edition, attributes nineteen works on sūtra and tantra to Āryadeva and a different list of fifteen works on sūtra and tantra to *'phags pa lha*. The *Treatise of Four Hundred* is attributed to the latter.

According to modern Buddhologists there were two Āryadevas, and the works on tantra are not considered to be by the author of *The Four Hundred*. There appears to be a consensus, however, that at least two other works may be attributed to the author of *The Four Hundred*. One is a text called *The Hundred*,[17] found in the Chinese but not in the Tibetan canon, which, together with the works of Nāgārjuna, was considered of great importance for the study of the Mādhyamika system in China and Japan. The other is *The Hundred Syllables*,[18] an extremely terse refutation of Sāṃkhya and Vaiśesika assertions, attributed to Āryadeva in the Chinese canon and to Nāgārjuna in the Tibetan canon. *The Four Hundred, The Hundred* and *The Hundred Syllables* display a certain homogeneity in style and subject-matter which supports their attribution to Āryadeva.

Tibetan scholars, on the other hand, believe that Āryadeva was a practitioner of both sūtra and tantra, and that he could well have employed diverse literary styles when writing on different subjects. They therefore traditionally attribute many more works to him. In his preface, Gyel-tsap refers to the *Lamp for the Collection of Deeds*,[19] a Vajrayāna work by Āryadeva, pointing out that the author of our text mentions his level of attainment in it. Among all these works only some fragments of *The Four Hundred* and of a Vajrayāna text are extant in Sanskrit, which further complicates the task of attribution.[20]

The Chinese canon contains ten chapters of *The Hundred*, each consisting of five stanzas, and the last eight chapters of *The Four Hundred*. It also contains a translation of Dharmapāla's commentary on these eight chapters. In his commentary, Candrakīrti criticizes such a division of the work into two parts, but both Dharmapāla and Hsüan tsang, the Chinese translator of his commentary and of *The Four Hundred*, had no qualms about such a division, since their interest seems to have lain primarily in Āryadeva's refutation of heterodox views.

The topics covered by the translated portion of *The Hundred* closely resemble those covered in the second half of *The Four Hundred*. There are additional correspondences with other parts of *The Four Hundred*.[21] This has led to speculation regarding the authenticity of *The Hundred*, particularly in view of the fact that Candrakīrti, commenting on the title *The Four Hundred*, says the treatise was also called

The Hundred(s) and explains the reason for this.[22] In his commentary on Nāgārjuna's *Fundamental Wisdom* called *Clear Words,* he refers to *The Four Hundred* in the colophon as *The Hundred(s).*[23]

There are, however, also differences in the order in which the topics are presented and in the arguments put forward to refute the opponents' theses. Whereas *The Four Hundred* has only a few analogies in the second half, *The Hundred* contains many, perhaps added by Kumārajīva who translated the work into Chinese. Thus, *The Hundred* could be an independent work or a rearranged and abridged version of *The Four Hundred* with some additions.[24]

The topics treated in *The Hundred Syllables* are considered in the same order as they appear in the second to tenth chapters of *The Hundred.*[25] On account of its similarity in subject-matter to *The Hundred* and *Four Hundred,* the attribution of *The Hundred Syllables* to Nāgārjuna is considered mistaken.

THE FOUR HUNDRED STANZAS

The title of Āryadeva's work, *The Four Hundred on the Yogic Deeds,* is interpreted variously by different commentators.[26] In his commentary Gyel-tsap says, "Moreover, this treatise was written to facilitate understanding of the Master Nāgārjuna's assertion that these stages of the path of practising the yogic deeds enable those with a Mahāyāna disposition to attain Buddhahood."[27] In this context "yogic deeds" refers to the spiritual paths or insights to be developed by someone with a Mahāyāna disposition, i.e. one who has great compassion encompassing all sentient beings but who is not necessarily yet a Bodhisattva.

The title of Candrakīrti's commentary refers to the work as *The Four Hundred on the Yogic Deeds of Bodhisattvas.*[28] In this case the one who practises the yogic deeds is clearly identified as a Bodhisattva. The text is also said to be called *The Yogic Deeds* because it describes the deeds of a yogī or adept of the Middle Way. According to Gyel-tsap and Candrakīrti *yogic* describes the paths which these deeds constitute while in the latter case *yogic* refers to the kind of person who practises them.

In Tibetan the word for *yoga* is *rnal 'byor.* According to an interpretation generally accepted by Tibetan scholars, the first syllable is part of the word *rnal ma,* meaning real or authentic. It is sometimes also taken to refer to the actual or fundamental mode of existence of phenomena. The second part, in this context, belongs to the phrase *dbang 'byor ba 'gyur ba,* to gain control. Thus *yoga* may also be interpreted as gaining control over authentic paths or practices, which in this case refers both to paths necessary for the attainment of liberation by those who seek only personal freedom and to paths leading to highest enlightenment which must be practised by those with a Mahāyāna disposition.

In his commentary Gyel-tsap points out that *The Four Hundred* is a commentary to Nāgārjuna's *Treatise on the Middle Way* and not an independent text. This, he says, is evident from the fact that the usual expression of worship at the beginning has been omitted. Āryadeva's text is, however, not merely a commentary on Nāgārjuna's work, presenting the two truths through refutation of others' assertions and establishment of the Mādhyamika position. It also acts as a supplement. Nāgārjuna's *Treatise on the Middle Way* deals mainly with ultimate truth and concentrates on Buddhist philosophical systems, refuting primarily Vaibhāṣika and Sautrāntika tenets. Āryadeva supplements this by also directing his attention to non-Buddhist systems. He further supplements Nāgārjuna's text by explaining in the first half of *The Four Hundred* the extensive paths associated with conventional truths. In doing so he draws upon Nāgārjuna's *Precious Garland*.

Candrakīrti's *Supplement to the "Treatise on the Middle Way"* performs the same function but approaches it in a different way. Candrakīrti interprets Nāgārjuna's text from a specifically Prāsaṅgika-Mādhyamika standpoint and concentrates on refuting Cittamātra and Svātantrika tenets.

Like Nāgārjuna, Āryadeva is accepted by all proponents of Mādhyamika tenets as a model Mādhyamika because theses unique to the Prāsaṅgika position are not explicitly stated in his texts. Candrakīrti's *Commentary on the "Four Hundred Stanzas on the Yogic Deeds of Bodhisattvas"*, however, explains Āryadeva's text from the radical Prāsaṅgika-Mādhyamika point of view that phenomena do not have intrinsic or objective existence of any kind but are entirely dependent on other factors. He emphasizes the use of consequences as the way to generate the view of the Middle Way in the opponent.

Both Nāgārjuna and Āryadeva urge those who want to understand reality to approach it and induce direct experience of it through philosophical enquiry and reasoning. Although such direct experience of reality cannot be communicated as it is, reality is not considered ineffable and unknowable nor are language and conceptuality seen as hindrances preventing such an experience. On the contrary they are

seen as essential tools, since it is vital first to gain a sound intellectual understanding of the fundamental nature of things, their emptiness of true existence. The practitioner is thus engaged in removing misconceptions and becoming familiar with correct conceptions.

Since Nāgārjuna's *Treatise on the Middle Way* is concerned with
ultimate truth and does not explicitly deal with the extensive paths
practised by Bodhisattvas, the question of whether it is a Mahāyāna
text arises. Nāgārjuna establishes selflessness by adducing a multitude of reasons. A more limited approach is sufficient for practitioners who wish to rid themselves only of the obstructions preventing liberation; Mahāyāna practitioners who must eliminate obstructions to the perfect knowledge of all phenomena require an extremely powerful understanding of selflessness. This can only be
gained by employing such an extensive and varied approach. In order to develop this powerful perception of reality a vast accumulation of merit or positive energy is necessary. This is created through
the kind of love, compassion and altruistic intention cultivated by
Bodhisattvas.

By describing, in the first four chapters of *The Four Hundred*, the
four basic misconceptions which are responsible for our suffering in
cyclic existence, Āryadeva prepares the student to develop the altruistic intention. We need to understand our own suffering clearly
and recognize how actions based upon disturbing attitudes and
emotions fetter us to the cycle of involuntary rebirths. For unless we
feel a genuine distaste for this recurrent process ourselves, we will
not have heartfelt compassion for others who constantly experience
similar suffering, nor will we feel the love that wishes to ensure their
happiness.

Although Āryadeva does not explicitly indicate how overcoming
these four misconceptions—which distort our perception of what is
actually impermanent, suffering, unclean and selfless—leads to the
development of the aspiring altruistic intention, this progression is
implicit, since he continues by discussing the qualities of a Buddha
as well as the activities of a Bodhisattva. Gyel-tsap draws our attention to this progression toward the end of the second chapter.[29]

In *The Supplement* Candrakīrti uses another device for the same
purpose. Through the analogy of a bucket in a well or on a water
wheel, he demonstrates how we and others move helplessly from
one rebirth to another buffeted by different forms of suffering.[30] By
thinking deeply about this process with regard to ourselves, compassion for others will also arise. There is, however, one important

prerequisite if this is to happen, which is mentioned neither in *The Four Hundred* nor in *The Supplement*. We know from experience that the more lovable we find someone, the more unbearable it is to see them suffer. Therefore unless other living beings seem close and dear to us, their suffering will not stimulate the urgent wish to help them. There are two traditional techniques specifically designed to develop that feeling of closeness to others: recognizing the drawbacks of self-ishness and the great benefits of cherishing others by understanding that it is appropriate to do so for a great number of reasons, among which is our total dependence on them for survival. When this sense of closeness grows, it helps us to begin shifting the focus of attention in our life from self to others. The second technique involves recognizing the close connection between ourselves and others on the grounds that there is no living being who has not been our mother, father, brother, sister, son or daughter during a previous life. Candrakīrti's commentary on *The Four Hundred* emphasizes this fact.[31]

Both *The Four Hundred* and *The Supplement* deal not only with ultimate truth, but also with conventional truths in the form of the paths a Bodhisattva must practise to accumulate the merit which provides the vital foundation for a powerful insight into the nature of reality, capable of destroying the obstructions to knowledge of all phenomena. *The Supplement* does this by discussing the first five perfections of giving, ethical discipline, patience, effort and concentration in the context of the Bodhisattva grounds on which special facility in each of these is developed. Āryadeva's text, on the other hand, begins by discussing the misconceptions which someone with a Hīnayāna disposition must overcome in order to attain liberation and which must also be overcome by an aspiring Bodhisattva. Although the perfections are not all discussed individually, the text examines Bodhisattva conduct and how to overcome obstacles to it.

Through their diverse approaches to Nāgārjuna's text, *The Four Hundred* and *The Supplement* enrich our understanding of the conventional and ultimate.

The Four Hundred, like *The Treatise on the Middle Way* and many other great Indian basic or "root" texts, is written in an extremely terse style. The stanzas of the Tibetan version have four lines each consisting of seven syllables. In many cases some of these seven syllables only serve to preserve the meter and do not affect the meaning. This characteristic terseness gives the texts a flexibility and ambiguity which permits many interpretations. Tibetan scholars compare their elasticity to that of a musk deer's skin which can be stretched this way and that. Occidental scholars frequently find this ambiguity a source of frustration and search for a definitive meaning. Oriental scholars can more easily accommodate such a variety of interpretations since they take into consideration the different purposes which such interpretations might serve.

Terse and strongly negative statements, which abound in Nāgārjuna's and Āryadeva's work, speak of having "no view," "no position" or claim that a thing or the self "does not exist." These are open to misconstruction and indeed have been misconstrued in that the Mādhyamika position is regarded as a nihilist philosophy by scholars who take these statements literally. The commentaries, however, elucidate their true meaning.

BA-TSAP'S LIFE

The Four Hundred together with Candrakīrti's commentary on it was translated into Tibetan by the great translator Ba-tsap Nyi-ma-drak *(spa tsab nyi ma grags)* in collaboration with Sūkṣmajana. According to the *Blue Annals*,[32] Ba-tsap Nyi-ma-drak was born in 1055 in the upper district of Ba-tsap in Pen-yul *('phan yul)* in central Tibet. As a young man, he braved the long and arduous journey to Kashmir and remained there for twenty-three years, first becoming thoroughly conversant with the Sanskrit language, then studying the Buddha's teaching and translating works by the great Indian Buddhist masters. Among the illustrious teachers with whom he studied were Sajjana's two sons, one of whom was Sūkṣmajana.

Ba-tsap Lo-tsa-wa's greatest contribution lies in his translation and revision of a number of seminal Mādhyamika texts.[33] He translated Nāgārjuna's *Sixty Stanzas of Reasoning*[34] and revised a translation of his *Treatise on the Middle Way*.[35] He also revised a translation of his *Precious Garland of Advice for the King*.[36]

Of Candrakīrti's works, in addition the commentary on *The Four Hundred*, Ba-tsap also translated *Supplement to (Nāgārjuna's) "Treatise on the Middle Way"*,[37] the *Autocommentary on the "Supplement"*,[38] and *Clear Words, Commentary on "Treatise on the Middle Way"*.[39] The first two of these he initially translated with the Indian scholar Tilakakalaśa and the third with Mahāsumati. After his return to Tibet, Ba-tsap revised all three translations with Kanakavarman when the pandit visited Tibet at Ba-tsap's invitation.

Ge-shay Sha-ra-wa *(dge bshes sha ra ba)*,[40] one of the great Ga-dam-ba *(bka' gdams pa)* masters, sent many of his students to Ba-tsap to study Mādhyamika. Ba-tsap and his four closest students, known as the "Four Sons of Ba-tsap,"[41] did much to establish the Prāsaṅgika-Mādhyamika system in Tibet. Ba-tsap also taught the Guhyasamāja Tantra extensively and revised Rin-chen-sang-bo's *(rin chen bzang po,* 954-1055) translation of an important commentary on it by Nāgabodhi with which he felt dissatisfied.[42]

One of the first works Ba-tsap translated after his return to Tibet was a commentary on Vasubandhu's *Treasury of Knowledge* by Pūrṇavardhana.[43] He also translated Nāgārjuna's *Essay on the Mind of Enlightenment*,[44] and a number of other works on tantra. Of the works by Atīśa who was active in Tibet just before Ba-tsap's birth, he translated the *Great Compendium of Sūtra*.[45] Along with Muditaśrī he also revised a substantial part of Candrakīrti's commentary on Nāgārjuna's *Seventy Stanzas on Emptiness*. The exact date of Ba-tsap's death is unknown, but it was probably in the second decade of the twelfth century.

Contemplating the lives of the great translators, one marvels that they undertook the difficult journey from Tibet to India, in a number of cases even several times. Not only was the journey fraught with hazards, but the climate and conditions to which they had to accustom themselves were very different from those of their own country. Many aspiring translators who set out for India died far from home. The contribution to Tibetan civilization of those who survived is unequalled. Their thirst for knowledge of sūtra and tantra and of the commentaries by the great Buddhist sages of India which they could not acquire in Tibet, and their determination to then make that knowledge available to others through translation and teaching cannot fail to move and inspire the modern reader.

CANDRAKĪRTI'S COMMENTARY

The only Indian commentary on *The Four Hundred* which was translated into Tibetan is Candrakīrti's comprehensive *Commentary on the "Four Hundred Stanzas on the Yogic Deeds of Bodhisattvas"*, upon which all the Tibetan commentaries are based. Candrakīrti, who is thought by most Western scholars to have lived in the seventh century, mentions other earlier commentaries on Āryadeva's text. He criticizes a commentary by Dharmapāla which divides the text into two distinct parts, pointing out that to do so ignores the fact that the two truths are interconnected and integral parts of a whole. Candrakīrti further criticizes this commentary as a misinterpretation for its explanation of Āryadeva's text from a Cittamātra standpoint, since to Candrakīrti it is self-evident that Āryadeva's philosophical position accords with Nāgārjuna's and is thus Mādhyamika.[46]

Candrakīrti's explanation of the text uncompromisingly presents the Prāsaṅgika-Mādhyamika position that phenomena do not have intrinsic or objective existence of any kind but are entirely dependent on other factors. The very core of the Prāsaṅgika system concerns the compatibility of dependent arising and lack of inherent existence. Although things are utterly unfindable when subjected to scrutiny regarding their fundamental nature, this in no way impairs their ability to function. Indeed it permits them to function. When the ultimate, the emptiness of things, is understood correctly it supports the presentation of the conventional, dependently arising phenomena, and when the conventional is understood correctly as meaning that which arises in dependence on other factors, it supports the understanding that things which arise in such a way necessarily lack inherent existence.

In his commentary Candrakīrti explains that the analogies which illustrate every stanza of the first eight chapters and which he elucidates are drawn from an earlier commentary by the master Dharmadāsa of whom little is known.[47] These vivid and unusual analogies frequently reveal the seamier side of ancient Indian life.

Dzong-ka-ba (*tsong kha pa blo bzang grags pa*, 1357-1419) cites Candrakīrti's commentary on *The Four Hundred* many times in his *Great Exposition of the Stages of the Path* and clearly considered it and *The Four Hundred* as texts of major importance.

TIBETAN COMMENTARIES ON *THE FOUR HUNDRED*

Commentary to Āryadeva's "Four Hundred Verses"[48] by Ren-da-wa (*red mda' ba gzhon nu blo gros*, 1349-1412) is the earliest available commentary on *The Four Hundred* by a Tibetan author. It is a lucid and concise commentary which omits Dharmadāsa's analogies. Ren-da-wa does not always qualify the object of refutation as clearly as does Gyel-tsap nor does he give as great importance to the establishment of conventional truths. Since Ren-da-wa was Gyel-tsap's teacher, it is possible that Gyel-tsap had access to this commentary and chose to stress points which he felt required more attention, at the same time presenting the material in a different format. Ren-da-wa concentrates on the meaning of the text, closely following Candrakīrti's presentation. He is not as intent as Gyel-tsap on summarizing the arguments and formulating them according to the dialectic code.

There are instances where Ren-da-wa's interpretation is at variance with Gyel-tsap's more usual version of the Prāsaṅgika system based on Candrakīrti's works. For example, in his commentary on stanza 298 (chapter XII), Ren-da-wa says that on seeing reality, nirvāṇa is made manifest. He further specifies that from the path of seeing onwards the meditative equipoise of the Exalted constitutes nirvāṇa with remainder. The reason he gives is that to the Exalted in meditative equipoise the characteristics of products such as the aggregates do not appear, whereas nevertheless the meditator's aggregates do appear to an observer and have not ceased. Nirvāṇa without remainder is achieved when that Exalted person dies and attains a mental body in a pure land.[49] According to the more usual interpretation, a unique feature of the Prāsaṅgika presentation is that nirvāṇa without remainder is attained before nirvāṇa with remainder. "With" and "without remainder" are taken to refer to remaining appearances of true existence. Thus during meditative equipoise on emptiness an Exalted person does not perceive any appearance of true existence, whereas in the subsequent period such appearances are once more present.

Nāga King's Ornament for Thought, Explanation on the "Four Hundred on the Middle Way"[50] by Bö-drül-den-bay-nyi-ma *(bod sprul bstan pa'i nyi ma,* ca.1905?-1960?) also omits Dharmadāsa's analogies. It deals briefly with the first eight chapters and concentrates mainly on the second half of the text. Bö-drül's explanation of the stanzas also includes some unusual interpretations of the Prāsaṅgika system, a few of which are included here. He identifies conceptions of a self of persons as the root of obstructions to liberation and conceptions of a self of phenomena as the root of obstructions to omniscience, thus distinguishing between these two misconceptions on the grounds of subtlety.[51] He further says that Hīnayāna nirvāṇa is attained by understanding the person's lack of true existence while Mahāyāna nirvāṇa, complete enlightenment, is attained by understanding the selflessness of phenomena.[52] More usually the conception of a self of persons is said to arise from the conception of a self of phenomena, both of which are said to act as obstructions to liberation. It is therefore asserted that Hearers and Solitary Realizers must meditate on both the selflessness of the person and of phenomena in order to attain liberation.

Describing the Mahāyāna paths, Bö-drül states that both obstructions to liberation and omniscience can be divided into speculative and innate obstructions. The speculative ones in both categories are eliminated on the first Bodhisattva ground while the innate ones in both categories are eliminated gradually from the second ground onwards.[53] In this context a more commonly accepted interpretation of the Prāsaṅgika system is that there are speculative and innate obstructions to liberation. Such a division however is not made regarding obstructions to omniscience which are divided into the manifest and that part composed of seeds. Furthermore those who have a Mahāyāna disposition from the beginning do not start to eliminate obstructions to omniscience until they reach the eighth Bodhisattva ground when all obstructions to liberation have already been eliminated.

Bö-drül writes that the emptiness of one aggregate, one source and one element is the emptiness of all knowable phenomena.[54] Gyel-tsap emphasizes that the nature of emptiness is always the same but that the emptiness of one thing is not another thing's emptiness, otherwise when an inferential awareness cognizes the emptiness of a pot it would necessarily also cognize the emptiness of a piece of woollen cloth.[55]

In an interesting section at the end of his commentary on the sixth chapter Bö-drül explains how specifically understanding the true nature of the mind acts as the most powerful antidote to disturbing attitudes and emotions.[56]

Sea Spray, Explanation of the "Four Hundred on the Middle Way",[57] by Gah-tok Nga-wang-bel-sang (*kah thog ngag dbang dpal bzang,* 1879-1941), includes explanation of the analogies for the first eight chapters and is closely based on Gyel-tsap's commentary, which is used verbatim in many places. Gah-tok cites copiously from texts by Maitreya, Bhāvaviveka and others and also from Candrakīrti's *Supplement.* In addition he introduces his own personal interpretations, sometimes at variance with Gyel-tsap's. For instance, commenting on stanza 180 (chapter VIII), he states that to attain liberation one does not need to cognize that emptiness and dependent arising lack inherent existence because the conception of a self is the root of cyclic existence. Thus the antidote is to understand selflessness.[58] In saying this he makes a distinction regarding the subtlety of what is negated when the selflessness of persons and the selflessness of phenomena are cognized.

He appears to make a similar distinction when pointing out how stanza 190 (chapter VIII) shows the complete paths of persons of the three capacities. The first line indicates how, as part of the practices of a person of the least capacity, demeritorious action must be stopped in order to ensure a good rebirth. The second line shows the main practice of a person of intermediate capacity—the understanding of selflessness which is the training in wisdom. Implicit in this are the other two kinds of training, in meditative stabilization and in ethics, and thus everything necessary for the attainment of liberation is included. He then goes on to say that the third line encompasses all Mahāyāna paths of method and wisdom. It does this by indicating the basis of the view which is the non-inherently existent nature of the emptiness and dependent arising of all phenomena. This pacifies all elaborations, is free from all assertions and shows the true state of the two truths.[59] He thereby again distinguishes between selflessness of the person and selflessness of other phenomena on the grounds of subtlety. This is not in keeping with the more common interpretation of the Prāsaṅgika system where a distinction is made only with regard to the basis, i.e. persons and phenomena, but not regarding what is negated.

Gah-tok reiterates this point in his commentary on stanza 288 (chapter XII), when he says that usually emptiness is regarded as a mother, its understanding being the cause for enlightenment in any of the three vehicles. Skillful means is regarded as a father, responsible for the distinctions between the three vehicles. Since two kinds of selflessness were taught, it is his opinion that skillful means is not the only criterion for making such a distinction.[60] This implies a difference based on the kind of selflessness cognized by practitioners of a particular vehicle.

In an inspiring passage commenting on stanza 375 (chapter XV), Gah-tok emphasizes that it is foolish to imagine that we can begin with placement meditation and stresses the great importance of first doing analysis which employs reasoning in order to ascertain the ultimate properly. The stronger our ascertainment of the ultimate grows, the more the conventional will seem to resemble an illusion. The more skillful we become in establishing the conventional, the better we will be able to distinguish to what ultimate analysis is and is not applicable. Our activity and view will become pure and we will be able to overcome all confusion with regard to the two truths.

Compassion for all those who suffer through not understanding how things are will then arise. Although it is said by some that investigation is a fault, it is impossible to do true meditation without having heard and thought about the subject-matter sufficiently.[61]

Interlinear Commentary on the "Treatise of Four Hundred Stanzas"[62] by Shen-pen-nang-wa (*gzhan dga' gzhan phan chos kyi snang ba*, 1871-1927) draws primarily on Candrakīrti's commentary and illuminates Āryadeva's text in an effective and concise way.

GYEL-TSAP'S LIFE AND WORKS

According to traditional biographical sources Gyel-tsap Dar-ma-rin-chen (*rgyal tshab dar ma rin chen*) was born in 1364 at Ri-nang (*ri nang*) in the Nyang-tö (*myang stod*) area of Dzang (*gtsang*) where his father was an official. At the age of ten he was given the vows of a novice monk and received the name Dar-ma-rin-chen. He then learned to read and write and studied valid cognition, Maitreya's *Ornament for Clear Realization* and its commentaries as well as texts on higher knowledge and discipline with different masters but especially with the great Sa-gya (*sa skya*) master Ren-da-wa. Ren-da-wa also taught him Mādhyamika philosophy and gave him extensive instruction on tantra. Along with Dzong-ka-ba, Gyel-tsap became one of Ren-da-wa's seven closest disciples and is said by the Sa-gyas to have held the complete teaching of their tradition.

While visiting a famous Sa-gya monastery in Dzang Gyel-tsap distinguished himself by debating on ten different texts. At the age of twenty-five he took the vows of a fully ordained monk and then travelled to central Tibet where he gained a high reputation for scholarship and prowess in debate. Having defeated two Sa-gya masters, Gyel-tsap decided to challenge Dzong-ka-ba. When he arrived at Nyel-tö Ra-drong (*gnyal stod ra grong*) where Dzong-ka-ba was teaching, he entered the hall while the discourse was in progress without removing his hat in the customary way. Dzong-ka-ba noticed him but continued to teach. Gyel-tsap strode up to the throne on which Dzong-ka-ba was seated and began to mount it. Totally unruffled by this uncouth behavior, Dzong-ka-ba simply moved over to make room for him and continued. As he listened, Gyel-tsap heard many things he had never heard before from any other scholar and his arrogance began to subside. First he removed his hat, then he got down from the throne and seated himself among the listeners.

The desire to challenge Dzong-ka-ba had left him completely; instead he felt the burning wish to become his student. Dzong-ka-ba, it is said, saw in him a jewel-like disciple and accepted him. He taught Gyel-tsap the scriptures, explaining the most difficult points with stainless logic. This inspired Gyel-tsap with such faith and devotion that he decided he would seek out no other masters but would remain with Dzong-ka-ba for the rest of his life.

In due course he received the complete transmission and explanation of Dzong-ka-ba's *Great Exposition of the Stages of the Path*. Later he wrote the following in his *Gateway for Conqueror Children, Explanation of (Śantideva's) "Engaging in the Bodhisattva Deeds"*:

> Until I found the foremost holy [Dzong-ka-ba]
> I did not understand even one aspect
> Of the path that cuts through worldly existence,
> The Middle Way of dependent arising free from extremes.
> Whatever good explanations I possess
> Are all due to my master's kindness.[63]

When Dzong-ka-ba was establishing Gan-den *(dga' ldan)* Monastery, Gyel-tsap assumed responsibility for its construction and participated personally in the work as far as the rules of discipline for a fully ordained monk permitted. The main construction was completed in 1410. During this great enterprise and in all respects he carried out Dzong-ka-ba's wishes with perfect obedience and became his foremost disciple. Even during Dzong-ka-ba's lifetime, many of his students also studied with Gyel-tsap.

When Dzong-ka-ba was near death he gave his pandit's hat, his yellow robes and his cape to Gyel-tsap as a sign that he was to succeed him. In retrospect it was said that Gyel-tsap's act of mounting the throne with him during that early encounter was an auspicious indication that he would be Dzong-ka-ba's successor as holder of the Gan-den throne. He took on this responsibility at the age of fifty-six when Dzong-ka-ba died and held the position for thirteen years. Through his teaching and example Gyel-tsap led many toward liberation. During this period he spent the summer and winter months meditating and taught during spring and autumn. At the age of sixty-eight he installed Kay-drub Ge-lek-bel-sang-bo *(mkhas sgrub dge legs dpal bzang po, 1385-1438)*, Dzong-ka-ba's other closest disciple, as the next holder of the Gan-den throne. Gyel-tsap lived for one more year which he spent mainly in meditation. He died in 1432 at the age of sixty-nine according to Tibetan calculation.

Among Gyel-tsap's most important works are *Ornament for the Essence, Explanation (of Maitreya's "Ornament for Clear Realization")* *(rnam bshad snying po rgyan); Commentary on (Maitreya's) "Sublime Continuum of the Great Vehicle" (theg pa chen po rgyud bla ma'i ṭik ka);* a commentary on Nāgārjuna's *Precious Garland* called *Clarifying the Essential Meaning (snying po'i don gsal bar byed pa);* a commentary on Nāgārjuna's *Sixty Stanzas of Reasoning;* and a number of commentaries on valid cognition, including *Elucidation of the Path to Liberation (in Dharmakīrti's) Commentary on (Dignāga's) "Compendium of Valid Cognition" (rnam 'grel thar lam gsal byed).* He wrote a commentary on Asaṅga's *Compendium of Knowledge* called *Essence of the Ocean of Knowledge (chos mngon rgya mtsho'i snying po).* He also wrote many works on tantra.

GYEL-TSAP'S COMMENTARY

In his preface to the *Essence of Good Explanations, Explanation of the "Four Hundred Stanzas on the Yogic Deeds of Bodhisattvas"* Gyel-tsap provides a complete overview of the text and in keeping with a unique contribution made by Tibetan masters, he has also created a detailed outline which enhances the clarity of his work and serves as an aid to memory. This outline may be found in the appendix.

Gyel-tsap's commentary takes the form of a lively and pithy dialogue in which the words of Āryadeva's text are used to answer hypothetical and actual assertions, questions and objections. This device is effective since one frequently identifies with the protagonist's psychological or philosophical position, which Gyel-tsap states incisively and succinctly. Each attempt to secure oneself fails as irrefutable arguments demolish the successive positions one takes, making them untenable. This constant shifting of ground, expressed in the protagonist's search for new approaches to justify his position, is a defense against recognizing the truth which Gyel-tsap skillfully induces us to face.

In the second half of his commentary, Gyel-tsap usually identifies the system of tenets to which the opponent adheres, and refutes the opponent's arguments by means of a clear and concise statement of syllogisms and unwanted consequences. The pace is fast and there are few long or convoluted passages. This presentation is ideal for those with a facility in Buddhist logic, which in the scholarly tradition of Tibetan monasteries was considered prerequisite. For those with no training in this form of logic the arguments may at times appear somewhat elliptical and difficult to follow.

In accordance with the tradition of a "word commentary," Gyel-tsap includes all the words of Āryadeva's text, though not necessarily in the order in which they occur. He does not, however, merely explain them, but also elucidates the underlying meaning in the manner of a "meaning commentary."

Unlike Ren-da-wa, Gyel-tsap places a very strong emphasis on the valid establishment of conventionalities, repeatedly stressing that Prāsaṅgikas in no way deny the existence of dependently arising phenomena. There is a continual process of calibration between refutation of what in reality does not exist and establishment of what exists conventionally. In thus valuing the conventional he closely follows Dzong-ka-ba, who gave equal importance to appearances, namely dependent arising, and to emptiness, the lack of intrinsic existence.

Gyel-tsap always clearly defines the object of negation, stating precisely what kind of existence is being refuted. This acts as an important safeguard against negating too much.

He mentions at the end of the sixteenth chapter that he has given the analogies in an abbreviated form since he feared that otherwise they would take up too much space. In fact his rendition of them is frequently quite cryptic and in translation they have therefore been elaborated from Candrakīrti's commentary.

SUMMARY OF GYEL-TSAP'S COMMENTARY ON
THE FOUR HUNDRED

Although we do not think of our bodies as permanent, we are unaware of the subtle changes they undergo moment by moment. We are, of course, aware of the less subtle changes which take place and know that we must die. However, death does not demand our immediate attention, since it doesn't seem imminent. We therefore continue to act in accustomed ways, making plans that we are unwilling to relinquish.

This appearance of stability is an illusion which we take for reality. Everything we base upon it is based on a misconception, an erroneous conception of permanence, for in fact the psycho-physical aggregates are in constant flux.

The first chapter urges us to consider primarily the coarser aspects of impermanence which an ordinary person can recognize with relative ease. In his commentary Bö-drül points out that this first chapter presents four main topics for meditation on impermanence: the fact that death follows birth, that rise is followed by fall, accumulation by dispersal and meeting by parting. Subtle impermanence is introduced only briefly, since it is much more difficult to recognize.

The chapter begins by reminding us of our own impending death and its inevitability. Our reasons for not fearing death are all invalid. Ultimately we cannot ward off death, no matter what means we employ; we should acknowledge that our efforts to do so simply mask our fear. It is foolish to risk this life for prosperity and fame or endanger the happiness of future lives for the sake of the present one and its brief pleasures, since none of this brings lasting benefit. Life is just a succession of moments which lead relentlessly toward old age.

We notice and feel sad when those we love grow old, but fail to remember that the same is happening to us. Grief when they die is unreasonable, for death is the natural consequence of birth, and living beings come into and go from this world of their own accord. Our attachment to them is an unreliable emotion, contingent upon all sorts of other factors; it can vanish swiftly. We yearn for relationships and to meet with those who are dear to us, yet meeting is inevitably followed by parting. We should therefore willingly separate from all that we cling to at present, before such a separation is forced on us.

Here the emphasis is placed on recognizing that people, things and situations are not static. Clinging to them and wishing them to remain unchanged is unrealistic and a cause of fear. Once we are able to acknowledge this, our attachment and thereby our fear will diminish, and we will be better prepared to face both life and death.

The second chapter explains that even though the body clearly gives rise to disturbing attitudes and suffering, it can be used constructively and must therefore be cared for in an appropriate and moderate way. While we do not actually think of the body itself as pleasurable, we feel that if only the circumstances were right, we would be able to experience physical well-being and pleasure. This is an illusion, since we mistake what is in itself suffering and a source of suffering for a source of pleasure. Different forms of pain and discomfort are abundant and arise without any effort on our part, whereas pleasure is rare and difficult to induce. Most of the pleasure we experience requires effort and is due to external factors. It is therefore like something foreign to the body. Pain and suffering, on the other hand, frequently arise without any external provocation, indicating the body's intrinsic disposition toward them. In this way the coarsest and most easily recognizable form of suffering is identified.

However, what we normally think of as pleasure is not as it appears, for when it is intensified, it turns into pain. Protracted discomfort does not follow the same pattern; its intensification gives rise to increasingly severe pain. When the body is in the process of disintegrating, is vulnerable, composed of conflicting elements, impossible to keep comfortable, and when every action requires effort, how can it be considered a source of pleasure? Do we ever experience pleasure intense enough to override pain? We mistake the alleviation of discomfort for pleasure, but the relief experienced simply disguises the beginning of a new form of discomfort. How can the mere alleviation of pain be considered "real" pleasure? Thus what is conventionally regarded as pleasure is, in fact, the suffering of change, since it does not last.

The body, which is the basis for these experiences, is the result of past actions motivated by disturbing attitudes and is thus contaminated. Even when not overtly present, suffering may arise at any moment. This constant potential for suffering reveals that the body itself constitutes the pervasive suffering of conditioning. Without recognizing that the contaminated psycho-physical aggregates themselves are the subtlest form of suffering, we cannot develop the genuine wish to free ourselves from the cycle of birth and death. Understanding the other two kinds of suffering leads toward an understanding of this.

Desire for sensual pleasures is unlimited and inexhaustible; no matter what pleasures we enjoy or how long we indulge in them, our thirst will never be quenched. The only effect of sensuality is to increase craving. In demonstrating the undesirability of what we desire as well as the unwholesomeness of desirous states of mind, the third chapter focuses mainly on attachment to sexual pleasure and on the unclean nature of the body.

In doing so, discussion centers on women's bodies and on men's desire for women. To understand the reasons for this one must bear in mind that Āryadeva's text and the subsequent commentaries on it were addressed to what was probably an exclusively male audience consisting almost entirely of monks trying to observe vows of celibacy. Since most human beings are not naturally celibate, one can assume that preoccupation with women's bodies and sexual desire was a pertinent issue for them. One must also recall the status of women throughout recorded history, both in Indian society and most other societies, as possessions first of their fathers and then of their husbands. This enforced passivity, which deprived them of any effective rights within or control of the society in which they lived, left them with very limited means of exercising influence, among which was their sexual desirability. The almost exclusive emphasis on the uncleanness of women's bodies is perhaps a reaction to this manipulative power, since the arguments concentrate primarily on establishing the undesirability of sexual contact with women rather than on the undesirability of a lustful state of mind.

Since learning to apply the appropriate antidotes to disturbing states of mind is a lengthy process, beginners are usually advised to deal with disturbing attitudes and emotions temporarily by putting distance between themselves and whatever stimulates these states. Although reviling women's bodies and behavior may act as an incentive to do this and may to some extent counteract lust, it could also have the unwanted effect of provoking antipathy to women. Since Āryadeva was a practitioner of the Great Vehicle and therefore motivated by love and compassion for *all* living beings, one can rest assured that this was certainly not his intention. However, one wonders why the uncleanness of the male body is not stressed to the same extent, since contemplation of the true nature of one's own body can also effectively counteract sexual desire. In any case we must be wary of superimposing modern values and sensibilities on the text but instead draw from it what is relevant and view it within a historical context.

Āryadeva points out that none of the reasons we use to justify our desire, such as the other's attractive appearance, good qualities or behavior, are valid reasons. Moreover we often feel embarrassed when we recall how shamelessly we acted when we were younger. How can the obsessive state of mind associated with desire be called pleasurable? If desire itself were pleasurable we wouldn't feel compelled to satisfy it. On the contrary, it is like an itchy rash—scratching it brings temporary relief, but only aggravates it in the long run. Infatuation makes us act in ways we would normally find humiliating and causes unreasonable jealousy.

To counteract our misconceptions about the body, we must consider how it has come into being through unclean causes and produces unclean substances. Nothing can alter this unclean nature, no matter what artifice we employ. If it is possible to rid oneself of desire for other's bodies, how can we claim that the body really is clean? When we become aware of the defects of what is desired, desire for it ceases.

The misconception of the self, the view of the transitory collection as real "I" and "mine," is one of the fundamental disturbing attitudes. While the tenth chapter refutes various wrong views regarding the self, the main topic of the fourth chapter is pride and egoism, which are manifestations of the coarsest forms of this misconception. Since the effects of egoism and pride are most evident in the autocratic behavior of those who hold power, this chapter examines the conduct of kings to demonstrate that such feelings are unjustified and to show how they may be overcome.

A king has no reason to feel arrogant, since he is actually an employee of the people and holds his position by common consent. His apparent authority and control over the finances and activities of his country are an illusion, for he is invested with these powers by his subjects. It is totally unjustified for him to use the protection of his subjects as an excuse for irreligious actions. He may think that protecting them, their affairs and customs is a religious practice, but it is merely his duty and no more of a religious practice than any other form of work.

Kings are in a perilous position, for they are easily tempted to abuse the power they wield. Manuals on statecraft are frequently misleading, and the advice they contain is not necessarily for the well-being of the people. Violence toward enemies and harsh punishment of law-breakers is inadmissible behavior for a king; such actions will bring him only infamy and suffering.

Neither a royal birth nor wealth and power are reasons for egoism and pride, since all of these are unreliable and essenceless. Arrogance regarding such things is quickly deflated when confronted with the greater wealth, social standing and authority of others.

Understanding the actual nature of the contaminated psychophysical aggregates and how these four kinds of misconceptions regarding them create suffering makes us wish to free ourselves from cyclic existence. When we then consider the situation of others, which essentially is like our own, we will feel compassion, if a sense of closeness with them has been established. Development of this compassion gives rise to the aspiration to attain enlightenment for the sake of others. A profound personal recognition of the unsatisfactoriness of cyclic existence forms the basis for this, otherwise we will not empathize with them nor wish to help them.

If becoming a Buddha allows us to help living beings in the most effective ways, what is a Buddha like? The fifth chapter describes a Buddha's compassionate and powerful activity, whose well-spring is perfect knowledge. Every action is an expression of compassion. An enlightened being's power is so great that even the word "Buddha" can ward off death in that it implants a seed for the attainment of liberation from the cycle of involuntary birth and death. The Buddha Śākyamuni's silence in the face of certain questions shows his consummate skill resulting from omniscience, rather than demonstrating his lack of omniscience. A Buddha is thus the embodiment of perfected compassion, power and wisdom.

The quality of one's mind and motivation is crucial in determining the value of actions. Bodhisattvas control their minds so effectively that they never do anything harmful. Through the power of their conventional altruistic intention to attain enlightenment for the good of all others, actions which would normally be harmful are transmuted and become constructive and beneficial. The merit of Bodhisattvas who have developed the ultimate altruistic intention and attained the first Bodhisattva ground is then discussed.

The fifth chapter thus first describes enlightenment, mainly in terms of enlightened activity. Then, to encourage us to attain that state and to develop a profound appreciation of Bodhisattvas, it describes the transformative effects of the altruistic intention.

Implementing this intention through actions which benefit others requires imagination and sensitivity toward their needs and capacities. Bodhisattvas use others' natural affinities and interests as a means of gradually leading them toward an understanding of reality. The more obstinate and confused they are, the greater the Bodhisattva's compassion. Bodhisattvas do not hesitate to assume whatever role or relationship allows them to help most effectively, since this is their only concern. There is nobody with whom experienced Bodhisattvas cannot communicate constructively. This places a great responsibility on them, which they should never neglect. How can we fail to admire and appreciate them, when we realize their true qualities? Not to do so and to feel hostility toward them is a grave error.

A Bodhisattva's training consists of practising the six perfections and the four ways of gaining others' trust in order to help them. Practice of the perfections creates the two great stores of merit and insight which give rise to the Wisdom and Form Bodies of a Buddha. Āryadeva then discusses the merit created by giving, the first of the perfections. We should not be daunted by the magnitude of the Mahāyāna perspective nor by the profundity of its teaching, but should understand that perfect enlightenment is possible, since exceptional causes yield exceptional results.

However, while we are dominated and troubled by disturbing emotions, it is not possible to accomplish our own good, let alone others'. In the sixth chapter Āryadeva identifies these disturbing emotions which interfere with a Bodhisattva's practice. He also describes how Bodhisattvas treat those who are affected by these turbulent emotions. Unless we recognize these states of mind clearly, we will be unable to get rid of them. Mortification of the body cannot free us from them or from the contaminated actions instigated by them, for they are rooted in the mind. It is therefore vital to understand particularly how the three main disturbing emotions, desire, anger and confusion, operate and what their effects are. Our inability to recognize the suffering they cause when we are overwhelmed by them is, in fact, the greatest suffering, for it robs us of the incentive to get rid of them.

Since anger and desire require their own specific antidotes, students dominated by either must be treated accordingly. Moreover, confusion, anger and desire predominate at different times of the day; if we understand what stimulates them, we will be better prepared to counteract them.

Desire is extremely difficult to overcome, because initially it seems agreeable. This blinds us to its disastrous effects. Deeply ingrained habitual desire is much more difficult to counter than desire stimulated by a particular circumstance, for the latter can be dealt with by avoiding the stimulus. The destructive force of hatred and anger is far easier to recognize. At the root of all negative emotions lies confusion which can only be eliminated by understanding dependent arising. Eradicating confusion uproots the other disturbing attitudes and emotions as well.

Bodhisattvas must recognize behavior that indicates someone in whom desire, for instance, is predominant and should know how to help such a person. The destructiveness of anger and its inappropriateness as a response to harm inflicted by others are then examined. Such harm is the result of our own previous negative actions. By experiencing the fruit of those actions, their momentum comes to an end, while retaliating simply creates more negative karma. None of the reasons put forward to justify an angry response to real or imagined injuries are valid. Understanding the enormous ben-

efits of patience helps us to overcome anger, for patience and tolerance give rise to many remarkable accomplishments.

While it is important to apply the different techniques described
to overcome manifest forms of these disturbing emotions, we must
endeavor to gain a correct understanding of reality, for only this will
allow us to eliminate them completely. The sixth chapter thus clearly
describes how and why we should rid ourselves of the disturbing
emotions and help others to do so too, for these emotions act as the
source of our continued rebirth within cyclic existence.

The seventh chapter explains that the unbroken cycle of involuntary births and deaths is caused by actions based upon these disturbing emotions. Cyclic existence is fraught with suffering. Though temporarily we may be reassured by our youth, youth does not last long.
Soon we will be compelled to take another rebirth over which we
have no control since it is determined by past actions. Countless lives
have been thus wasted but at present we have a rare opportunity to
break this cycle. If the right conditions are assembled, we can certainly end our cyclic existence, but in the case of someone for whom
they are not assembled, no such end can be foreseen. We should
therefore recognize how difficult it is for the necessary teaching, a
competent exponent and a recipient with the prerequisite qualities
to come together at the same time.

Since contaminated actions are responsible for our continued rebirths, we must stop performing them, but our blindness to the horror of cyclic existence prevents us from doing this. In striving for a
desired result, we do much that is negative and that inevitably brings
suffering. No matter how much energy we invest, we can never be
certain our actions will yield the fruit we wish. What we do achieve
perishes of its own accord and is impermanent. Then why do we
waste so much effort?

Even good rebirths are unsatisfactory, because they too entail suffering, and it is a mistake to perform positive actions out of attachment to the pleasure, prosperity and authority one hopes to experience in them, for attachment will eventually bring suffering. Renunciation, not the acquisition of such pleasures and prosperity, is what
brings true and lasting happiness. Only by seeing the illusory nature of the world and of the pleasures it offers can we free ourselves
from suffering and attain the highest state of freedom.

The eighth chapter provides advice on how to make the student's
mind ready for instruction concerning the fundamental nature of all
phenomena. When the identity and causes of disturbing emotions

are examined, it becomes evident that the mind can be purified of them, and that we are not forced to continue taking involuntary re-births under their influence. The fact that most people have not got rid of them is due to their lack of interest.

Whether we attain liberation or remain caught in the cycle of birth and death depends on whether or not we gain a correct understanding of reality. Even a doubt which tends in the right direction causes the fabric of cyclic existence to begin disintegrating. Fear of empti-ness and prejudice make us cling to our habits and are obstacles to the attainment of liberation. Only a sense of strong antipathy to the process in which we are trapped can act as the necessary spur to at-taining freedom.

Although understanding the nature of reality is of such vital im-portance, it is not taught to everyone at once because most people are not ready to understand it. If it is misunderstood or rejected the consequences are extremely grave. It is therefore wise to proceed cautiously. First people should be discouraged from doing unwhole-some things and encouraged to do what is wholesome. They should then be helped to overcome gross misconceptions regarding the self and finally the subtler ones, until all wrong views have been eradi-cated. In doing so, great skill must be employed to ensure that stu-dents understand conventional reality correctly. Unless they do, they will not be able to understand ultimate truth. Even if we cannot at-tain liberation in this life as a result of receiving instruction on emp-tiness, it will leave a profound imprint which will bear fruit of its own accord in future. Just as our attachment to the body ends when we recognize that it is bound to disintegrate, all other disturbing emo-tions will end when we understand the dependently arising nature of all phenomena. Cyclic existence comes to an end when the causes that produce it are incomplete. Liberation is therefore possible.

Having gained a sound understanding of conventional truths as they actually are, and having purified the mind by developing the prerequisite Mahāyāna intention, the student is ready to be intro-duced to ultimate truth. Though there are as many permanent as im-permanent phenomena, the former are more subtle and thus more difficult to comprehend. This is because they cannot be apprehended by the senses, but only by mental perception and primarily by con-ceptual awareness.

Inability to identify correctly what is permanent leads to the mis-identification of permanent phenomena as functional things and of certain impermanent things as permanent. The ninth chapter presents a general introduction to the refutation of true existence by refuting that the self, space, time, particles and liberation are permanent functional things. This is shown to be a contradiction in terms. The refutation of misconceptions regarding the self and time are treated briefly here and at length in the tenth and eleventh chapters.

The protagonist in Gyel-tsap's dialogue argues that there are certain phenomena which are both functional and permanent and are neither produced by other factors nor give rise to effects, while others are causes but not effects. It is impossible for anything to be permanent and also a functional thing as is claimed, for whatever arises in dependence upon other factors, i.e. causes and conditions, is not permanent. A functional thing always has a cause, while that which is permanent never has. It is impossible for a functional thing to be neither cause nor effect, nor for it to be only a cause but not itself an effect as is claimed, since both are contrary to the normal operation of cause and effect. Anything that undergoes a transformation to produce an effect cannot be permanent, nor can a cause and an effect have totally disparate natures such that the one is permanent and the other impermanent.

To demonstrate that particles are not truly existent partless phenomena as asserted, it is shown that they have sides and do not therefore interpenetrate completely when they come together to form a composite. Moreover, in forming such a composite, particles could not move unless they had parts, such as a fore and rear. Since they undergo change during the formation of the composite, how can they be permanent? The causal particles no longer exist once the effect has been produced.

Finally the chapter presents a critique of liberation as asserted by the opponent. It cannot be a functional phenomenon as claimed, for then it should produce an effect, but none can be identified. This is followed by a discussion of what attains liberation and what exists as a basis when liberation occurs, in the course of which it is demonstrated that the basis cannot be a permanent truly existent self. Although the objects refuted in this chapter are those of speculative conceptions of true existence, their refutation is a vital step toward undermining the innate conception of true existence.

Both Buddhists and proponents of non-Buddhist systems in which there is a belief in liberation from suffering posit the self as the basis both for the states of bondage and release. The identity and attributes of this self, which is therefore of great importance, are variously described, supported by numerous reasons. Most of these systems identify the self as a permanent functional thing. The tenth chapter shows the impossibility of the self's existence according to these assertions.

Chapter ten begins by examining the self as asserted by the Vaiśeṣikas. First it is shown that gender, which differs from one life to the next, is incompatible with the idea of a permanent self. Nor can a permanent intangible self act as agent of the body's movements, as is claimed, since only something tangible can cause motion. A permanent self would be invulnerable to harm of any kind and would therefore not need to seek spiritual practices as a means of protection. Nor does memory of past lives establish the self as permanent, but demonstrates the presence of a continuum of consciousness, consisting of moments which arise in dependence upon each other. If, as is claimed, the person were mindless matter only capable of memory through an association with consciousness, then the person could not be permanent and unchanging, since it would first lack and then possess the faculty of remembering. Moreover something which at different times has different attributes, such as pleasure and pain, cannot be permanent either.

The Sāṃkhya assertion that a permanent conscious person exists is then examined and its flaws are revealed. What role would the eyes and other senses play, if such a continually conscious person existed? If the person is claimed to be potentially conscious, the self and consciousness could not be a permanent indifferentiable entity, for then the person but not consciousness would exist before an object is experienced. Any transition from potential consciousness to actual consciousness indicates that the person is not permanent.

The Naiyāyika assertion that there is a vast permanent partless self which is present in each being is next shown to be illogical, for then that which is one person's self should also be another's. This is followed by an examination of the Sāṃkhya belief that the creative force is unconscious matter with the capacity to produce virtue and nonvirtue but with no capacity to experience their effects. On the other hand if, as the Vaiśeṣikas claim, the self is the doer of actions and experiencer of their results, how can it be permanent, for this necessarily entails transformation from a previous state to a subsequent one.

A permanent self would be invulnerable to the suffering of cyclic existence and would therefore not need to seek release. Moreover, if the self were truly existent, how could giving up conceptions of a self be the means to attain liberation, as is claimed?

All these views are based on a failure to understand that impermanence does not necessitate discontinuation. Nothing impermanent can be produced from a permanent cause. Therefore a permanent self is not feasible as an initiating cause of activity. Products which undergo change moment by moment are neither permanent nor do they discontinue. This becomes clear when we correctly understand the nature of dependent arising, for though the cause ceases to exist when the effect is produced and is therefore not permanent, an effect has arisen from it and thus there is continuity.

Although the views of the self refuted in this chapter are speculative ones, their refutation is an essential step toward the refutation of the innate conception of the self. If the self existed as it appears to the innate conception, it would necessarily exist in the ways refuted here.

The eleventh chapter continues the refutation of truly existent time, begun in the ninth chapter, as part of the extensive presentation of the selflessness of phenomena with specific reference to products. By refuting the true existence of functional things existing in a temporal context, it is shown that time itself cannot have true existence. Time can neither be a permanent functional thing nor an independent cause, because past, present and future can only be posited in dependence on one another. Neither time nor that which exists within a temporal context can be posited except in relation to each other. Since time operates and can be understood only in relation to things and events, it is not an independent phenomenon. If it were truly existent, things could undergo no change and there would be nothing impermanent.

Time cannot be a permanent cause and produce an impermanent effect, for then cause and effect would be totally disparate in nature. If a thing existed while in the future, as is claimed by the Vaibhāṣikas, for example, the effect would already exist at the time of the cause, and there would be no sense in making any effort to accomplish a particular result. Effects would, in that case, exist without the need for causes, contrary to the normal operation of actions and their results. On the other hand, if future effects were utterly non-existent, it would be senseless to try to develop insights in order to overcome future disturbing emotions and suffering.

Refutation of truly existent permanent time indirectly also refutes the arising of effects from incompatible causes as well as their fortuitous production. In order to understand and gain conviction regarding the relationship of actions and their effects, we must gain a sound understanding of the relationship between the past, present and future.

The twelfth chapter begins by examining what qualities make one an ideal recipient for explanations concerning emptiness. Only benefit ensues for both student and teacher when the nature of reality is explained to such a person, while in the absence of these qualities the consequences may be grave.

Someone who is not genuinely open-minded and unbiased easily misunderstands even what has been well and clearly explained. Although one may accept that liberation can be achieved by overcoming faulty states of mind, lack of open-mindedness prevents one from recognizing that only a correct understanding of reality can eradicate them completely. To attain freedom we need to know the correct means. It is thus vital to gain conviction in the importance and efficacy of understanding emptiness.

Through lack of intelligence people follow misleading teachers and are led astray into thickets of wrong views. Lack of interest prevents one from finding out how to gain liberation and from following what was explained by the Buddha who taught from his own experience. The ideal recipient for instruction on emptiness is therefore openminded, intelligent and interested.

Ingrained ideas about the self prevent ordinary people from considering the possibility of emptiness and cause them to fear it. Since rejecting emptiness makes it difficult to attain a good rebirth and impossible to achieve liberation, great care must be taken to prepare students sufficiently and ensure that they are receptive, otherwise this precious teaching acts as a poison instead of a panacea. A skilled teacher can recognize who is and who is not ready to receive such instruction.

The text continues by briefly identifying the nature of reality and explaining its importance, since neither liberation nor enlightenment can be reached without understanding it. The purpose of studying it is soteriological and not to outshine opponents in debate. Nevertheless, since a person who understands emptiness cannot be beguiled by wrong views based on false arguments, understanding it automatically destroys the deceptive reasoning used by others. How could such a person not fail to pity those who are led away from the truth by false teachers?

Since emptiness is difficult to understand, and since the transformation of one's attitudes, the focus of Buddhist practice, is hard to achieve, many people choose physical and verbal forms of practice by which they hope to attain liberation. Although non-violence and emptiness are the salient principles of the Buddha's teaching and the only way by which a good rebirth and liberation can be attained, attachment to their own particular religious practices and views prevents people from adopting what the Buddha taught. The wise, however, are unprejudiced enough to adopt whatever is truly beneficial, even if it belongs to a tradition other than their own.

Our senses and what they experience exercise a compelling influence over us, because they seem to have true and objective existence. The thirteenth chapter demonstrates that neither the senses nor their objects exist as they appear. We feel that since objects are directly perceptible they must have true existence. In that case we should see every aspect of an object, such as a pot, at once. A pot, however, consists of many diverse elements of which visual perception apprehends only one, its visual form. Yet this visual form too has its specific components. Therefore the pot and its constituents are merely imputed to a collection of components and do not exist in and of themselves as directly perceptible objects. This same analytical procedure should be applied to the objects of the other senses: to sounds, smells, tastes and tactile objects. One will discover that none of these are truly existent directly perceptible objects. A closer analysis then follows which establishes that all the components that make up a composite, even particles, have parts. Thus each is simultaneously a component as well as a composite. An analysis of the relationship between the four elements and their outcome, visual form, is then made to demonstrate that they are neither inherently one nor different.

The senses and the process of perception are examined next. Confusing lack of true existence with total non-existence, the opponent argues that the Mādhyamika presentation of the senses contradicts what was said by the Buddha about the eyes and so forth being the maturation of past actions. In answer it is established that although nothing can sustain ultimate analysis, since nothing is findable when subjected to this kind of investigation, our experience confirms the existence of our senses and other phenomena. Thus the Buddha's statements about the relationship between actions and their effects are in no way contradicted, since such statements refer to the conventional existence of actions and their effects.

Inquiry is then made as to whether the eye and the visual perception it induces function simultaneously or consecutively, and whether the eye goes toward its object or not; if motion is involved, does it occur before, during or after perception? If no motion is involved, all objects should be equally visible. If the eye were an inherent instrument of perception, its function would not depend on a multitude of other factors. In that case it should also see itself. None of the factors involved in the process of perception—neither objects, sense organs nor their related perceptions—exist inherently or operate independently.

A similar investigation is then carried out in relation to sound and its perception. Does sound emit noise or travel silently? Is it apprehended through contact or not? Does the mind travel toward objects or not? What is the mind's relationship to the senses? How does recognition, which identifies things, function if things do not exist inherently? In each case the conclusion is the same: nothing is findable nor can be pin-pointed under such analysis. Yet events, objects and perception occur, arising in dependence on a combination of many different factors. Their dependent arising is a true source of wonder and amazement. We must learn to recognize that though things appear in one way and exist in another, and though they cannot be found when subjected to a scrutiny that examines their fundamental nature, they do exist and operate.

The fourteenth chapter continues by refuting extreme conceptions of reified existence and total non-existence. If phenomena were inherently existent, they should be independent and findable when sought by a reasoning consciousness analyzing their final mode of existence, but they are neither. Emphasis is placed on the fact that ultimate or inherent existence is being refuted, and that this should not be misinterpreted to mean that things do not have valid conventional existence.

The reason of not being inherently one or many is first presented concisely and then applied to refute non-Buddhist as well as Buddhist contentions, in order to establish that neither what is imputed nor its basis of imputation has true existence.

The text first examines whether the pot and its constituents, like visual form, are inherently one or different. If they were inherently one, there should be a pot wherever there is a visual form. Alternatively, if the pot possessed visual form as something inherently different from itself, the two would be unrelated, and we should be able to see a pot without necessarily seeing its form. In developing this examination of the relationship between the pot and its parts, the text investigates Vaiśeṣika contentions regarding the relationship between the generality "existence" and specific instances such as a pot. Here, the relationship between a substantial entity (a pot) and its attributes and the relationship between one attribute and another are also investigated.

According to Vaiśeṣika contentions one would not be able to say that the pot exists because the pot and existence are inherently different and thus unrelated. Neither could one say "one pot," since a substantial entity and its attributes, in this case the pot and one, are asserted to be inherently different and possession between them not reciprocal. When we say a "large pot" we mean its form is large. According to the Vaiśeṣikas, however, both form and size are attributes and one attribute cannot qualify another, with the absurd consequence that a large pot could not exist.

Next Sautrāntika assertions regarding the relationship between characteristics and what they characterize is examined.

The pot, for instance, is not a truly existent single unit, since it is composed of eight constituents with their own individual properties. Nor is it a truly existent plurality, since there is not a separate pot for each of these constituents. The opponent argues that the constituents combine to form a truly existent pot. Yet how do tangible constituents such as the four elements combine with intangible ones such as visual form? These constituents are merely components and not the compound itself. If the compound is not truly existent because it depends on its parts, neither are the components, since they too depend on their parts.

If form is truly existent, why is one form a pot and another not a pot? Surely all forms should be pots, since distinctions would indicate dependence on other factors. A pot comes into existence through causes which require their own causes. How can anything which is produced in this way be truly existent? When the components retain their own particular properties, how can their combination form a truly existent single unit? The components themselves, for instance visual form, depend on their constituents, such as the four elements; the elements too exist only in dependence upon each other and not in and of themselves. Even elemental particles, when subjected to similar scrutiny, are found to depend on their parts and other factors. Finally the "diamond fragments" reason, which examines production by focusing on the effect, and the reason of dependent arising are reiterated to establish lack of true existence.

Through inability to understand the continuum of things or the nature of composites correctly, they are thought to be permanent and truly existent. However their lack of true existence should not be confused with non-existence. Things are like magical illusions, in that they appear to exist in and of themselves, but actually depend upon each other. Inherent existence implies permanence which precludes the coming into existence of things in dependence on other factors. Only by understanding that things do not exist as perceived by conceptions of true or inherent existence can the seed of cyclic existence be destroyed. We should therefore make a great effort to develop a correct understanding of reality.

The fifteenth chapter examines the production, duration and disintegration of impermanent phenomena, since the opponent uses the existence of these characteristics to support the argument that products are truly existent. Refutation of inherent production is the main focus, since by refuting this, inherent duration and disintegration are automatically also refuted.

Inherent production of a thing is impossible, for neither that which exists nor that which does not exist at the time of its causes is produced by way of its own entity. Something non-existent at the time of its causes cannot come into being in and of itself. If it could, even totally non-existent things like rabbits' horns could occur, since they would not depend on producing causes. On the other hand, neither would something already existent at the time of its causes require anything to bring it into existence. A thing is not produced while it exists nor while it is non-existent. Since there is no other possibility, how can production be truly existent, for when analyzed nothing is findable.

Do the three characteristics—production, duration and disintegration—occur sequentially? They cannot, for they are simultaneous aspects of an on-going process, dependent on one another. Unless a thing has all three of these features, it cannot be a product.

Moreover inherent production is impossible, since things are not produced from themselves, i.e. from that which has the same nature, nor from that which has a different nature, for neither have inherent existence. Since production, duration and disintegration cannot be found to exist before, simultaneously or after that which they characterize, they cannot exist inherently. Even aging is relative, for a product constantly undergoes production. Are these characteristics and that which they characterize inherently one or different? If they were one, they would lose their specific identities, while if they were different, things could not be impermanent.

Something that already exists is not produced again, nor do its causes still exist, when it has been produced. The relationship between cause and effect and the function of production are then examined to establish their lack of inherent existence. The opponent argues that if neither that which is already produced and therefore functional nor that which is unproduced and therefore non-functional is being produced, what is being produced must be that which is presently undergoing production. To demonstrate that this too is not produced in and of itself, that which is in the process of being produced is next investigated. Is it identifiable as half produced or half unproduced? Does it already have an identity or not? Is it findable as something between the past and the present? Can one find anything, when an attempt is made in this way to identify the process of production and that which is being produced? What is the criterion for existence and non-existence? Through this investigation it becomes clear that causes and effects are interdependent, and that neither the arising of an effect nor the cessation of a cause occurs in and of itself.

The sixteenth chapter once more reviews the purpose of the text, explaining that it is to lead us to liberation by overcoming attachment to cyclic existence. Liberation can only be attained through a correct understanding of reality, but those who are unintelligent or lack sufficient instruction regarding the nature of reality fear emptiness. It is therefore essential to prepare their minds sufficiently by helping them to gain an undistorted understanding of conventional reality. Only then should the path which frees one completely from the cycle of involuntary birth and death be revealed to them.

The preceding chapters refute all kinds of innate and speculative misconceptions about things which are in fact empty of inherent existence. Some final arguments raised by opponents of the Mādhyamika system are examined. Opponents support the contention of true existence by pointing out that both the author, his subject-matter and the words he uses exist. Of course they exist, but not inherently as is claimed, because they depend upon one another. One can only refute another's thesis by convincingly establishing one's own, but the arguments advanced by the opponents to establish their theses remain as unproven as the theses themselves.

As part of a final refutation of extreme views, the fact that even emptiness lacks true existence is emphasized. If Mādhyamikas as-

serted that emptiness were truly existent, the phenomena which act
as its basis would necessarily also be truly existent. However since
no such assertion is made, how can these phenomena have true
existence?

This is followed by a summary of various refutations of true existence introduced in previous chapters. When one examines how fire
exists, whether a thing and its parts are inherently one or different
or how particles exist, one finds that nothing is truly existent but that
everything depends on other factors. From the point of view of their
fundamental nature, there are no distinctions among phenomena,
for everything is equally empty of true existence. If opponents of the
Middle Way nevertheless choose to dispute this thesis, they must
convincingly establish their own position, yet they repeatedly fail to
do so. Thus finding cogent arguments that invalidate the Mādhyamika position is obviously not as simple as they claim. If things
were truly existent merely because one says they are, they would,
by the same argument, be empty of true existence merely by saying
they are; words alone do not affect reality. It is a mistake to think
that things were previously truly existent, but are rendered non-existent through refutation of their true existence. They never existed
in this way in the first place. Neither the existence of reasons nor
analogies establishing emptiness can be used to support the thesis
that things are truly existent, for the reasons and analogies themselves lack true existence. Though things do not exist in and of themselves, they nevertheless exist. Through understanding their true
mode of existence, we can gain freedom.

THE TRANSLATION

The translation consists of Gyel-tsap's preface, Āryadeva's verses and
Gyel-tsap's commentary on them. Gyel-tsap's outline of the text has
been presented as a separate appendix to show the structure of the
whole and to serve as a guide to contemplation of the subject-matter. It therefore does not appear at the head of and throughout each
chapter as in the original work.

Each section of Gyeltsap's commentary appears with the relevant
stanza by Aryadeva and stands on the page as a discrete unit. These
units of commentary correspond to the sections of the outline in the
appendix which bear the stanza numbers.

In his commentary Gyel-tsap frequently refers to Candrakīrti's
commentary and additional references to it have been made

throughout this translation both in the form of interpolations and in the endnotes. Interpolated material is indicated by brackets or notes.

A section of further commentary has been placed after each of the first eight chapters. This additional commentary incorporates material from other sources which is relevant to the topic discussed within the chapter and suggests further approaches for contemplation and practical application. These sections have been written by the Venerable Geshe Sonam Rinchen and myself.

In translating Āryadeva's text, as little extraneous material as possible has been interpolated in an attempt to preserve something of the original style and to allow Gyel-tsap's commentary to demonstrate fully the function of the hermeneutic tradition. The presence of interpolated words is, for the most part, clearly indicated by the use of brackets.

There are some variations among the extant Tibetan versions of the text, for instance those included in the different editions of Candrakīrti's commentary. On account of the text's terseness and frequent ambiguity, during the process of translation the commentaries, particularly Gyel-tsap's, have been used to provide a key to the meaning. When a choice between different versions of a stanza has had to be made, the version used by Gyel-tsap has generally been preferred. Where such differences change the essential meaning, the alternative reading may be found in the endnotes.

I wish to mention Karen Lang's translation of the text, *Āryadeva's Catuḥśataka, On the Bodhisattva's Cultivation of Merit and Knowledge,* Indiske Studier VII, (Copenhagen: Akademisk Forlag, 1986, also published in India by Motilal Banarsidass). This is a new edition of the Tibetan of Āryadeva's text which includes variants as well as the surviving Sanskrit fragments, constituting less than a third of the four hundred stanzas. Her introduction gives a comprehensive list of previous editions and translations of the text, which has not been repeated here. She provides excellent scholarly and illuminating annotations which indicate the correspondences between Āryadeva's text and Nāgārjuna's *Treatise on the Middle Way* along with copious references to other Indian Buddhist and non-Buddhist texts.

Repetition is a stylistic device favored and used to good effect in Tibetan, and a particular word or phrase is often repeated many times within a short passage. While every effort has been made to preserve Gyel-tsap's style, English synonyms have occasionally been introduced to relieve the monotony of such repetition.

Since the Tibetan third person singular pronoun is not gender specific and therefore when, for instance, it refers to a Bodhisattva, there is no clear indication of the Bodhisattva's gender, the use of "s/he" and so forth has been avoided, both in the translation of Āryadeva's text and of the commentary, by using plural forms. This has only been done where the intended sense is not affected and statements of a general kind are involved.

May all who are oppressed by unhappiness and suffering
find freedom and lasting joy.

Acknowledgments

Work on this translation first began in 1978 after the Venerable Geshe Ngawang Dhargyey taught the whole of Gyel-tsap's commentary on *The Four Hundred* at the Library of Tibetan Works and Archives in Dharamsala, India. I attended this series of lectures and his excellent presentation stimulated my interest in the text. I was also present later in the year when he was requested to teach the first eight chapters again.

The text proved much more difficult than I had originally anticipated and I quickly discovered both that my knowledge of Tibetan was insufficient and that my understanding barely skimmed the surface of Aryadeva's text and the commentary which I was attempting to translate. But for the Venerable Geshe Sonam Rinchen's enthusiastic encouragement I would have abandoned the project. However his generous offer to help me understand the text gave me the courage to continue and so we began the long process which has finally culminated in this translation.

Paradoxically the more my understanding grew, the more evident it became how little I had actually understood. Thus having completed an initial draft after going through Gyel-tsap's commentary together, it was obvious that I needed to re-examine many parts. With infinite patience Geshe Sonam Rinchen undertook to explain the whole text to me once more, word by word. We simultaneously read Ren-da-wa's commentary and repeatedly consulted Candrakīrti and the other Tibetan commentaries mentioned earlier to throw light on passages which appeared ambiguous or difficult to understand. We examined the complete text together in this way many times. I asked innumerable questions, often repeating the same ones, in my attempts to cross the barriers raised by language and alien concepts. Geshe Sonam Rinchen responded with unfailing compassion and untiring generosity.

In 1988 His Holiness the Dalai Lama taught *The Four Hundred* as part of the spring teaching in the main temple in Dharamsala. This proved an inspiration to persevere with the translation despite the many difficulties it presented.

During our work together I have come to recognize that Geshe Sonam Rinchen is a great Mādhyamika master whose personal quest to understand reality has given him the ability to inspire others and to explain this most difficult subject with uncommon clarity. His simplicity, amazing openness and constant loving kindness are the evidence of his profound insights. Without his presence, encouragement and care this translation would never have been completed and so I thank and pay homage to him from the depths of my heart.

I would like to express my gratitude to all those who over the years urged me to complete this work. I particularly wish to thank the Tibetan interpreters at the Library of Tibetan Works and Archives, Dharamsala, India, who helped me at different times during the early stages of preparing this translation — Losang Choephel, Losang Dawa and Losang Gyaltsen.

I would like to acknowledge the inspiration and guidance provided by Professor Jeffrey Hopkins and Dr. Elizabeth Napper through their excellent translations of Mādhyamika literature and thank them too for their personal encouragement.

My thanks are also due to Dr. John Newman, the scholars Losang Shastri and Tashi Tsering at the Library of Tibetan Works and Archives and to Losang Norbu Shastri, editor of the translation unit at the Central Institute of Higher Tibetan Studies, Sarnath, India, for information on various subjects.

I am grateful to my editor, Susan Kyser, for her useful suggestions and for kindly and skillfully inserting all the commas that I blithely omitted.

Sallie Davenport, like a wish-fulfilling jewel, offered to process the manuscript when the task of preparing it for publication seemed overwhelming. It is impossible to express the deep appreciation and gratitude I feel for her unfailing graciousness, patience, meticulousness, valuable suggestions and friendship.

Ruth Sonam
Dharamsala, India
November 1993

Technical Note

The system of transliteration used, with minor modification in that no letters are capitalized, is that devised by Turrell Wylie (see "A Standard System of Tibetan Transcription," *Harvard Journal of Asiatic Studies*, Vol.22, 1959, pp.261-67).

The pronunciation system used is the "essay phonetic" system developed by Jeffrey Hopkins (see the technical note in *Meditation on Emptiness*, London: Wisdom Publications, 1983, pp.19-21). This approximates Lhasa pronunciation but is a simplified phonetic system in that it does not try to mirror all minor variations. Hopkins' system indicates a high tone in Tibetan by placing a macron over the consonant. These macrons have been omitted here for the sake of further simplicity although this diminishes the accuracy of the system.

Throughout the text, the first occurrence of any Tibetan name in phonetics is followed by the transliteration. In the following chart of the transliteration and phonetic systems, the Wylie transliteration is given first followed by its equivalent in Hopkins' phoneticization, where the placement of the macrons may be seen as a guideline to more accurate pronunciation.

ka	g̱a	kha	ka	gsa	ga	nga	nga or ṅga
ca	j̄a	cha	cha	ja	ja	nya	nya or ñya
ta	ḏa	tha	ta	da	da	na	na or ña
pa	ḇa	pha	pa	ba	ba	ma	ma or m̄a
tsa	ḏza	tsha	tsa	dza	dza	wa	wa
zha	sha	za	sa	'a	a	ya	ya
ra	ra	la	la	sha	s̄ha	sa	sa
ha	ha	a	a				

In Hopkins' system the nasals (see far right-hand column) are low in tone when not affected by a superscribed or prefixed letter and high tone when there is a prefix or superscription.

A subjoined *la* is pronounced *la,* except for *zla* which is pronounced *da.* *dbang* is phoneticized as *wang* and *dbyangs* as *yang.*

The letters *ga* and *ba* are phoneticized as *k* and *p* in suffix position.

Sanskrit names that were reconstructed from the Tibetan are preceded by an asterisk.

Gyel-tsap's Commentary on
The Four Hundred Stanzas of Āryadeva

with additional commentary by
Geshe Sonam Rinchen

༄༅། བཞི་བརྒྱ་པའི་རྣམ་བཤད་

ལེགས་བཤད་སྙིང་པོ་ཞེས་བྱ་བ་བཞུགས་སོ།

Prologue

Homage to the foremost excellent ones
who possess great compassion.

I pay homage at the feet of the Subduer, spiritual guide to
transmigrators,
Renowned on this earth as the Omniscient One,
Who for the very white collection of virtue, like the face of a
snow mountain,
Is as a wish-fulfilling gem, the source of everything desired.

With respect I bow at the feet of the Protector Nāgārjuna,
The only eye with which to see the Buddha's infinite teaching,
Who ascended to the state of omniscience, having fully
elucidated
The Subduer's doctrine, such as the ultimate essence of the
Conqueror's teaching and so forth.

I bow my head at the feet of the foremost father and son:
Who from early youth perfected learning,
Whose boundless knowledge and wisdom flourished,
Whose wisdom overcame the dangers of worldly existence,
And whose beneficent compassion removed the dangers of
peace;
The radiance of whose renown dispels the obscuration of
transmigrators.[1]

Though the thought of the great trailblazers[2] is hard to
understand,
I take pleasure in the exposition of this great treatise,
To increase my familiarity with the good explanation,
And also to benefit others who are fortunate.

Preface

This *Treatise of the Four Hundred Stanzas on the Yogic Deeds of Bodhisattvas* has four parts: (1) the title, (2) the translator's homage, (3) the text and (4) the conclusion.

THE TITLE

> In Sanskrit, *catuḥśatakaśāstrakarikanāma;*
> in Tibetan, *bstan bcos bzhi brgya pa zhes*
> *bya ba'i tshig le'ur byas pa,* The Treatise
> *Called Four Hundred Stanzas.*

Catuḥśataka in Sanskrit is translated as "The Four Hundred," *śāstra* as "Treatise," *kārikā* as "Stanzas," and *nāma* as "Called".

This treatise has sixteen chapters of twenty-five stanzas each, and almost every stanza explains one complete point. Since it has four hundred stanzas, it is called *The Four Hundred.* The original text was entitled *śatakaśāstra, The Treatise of Hundreds.* Candrakīrti's commentary says:

> Regarding this *Treatise of Four Hundred* [in the title
>   of the original text],
> The word "four" is not explicit;
> And in order to dispel ideas,
> It is called *The Hundreds.*
> Because it corrects conceptions,
> It is called a *Treatise.*[3]

The reason why the word *catuḥ,* "four," has been omitted is because it dispels countless hundreds of wrong ideas. It was therefore entitled *The Treatise of Hundreds* in view of its effect; Candrakīrti has explained the invalidity of an erroneous interpretation based on the word "hundreds" by another commentator. Candrakīrti, the author of the commentary, by discerning the intention implicit in the text, has clarified the meaning of this version of the title to preclude others' wrong ideas.

THE TRANSLATOR'S HOMAGE[4]

Homage to the Exalted Mañjuśrī

It says, "Homage to the Exalted Mañjuśrī" to indicate that the treatise deals extensively with the training in special wisdom by way of its focal object[5] and since this is its principal topic, it is a treatise of knowledge.

Presentation of the general meaning of the text begins by showing the author's greatness, then dispels another commentator's wrong ideas and briefly shows the actual intention.

SHOWING THE AUTHOR'S GREATNESS

Candrakīrti's commentary says:

> Since the Master Āryadeva is accepted as the Master Nāgārjuna's[6] main disciple, his system does not differ from the latter's system. The Master Āryadeva was a prince born on the island of Siṅhala. Later he gave up his royal inheritance and took ordination. Then, after travelling through the south of India, he became Nāgārjuna's disciple.[7]

Having gained a profound understanding of the teaching of sūtra and tantra, he practised their meaning and thereby definitely reached the state of Buddhahood in that very life. In *The Compendium of Deeds*,[8] written by the Master Āryadeva himself, he confirms attainment of the illusory body, exclusive to the Highest Yoga Tantra. The Protector Nāgārjuna asserts that the supreme accomplishment will be attained in the very life in which that illusory body is attained. While some versions say he attained the stages of completion, preceded by the stages of generation, this is accepted to mean the same as the previous assertion by Nāgārjuna. Thus there is also no contradiction when he is described as a common being during the early part of his life. The *Commentary on the "Compendium of Vajra Wisdom"*[9] states that this master attained the eighth Bodhisattva ground. There are many texts on sūtra and tantra by him which have not been mentioned here.

DISPELLING ANOTHER COMMENTATOR'S WRONG IDEAS

Candrakīrti's commentary says:

> A contemporary author[10] has divided this treatise into two.

Based on the word "Hundreds," the Venerable Dharmapāla divided the body of the text into two, calling the first eight chapters "Teaching Hundreds," and the last eight "Disputation Hundreds." Furthermore, he has interpreted the essential meaning in a Vijñaptivāda[11] way as a refutation of imaginary phenomena existing by way of their own characteristics. This is not the intention of the text. Candrakīrti's commentary says:

> Statements regarding individual textual systems by one who has taken them as separately defined textual systems are nonsense.[12]

This is because the text shows the stages of the path by which a person of Mahāyāna disposition proceeds to unsurpassable enlightenment as an integrated sequentially connected totality. Furthermore, since it clearly establishes the essential meaning to be dependent arising without even the slightest inherent existence, no doubt can remain as to whether truly existent other-powered phenomena are accepted in this system. In addition, those systems assert that there is no need to understand subtle selflessness in order to gain release from worldly existence, whereas the need to do so is clearly established in this treatise.

BRIEFLY SHOWING THE ACTUAL INTENTION

Objection: In that case there was no need to write the treatise, because the Master Nāgārjuna has explained this extensively in the *Fundamental Treatise on the Middle Way, Called "Wisdom"* and so forth.

Answer: There is no fault. When our own and others'[13] contentions are refuted in the Master Nāgārjuna's treatises by many collections of reasoning, it might be thought that the *Treatise on the Middle Way* is a treatise provoking debate, intended to defeat opponents. The *Fundamental [Treatise Called] Wisdom* and so forth are not intended to provoke debate, but to enable those seeking liberation to understand the suchness of things. Moreover, this treatise was written to facilitate understanding of the Master Nāgārjuna's assertion that these stages of the path of practising the yogic deeds enable those with a Mahāyāna disposition to attain Buddhahood. At the same time it shows that the attainment of liberation by persons of the Lesser Vehicle also depends on understanding the suchness of things.

Objection: Have these points, too, not already been explained in Nāgārjuna's *Precious Garland on the Middle Way* and so forth?

Answer: There is no fault. The text shows very clearly and extensively how development of the altruistic intention to attain enlight-enment must be preceded by abandoning the four errors of think-ing of the aggregates as clean, pleasurable, permanent, and as hav-ing a self; also by training in the attitudes of persons of small, inter-mediate and great capacity. Moreover, since the text is written in an explicit and comprehensive way that refutes others' wrong ideas about the Protector Nāgārjuna's presentation of the two truths, it is not superfluous. The omission of any expression of worship in the text is to indicate that it is merely a supplement to dispel doubts concerning the Master Nāgārjuna's text.

Question: How does this treatise explain the stages of the path?
Answer: Candrakīrti's commentary says:

> By exposing conventional things just as they are, it teaches the ultimate gradually.[14]

The first four chapters, showing that it is erroneous to consider the five aggregates as permanent and so forth, explain extensively how to develop aversion to cyclic existence. Of these, the first chapter shows that since the five contaminated aggregates are produced in dependence on causes and conditions, they are impermanent. By describing extensively how to meditate on death and impermanence, it shows the need to abandon the erroneous belief in permanence.

The second chapter shows how it is erroneous to consider what is contaminated and impermanent to be really pleasurable. Anything impermanent is unsuitable as a trustworthy source of one's ultimate well-being; moreover, the contaminated aggregates are vulnerable by nature.

The third chapter shows how to eliminate the error of consider-ing cyclic existence [i.e. the contaminated aggregates] as clean, for suffering always arouses aversion.

Since it is inappropriate to feel proud by considering as the self and self's that which is unclean and to be discarded, the fourth chap-ter shows how to eliminate the conceived object of pride, the dis-torted self which it is appropriate to negate.

Thus these four chapters, by properly training one in the attitudes of a person of intermediate capacity, produce the realization that to remain in cyclic existence under the influence of contaminated ac-tions and disturbing emotions is like being trapped in a pit of fire. Indirectly they show how those with a Mahāyāna disposition gen-erate the aspiring altruistic intention[15] that makes them want to at-tain Buddhahood.

Seeing that the attainment of Buddhahood depends on Bodhisattva deeds, once the practical altruistic intention[16] has been generated, the fifth chapter shows how to engage in such deeds.

Seeing that one cannot fully accomplish one's own well-being, let alone others', because of being dominated by disturbing emotions, the sixth chapter extensively shows how disturbing emotions arise and so forth.

Since objects such as visual form cause disturbing emotions to arise, remain and grow, the seventh chapter shows how to prevent the arising of overt disturbing emotions that focus on these objects.

Since objects such as visual form cause disturbing emotions to arise in those who do not understand their fundamental mode of existence and who have an incorrect mental approach, the eighth chapter shows how to make the students' mindstream receptive, with advice about developing the wish to get rid of disturbing emotions and about the appropriateness of approaching the meaning of reality even by way of a positive doubt, and so forth.

Thus the first eight chapters show how to ripen the mindstream fully, while the last eight show the stages of the paths dependent on ultimate truth, which destroy obstructions formed by disturbing emotions[17] and obstructions to omniscience.[18]

The ninth chapter shows how to meditate on the refutation of permanence to demonstrate that products do not have even the slightest essence of permanence.

The tenth explains internal and external selflessness. The refutation of permanent time is explained in the eleventh. The refutation of extreme views is extensively explained in the twelfth. In the thirteenth the absence of true existence of the sense organs and their objects is explained in detail. In the fourteenth chapter the refutation of extreme conceptions is explained by showing the feasibility of attaining liberation and enlightenment in that all dependently arising phenomena, which resemble the ring of light formed by a whirling firebrand, do not have even the slightest inherent existence.

The fifteenth shows extensively how to meditate on the production, abiding and disintegration of products as being empty of inherent existence.

The sixteenth, in showing the purpose of writing this treatise and eliminating remaining counter-arguments by misguided opponents, explains how to meditate on settling [the procedure between] spiritual guides and students. Thus the treatise extensively explains the stages of the paths that depend on conventional and ultimate truths by describing the focal objects of those paths.

The specific meaning of the text has two parts. The first explains the stages of the paths dependent on conventional truths. The second explains the stages of the paths dependent on ultimate truth.

Explaining the stages of the paths dependent on conventional truths has two parts. The first shows how the aspiring altruistic intention is developed after training in the attitudes of a person of intermediate capacity, by explaining elimination of the four errors. The second explains how to train in the deeds after developing the practical altruistic intention.

Chapter I

Abandoning Belief in Permanence

The main obstacle to generating effort to gain the paths of the Exalted[19] is the erroneous idea that what must die will not die. Therefore, by repeatedly thinking about death and impermanence, one should strive to attain these paths, for through familiarity with this it will be easy to understand suffering and so forth as well.

> 1. If those whose lord is Death himself,
> Ruler of the three worlds, without a master,
> Sleep soundly like true [vanquishers],
> What could be more improper?

Those who are not free from the bonds of the three realms because they cling to things as truly existent and who are in the power of the demon Death, have as sovereign the Lord of Death himself. He is the willing ruler of the Desire, Form and Formless Realms, and of the three worlds beneath, upon and above the earth. He has no master who commands him nor does he command others but carries out the punishment himself. He is therefore referred to as the "Lord of Death *himself.*" If those under such a lord, who like a butcher brandishing his sharp knife is engaged in killing, and on whom their life or lack of it depends, do not make effort to gain the paths of the Exalted with as much urgent care as though they were already marked by death or their heads were on fire, but instead sleep soundly like Buddhas and Foe Destroyers—the true vanquishers of the demon Death—and if they make no effort to find a means to avert Death, what could be more improper, reckless and foolish? Therefore, contemplating impermanence repeatedly, make meaningful use of your leisure and fortune.[20]

It is like the following analogy: A certain minister had failed to please some of the king's torchbearers. Wanting to have him put to death, the torchbearers misled the king, but the minister, suspecting the king might kill him, remained attentive. Like him, we must take care and pay attention to the means of avoiding Death's harm. It is also like a man who lost his way and, thinking himself safe in a very frightening hamlet in a desolate place, was overpowered and killed. Similarly, if one is careless in the hamlet of the three realms where the Lord of Death's punishment is near, Death will certainly overpower one. Therefore make effort to practise the excellent teaching.

Assertion: The Lord of Death who rules the three worlds does exist, but meanwhile one has life, which wards off death; so while one is alive, there is no need to fear death.
   Answer:

2.   **Those who are born only to die**
     And whose nature is to be driven,
     Appear to be in the act of dying
     And not in the act of living.

Life does not ward off death because it is doing death's work, since aging and dying are simply preconditioned by birth. All children are in the first place born to die and, like animals led to slaughter by the butcher, it is then their nature to be driven towards death without a moment's respite by aging, sickness and decline. Since they appear to be in the act of dying, like victims in the throes of decapitation, and not in the act of living, such life is not in the least trustworthy. In the life stories [of Buddha Śākyamuni] it says:

> Heroic ruler, from that first night
> Of entering an earthly womb from elsewhere,
> Starting then and day by day
> One approaches death unceasingly.

It is like a messenger who, threatened by a fierce and merciless king that he will be killed unless he arrives at a certain time, keeps on the move and never stops. Similarly, whatever one is doing, whether walking purposefully, strolling, sitting or lying, there is not even the briefest moment when one's life span is not decreasing. Therefore, do not trust life. A Parivarājakā[21] wanted to enter her home and was stepping over a camel lying at her door, when it jumped up in fright and bolted. Just as she was in its power, understand that we who have been born are in death's power. It is also like an assassin hired to kill someone but, unable to do so, he kills his employer instead. Understand that what has been born is performing the function of dying and not of staying alive.

Assertion: These days people live to be a hundred years old. When sixteen years have passed, there are still eighty-four during which one can first enjoy oneself and then try to ward off death. Since life is long, it is reasonable to place hope in it.

Answer: It is most unreasonable.

> 3. **You see the past as brief**
>   **Yet see the future differently.**
>   **To think both equal or unequal**
>   **Is clearly like a cry of fear.**

If you see the past as brief and see your future life span differently— not as brief but long—and act recklessly because of such an idea, it is quite unreasonable. *The Precious Garland* says:

> The causes of death are many,
> Those of staying alive are few, and
> These too can become the causes of death.
> Therefore always perform the practices.[22]

Since the time of one's death is uncertain, thinking of your past and future as equal in length, or unequal in that the past is short and the future longer, clearly indicates that you are frightened of death. It is like a man on a dangerous road who is afraid of robbers but pretends not to be afraid, crying out boldly and singing. It is also like a band of childish people who spent the night in one room in a town. They got up early in the morning and left after defecating in different parts of the room. Only several Brahmins remained behind. The caretaker scolded them, saying, "Remove this excrement, you louts, before I give you a thrashing!" It is said they each agreed to remove their own excrement but not the others'. To regard one's future life span as longer when the time of one's death is uncertain is as irrational as considering one's own excrement cleaner and thinking of it as "mine," when it is all equally filthy.

Assertion: Though one cannot be certain that the future will be longer, since death is common to all sentient beings, there is no need for one alone to fear it.

Answer: That is most unreasonable.

4. Since death is common to others too,
    You have no fear of it.
    Does jealousy cause suffering
    When only one is harmed?

If you do not fear death because it is common to other sentient beings too, and suffer when you see the Lord of Death harm one person and not others, but do not suffer when all are harmed, your suffering in the first case is through jealousy. Yet does death cause suffering through jealousy? No, it causes suffering by its very nature. Therefore its commonness does not prevent suffering and so it is proper to fear the fearful.

A householder suffered when the king initially collected a tax only from him, but when it was collected from everyone, he did not suffer. The suffering first was because of jealousy. The suffering of death is not like that, but like this: even if many of one's friends are in hell, it will not lessen the suffering.

Assertion: Death does not occur without sickness and aging. As these can be remedied by medical treatment and taking essential nutrients,[23] death need not be feared.

Answer:

5. Sickness can be cured and aging treated,
    Therefore you do not fear them.
    Yet there is no cure for the last ordeal;
    Thus obviously you fear it.

It is unreasonable not to fear death just because sickness and aging can be remedied a little. Though the fact that medical treatment can cure sickness and taking essential nutrients can somewhat retard old age may allow you not to fear them for the moment, there is no cure by any method for the horror of death, the last ordeal, and thus obviously you should fear it. It is like the following analogies: A king's rebellious minister bribed some envoys who had been sent, but when the king himself went to war there was no remedy. When a washerman spoiled some Brahmins' clothes, he was able with skill to reach a compromise, but when he ruined the king's robes, there was nothing he could do to please.

In Candrakīrti's commentary, an analogy of contrast is used: the stanza he cites says when a king's robes are ruined, a plea well-couched in poetic words of flattery may be effective. Death, however, cannot be affected by pleas.[24] This shows the need to be extremely apprehensive of death, for though even that which is difficult to remedy can be remedied, one cannot plead with death.

Assertion: Though death will come and common beings cannot avert it, one does not fear it because at present one has no certain knowledge of it.
　Answer: It is not difficult to know death.

6.　Like cattle intended for slaughter,
　　Death is common to all.
　　Moreover when you see others die
　　Why do you not fear the Lord of Death?

Death is common to all cattle intended for slaughter, and one sees another die; just so, death also is common to all of us ordinary beings. Moreover, you have seen many die, see many who are dying at present, and will see many die; how can you have no reason to fear the Lord of Death on the grounds that you have not seen death? Consider the fearfulness of death, and instead of acting like cattle for slaughter who, seeing the butcher kill one, wait to be killed themselves, be conscientious in the practice of virtue.

It is unreasonable to doubt the need for such great concern to avert death on the grounds that, though obvious, the time of one's death is uncertain.

7.　If because the time is uncertain
　　You think you are eternal,
　　One day the Lord of Death
　　Will do you injury.

It is extremely foolish to think you are eternal because the time of your death is uncertain. On account of death's unpredictability, you should be on guard from today. Though you may not have died today, one day the Lord of Death will do you an injury. Therefore, giving up all hope to stay alive, and thinking of death, be conscientious about practising the path to liberation. Just as all the people of a certain place went one by one in turn to be devoured by the ogre Bagasu, all who are born will die.

Assertion: Though death is certain here, fear of death arouses aversion only in the cowardly, while the brave, to gain reward and honor, are undaunted even when sharp weapons rain down on their bodies in battle. Thus, they do not fear death.

Answer: That is most improper.

8. If you consider future goals
    But not your waning life,
    Who would call intelligent
    Such selling of yourself?

If you avidly consider future goals such as rewards and honor, but do not consider the waning life of the body which is the basis for such acquisitions, you are acquiring rewards and honor by selling your life. Who would call you intelligent? No one; you will only be called stupid. Therefore examine whether you risk losing your life and do not be attached to rewards and honor.

The use of "having love" is not in accordance with the meaning of Candrakīrti's commentary.[25]

It is like the following analogies: A merchant's son who had many love affairs considered only his attachments to others, not their reciprocation, and was soon ruined by the merrymaking and quarrelling of his affairs. A Brahmin had three sons. During a time of famine he told his wife they should sell one son. A king's son heard about it and asked for the boy. Since their father held on to the oldest and their mother to the youngest, the middle one said to the king's son, "Since I am being sold, take me," which is like selling oneself.

Assertion: If it is reprehensible to sacrifice one's life for wealth, it must be alright to perform ill deeds to safeguard one's life.

Answer: It is not appropriate.

9. Why do you do ill deeds,
    Pledging yourself as security?
    Of course, like the wise, you must be
    Free of attachment to yourself.

Why do ill deeds for the sake of a little food and drink in this life, pledging yourself to experience great suffering later? Of course, like wise Foe Destroyers, you must be free from attachment to yourself.

It is like the prostitute who sold the swindler, and like being held as security because of drinking a lot of beer and not paying for it.

A swindler took advantage of a prostitute, using up all her savings but giving her nothing in return. Eventually she had two children by him. Not long after that a travelling merchant was staying in their home. She told the swindler, "The two of us will have more children. Let's sell our children to the merchant," and indeed, that is what they did. Later, when the merchant was about to leave, the prostitute told the swindler, "I will go and stay in the merchant's home as security and you take the two children. Be sure to wash and feed the youngest one properly." The swindler replied, "No, you take the two children and I will stay in the merchant's home as security." She agreed and, having retrieved the children, went and hid in a remote place. On the second day the merchant tied up the swindler and left with him for home. Similarly, childish people do ill deeds, pledging themselves as security; they alone will experience the maturation.[26]

Someone with no money went to a drinking house and, promising to pay, drank a lot of beer. However, when he did not pay, he was kept there and made to suffer.[27]

It is unreasonable to sell oneself for the sake of this life by performing ill deeds in the hope of staying alive long.

> 10. No matter whose life, it does not
> Differ from the moments of mind.
> This people certainly do not perceive.
> Thus it is rare to know the self.

Since the nature of functional things is not to remain unchanged for a second moment, the life of any sentient being, no matter who, does not differ from the individual moments of mind [whose momentary changes are not too difficult to understand—the mind quickly moves from one focal object to another, as when rapidly reciting the alphabet[28]]. People in the grip of causes for the misconception of permanence, [mistaking as alike the sequence of unalike moments of a product that occur without interruption,[29]] certainly do not perceive this. Thus, in the world it is rare to know the nature of the self, so make effort to meditate on subtle impermanence.

It is like looking for clothes that fell into a river a long time ago at the spot where they fell into the water, and like the swiftness of the son of the gods Aśvaka, which was unrivalled by any of the gods and others that travel in the sky. Nothing is briefer than this life, disintegrating moment by moment.

Assertion: Being alive consists of a series of brief moments, but since the continuity is uninterrupted, life is long. Therefore, attachment to it is reasonable.

Answer: That is an erroneous idea.

11. You would like to live long
    But dislike old age.
    Amazing! Your behavior
    Seems right to people like you.

If you would like to live a long life but dislike old age with its white hair and wrinkles, it is pitiful and amazing. Your contradictory behavior seems right only to unwise people like you, not to the wise. Since you don't want old age, don't be attached to the continuation of life.

It is like some youths who made fun of an old man sitting in a park. "You look old," they jeered, but they were hoping to live a long time.

Assertion: Though one does not want to age and die, when these two happen to one they are not as much a cause for grief as when they happen to one's son. It is therefore appropriate to grieve at the death of one's son and others.

Answer: It is inappropriate.

12. Why do you grieve at death
    On account of your son and others?
    When the one that laments is a victim,
    How is that not reprehensible?

When it is fitting for you, a person in the Lord of Death's power who does ill deeds, to grieve about dying, why do you grieve on account of your son's and others' deaths while neglecting to remember your own? If one laments about another person's death, when one is a victim of the Lord of Death oneself but ignores it, how would one not deserve censure from the wise? Since it is only reprehensible, endeavor to remember your own death.

A Brahmin's servant wearing a peacock's feather as a badge recognized others' servants by this sign, but did not think of herself as a servant. Forgetting it is one's own nature to die, but lamenting that one's son is dead, is like that.

Assertion: Though it is proper to grieve about dying, it is nevertheless reasonable to grieve when the son one has considered one's own goes to the next world without asking.

Answer: Even that is not admissible.

13. If, unrequested, someone has
    Become your son, it is not
    Unreasonable if he leaves
    Without having asked.

If someone whom you have not requested to become your son does so through the force of his own actions, it is not unreasonable if he leaves without having asked his father whether he may go, because it is his nature to come and go arbitrarily.

It is like the following analogy: A girl who had newly arrived agreed to be the wife of a man staying in a park. When she later left without having asked him, he grieved. Someone inquired whether he knew from where she had come. He replied that he didn't. "Then since she left just as she came, why grieve?" It is unreasonable to grieve over the dead when one does not know from where they have come nor where they are going.

14. Only because of your confusion
    You did not notice your son's [indications].
    His enthusiasm to go
    Is shown by his growing old.

Perhaps it is not that he did not ask to go, only that, because of your confusion, you did not notice when your son showed indications of going. His enthusiasm to go to the next world is implicitly shown by his growing old with white hair and wrinkles.

It is like the following analogy: A father sent his only son on an assignment, but grieved when he was about to go. Similarly, having been eager to produce a son, it is unreasonable to grieve at death, the outcome of having been born.

Objection: Although he showed his enthusiasm to go, great attachment to one's son causes one to grieve.

Answer: Attachment is not appropriate.

15. A son does not love [his father]
    As much as his father loves him.
    People in the world go down;
    Thus, a high rebirth is hard to find.

A son does not love his father as much as a father loves his son. Ordinary people feel attracted to the young, like their children, but the young do not feel as attracted to their elders. Hence those such as one's son, whose upbringing has entailed hundreds of hardships, because of their weak sense of gratitude will reject their father and so forth in an instant. One's actions precipitate one downwards like that attraction [since a mind directed by attachment runs downhill like water[30]]. Therefore most people in the world go down to the hells and so forth. Thus, no need to mention liberation, even a high rebirth is hard to find, so willingly respect your elders.

It is like the asafoetida[31] and the sound of a bell which are gradually used up and dissipate. Similarly, lack of gratitude for what has been done destroys one's practices, making even a high rebirth hard to find.

Taking a small amount of asafoetida at a time from the traders' source, it was used up little by little until all of it had been dissipated. The sound of a bell gradually dies away. Similarly, ingratitude and other kinds of bad behavior gradually destroy one's practices.[32]

Moreover, attachment to an obedient or disobedient son, whichever, is inadmissible.

> 16. When he is disobedient
>   No one will call him lovable.
>   In that case attachment is
>   Nothing but a transaction.

No one will call a son who disobeys his father lovable.

Objection: But one is attached to an obedient one.

Answer: In that case the attachment is nothing but a business transaction and is not due to your son.

It is like the following analogy: A king had a very beloved son who died. His ministers informed him that his son had rebelled, which upset the king and he made plans to kill his son. They then told him that he had died. The king was pleased [and beat a great drum for joy. Likewise obedience appeals to the worldly; its opposite does not.[33]]

Objection: A father's attachment to his son is steadfast, irrespective of whether he is obedient or disobedient.

Answer: Attachment is not steadfast.

> 17. Suffering caused by separation
>   Is quickly gone from human hearts.
>   See, too, attachment's instability,
>   Indicated by suffering's end.

The suffering caused by separation from the object of one's attachment, such as one's son, is quickly gone from human hearts and does not last long. If the bonds of attachment did not loosen, the suffering it causes would not stop; but by seeing the suffering—its effect—end, consider the instability of attachment too, which is indicated by this.

It is like the following analogy: A king was crossing the water when a non-human spirit captured his boat. One of his ministers, entrusting his children to the king's care, jumped into the water shouting, "Take me and let the King go!" The boat was released. When the children heard of their father's death, they suffered, but because the king cared for them well, they came to regard their father's death as an advantage. As in this case, even grief does not last forever.

Objection: Though it is inappropriate to grieve in one's heart for a dead son and others, for the sake of convention one must beat one's breast and so forth.

Answer: That is not appropriate.

>   18. Knowing it is of no benefit,
>   Still you have injured yourself.
>   You make yourself a hypocrite,
>   Which also is improper.

Knowing it is of no benefit whatever, still you have injured your body by tearing your hair and so forth. If you injure yourself hypocritically, it is merely in keeping with deceitful people's ways and therefore improper of you.

It is like one woman who promised to teach another woman how to commit suicide and, proud of being the teacher, killed herself.

Objection: Though self-torment is of no benefit, nevertheless it cannot be dispensed with if one is to have a relationship with the surviving relatives.

Answer:

>   19. People in this world wander,
>   Full, as it were, of suffering.
>   Why fill with suffering
>   People who already suffer?

Through the force of their actions ordinary beings become men and women and continue to wander, full, as it were, of suffering. Why fill with more fresh suffering beings who already suffer of their own accord? It is like rubbing salt into a wound. Since there is not the slightest use in having relationships with them, put effort into the means of freeing yourself from cyclic existence.

It is like the following analogy: There were two brothers whose father had died in the presence of one and whose mother had died in the presence of the other. When they met they made each other miserable, which was not of the slightest use.

Objection: Though parting causes suffering, being with one's family causes happiness. Therefore attachment is reasonable.

Answer: It is not.

> 20. **If meeting is a joy to you**
>   **Why is parting not also a joy?**
>   **Do not meeting and parting**
>   **Both seem to go together?**

If meeting is a source of joy to you, why would it not be appropriate for you to consider parting also as a source of joy? It should be, for do not meeting and parting both seem to go together? They only ever go together. Understand that it is like the following analogies: Mistress Black Nose follows Lady Luck. Though poisonous food may bring a little pleasure, in the end it produces suffering.

A man went to propitiate his tutelary deity and prayed for good luck. He received a promise. That night Lady Luck followed by Mistress Black Nose entered his home. The man asked Lady Luck, "Who is this?" She replied that it was Mistress Black Nose. He protested that he had received no promise regarding her. Lady Luck answered, "Wherever I am, she inevitably is too." Similarly, wherever there is meeting, there is also parting.

Anyone who eats poisonous food will undoubtedly die or experience mortal suffering. Similarly, all the pleasures of meeting are connected with the suffering of parting.

Objection: The suffering of separation can be discounted, for though an eventual parting is certain, the time spent as friends is long.

Answer: The periods of separation are not short, nor are those of being together long.

> 21. **When the past is beginningless**
>   **And the future endless,**
>   **Why do you notice being together**
>   **But not the separations, though they be long?**

When beings in cyclic existence have a beginningless past and an endless future, why do you notice the very short periods of being together but do not notice the separations, although they are long? Why are you not depressed by them? Whoever is attached to such brief periods of being together should be depressed by the long separations.

Someone who had been living abroad, and whose wife had become another man's partner, began to suffer as soon as he reached home. It is just as unreasonable when ordinary people who do not grieve over lengthy separations grieve over brief ones.

A man who had gone to another country and lived abroad left behind a wife who became another man's partner. When the man came back he heard about it from people living near his village, but nevertheless went to the seducer's house. He suffered from the pangs of separation that arose then and there, though he had not suffered because of the preceding separation. He even got involved in a dispute about it.[34]

Objection: Though separations are long, the suffering of separation vanishes when the mind is distracted by the marvels of the different seasons, such as the flowers blooming in spring and the bright autumn moon.
   Answer:

> 22. Time, [consisting of] instants and so forth,
>   Is certainly like an enemy.
>   Therefore never be attached
>   To that which is your enemy.

Since time, consisting of instants, moments, brief spans and so forth which gradually add up, consumes the moments of your life, it is certainly like an enemy which robs you of life. For that reason do not be attached to that which is your enemy.

An old servant, made to suffer continually by her mistress, was attached to her and did not complain. Ordinary people who are attached to the different seasons in spite of the heat, cold and so forth are just like this.

Objection: Though what has been said is reasonable, separating from one's family is hard, and fearing that, one cannot go off to the forest.
   Answer:

23. Fool, because you fear separation,
    You do not leave home.
    Who that is wise does under punishment
    What must certainly be done?

Fool, if you do not definitely leave family life behind to live in seclusion because of your fear of separation from family and friends, the
Lord of Death will certainly separate you from your family and
friends. Therefore who that is wise about what must be adopted and
discarded does what must be done in any case because of being
forced definitely to do it by Death's punishment? Go off to the forest therefore, before Death threatens you with punishment, and
make effort to attain liberation.

Do not act like villagers who would not pay the taxes they definitely had to pay until they were made to suffer.

Objection: Though one must certainly leave one's relations, nevertheless only after bringing up one's son and handing over responsibility for the family to him can one definitely go off to the forest.
  Answer:

24. You may think you must obviously
    Go to the forest once this has been done.
    Whatever you do must be left behind.
    What is the value of having done it?

You may think that later you must obviously, that is definitely, go
off to the seclusion of the forest once you have done tasks like bringing up your son and so forth, but whatever you do must inevitably
be left behind. What is the value of having done that which does not
yield even the slightest desired result? It is right to give it up from
the start.

It is like the following analogies about throwing away a useless
stone and discarding a mango covered with dirt after washing it.

A traveller stopped on his journey and began to file a stone. Asked
what he was doing with it, he simply said he was filing it down. After his companions left him, he had many difficulties without man-
aging to make the stone square. Understand that the domestic activities of travellers in cyclic existence are like this.[35]

Someone picked up a mango that had fallen in the dirt. Somebody
else asked him, "What will you do with that?" "I'll wash it and throw
it away," was his answer. Likewise, if things must be relinquished,
why take such trouble to get them?[36]

Objection: Though going off to the forest is of greatest importance, fear because of attachment to "I" and "mine" makes one unable to go.
   Answer:

> 25. **Whoever with certainty has**
> **The thought, "I am going to die,"**
> **Having completely relinquished attachment,**
> **Why would they fear even the Lord of Death?**

If you make effort to meditate on death and impermanence, you will become free from attachment to both "I" and "mine," for it is like this: whoever thinks, "It is uncertain when I'll die, but I will die soon," and has certainty about it, will abandon busyness. Having also completely given up attachment to the existence of the self, why would such a person fear even the Lord of Death? Since you will attain liberation through abandoning fear, you will not be afraid to go off into the forest and part from your son.

It is like the following analogies of wearing a ring to detoxify food and giving up poisonous foods.

Like wearing a ring on one's hand to detoxify food, the wise maintain awareness of impermanence to destroy disturbing emotions.[37]

Just as one will enjoy well-being through giving up poisonous foods, one will achieve definite goodness by giving up all attachments.[38]

Although some versions of the text read "certainly has," this does not contradict what has been explained.[39]

Therefore, as has already been explained, think again and again that, being in Death's power, you are certain to die and that the time of your death is uncertain. By establishing a sound basis regarding this, more advanced paths will arise effortlessly. Furthermore, according to the Spiritual Friend Bo-do-wa,[40] since the path to generating insights is blocked until an awareness of death and impermanence has arisen in the mind, continually meditate on coarse and subtle impermanence.

The summarizing stanza:

> That which cuts craving for reward and honor,
> The best spur to practise with effort in seclusion,
> The excellent secret of all the scriptures,
> Is initially to remember death.

This is the first chapter of the *Four Hundred on the Yogic Deeds*, showing the means to abandon the belief in permanence.

This concludes the commentary on the first chapter, showing the means to abandon the belief in permanence, from the *Essence of Good Explanations, Explanation of the "Four Hundred on the Yogic Deeds of Bodhisattvas"*.

COMMENTARY TO CHAPTER I
BY GESHE SONAM RINCHEN

Unless we remember death, there is no real incentive to practise, because we will not think about future lives nor about the need to ensure our well-being during them. Even if we recognize the need to practise, without remembering death we will procrastinate. There will be no sense of urgency. Though we may actually begin, unless we are mindful of death, what we do will not be pure in that it will remain directed primarily towards benefits in this life such as prosperity, good health and longevity. While practices may accomplish these things, they are not pure unless, having understood the narrowness and triviality of our normal concern for this life, we maintain a long-term perspective and direct our activities towards the achievement of future well-being, liberation and enlightenment. Without constant mindfulness of death, even properly directed practices will not be undertaken with sufficient energy to leave a strong and lasting imprint. Our practices should not be like writing on water, but should leave an indelible impression, like an engraving on stone. The thought of death is sobering and helps us to keep a sense of proportion. Without it, we may be tempted to act in an irresponsible and destructive way.

Though none of us think we will live forever, we act as if certain we will not die today, tomorrow, next month or next year. In fact our hopes and plans are based on the assumption that we will live for a long time. We plan to secure our livelihood, possessions, wealth, friends and status. Our pursuit and acquisition of these things involves craving and attachment. Inevitably, therefore, hostility arises towards anyone or anything that could deprive us of what we seek or damage what is ours. Unaware of the destructiveness of attachment and anger, we create much harm which causes us trouble in this life and destroys our chances of happiness in future lives. Thus the possibility of attaining liberation, or even good rebirths, grows more remote.

If we have wasted our energy pursuing the ephemeral happiness of this brief life, when death comes we will feel helpless and regret our failure to practise in a way that could have brought about a radical transformation in this life and provided a favorable setting for growth in the future as well.

Cultivating an awareness of death's closeness is of great benefit. It encourages us to use our property and wealth generously for others' well-being, to be conscientious about preventing harmful physical, verbal, and mental activity, and to live in a constructive way, making best use of each moment.

Our harmful physical and verbal actions stem from disturbing emotions which make the mind unruly. The only effective way to rid ourselves completely of these emotions is through understanding reality. Since this takes time, we need a powerful means to combat their manifest form. Mindfulness of death provides this, for the more we bear in mind our own impending death, the less these disturbing emotions or their physical and verbal expressions will manifest, and our positive practices will become purer through being less contaminated by the three poisons.

Initially, awareness of death spurs us to practise. It then induces us to persevere. Finally it ensures the successful completion of whatever was undertaken. Such attentiveness has the power to transform each moment, making every day precious and meaningful.

Fully understanding the many advantages of remembering death and the disadvantages of not doing so, we should cultivate an awareness of coarse and subtle impermanence. By doing so we will realize how we undergo change constantly, and that such change is an involuntary process governed by factors beyond our control. This will lead us to an understanding of coarse and subtle suffering and toward that of coarse and subtle selflessness.

Chapter II

Abandoning Belief in Pleasure

The contaminated body is a source of suffering because it is damaged by internal causes of harm in the form of four hundred and twenty-four diseases and external causes of harm such as sticks, clods and so forth. Therefore the Exalted with direct perception of its suffering nature see it like a foe. Nevertheless, this body should be properly protected from deterioration.

> 26. Although the body is seen like a foe,
>   Nevertheless it should be protected.
>   By long sustaining a disciplined [body]
>   Great merit is created.

By sustaining an ethically disciplined body for a long period, great merit is created in completing the vast stores of merit and wisdom. This dispels doubt as to whether perhaps it should not be nurtured since it is like a foe. As a result of the discussion about impermanence, one may feel aversion and wonder what is the value of the body which gives rise to much senselessness. Thus, alternatively, one can interpret the words "Although the body is seen like a foe" and so forth as being intended to get rid of such contempt.

It is like a merchant's son who protected a thief to whom he was bound by a close tie. [He established this close tie with the thief because he was afraid to lose his companionship on outings, and protected him even when he was put in jail.[1]]

Assertion: If the body is to be protected, one should pamper it with food and clothing.

Answer: There is no such fault.

27. When human suffering is produced
    By the body, and pleasure by other [factors],
    Why are you devoted to
    This hull, a container of suffering?

When even the slightest human suffering, such as hunger or thirst, is produced by the body, and the slightest physical pleasure, such as satisfaction from food and drink, is entirely due to external factors, why are you devoted to this hull of a body which is a container of all kinds of suffering? You should care for it just enough to practise virtue energetically and not be at fault in your use of food and clothing.

It is like the following analogy: A man gave a ride in his chariot to an ogress who showed herself in a beautiful form. A little later an ugly ogress appeared ahead. He slashed her with his sharp sword, and there were two. When he also slashed those two, there were four. Then a deity spoke from the sky, saying, "If you kill that woman, they'll all be killed!" He acted accordingly. Similarly, if by meditating on impermanence and suffering one gets rid of attachment and makes effort to prevent the body from coming into existence, all suffering will end.

Assertion: Although pain occurs only because of the body, since it can be alleviated, it is weak and pleasure greater. Therefore one does not fear pain.
Answer:

28. When humans do not have
    As much pleasure as pain,
    Should so much pain
    Be considered negligible?

If a wasp stings Devadatta while he is sitting on a soft cushion and experiencing the pleasure of enjoying attractive objects, his pleasure will vanish and he will be miserable with pain. Similarly, when humans do not mainly have pleasure because pain is very strong, should one consider so much pain as negligible? Since it is inappropriate to do so, think about suffering and feel aversion.

Bāli stole Sugrīva's wife with much difficulty. It brought him only suffering and not even a little pleasure. To think of cyclic existence as pleasurable when one founders in a morass of suffering is like that.

29. Ordinary people are bent on pleasure;
    Those who have pleasure are hard to find.
    Thus it is as if transitory
    Beings are pursued by suffering.

Since pleasure is weaker and outweighed by suffering, ordinary people are bent on attaining pleasure and run from suffering. Yet it is hard to find those whose suffering body is comfortable, for in the hope of pleasure, they create the causes for suffering. Although common beings, who are impermanent and disintegrate moment by moment, keep running from suffering, suffering pursues them like a shadow and is therefore hard to abandon.

It is like climbing down a well out of fear of a mad elephant and thinking one is safe. [Ordinary people, whose connection with suffering is constant, out of ignorance think they are happy.[2]]

30. Suffering is found at will,
    But what pleasure is there at will?
    Why do you value the rare
    But do not fear the plentiful?

Suffering is always close by, and if not, can be found at will without the need of effort to acquire it. But what pleasure is found at will? It is something rare for this suffering body—as rare as coolness in the sun's heat. Why do you ordinary people value pleasure which is rare but do not fear suffering which is plentiful? If you value rare and desired pleasure, it is appropriate to feel aversion for undesired and plentiful suffering. It is like the following analogy: Someone who breaks into the king's treasury has wished suffering on himself and does not gain any happiness.

31. A comfortable body
    Is a container of suffering.
    Thus valuing the body and
    Valuing a foe both seem alike.

Even a thorn causes the body with its delicate flesh great suffering. [It reacts like a new leaf at the touch of a flame.[3]] Even a somewhat comfortable body is a container of great suffering. For a person to value the body and to value a foe seems similar, since both are alike in comprising causes of suffering.

It is like the following analogy: A king saw a man asleep in a chariot in the noonday heat. Feeling pity, he took care of him, with the result that later even the touch of a mustard seed prevented the man from sleeping. The more one indulges in comfort, the more suffering it provokes.

> 32. The body, however long one spends,
>   Will not in itself become pleasurable.
>   To say its nature can be overruled
>   By other factors is improper.

Moreover, even if one cossets the body for a long time with comforts intended to cause pleasure, however long one spends, it will not in itself become pleasurable, because its nature is suffering. To say that its nature can be overruled by other factors is improper. No matter how much a mother crow nurtures a cuckoo fledgling, it will always be a cuckoo and never a crow. To assert that the body is by nature pleasurable is like that.

Though lead, brass, silver and gold, when smelted temporarily assume a liquid form, they are hard by nature, and it is not their property to be liquid.[4]

Objection: Its nature cannot be suffering, for those of royal caste and so forth have nothing but pleasurable feelings from birth to death.
Answer:

> 33. The high have mental suffering;
>   For the common it comes from the body.
>   Day by day, both kinds of suffering
>   Overwhelm people in the world.

The high, such as kings with many attendants and possessions, have constant mental suffering from fearing the decline of their own prosperity and being unable to bear others' prosperity. For common people who lack the necessities of life, the experience of suffering arises from the body. Day by day, people in the world are overwhelmed in this way by both mental and physical suffering.

It is like the following analogy: A king was pleased with an expert trainer who managed to ride a difficult elephant. Seeing this, the elephant keeper felt uneasy. Another man without expertise was punished by the king, which caused him physical suffering.

Assertion: Though these two kinds of suffering exist, one does not notice them because great pleasure makes them insignificant.
Answer:

34. Pleasure is governed by thoughts;
   Thoughts are governed by pain.
   Thus there is nothing anywhere
   More powerful than pain.

There is no pleasure so great that it can make pain insignificant, because pleasure depends on thoughts, which are governed by pain. It is like this: when one thinks of oneself as a benefactor, mental pleasure arises, but that pleasure is stopped by the fear that, though one has wealth, it might come to an end. The arising and cessation of pleasure are governed by thoughts, and since pleasurable thoughts are destroyed by pain, they are governed by pain. Therefore nowhere in the world is there pleasure more powerful than pain. It is like the following analogy: There were two wives, a senior and a junior one. The one suffered more about seeing the other's son being shown respect than about the death of her own.

When the senior wife saw the junior wife's son being decked out and shown respect, she cried bitterly. When asked what was the use of crying about her dead son, she answered that she was not crying about him, but about the junior wife's living one. Some time later, the junior wife's son fell ill and was taken to another village. After a few days, when the senior wife was near that village she saw a dead body being carried out. She thought the junior wife's son had died and felt very happy.[5]

Assertion: Although pleasure is hard to find, it does no harm, but since pain harms, it is as if alien to the body.
Answer:

35. With the passage of time
   Pain increases.
   Pleasure, therefore, seems as if
   Alien to this body.

Pleasurable sensations are not natural to the body, for with the passing of time from childhood to youth, maturity and old age, suffering—such as that of aging—increases and pleasure vanishes. Therefore pleasure seems as alien to this body as a visitor who only stays for one day.

It is like a traveller on a long journey whose suffering increases as he grows tired and runs out of provisions.

Assertion: Although the body's nature is suffering, causes of pleasure act as a remedy. Therefore one need not feel aversion.
Answer: That is incorrect.

> 36. There seem to be many causes
>   Of suffering, like sickness and others,
>   But humans do not seem to have
>   As many causes of pleasure.

There appear to be many causes of physical suffering—internal causes such as sickness, as well as many external ones. But humans do not seem to have as many causes for pleasure. Since suffering occurs constantly, one ought to feel aversion. It is like a certain man who wanted a king's daughter as his wife and because of that got involved in a lot of suffering.

Assertion: If pleasure did not exist it could not intensify, but since it is seen to intensify, real pleasure does exist.
Answer: That is not so.

> 37. With the intensification of pleasure
>   Its opposite is seen to occur.
>   With the intensification of pain
>   There will not likewise be its opposite.

Through the intensification of pleasure, its opposite, pain, is seen to occur; but through the intensification of pain, there will not likewise finally be just pleasure, its opposite. As pain intensifies, body and mind experience agony. It is like King Māndhātṛ who fell because he wanted Indra's half of the throne and was not content to share power with him.

> 38. With the conditions for pleasure
>   Its opposite is seen.
>   With the conditions for pain
>   There is not its opposite.

When one overindulges in the causes of pleasure such as food and so forth, the opposite of pleasure, just pain, is seen to occur together with the conditions for pleasure. But when one has prolonged contact with the causes of pain, together with these conditions for pain, there is no change to pleasure, its opposite. It is like King Aśoka's prison called the "Pleasant Abode" where one could first choose one's favorite form of behavior, but since no other could then be adopted, this eventually became painful.

Assertion: Since the expression "Devadatta has pleasure" is used, pleasure does exist.
　　Answer:

> 39. When you have spent, are spending
>   And will spend time dying,
>   It is not at all proper to call
>   The process of dying pleasurable.

Composite things by nature disintegrate moment by moment; furthermore this is true with regard to the three times. When you have therefore already spent, are spending and will spend time disintegrating and dying, it is not at all proper to call the process of dying pleasurable.

It is like the following analogy: A householder accused a bad servant who kept spoiling his things of ingratitude. The servant replied, "You wasted your actions trusting me." Similarly, childish people think of the process of dying as pleasurable [and of themselves as happy, though they have been dying from the time they were a fetus.[6]]

> 40. When beings with bodies are constantly
>   Afflicted by hunger and so forth,
>   It is not at all proper to call
>   Being afflicted pleasurable.

Furthermore, it is inappropriate to think of suffering as pleasure, for beings with bodies are constantly subject to different kinds of affliction such as hunger, thirst and so forth. It is therefore not at all proper to call being afflicted by the causes of suffering pleasurable.

It is like a new wife who wanted to have control of the household, and when she did, though it gave her trouble, thought of it as happiness.

41. Though powerless, the combining of
    All the elements produces [the body];
    Thus it is not at all proper to call
    What is incompatible pleasurable.

[Pleasure and pain depend on the body which depends on the elements.[7]] Each of the four elements on its own is powerless to produce the body, which is produced through the combining of the elements. [During the development of the fetus the earth element stabilizes the other three, preventing abortion. Thus the earth element holds the fetus. The water element binds, creating solidity; otherwise the particles would disperse like sand. The fire element prevents decomposition of the fetus, while the wind element enables growth and development to take place.] However the elements harm each other. [The earth element inhibits the movement of wind.] Wind disperses the others, and fire [which water harms] burns earth and dries up water. It is thus not at all proper to call a collection of incompatible and conflicting factors pleasurable.

It is like the following analogy: There can be no pleasure when a horse, jackal, snake, bird, deer and child-eating crocodile are confined together.

42. When there is never that
    Which will relieve cold and so forth,
    It is not at all proper to call
    Being destroyed pleasurable.

When beings with bodies never have effective means to do away with cold, heat and so forth, it is not at all proper to call being destroyed by harmful agents pleasurable.[8]

A band of thieves harried with nooses and sticks will find no comfort [wherever they turn for protection. Similarly, when ordinary people harassed by suffering turn to its antidotes, they still do not have pleasure.[9]]

Assertion: Since conventionally one uses the expression "Devadatta is lying down comfortably," real pleasure does exist.
Answer:

43. When on earth no action is
    Done without exertion,
    It is not at all proper to call
    Performing actions pleasurable.

When on earth there are no activities—lying down, walking, sitting and so forth— done without mental and physical exertion, it is not at all proper to call performing tiring actions pleasurable. [When one is weak and incapable of effort, even raising one's arm requires someone else's assistance. When one is strong, however, one does not notice the suffering involved in lying down or in extending and flexing one's limbs. Daily one performs many actions to ensure the body's survival; they are not performed for pleasure.[10]]

It is like the following analogy: A prince with five tutors for different subjects such as grammar is always miserable, [because when one releases him another one catches him. Similarly, common beings who perform actions associated with the five aggregates, which are like thieves and executioners, are always miserable.[11]]

Assertion: If there were no pleasure, it would not be feasible to experience suffering for the sake of pleasure, but since suffering for pleasure's sake is seen, pleasure does exist.
   Answer:

44.   In this [life] and in others, always
      One should guard against ill deeds.
      Calling them pleasurable is not at all
      Proper when there are bad rebirths.

The unwise do ill deeds for the sake of a little pleasure, and as a result experience such sufferings as being put to death in this life and bad rebirths later. Since the wise want happiness, they should always, in this and other lives, guard against suffering caused by ill deeds. When there are bad rebirths resulting from actions done by the unwise for the sake of pleasure, calling them pleasurable is not at all proper. One should guard against ill deeds just as one guards against an unknown enemy who is a constant source of fear.

Assertion: One sees that those intent on pleasure ride horses and elephants, considering it a discomfort to walk on their own two feet. Therefore, pleasure does exist.
   Answer:

45.   There is never any pleasure
      For humans in riding and so forth.
      How can that which at the start
      Does not begin, in the end increase?

On examining accepted causes of pleasure one finds that, right from the start, slight discomfort is beginning. For humans there is never, even at the outset, pleasure in riding, eating or drinking. If done in excess they only become painful. How could something which at the start was not a beginning of pain in the end increase and become intense pain? That which from the start was a small incipient cause of pain is mistaken for pleasure.

It is like a fool who thinks the last half-ladle of his parents' fried bread will satisfy his hunger.

Assertion: Pleasure caused by the alleviation of pain exists.
Answer:

> 46. **Thinking the alleviation**
> **Of pain is pleasure**
> **Is like someone who feels delight**
> **Vomiting into a gold pot.**

When a rich man, vomiting into a gold pot, sees his servant vomit into a clay one, though vomiting is equally unpleasant for both, he thinks how prosperous he is. Like the rich man who feels delighted, one mistakes for real pleasure the feeling of satisfaction when pain has been alleviated and becomes less acute; but there is no real pleasure. For instance, the feeling of satisfaction, as the pain of being burnt somewhat decreases when one moves out of the scorching sun into the shade, is called the pleasure of alleviated pain; but the suffering of cold begins as soon as the discomfort of heat diminishes. Thus there is no pleasurable sensation entirely free from discomfort. Since ordinary people's pain does not require even a weak pleasurable feeling as a basis in relation to which it is established, it is said that ordinary people have real suffering but no real pleasure. However it is incorrect to assert that nominally pleasure does not exist, for that would be to deny fact.

The difference should be understood as illustrated by the following analogy: Even when blue and yellow are juxtaposed, the perception of blue as blue and not as yellow arises, whereas when a long thing is placed beside a much longer one, the perception of it as short arises.

The use of "real" in this context should not be confused with "real" as the object of refutation by reasoning.[12]

It is like a man who eagerly swallows horse dung, regarding it as pleasant [because he thinks it will calm the suffering caused by his illness.[13]]

Assertion: Pleasure does exist because when, for instance, one moves a load from one shoulder to the other, a sense of pleasure arises. If there were no pleasure, one would not move it.
   Answer:

   47. **By beginning it stops the produced —**
       How can pain that begins be pleasure?
       It seems the Subduer therefore said
       Both birth and cessation are suffering.

When the discomfort of carrying a load on the right shoulder for a long time becomes intense and one moves it on to the left one, it is merely that a slight pain which is beginning stops the intense pain already produced, not that there is no discomfort at all. How can there be pleasure while a new and different pain is beginning or while intense pain is stopping?

   Although when one takes birth some forms of suffering stop, it is inappropriate to regard that as pleasure. The author Āryadeva says it seems this is why in the *Sūtra of Advice to Kātyāyana*[14] the Subduer said:

   When Kātyāyana's son is born, only suffering is born.
   Also when he ceases, only suffering ceases.

One should understand this as explained extensively in the *Nanda Entering the Womb Sūtra*[15] and through the analogy of carrying a load.

Assertion: Real suffering exists but is not apparent because pleasure conceals it.
   Answer:

   48. **If common beings do not see suffering**
       Because pleasure disguises it,
       Why is there no pleasure
       Which obscures suffering?

If real suffering exists but common beings do not notice it because pleasurable feelings disguise it, there should be pleasure which is stronger than suffering. Why is there no pleasure that can obscure suffering? Because ordinary people do not have real pleasure.

It is like the following analogy: A man pursued by an elephant falls into an old well. He stops his fall halfway down by catching hold of some couch-grass at whose root a rat is gnawing. Below a large snake lies in wait and from the sides pythons writhe toward him. Meanwhile he is absorbed in tasting the honey which drips from above and thinks of that as pleasure. When childish beings in cyclic existence, pursued by the elephant of death, fall into the well of old age, they stop their fall halfway by catching hold of the couch-grass root of virtuous paths of action. Below the snake of bad rebirths lies in wait and pythons of disturbing emotions writhe toward them from all sides. While the rat of maturation is gnawing at the couch-grass root of life, they are absorbed in tasting the honeyed drops of craving for attractive objects, but as in the analogy, there is only suffering and not even the slightest real pleasure.

The other analogy should be understood from Candrakīrti's commentary. A crow perched inside the carcass of an elephant and was drowned when a sudden rainstorm flooded it, paying a heavy price for small gain. Children absorbed in the enjoyment of attractive objects overlook the dangers involved and are drowned in the ocean of cyclic existence.[16]

Assertion: If the body's nature were suffering, it would be unnecessary for the Teacher [Buddha] to say that the body is suffering, just as there is no need to point out that the sun is hot.

Answer: There is no such fault, for though the body's nature is suffering, because of confusion one does not realize it and, thinking it pleasurable, one circles in cyclic existence.

> 49. Common beings must be told, "You are not
>   Free from attachment to suffering."
>   Certainly Tathāgatas therefore have said
>   This is the worst confusion of all.

Our Teacher therefore said, "Mistaking suffering for pleasure, you are not free from attachment." Common beings need to be told this. Certainly that is why the Tathāgatas[17] have said, "Sister, the foremost of all obstructions is ignorance." In other words, they have said that confusing real suffering with pleasure is the worst confusion of all.

It is like the following analogy: Taking her wages, a servant girl did only half the work and then left it. Her mother told her that whatever she took hold of, she should hold on tight. One day she took hold of a donkey's tail and though others told her not to hold on, she did not let go but repeated, "Whatever you take hold of, hold on tight." Similarly, the Teacher instructed those in the grip of confusion's errors, who cling to the idea of suffering as pleasure, to develop aversion to suffering.

Assertion: Though the body is impermanent, it is pleasurable.
  Answer: That is not so.

> 50. **The impermanent is definitely harmed.**
>   **What is harmed is not pleasurable.**
>   **Therefore all that is impermanent**
>   **Is said to be suffering.**

Whatever is impermanent, like the body which is a maturation of contaminated past actions and disturbing emotions, is definitely damaged by factors causing disintegration and therefore produces aversion. Anything affected by causes of harm, whose character is to produce aversion, is not pleasurable. Therefore all that is impermanent and contaminated is said to be suffering, just as anything that falls into a salt-pit becomes salty.

Having aroused in trainees aversion to cyclic existence, the author Āryadeva quotes sūtra saying that birth is suffering, to bring them to enlightenment. Also in the treatises of knowledge[18] the Teacher says that the five contaminated aggregates are suffering:

> They are suffering, its sources, the world,
> The basis of views and also existence.[19]

And:

> Whatever without exception has any of
> The three kinds of suffering is thus suffering.

And:

> The attractive, the unattractive, and
> All else that is contaminated ...[20]

The author Āryadeva explains the faults of cyclic existence, establishing the intended meaning of these statements to bring those who are afraid and desire liberation into the Great Vehicle.

Moreover the Teacher said, "Monks, while you have been circling in cyclic existence there is no one who has not been in the position of your father, mother and so forth." Realizing this, just as Bodhisattvas willingly make sacrifices to rescue sentient beings from cyclic existence in the ship of the Great Vehicle, the author of the treatise shows extensively in the first four chapters how to generate the aspiring altruistic attitude intent on highest enlightenment by explaining the faults of cyclic existence.

Although the lines quoted here are from the Master Vasubandhu's *Treasury [of Knowledge]*, they are clearly words from the sūtras on knowledge. With reference to this, some learned teachers say that although the Master Vasubandhu holds that the seven treatises of knowledge[21] are not sūtra, the spiritual father and son, Nāgārjuna and Āryadeva, seem to hold that some parts are.

According to the Protector Nāgārjuna, who asserts that phenomena do not have even an atom of inherent existence, there is real suffering but not the least real contaminated pleasure. If there were, it would entail many errors. Therefore, as has already been explained, the pleasure of alleviated suffering, namely the arising of a feeling of satisfaction when suffering is somewhat weaker, is posited as pleasure.

The Master Vasubandhu refers to the Master Āryadeva in his commentary on the *Treasury*, saying, "The one who denies the existence of pleasure should be asked this ...."[22] He presents numerous parallel reasons for either the existence or non-existence of both real pleasure and real suffering, the need to accept the true existence of functional things being a foregone conclusion in that system. With regard to this, the author of the commentary, Candrakīrti, states numerous refutations here.[23] If pleasurable feelings existed inherently, [clearly] it would be senseless for them to arise again. Moreover, if collective effects existed truly as functional things, they would not need to be produced by causes, and if they existed truly as non-functional things, they could not be produced and so forth. If past and future functional things existed inherently, they would be present [now]. Stating many such damaging consequences, he says that there is no opportunity for criticism of the Master Āryadeva.

The *King of Meditative Stabilizations Sūtra* says:

> A person who is tormented by thirst
> In summer at noon—that transmigrator
> Sees mirages as a body of water.
> Understand all phenomena are like this.
>
> Although a mirage contains no water,
> Confused sentient beings want to drink it.
> Unreal water cannot be drunk;
> Understand all phenomena are like this.[24]

Accordingly, accepting that which arises dependently as empty of inherent existence, make effort to consider conceptions of cleanness, pleasure, and so forth in relation to the nominal as erroneous.

The summarizing stanza:

> Abiding in this fathomless ocean of cyclic existence,
> Utterly tormented by the crocodiles of disturbing
>   emotions,
> What sentient being would not feel aversion?
> With effort endeavor to attain enlightenment.

> **This is the second chapter of the *Four Hundred on the Yogic Deeds*, showing the means to abandon belief in pleasure.**

This concludes the commentary on the second chapter, showing the means to abandon erroneous belief in pleasure, from *Essence of Good Explanations, Explanation of the "Four Hundred on the Yogic Deeds of Bodhisattvas"*.

COMMENTARY TO CHAPTER II
BY GESHE SONAM RINCHEN

Although none of us wants suffering, we experience it involuntarily. This is because we do not identify suffering and its causes properly and thus cannot take effective measures to prevent it. It is therefore of prime importance to recognize suffering and the kinds of activity and attitudes that give rise to it. By thinking about this sufficiently, we will begin to find the whole process intolerable and want to get rid of the state which it characterizes, namely cyclic existence.

It is impossible to eradicate suffering completely unless one has recognized the most subtle kinds. We tend to mistake these for pleasure and happiness, which leads to many problems. For this reason the author emphatically denies the existence of "real" pleasure or happiness of a contaminated kind.

In many texts different kinds of suffering are described, for instance six pertaining to cyclic existence in general and eight pertaining specifically to the human condition. These are enumerated to help us identify suffering within our own experience. All kinds of suffering can be subsumed under the suffering of pain, the suffering of change, and the pervasive suffering of conditioning.

Birth, sickness, aging and death are processes which clearly constitute suffering. In addition, while we are alive, we suffer the pain of separation from that which we love and from which we cannot bear to be separated. We suffer separation from our spiritual teachers, students, parents, children, partners, friends, riches and status. We also suffer from coming into contact with that which we wish to avoid and find unpleasant and frightening even to hear about, such as enemies, robbers, sickness and other calamities. We may be forced to live with or near those we dislike or fear. We suffer too through not finding what we seek and desire, such as status, profit, good crops, adequate payment for work done, others' appreciation or companionship.

When we experience suffering, we normally blame other factors—our surroundings, friends and associates, or resources—but we suffer even when all of these are exceptionally good. The poor think that the rich and influential must be happy, but they too experience suffering associated with the very things for which they are envied. Those with many possessions and much wealth suffer when they are taxed or robbed and because others constantly seek their financial assistance. They face problems accumulating and safeguarding their wealth, while the influential suffer trying to acquire and protect their status. Those who are poor have trouble making a living and suffer oppression from others.

Physical and mental pain are quite coarse forms of suffering, characteristic of cyclic existence and experienced because we have a contaminated body and mind. They arise again and again in different forms and indicate the presence of an underlying constant subtle kind of suffering. The pleasurable feelings induced by what are usually called "pleasures" constitute the suffering of change because they are characterized by instability and have the tendency, when intensified, to turn gradually into suffering. Our body and mind are governed by activities and disturbing emotions over which at present we are unable to exercise proper control. At any moment severe suffering may arise. Since body and mind are thus controlled by other factors, namely by previous contaminated actions and disturbing emotions, and are not under our own control, they are referred to as pervasive suffering of conditioning. We are not free but ruled by an enemy and thus suffer.

It is essential to recognize these various kinds of suffering in ourselves. Suffering will not stop of its own accord simply because we do not want to suffer. The only way to end it is to search for and rid ourselves of its causes. This should be done now while we have a precious human life and the opportunities it offers. Only when we have recognized our own suffering and find it unbearable can we truly begin to empathize with others and find their suffering intolerable. This leads to great compassion, the urgent wish to free all others from suffering, the root of the Great Vehicle.

Chapter III

Abandoning Belief in Cleanness

Assertion: Though the body's nature is suffering, it gains pleasure from satisfaction through the experience of attractive objects. Thus the use of such objects is appropriate.

Answer:

> 51. **Regardless of the amount of time,**
> **Concerning objects there is no limit.**
> **Your exertion for the body's sake**
> **Is, like a bad physician's, useless.**

Having enjoyed things fully during one's youth and then amassed wealth, it does not follow that one will later turn to religious practices when free from attachment to such things. Regardless of the amount of time spent, be it aeons, one will not come to an end of the objects one craves by reaching their limit, for there is none. Though a bad physician who is incapable of healing gives treatment, his efforts are fruitless. Your exertion to satisfy the body with pleasure is similarly fruitless.

It is like the following analogy: A monkey wearing a leopard skin is a source of constant anxiety to other monkeys. [Just as they cannot tell how long this anxiety will last, those who make use of sensual objects cannot set a limit regarding how much is needed to satisfy them.[1]

Assertion: [Just as thirst disappears after drinking sufficient water[2]], those who are satisfied by sensual pleasure will not crave things.

Answer:

52. Just as the craving for earth
    Does not stop in those that subsist on it,
    Similarly, longing for sensual pleasure
    Grows in people as they indulge.

An earthworm never stops craving the earth on which it subsists. Similarly human beings indulging in the things they crave are not only not satisfied by them, their longing for sensual pleasure keeps growing. [Indulgence in sensual pleasure makes desire stronger because it nurtures the seed.[3] How can people swept away on a tide of desire experience satisfaction?[4] They are like deer tormented by thirst.

In a dry stony place, with the sun beating down on them from a cloudless sky, thirsty deer see the mirage of a river and thinking they have found water, run toward it eagerly. But their thirst, far from being quenched, will only increase. Similarly, how can those who do not realize that sensual pleasures are like a mirage, but think of them as real and seek them, overcome disturbing attitudes?[5]

Objection: Even if pointing out the above mentioned disadvantages can stop one desiring ordinary women, it cannot stop desire for women whose appearance and behavior are exceptionally beautiful.
   Answer:

53. Among all women there is not the least
    Difference in sexual intercourse.
    When others, too, enjoy her appearance,
    What use is this perfect woman to you?

What use is this perfect woman with her beautiful appearance and behavior to you who lust for a woman's body?[6] It is inappropriate to feel particularly attracted to her, since the unclean part of all women stinks and constantly drips of its own accord. It is a sewer for the body's filth, and like a lavatory readily receives the filth emptied into it by many people. Except to erroneous perception, there is not the least difference of good or bad regarding the sensation of intercourse with this cesspit-like dark filth. Since a woman's appearance may also be enjoyed by other men and even by dogs, crows and so forth, it is unreasonable to feel particularly attracted by beauty.

It is like the following analogy: An unattractive woman's husband told her she was ugly-looking. She replied that ugly or good-looking, when it came to sexual intercourse there was no difference. More about the analogies may be found in Candrakīrti's commentary.

Her husband, however, did not understand what she meant, so she put cooked peas into different bowls and placed them before him when it was time to eat. He asked her, "What is all this about?" She answered, "I've put the peas into nice-looking bowls." "What's the difference?" "It's just the same with intercourse," she replied.[7]

A certain man saw someone else's wife and lusted to have intercourse with her. One of his friends later told him that the woman he wanted was there but that he should not speak to her, as she was a modest woman of good caste. In the dark he lay with the woman, who was his own wife, and having thoroughly enjoyed himself, claimed no woman could equal her.[8]

For what reason does it follow that an unintelligent and misguided person like you will only be attracted to someone beautiful? It does not [for if beautiful women were the cause of desire, it would never arise toward others; but desire arises toward ugly women too. Confusion alone causes desire.[9]]

> 54. Whoever sees her as appealing
>   Thinks himself satisfied with her.
>   Since even dogs and the like share this,
>   Why, fool, are you attracted?

Just as grandma appeals to grandpa, any man who finds a woman attractive feels satisfied with her. Even dogs, crows and the like share this desire for their own mates. It is like the evil spirits who were prejudiced about the attractiveness of their wives [and, arguing about it, went to ask a monk whose was the best looking. He said to them, "The one you find most attractive is the best looking."[10]]

Assertion: A captivating woman is hard to find and since finding one is remarkable, it is reasonable to desire her.
  Answer:

> 55. This woman, every part of whom is
>   Lovely to you, was common to all before.
>   Finding her is not as
>   Astonishing as it is for you.

When this woman, every part of whom seems lovely to you, was common to all before she met you, how can finding what is common to all astonish you? It is absurd. It is like King Udayana's amazement at his discovery of a woman who was common property.

Assertion: Although desire for women in general is inappropriate, it is reasonable to be attracted to a woman with good qualities, such as an honest nature.

Answer:

> 56. If those with good qualities seem attractive
>   And their opposite the reverse,
>   Which is true, former or latter?
>   For neither alone persists.

When those with good qualities seem attractive and a cause for desire, while the opposite, those with faults, seem the reverse and a cause for aversion, desire for those with only good qualities is nevertheless unreasonable, for in the same person both faults and good qualities occur successively, and neither faults nor good qualities alone persist. When someone first has good qualities and later faults, which is true? If one is true, the other must be false. Thus both desire and aversion are definitely inappropriate. It is like the following analogy: One feels happy enjoying a good meal but unhappy going to the lavatory.

It does not follow that only a woman with good qualities, because she conforms to one's ideas, is a cause for desire, for one sees that a fool's desire arises not only toward those with good qualities but also toward those with faults.

> 57. A fool's desire does not arise
>   Only for those with good qualities.
>   How can reason prevent
>   Those involved in it without reason?

How can the desire of those involved in it without good qualities as reason be prevented by reason of the absence of such good qualities? The shameless are not consistent. It is like the analogy of a sexually abnormal Brahmin woman who cried because she did not experience the pleasure other women enjoy.

Assertion: Women commit suicide when their husbands die, but men are not like that. Therefore it is reasonable to form a relationship with a woman who desires one.

Answer: A woman does not desire one alone.

58. As long as she knows no other
    She will remain with you.
    As with disease, women should always be
    Kept from opportunity.

As long as she has not experienced the taste of other men, she will remain with you and be loving, but once she experiences the taste of others, she may even reject you. Therefore, as with a bad disease, since women must always be kept from opportunity in the form of other men, they are not to be trusted. It is like the following analogy of a Brahmin woman who did wrong with a man who was interested in her.

A certain man was interested in a Brahmin woman who told her husband that she had been approached and was frightened. She said she would tell him if the man came again. When he came and did wrong, she felt desire for him and did not tell her husband.[11]

Assertion: Texts on social conventions recommend indulgence in sensual pleasure during youth; thus it is acceptable.

Answer: It is inappropriate to act according to conventions which encourage one and others to act improperly.

59. In old age one dislikes
    What one did during youth.
    Why would the liberated not
    Be extremely saddened by it?

If the passionate, in their old age, despite not having achieved freedom from desire, dislike the mere memory of the bad things they did during their youth, why would liberated Foe Destroyers not be extremely saddened by and deprecate lascivious behavior? Since they see it as utterly reprehensible and a source of aversion, those interested in their own good should give it up. It is like the following analogy: During festivities a woman absent-mindedly tied a calf to her father-in-law's neck because she was in a hurry. When he asked her what she was doing, she felt extremely embarrassed.

Assertion: Since pleasure in relation to women is the best pleasure in the Desire Realm, one should keep a woman for that purpose.

Answer: That is incorrect.

60. Those without desire have no pleasure,
    Nor do those not foolish have it.
    How can there be pleasure for one
    Whose mind constantly strays?

How can the pleasure of one who desires a woman and whose mind constantly strays from reality be the best? It is not best. Those without desire for women do not have pleasure focusing on them. Moreover those who are sensible do not have desire. [Since that which is not pleasurable is thought of as pleasure due to desire, the cause of the pleasure is desire which in turn is caused only by confusion erroneously conceiving its object.[12]]

It is like the following analogy: A young man desired a king's queen and although he experienced suffering for a long time on her account, he was not able to accomplish what he wanted.

A young man saw the king's queen and desired her. He gave one of her servants gifts and asked if it would be possible to meet the queen. She replied that it would and told the queen who said, "The palace is heavily guarded but when the time comes for the queen's outing, it will be possible." The maid told the young man. He prepared perfume, incense, flowers, garlands and so on for the lady while the year was passing. When the time for the queen's outing drew near, he thought that he and the queen would meet the next day and arranged his house carefully. That day his employer lost a cow and ordered him to search for it. While he was gone, the queen came to the young man's house and then returned home. Like this young man whose mind was distracted all year, how can those distracted by desire find happiness?[13]

Even if you make a woman your own, why keep her possessively out of jealousy toward other men with the thought that she is yours and no one else's? It is unreasonable to do so.

61. You cannot have intercourse constantly
    With a woman to match your attentiveness to her.
    Why keep her possessively with the thought,
    "She is mine and no one else's."

You lustful person, you are not capable of constant sexual intercourse with a woman to match your attentiveness toward her in the hope of enjoyment.

It is like the following analogies: An old Brahmin whose digestion was weak found a lot of good food. Though he was unable to eat it, he did not give it to anyone else but took still more.

A certain king kept hundreds of women in his palace but did not sleep with them, nor give them to anyone else. One day a monk asked him whether he slept with all the women and he said he did not. The monk, in order to have them set free, spoke to the king about religious practice and they were freed.[14]

Assertion: Conventionally, desire is said to be pleasurable, and since it does not occur without women, one should desire women.
   Answer:

> 62. **If desire were pleasurable**
>   **There would be no need for women.**
>   **Pleasure is not regarded as**
>   **Something to get rid of.**

If desire were pleasurable one wouldn't need women as a means to quell it, for pleasure is not regarded as something of which to rid oneself. [Desire is like a poison which requires another poison, women, as its antidote.[15]]

It is like the following analogy: A hungry man entered a house at night and saw a pot of ash, which he mistook for flour, and another of water. He mixed them together and ate. When his hunger was gone he realized it was ash. Feeling disgusted, he threw the remainder away and left.

Assertion: Pleasure occurs through intercourse with a woman.
   Answer:

> 63. **Even in intercourse with a woman**
>   **Pleasure arises from other [factors].**
>   **What sensible person would say**
>   **It is caused just by his lover?**

Who but a fool would say that his lover alone is the cause of pleasure during intercourse? [If intercourse with a woman were a cause of pleasure, both those with and without desire should all experience that pleasure, but they do not. Those who respect their precepts, though they may not be free from desire, will not feel pleasure but suffering if a woman forces them to have intercourse.[16]] The pleasure from intercourse is caused by other factors, namely [by contact of the sexual organs[17] and] by an incorrect mental approach. It is like the following analogy: A simpleton's wife made him work and he enjoyed it.

She made him fetch wood and water for her bath. She then made him heat the water and had him massage her and apply oil. She made him massage her private parts too and he even enjoyed it. Similarly the infatuated do not value their freedom but imagine happiness is to be found only through women.[18]

Assertion: Sensuality does give rise to real pleasure, because the infatuated seek sensual gratification again and again.
Answer: They do not seek it because desire is pleasurable by nature.

> 64. Blinded by desire they do not see
> Sensuality's faults, like a leper scratching.
> Those free from desire see the infatuated
> As suffering like the leper.

Like a leper who, because it gives a little pleasure, keeps scratching without seeing the harm it causes, like bleeding and oozing, those whose eye of intelligence is blinded by desire do not see sensuality's faults. Since the Exalted who are free from the itch of desire see the infatuated as suffering like the leper, desire cannot be pleasurable. It is like gambling and drinking which cause one to waste one's property.

Assertion: Though sensual pleasure is unclean, bearing insults from a woman, like being spat on, and responding with flattering physical and verbal behavior is pleasurable for those that [are under the influence of[19]] desire.
Answer: That is incorrect.

> 65. During a famine the destitute,
> Tormented by hunger, [bear] what occurs.
> This is how all the infatuated
> Behave when they are with women.

During a famine the destitute, tormented by hunger, bear what occurs, such as being insulted even a hundred times by a merciless rich man, in the hope that he will later give them a trifle. Since the behavior of the infatuated when they are with a woman is like that, it cannot be pleasurable. It is like someone in prison who wanted to drink the liquid from cow dung.

Assertion: There is real pleasure from women because those who are attached to the pleasure from women are seen to be jealous of others.

Answer: That does not establish the existence of real pleasure in relation to women.

66. **Through arrogance one may be**
Attached even to one's privy.
Anyone infatuated with
A woman will be jealous of others.

A rich man who is arrogant because of his wealth may be possessive about his privy and forbid others to use it. Similarly, anyone who is infatuated with a particular woman is seen to be baselessly jealous toward other men.

It is like the following analogy: King *Gambhīraśikhara, who was arrogant about his status, [out of jealous miserliness[20]] would not allow a serving woman to drink water.

Assertion: Though women's bodies are unclean, desire is reasonable because they are a source of pleasure.

Answer: When one realizes they are unclean, desire is inappropriate.

67. **It is reasonable for confusion**
And anger about the unclean to occur;
It is not at all reasonable
For desire to occur.

When one steps in excrement without noticing it, it is feasible that confusion could occur and that the offensive smell could give rise to anger. However it is not at all reasonable for incongruous desire to occur. [One does not realize the true nature of a woman's body because it is concealed by ornaments and so forth; thus one is unaware of it. Its bad smell might make one angry, but desire is never appropriate because of its unclean nature.[21]] Thus desire for a woman's body is unreasonable. It is like stepping in excrement at night.

Assertion: Though the body is unclean, it is not considered to be objectionable because conventionally it is without shortcomings. It is said: "Brahmins are purer than others and women purest of all."

Answer: This is incorrect.

68. **If, except to some people,**
A pot of filth is objectionable,
Why would one not think objectionable
That from which the filth comes?

When all except people not in their right mind find a pot full of filth, such as vomit, objectionable, why would anyone sensible not consider the body from which such filth constantly comes objectionable?

Where "people do not realize" occurs in the text it is explained as meaning that women's bodies are not commonly accepted as having shortcomings only because people do not realize this, but the meaning of Candrakīrti's commentary agrees with the foregoing.[22]

It is like some lustful men who saw attractive qualities in a beautiful woman but found fault with her when they saw her carrying a pot full of vomit.

A rich man had a beautiful maid who carried the slop-basin. Some lustful men wanted her and made advances, but one day they saw her come out carrying a basin full of vomit. This made them find fault with her, and they left holding their noses. That filth had come from nowhere but the body. Similarly, the childish do not see anything wrong with filth while it is in the body, but think of it as filth when it leaves the body.[23]

Assertion: Women's bodies are clean because people regard them as clean.

Answer: It is absurd for any intelligent person to assert that a woman's body is by nature clean.

> 69. Clean things are looked upon
> As the most worthless of all.
> What intelligent person
> Would say that it is clean?

Clean things like flowers, perfume, ornaments and so forth are looked upon as the most worthless of all by virtue of having been in contact with a woman's body, just as the sweet water of the Ganges becomes saline on meeting the ocean.

Assertion: The body is clean, because one sees people taking pride in it.

Answer:

> 70. Whoever has lived in a privy
> And without it would not have survived,
> In such a dung-worm, arrogance
> Arises only through stupidity.

Whatever is born from the womb has lived in the mother's womb between the stomach and intestines, which is like living inside a privy. Like a dung-worm, it has been nurtured by excremental juices without which it would not have survived. Pride thinking of that as clean arises only through stupidity. It is absurd to be proud of just that!

It is like the following analogy: A young man who had been put in a cesspit and lived on excrement escaped, and afterward thought it was unclean when someone else's clothing touched him.

A young man took up with the wife of another rich young man and went to his house. He was caught and put in a cesspit, where he survived on excrement. One day, during heavy rain, the sides of the cesspit collapsed and he escaped. Some relatives took him home and called a good doctor. After a few days his strength and color were restored. Some time later, after bathing and applying perfume, he went out to a busy road. A beggar inadvertently brushed against him with his clothing. He drew back indignantly and scolded him, saying, "Your vile clothing has made me unclean!"[24]

Assertion: The body is definitely clean since washing and so forth removes dirt from it.

Answer: ·

> 71. No means whatsoever will purify
> The inside of the body.
> The efforts you make toward the outside
> Do not match those toward the inside.

When whatever means employed, such as ritual ablution and washing, do not cleanse the inside of the body, [why make effort to clean what is by nature unclean?[25]] You do not make as much effort to clean the external filth that has come out of your body as you do to cleanse the inside of the body, but it would be reasonable to do so. [One might think the former cannot be cleaned because it is filthy by nature. In that case exactly the same applies to the inside of the body.[26]]

It is like the following analogy: [Two jackals were sitting under a palāśa[27] tree.] When a palāśa blossom fell, one of them thought they were all like that. The other thought that though the blossom that had fallen was not meat, the ones still on the tree were meat. This is like thinking what leaves the body is filthy while what remains in it is clean.

Assertion: Since ascetic sages do not give up women's bodies, craving for women is not something to abandon.
  Answer:

> 72. If, like leprosy, being full of
>   Urine were not common to all,
>   Those full of urine, just like lepers,
>   Would be shunned by everyone.

Although women are full of urine, these sages do not give them up because they themselves are the same. If only some and not all were full of urine, those full of urine would be shunned by those who were not, just as one holds one's nose and avoids contact with lepers. Women are not avoided because all are alike, not because they are clean. It is like the following analogy: A man without a goiter visited a place full of people with goiters and was thought ugly. The analogy of the king is as in Candrakīrti's commentary.

A soothsayer told a king that whoever used the water when it rained would go mad. The king had his well covered. When it rained the people of that place went mad after using the water and since only the king remained sane, they thought he was mad. When the king found out, he feared they might mock or harm him because they considered him mad, so he used the water too.[28]

Assertion: Though a woman's body is unclean, the uncleanness can be removed by beautifying it with perfumes and so forth.
  Answer:

> 73. Just as someone lacking a part
>   Is delighted with a substitute nose,
>   Desire holds that impurity is
>   Remedied by flowers and so forth.

It is like a man lacking a part because his nose has been cut off, who is delighted with and proud of a golden artificial substitute.[29] Attaching flowers and so forth to the body as a means to remedy its foulness and holding that this will make the body clean will not do so. [In lustful childish people who, because of their stupidity, do not see the body's nature, desire is stirred by flowers, perfume, jewelry and so forth intended to remedy uncleanness, and because of these they consider themselves and others clean.[30] Through stupidity people desire this body which is like a festering sore disguised by garlands of flowers and clothes.[31]]

It is like smearing butter on a cat's nose, which makes it think even a handful of insipid food is rich and tasty.

Assertion: There are fragrances and so forth for which one invariably feels desire.
Answer:

> 74. **It is inappropriate to call clean that**
> **Toward which freedom from desire arises.**
> **Nor is there anything which is**
> **A definitive cause of desire.**

There is no thing which is a definitive cause of desire since in the end one will become free of desire toward all things. [Even flowers and so forth, which are held to be clean, become unappealing when they wither, and one sees practitioners who are free from attachment to such things.[32]] To call clean the body, toward which exalted Foe Destroyers have generated freedom from desire, is inappropriate.

It is like the following analogy: A merchant, not recognizing his daughter, felt strong desire for her, but when he recognized her, he was free from desire.

A merchant was on a long journey when his daughter was born. On the day he returned, his daughter, who had grown up, was playing with other girls in a park on the outskirts of the town. On seeing her he felt strong desire, but when he heard from someone else that she was his daughter, his desire left him.[33]

Question: Is it possible or not for a single thing to comprise all four of these undistorted features, such as impermanence and so forth?
Answer:

> 75. **In summary, all four, that is**
> **Impermanence, uncleanness, suffering**
> **And selflessness are possible**
> **With regard to a single [thing].**

In summary, all four—impermanence, uncleanness, suffering and selflessness—are possible with regard to a single [contaminated[34]] thing, for whatever is a product is impermanent, because of being momentary. Whatever is impermanent is unclean because it produces aversion. Whatever is unclean is suffering because it harms. Whatever is suffering is selfless, because it is not under its own power.

[An ogress lived with a man, pretending to be his wife. He treated her as his wife until he realized that she made him suffer and was unpleasant, disobedient and unreliable. Then he realized that she was not his wife but an ogress, and his desire left him when he felt afraid. Similarly the intelligent become free from desire because they see the nature of products.[35]]

Therefore, developing aversion to cyclic existence, the uncleanness of which is exemplified by one's own body, make effort to gain the path to liberation.

The summarizing stanza:

> Understanding that sentient beings are also bound
> Like oneself in this unclean prison,
> With energy generate compassion observing
>   transmigrators,
> And make effort to accomplish highest enlightenment.

This is the third chapter of the *Four Hundred on the Yogic Deeds*, showing the means to abandon belief in cleanness.

This concludes the commentary on the third chapter, showing how to abandon erroneous belief in cleanness, from *Essence of Good Explanations, Explanation of the "Four Hundred on the Yogic Deeds of Bodhisattvas"*.

COMMENTARY TO CHAPTER III
BY GESHE SONAM RINCHEN

Along with ignorance, desire is the most serious cause of our problems. To overcome it completely we must gain effective knowledge of how things exist, but meanwhile we need to cultivate ways of dealing with and counteracting desire when it manifests. Whether directed toward things, experiences or people, desire arises from an incorrect mental approach which misapprehends its object. Distortion takes place in that the attractiveness and wholesomeness of the desired object are exaggerated, and this is accompanied by grasping. Desire inevitably creates difficulties because projection based on misconception without any basis in reality takes place. By observing it in action, we can discover the self-deception and fabrication in this process.

It is difficult but vital to distinguish desire and attachment from love and compassion, which are constructive emotions that we need to cultivate toward all beings, and to cultivate actively toward those with whom we have daily contact. The stronger these positive qualities become, the more ready we are to act unselfishly to alleviate others' suffering and ensure their well-being. Since love and compassion have a sound basis in reality, seeing others as they really are, they are not capricious but stable. Relationships governed by genuine concern of this kind do not constrict and are of lasting benefit.

When counteracting desire, the intention is not to provoke hatred and antipathy toward oneself or others. Indeed, for spiritual growth it is essential to see all living beings as valuable and lovable. There are many valid reasons to support the cultivation of these attitudes, such as our total dependence on others for survival. It is also important to value the body as a precious tool. However, desire of all kinds, particularly sexual desire, has a disturbing effect and prevents us from seeing things as they are. Our profound dissatisfaction with the body is revealed by our preoccupation with cleansing it, removing its natural odors, hiding its flaws, beautifying it, altering its shape and proportions and disguising signs of aging. Our unwillingness to accept that the body is unclean, which expresses itself in terms of our immediate response to any mention of that fact, shows the intensity of our attachment to and identification with the body. This makes us crave comfort and sensual pleasure and react with hostility toward anything which threatens to deprive us of these. Yet when we examine our own bodily processes and bodily excretions, it is difficult to cling to the idea of it as clean.

Desire and attachment cannot be driven out by subjugating the body through asceticism. The body must be nurtured appropriately, since good health enables us to be active for others' benefit. Our efforts should be directed toward subduing the mind and bringing about changes in our attitudes. This will bring us and others happiness, for there is no doubt that people and animals experience a sense of well-being and tranquillity in the presence of those who are not at the mercy of turbulent emotions but in whom the warmth of love and compassion is steady.

We respond to dependently arising phenomena that come about through contaminated actions and disturbing emotions as though they were stable and cling to them even though intellectually we are probably aware of their ephemeral nature. Nothing associated with cyclic existence is reliable. Friends become foes and foes become friends. Possessions and wealth merely stimulate our appetite for more and do not provide the lasting satisfaction we crave. Our status in society can change radically overnight and eventually we and our most loved friends and partners will be separated like autumn leaves scattered by the wind. Since these are all in constant flux and unreliable, they fail to give us comfort and enduring happiness. They are therefore disappointing and since, because of this, they stimulate aversion, they are referred to as unclean or unwholesome. Unless we acknowledge the unsatisfactoriness of this present situation, in which we are governed by contaminated actions and disturbing emotions and seek fulfillment in that which by nature is unstable and flawed, we will not feel any incentive to change.

Chapter IV

Abandoning Pride

The antidote destroying the seeds of conceptions of a self is explained in the last eight chapters [of this text]. Here, the antidote to overcome manifest conceptions of a self is explained. Moreover, since kings are very proud, the conceptions of "I" and "mine" are explained mainly with reference to them.

> 76. Who that is wise about worldly existence
> Would be arrogant, thinking "I" and "mine"?
> For all things belong equally
> To all embodied beings.

By considering oneself praiseworthy, arrogant pride arises, thinking, "I am the owner," which is a conception of the self, and, "These things are mine." This does not occur in the excellent who think correctly about the state of worldly existence. Generating such pride might be appropriate if a certain person could have control over a certain thing throughout all lives. However, all things, such as different places, are the same in that through the power of previous actions they will eventually be used by all ordinary embodied beings. For example forests and houses are common property.

It is also like an actor. An actor plays the part of a king for a while and then appears as a minister, a Brahmin, a householder and a servant. Similarly a king performs in the five transmigrations and will not remain in the same role forever.[1]

Assertion: Since all worldly enterprises are under the king's control, pride is appropriate.

Answer: After the crops of wild rice, which were not planted by the people of the first era, declined and land was apportioned, people began stealing each other's harvest. For protection, they gave one sixth of their harvest as payment to the person they appointed to guard their fields and called him the king.

> 77. Society's servant, paid with a sixth part,
>   Why are you so arrogant?
>   Your becoming the agent of actions
>   Depends on being placed in control.

How then can it be appropriate for you, the king, to feel arrogant, when you are the servant of a community of many people, paid with a sixth of the harvest? It is inappropriate to claim proudly, "I control all activities." Your becoming the agent of an action depends upon your being placed in control and appointed agent by the people. For instance, it is inappropriate for a servant to feel proud when his master delegates a task to him. When a servant is put in charge of a particular task, his master depends on him to do it, but this dependence does not justify pride on the servant's part.[2]

Assertion: Pride is appropriate because a king controls the giving and getting of wealth.
  Answer:

> 78. When those in his care receive their due,
>   They think of their master as the giver.
>   When the master gives what is to be given,
>   He thinks with conceit, "I am the giver."

When those in the king's care receive their annual wages due for service rendered, they think of themselves as inferior and of their master as the giver. Their master with conceit and arrogance thinks, "I am the giver," when he gives those in his care the wealth to be given. This is inappropriate and like feeling proud of being a benefactor because of paying employees their wages.

Assertion: Pride is appropriate because a king is free to enjoy all objects.
  Answer: It is not appropriate.

> 79. That which you wrongly regard,
>   Others [consider] a source of suffering.
>   Living by working for others,
>   What causes you pleasure?

What wrongly appears as a cause for superlative happiness to you, king, is seen as a source of suffering by those with discriminating wisdom and disciplined senses. Since you experience uninterrupted suffering in the process of protecting large communities of people and must live by working for others, it is not a cause only for happiness. How can this cause you pleasure when it is a source of many problems, like the craving for women, liquor and so forth? It is inappropriate, for instance, to feel glad at being appointed to punish thieves.

Assertion: Pride is appropriate because a king is the protector of his people.
   Answer: Pride merely because of that is inappropriate.

> 80. When a ruler seems to be the protector
>   Of his people, as well as protected,
>   Why be proud because of the one?
>   Why not be free from pride because of the other?

A king may feel proud because he protects his people but it also seems that the ruler himself is protected by the people, since he could not be the king unless they protected him. In that case why be arrogant because of the one? Why not be free from arrogance because of being protected? It is inappropriate to be proud. It is like the following analogy: When both husband and wife look after each other, pride is inappropriate.
   A husband told his wife, "I have to endure hundreds of difficulties, while you can just sit at home comfortably without any problems." She replied, "Why don't you stay at home for a day to do the work and you'll see what it's like." He did and felt depressed.[3]
   It is also like the lion and the forest. The lion protects the forest and the forest protects the lion.

Assertion: Pride is appropriate because a king has the merit of protecting everyone[4] like his own children.
   Answer:

> 81. Those in each caste prefer their own work;
>   Thus a living is hard to find.
>   If you become non-virtuous
>   Good rebirths will be scarce for you.

At present when people are strongly involved in the five degenerations,[5] most are untrustworthy and engaged in non-virtue, because in each caste, such as the Brahmin caste and so forth, people prefer their own work and it is therefore difficult to make a living without any problems. When you seize a sixth part of their merit you become non-virtuous because you also seize a sixth part of their ill deeds. Since good rebirths will therefore be scarce for you, arrogance is inappropriate. It is like a leper who instead of taking medicine wants to drink milk and eat fish, [which will aggravate his disease. Not only does a king perform many ill deeds, but he adds to these the wrong actions done by others.[6]]

Assertion: Pride is appropriate because a king is the protector of his people and independent.
  Answer: That is not so.

> 82. Those who act at others' insistence
>   Are called fools on this earth.
>   There is no one else at all
>   So dependent on others as you.

Someone who does not do work that must be done and which he can do, but acts only at the insistence of others is called a fool on this earth. Since a king's actions depend on the requests and insistence of others, there is no one else at all so dependent on others as you. Therefore it is unjustified to feel proud. For instance, it is not appropriate for someone who catches and frees dogs and monkeys for others to feel proud.

Assertion: Pride is appropriate because the protection of his people against harm from others depends on the king.
  Answer:

> 83. Claiming that "protection depends on me,"
>   You take payment from the people,
>   But if you perform ill deeds,
>   Who is equally merciless?

Who is as merciless as a king who performs ill deeds? None. Claiming that the protection of his people depends on him, when his people do not make a large payment, he takes by force and himself performs many ill deeds such as killing. He is like a bad physician who, greedy for money, does not relieve pain at once but only gradually.

A butcher was grinding bones when a splinter got into his eye. He went to a physician who, instead of removing the splinter, gave him medicine to relieve the pain. The splinter continued to cause trouble, necessitating numerous visits to the physician who charged for each consultation. Eventually the physician left town. The butcher's son managed to remove the splinter, which finally brought lasting relief. Likewise, kings take money from the people but do not do their work.[7]

Assertion: If wrongdoers are not punished, it is detrimental to others. Therefore, to protect the people it is proper to exact punishment.
  Answer: That is not so.

84. **If people who do ill deeds**
    Should not be treated with mercy,
    All ordinary childish people
    Would also not need to be protected.

If it is inappropriate to be merciful toward people who have done great wrong such as killing, ordinary childish people would also not need to be protected with compassion [since they are all engaged in wrongdoing.[8]] A king should be especially merciful to wrongdoers, otherwise although not called a brigand he will be one [because of taking payment without giving protection.[9]] A king must protect them just as he protects his own body and wealth [even though the wrongdoers are a source of trouble.[10]]

Assertion: A king who punishes wrongdoers to protect everyone is not a wrongdoer himself because he is engaged in helping the good.
  Answer:

85. **There is nothing that will not serve**
    As a reason for happiness.
    Reasons such as scriptural statements
    Will not destroy demerit.

There is nothing that through attachment to wrong ideas will not serve as a reason for happiness. Those who enjoy killing fish and pigs think, "This is the traditional work of my caste," and feel happy. Some deleterious Brahmin treatises say that animals were created by the lord of the nine transmigrations to provide sustenance, and killing them is therefore not an ill deed. Reasons such as scriptural statements, false arguments and the like will not dissipate or destroy the limitless ill deeds of those who exert themselves to kill and who hold such views.
  The words *yod mi 'gyur*[11] are a corrupt version of the text.
  It is like thinking one's undigested meal has been digested and eating more food. A greedy man, who thought he had digested his

last meal when he hadn't, asked some Brahmins whether it would be alright to eat again, drink water and go to sleep. They replied that it would and he suffered as a result. When his doctor asked him why he had done so, he replied that he had acted on others' advice. Actually he did it for pleasure, but he got very ill. Similarly, a king does ill deeds for pleasure and thereby creates the causes for great suffering as a hell being.[12]

Assertion: Since protecting his people is a cause for high rebirth and therefore a religious practice, a king needs no other.
  Answer:

> 86. If giving proper protection is
>   A ruler's religious practice,
>   Why would the toil of artisans too
>   Not be religious practice?

If it is a ruler's religious practice when, as a king paid with a sixth, he gives proper protection to his people and is acknowledged to do so, why would the work of artisans who toil to make weapons and moats for others' protection not also be religious practice? It too should be religious practice. If one agrees, there will be nothing that is not a religious practice. The king is like a man hired to protect the town.

Assertion: Since an intelligent king protects his people out of attachment, he is irreproachable.
  Answer:

> 87. This example shows the ruler on whom
>   The people rely as reprehensible.
>   The excellent see attachment to existence
>   As mother of all those in the world.

Being a ruler on whom the people rely for protection is a source of arrogance and all kinds of recklessness and is therefore reprehensible. The wise Exalted ones who see things without error regard attachment to existence as the mother of those in the world because it produces them. Recognizing attachment to existence as faulty, they eradicate it. For instance a trader in a wilderness who charges an exorbitant price for things is reprehensible.

A trader was responsible for getting equipment to protect his companions during a journey through the wilderness. He sold them the equipment at a high price. He is reprobate not for equipping his companions but for charging an exorbitant price. Similarly, although his people rely on the king because they benefit from his protection and so forth, he is nevertheless reprehensible because of his self-interest.[13]

Assertion: Because of his compassion, a king's protection of his people is his religious practice.
  Answer: That is not so.

> 88. The sensible do not acquire kingship.
>   Since fools have no compassion,
>   These merciless rulers of men,
>   Although protectors, are irreligious.

The sensible, who have not foolishly turned away from good paths like ethical conduct and are not attached just to power and wealth, do not acquire kingship. Fools, who are ignorant about actions and their effects, have no compassion. Kings, these merciless rulers of men, although they are protectors, are irreligious and a source of conceit and recklessness. It is like the merciless minister of a cruel king.

The minister of a cruel king was unable to make a man being punished pay a fine in gold. This angered the king. One of the man's associates was approached and he agreed to assist. Using violence he forced the man to pay, and the king made this associate his minister. Wishing to please the king further, he performed a terrible ill deed. Unable to kill the man with weapons, he set the whole area on fire and killed many thousands of creatures. The king was pleased even about this.[14]

Assertion: Treatises by sages state that even if, owing to the code of the royal caste, a king acts violently, he has not performed an ill deed.
  Answer:

> 89. Sages' activities are not all
>   [Actions] that the wise perform,
>   For there are inferior,
>   Mediocre and superior ones.

Not all the activities described in treatises by sages are performed by wise sages, for there are different kinds: inferior, mediocre and superior sages. For instance, treatises by some sages recommend intercourse with those with whom sexual intercourse is improper.

Assertion: Because past kings who took these social treatises to be valid looked after their people well, these treatises must be valid.

Answer: It is not certain that people will be happy by following these social treatises.

> 90. Virtuous rulers of the past
>   Protected the people like their children.
>   Through the practices of this time of strife
>   It is now like a waste without wildlife.

Former virtuous and kind rulers, such as universal monarchs who protected the people like their own children, increased happiness and prosperity. But those who rely on the practices of this time of strife nowadays devastate the world, making it like a waste without wildlife. Therefore treatises incompatible with religious practice are not valid. It is like a barbarian thief pressing unripe sugar-cane.

A barbarian thief stole unripe sugar-cane and pressed it but obtained no juice. Just as his action was futile both in terms of the present and the future, when he would have to bear the consequences of his theft, a king's failure to look after his people is futile both now and regarding the future because he creates much demerit.[15]

Assertion: Treatises state it is not irreligious even if a king harms his enemies when occasions to do so arise.

Answer:

> 91. If a king who seizes the occasion
>   To harm is not doing wrong,
>   Then others, too, such as thieves
>   Have not done so in the first place.

If a king who seizes the occasion to harm an enemy or anyone else that has acted improperly by beating him with sticks and the like is not doing wrong, others too, like thieves, have not done wrong in the first place—a thief finds an occasion to strike at someone rich first, and the king later finds an occasion to strike back. Finding an occasion to strike is explained as finding an occasion to harm. For instance, when the king died a certain minister killed the young prince and appropriated the kingship himself, which brought him many unwanted consequences.

Having seized the opportunity to do harm, he had a bad reputation in this life and was born in a bad transmigration in the next because of his demeritorious action. Then why would kings who seize opportunities to harm not be wrongdoers and infamous too?[16]

Assertion: By defeating the enemy in battle one acquires wealth and pleases the king, and if one dies for him in battle one will go to a high rebirth. Therefore a king should take pleasure in warfare.
   Answer:

> **92. If giving all one has for liquor**
> **And so on is not an offering,**
> **Why consider it an offering**
> **To give oneself in battle?**

If giving all one has for liquor, gambling and women is not an offering that pleases the excellent and if it is also demeritorious, why consider giving one's life in battle out of anger and greed an offering to please the excellent? For what reason would one take a high rebirth through this? It is not feasible. It is like a shepherd's wife who showed her body to her father-in-law.

A shepherd's wife was rude to her father-in-law while her husband was out visiting. When he came home the old shepherd told him about it and said, "If she behaves rudely to me again, I won't stay in your house." Considering his father more important than his wife, and wanting to please him, the shepherd angrily told her, "If you're rude to my father again, I won't let you stay in this house. In future you must do for him what is hardest to do and give him what is hardest to give." She agreed to this. The next time her husband was invited out, she served her father-in-law most respectfully. That day she bathed and massaged him with oil, garlanded him and gave him plenty to eat and drink. That night she washed his feet with lukewarm water and rubbed them with mustard oil. Then she took off her clothes and, stark naked, lay down on his bed in a provocative way. The old shepherd exclaimed, "Oh! You wicked girl! What are you doing?" She repeated what her husband had told her to do and said, "This is what is hardest for me to give." But he replied, "You did it to get rid of me. You can stay, but I am leaving right away!"

When her husband returned and found his father gone, she told him she had done just as he had said, but when he questioned further, she revealed what had happened. Out of respect for his father he drove her out and brought him back to the house. Giving her body to her father-in-law was not an offering. Similarly it is no offering when sentient beings sacrifice their lives in battle for a bad king.[17]

Assertion: It is reasonable to like being a king, because a king is the guardian of all his people.
   Answer:

> 93. You, the king, guardian of the people,
> Have no guardian yourself.
> Since your guardianship does not
> Release you, who would be happy?

Since a king is the guardian of his people, they follow his instructions, giving up unsuitable activities and engaging in suitable ones. However you, the king, have no guardian and, living in a morass of corruption without any guardian, your actions are arbitrary. Because you have guardianship yet have no mentor, the causes of suffering in bad rebirths hold you fast and have not released you. Therefore who would be happy about gaining kingship? It is unreasonable to be happy.

Most versions read this way and when the meaning is examined it may be explained as "does not release."[18] It seems appropriate also to say it is unreasonable to be happy because the causes of suffering do not let go and because of being without a friend or guardian.

For instance, a senior monk without a superior enjoys homage paid to him. [Likewise a king, having no superior, enjoys the obeisance and respect he receives.[19]]

Assertion: Since a king whose punishments are mild does not become famous, while one who punishes harshly is famous even after his death, it is appropriate to give harsh punishment.
   Answer:

> 94. Though a king is famous after his death
> It will bring no benefit.
> Do you, being worthless, and those who
> Cook dogs not have notoriety?

If posthumous fame brought some benefit, that would be all right, but even though a king is famous after his death, it brings no benefits, such as the elimination of ill deeds. If fame could wash away the stains of wrongdoing, why would you, because of your worthless actions like seizing others' wealth, and those who cook dogs, because of their awesomeness to dogs, not enjoy great fame? Therefore if one is interested in one's own good, it is not appropriate to punish harshly. It is like the following analogy: Seeing a rich woman's body being given an expensive cremation, another woman thought, "I will be rich too," and killed herself. A king who performs ill deeds for the sake of fame is like this.

Assertion: A prince of royal caste is fit to rule while others are not, therefore pride is appropriate.
   Answer: It is not.

> 95. When all power and wealth
>   Are produced by merit,
>   It cannot be said that this one
>   Will not be a basis for power and wealth.

When enjoyment of the power and wealth of all kingship is produced by merit, it cannot be said that this sentient being will never in any life act as a basis for power and wealth. It is therefore not appropriate to feel proud, since power and wealth belong equally to all who create meritorious actions. It is like a craft which belongs equally to all who learn it.

Assertion: Since the practice of kingship is only explained to those of the royal caste but not the other three and thus the royal caste alone should rule, pride because of caste is appropriate.
   Answer:

> 96. In the world caste is determined
>   With regard to the main means of livelihood.
>   Thus there is no division among
>   All sentient beings by way of caste.

Castes are not distinct by way of their own entity. Humans of the first era were born miraculously from mind and were endowed with luminosity. They had miraculous powers and could travel in space. They lived on the food of joy and did not have male or female sexual organs. Later, as they began to eat coarse food, they gradually developed different shapes determined by their male and female organs, and birth from the womb occurred.[20] Then, because of hoarding, stealing and so forth began. To protect against stealing, a man in his prime was appointed by the majority of the community to guard the fields. Those who agreed to do this work were known as the royal caste. Those who wished to subdue their senses left the towns to do ascetic practices and were called Brahmins. Those who carried out the king's orders were called the official caste, and those put to menial work like ploughing the fields were known as the common caste. Thus, in the world, caste was determined with regard to the main means of gaining a livelihood. There is no innate division among sentient beings based on castes distinct by way of their own entity. It is like pots distinguished by their different contents. [Each one in a set of identical clay pots is designated according to its content, such as the butter pot and the honey pot.[21]]

Thus it is very wrong to accept statements in treatises by sages that say even if a king uses violence it is not irreligious.

Assertion: Since there are four different ancestral lineages among humans, there are castes which differ by way of their own entity.
  Answer:

> 97. **Since it was very long ago**
> **And women's minds are fickle,**
> **There is no one from the caste**
> **Known as the royal caste.**

It is very difficult to find anyone whose caste is certain because of being born from parents of pure caste. Since the division into four castes occurred very long ago in the world, and women's fickle minds have turned toward other men, there is no one who definitely belongs to the caste known as the royal caste. Therefore pride on account of one's ancestry is unjustified. It is like the following analogy: Someone left a golden water pot in a Brahmin household for safe-keeping. In the long period that followed the owners of the house changed many times and the pots changed too.

Someone left a gold water pot in a Brahmin household for safe-keeping. After a long time the owner returned and asked whether a member of the Brahmin family was at home. He was told that there was no Brahmin family living in the house but one of royal caste. The man asked about the gold pot the Brahmins had kept for him, but was told there was no gold pot, only a silver one. He asked them to take care of it for him. After a long time he returned again only to find that the inhabitants of the house now belonged to the official caste and that they were keeping a copper pot. On another occasion when he went there, he found a family of the common caste and the pot was now an iron one. Castes change just like the pot and the family.[22]

Assertion: If one does not become royal through caste, one becomes a member of the royal caste through one's work of protecting everyone.
Answer:

98. If even one of common caste
Through his work could become royal caste,
One might wonder why even a commoner
Should not become Brahmin through his work.

If, by doing the work of the royal caste such as protection of the people, even people of common caste could become royal caste, one might wonder why even those of common caste should not become Brahmin by doing Brahmin work such as reciting the Vedas. Thus it is wrong to think that one belongs to the royal caste because of one's work. For instance, though one speaks of a boat going to "that bank" and coming to "this bank," neither this bank nor that bank exist by way of their own entity, [but are relative to one's position. Similarly caste is merely an attribution.]

Assertion: Through the power and wealth of kingship it is possible when the time is right to distribute possessions and so forth to a great many people. Therefore pride is appropriate.
Answer:

99. A king's ill deeds cannot be
Distributed like his wealth.
What wise person ever destroys
Their future for another's sake?

While it is true that he can distribute possessions accumulated over a long period, a king cannot distribute the ill deeds created in connection with them as he can power and wealth. When one alone must experience the effects of ill deeds, what wise person would destroy their future lives on account of something trivial for someone else's sake? Shame, not pride, is appropriate. It is like the following analogy: When a buffalo is killed, though many eat this sacrificial offering, the ill deed accrues to the killer alone.

A butcher's son was afraid to do wrong and refused to kill deer and other animals. His relations said, "Go ahead and kill. We will share any wrong there is in that." He answered, "I have an awful headache. Please share it with me." "We can't do that," they said. "Then how can the suffering of bad rebirths be shared?"[23]

Assertion: Since one lives with great power and wealth, pride is appropriate.

Answer:

> 100. **Pride caused by power and wealth**
> **Does not remain in the hearts of the wise,**
> **Once one has looked at others**
> **With equal or superior power.**

Regarding pride caused by the power and wealth of kingship and so forth, which thinks, "I am better than others," one must look at those with equal power and wealth as well as others much more mighty than oneself who have superlative power and wealth. Having done so, pride will not remain in the hearts of the wise, who understand how to analyze in detail the way things are. It is like the following analogy: The Brahmin Vasudhara's wife was proud of her body. The proud lady was made to join the retinue of a certain king's queens. Seeing the ladies-in-waiting decreased her pride.

The Brahmin Vasudhara's wife said, "Although there's no one on earth with a body like mine, you don't make me splendid by giving me the clothes and jewelry I deserve." In response he made her a member of the queen's retinue. Seeing the ladies-in-waiting, no need to mention the queen, decreased the pride she felt about her body.[24]

The summarizing stanza:

> Thinking about the impermanence and uncleanness
>   of the body,
> Understand the faults of attachment to it.
> Make effort to achieve unsurpassable enlightenment
> And give up pride in both "I" and "mine."

> **This is the fourth chapter of the *Four Hundred On***
> **the Yogic Deeds, showing the means to abandon**
> **conceptions of a self.**

This concludes the commentary on the fourth chapter, showing the means to abandon erroneous conceptions of a self, from *Essence of Good Explanations, Explanation of the "Four Hundred on the Yogic Deeds of Bodhisattvas".*

COMMENTARY TO CHAPTER IV
BY GESHE SONAM RINCHEN

Pride makes us look down on others as if surveying the surrounding countryside from a mountain top. The wise regard it as an enemy. Nāgārjuna has said that pride on account of our internal and external riches robs us of our wealth of virtue. It conceals our faults and makes us refuse to listen when others point out our weaknesses, depriving us of the chance to correct them. It also blinds us to others' positive qualities and prevents us from emulating them or learning what they can teach us. A person who lacks humility is like a tree without fruit: both stand bolt upright. But someone with humility is like a tree laden with fruit: both bow down. The Ga-dam (*bka' gdams*) masters said the water of good qualities will not stay on a ball of pride. In our case happiness easily leads to arrogance which makes us insensitive and callous to others. We despise them and their misfortunes and are disdainful or condescending in the way we treat them, which hurts their feelings. Pride makes harmonious relationships impossible because it prevents respect for others. It also makes us exercise whatever power we have to reinforce our own status and keep others in an inferior position.

Understanding the disadvantages of pride, we must first try to decrease it and then completely rid ourselves of it. It is essential to recognize the many forms pride can take and discover which we have. Feelings of superiority may arise in relation to those who are inferior, equal, or in fact superior. One may have an overwhelming sense of self-importance or conceit thinking one has attained qualities and insights which one does not possess. One may take pride in thinking one is only slightly inferior to those who are actually vastly superior, or may wrongly feel proud of possessing insights, for example, when one has gone badly astray. One may even be proud of one's humility. By consciously cultivating respect for others, recognizing and valuing their positive qualities, such as generosity, kindness, patience, stability or knowledge, we ourselves can come to possess the same riches because our admiration will make us want to acquire these qualities. Mahākāśyapa is said to have regarded all living beings as his teachers. Just as rivers flow down to the sea, good qualities come to one with humility. Instead of feeling proud because of our social status, possessions, appearance, reputation, knowledge or spiritual accomplishments, we should use these assets to help others, wishing that they too may in future enjoy similar advantages.

Pride must be distinguished from self-confidence. Pride can arise without any justification over something trivial. It is a destructive emotion, whereas self-confidence is a feeling of certainty based on sound reasons that one has the ability to do something. It is an aspect of wisdom and essential in giving us the courage to undertake difficult and challenging tasks.

Chapter V

Bodhisattva Deeds

The explanation of how to train in the deeds, having generated the practical altruistic intention, has four parts. The first is the actual meaning. The second explains the means to abandon disturbing emotions which prevent the deeds. The third shows how to abandon attachment to sense objects on which disturbing emotions focus. The fourth shows the methods of fully training the student's mindstream, making it receptive to the development of spiritual paths.

THE ACTUAL MEANING OF
HOW TO TRAIN IN THE DEEDS

Through the special features of the preceding good and precious explanation those of Hīnayāna disposition, feeling aversion toward cyclic existence, seek liberation. Those of Mahāyāna disposition, having developed great compassion, seek Buddhahood.
Question: Where are the causes for this found?
Answer: In the Buddha.
Question: What is a Buddha like?
Answer:

> 101. Not a single movement of Buddhas
> Is without reason; even their breathing
> Is exclusively for
> The benefit of sentient beings.

Such a supremely compassionate person performs inconceivable activities for the welfare of all sentient beings without exception.

Buddhas make no movement of the three doors[1] that is not for the benefit of sentient beings. *The King of Meditative Stabilizations* says:

> Countless hundreds and thousands of rays come from
> The soles of the King of the Teaching's feet,
> Cooling sentient beings in all the hells.
> Freed from suffering, they enjoy bliss.[2]

And:

> When a Conqueror places his foot on the threshold
> Those blind from birth, those whose ears do not hear,
> The protectorless and those with small merit—
> All of these gain eyes and ears.[3]

Even his breath, which flows naturally without depending on any intention, forms a huge rain cloud above the hell realms like a mound of eye ointment, fascinating the hell beings. From it falls a delicious cooling rain making the mass of fire in the hells die down. Freed from their suffering, the hell beings wonder whose power pacified it, whereupon they see the Buddha's body adorned with the major and minor marks.[4] The force of their admiration stills the suffering of the hells and produces in their minds virtue concordant with the attainment of liberation.

Thus if even his breathing is exclusively for the temporary and ultimate welfare of sentient beings, what need is there to mention the benefit of activities such as teaching? Those interested in their own good should have faith in and respect for Buddha, the Supramundane Victor.

The analogy of what happened when a monk of the Parāśara caste agreed to stay in a mechanic's house for the summer is as in Candrakīrti's commentary.

A master mechanic offered to support a monk of the Parāśara caste if he would stay in his house throughout the summer. In the basement of his house there were many machines doing mechanical work. The monk remained on the premises as his host wished and did not leave the house. Bidding him good-bye when the summer was over, his host gave him money for a set of robes and told him it was payment for his work. The monk replied, "I haven't done any work for you. Why should I accept payment?" His host told him he had done nothing but work during his stay and took him to see the machines and what had been manufactured.[5]

Those who trust the Buddha will gain freedom from all fears, even the fear of death.

102. Just as ordinary people are
     Terrified by the words "Lord of Death,"
     So the words "Omniscient One"
     Terrify the Lord of Death.

The words "Lord of Death" terrify ordinary people. Similarly, just hearing the words "Omniscient One" endow whoever hears them with the good fortune to attain nirvāṇa, thereby terrifying and subjugating Death as well. Sūtra says: Those who hear my name will attain nirvāṇa in any of the three vehicles.[6]

It is like the following analogy: When a son was born to a certain king he issued a decree freeing all prisoners. His subjects were happy [except for the prison guards, who were as frightened as if they had been exposed to a contagious disease. Similarly, when Tathāgatas come all beings except demons are happy.[7]]

Assertion: Surely he lacked omniscience since he did not answer fourteen questions such as whether the self and the world are permanent or impermanent and so forth.

Answer: Rather than disproving, it establishes his omniscience.

103. A Subduer has [perception of] that
     Which should and should not be done or said.
     What reason is there to say
     That the Omniscient One is not all-knowing?

A Subduer directly perceives the right and wrong time for temporary and ultimate actions, what actions should not be done, what is not beneficial, what is harmful, as well as all that should or should not be said.

Since the Buddha possessed such perception, he did not give an answer to these questions, which were based on a belief in the true existence of persons and phenomena. It is not feasible for a basis of attribution whose existence has been negated to have an attribute.[8] He did not answer, because he saw that they would not be receptive vessels for the profound, were he to teach selflessness. Thus there is no reason to say that the Omniscient One is not all-knowing. Indeed this substantiates his omniscience. *The Precious Garland* says:

> Asked whether it had an end
> The Conqueror was silent.
>
> Because he did not give this profound teaching
> To worldly beings who were not receptive vessels,

The all-knowing one is therefore known
As omniscient by the wise.[9]

It is like the following analogy: A certain king, wanting to penalize a rich Brahmin, told him that he would be punished unless he
quickly sent his family's well. The Brahmin's daughter replied,
"Wealth attracts wealth [and one elephant attracts another.[10]] Please
send us a well." In this way they avoided punishment. Similarly, a
Buddha acts for the welfare of sentient beings by skillful means.

Question: If Buddha does not say what should not be said, did he
not say, referring to Devadatta, "What of this boy who wears one
piece of cloth and has taken the bait?"[11]

Answer: Although he said this, it was not to harm others but to
turn them away from ill deeds. He saw that unless he deflated
Devadatta, many transmigrators would be harmed. [Words intended
to benefit, even if unpleasant, are entirely virtuous.[12]]

Mind should be understood as paramount or foremost in all activities of the three doors.

104. **Without intention, actions like going**
     Are not seen to have merit and so forth.
     In all actions, therefore, the mind
     Should be understood as paramount.

This is because actions like coming and going are not seen to be
meritorious or demeritorious except[13] through the power of the virtuous or non-virtuous intention motivating them. It is like the following analogy: A naked ascetic[14] entered a temple and prostrated
to one statue while touching another with his posterior, thereby creating virtue as well as an ill deed.[15]

105. **In Bodhisattvas, through their intention,**
     All actions, virtuous and non-virtuous,
     Become perfect virtue because
     They are in control of their minds.

Since mind is foremost in all activities, virtuous actions such as giving or even such actions as killing, which in others would be non-
virtuous, all become perfect virtue in Bodhisattvas who are in control of their minds, because of their motivation to help others. This
is because they have gained the ability at will to engage in virtue and
not to engage in non-virtue. [Cutting off a finger bitten by a snake

stops the momentum of much greater suffering and causes only a little pain. This does not make the doctors who do it non-virtuous. Bodhisattvas' deeds are like this.[16]]

It is like the following analogy: A Bodhisattva called Mahākaruṇā, who was a captain, used a short spear to slay a pirate captain who intended to kill a group of five hundred Bodhisattvas on board. He thereby turned his back on a hundred thousand aeons of cyclic existence.[17]

Question: When are such Bodhisattvas known as "ultimate Bodhisattvas"?

Answer: After they have attained the first ground.[18]

106. The merit of Bodhisattvas with
     The first intention far exceeds
     That which would make all beings on earth
     Become universal monarchs.

The special features of their good qualities are as follows: if the accumulated merit through which one becomes a universal monarch ruling the four continents is great, there is no need to mention that the merit required for all beings on earth to do so would be greater. The merit of a Bodhisattva who has generated the first ultimate altruistic intention far exceeds the merit that would make all beings on earth become universal monarchs.

It is like the following analogy: A king issued an edict which made it easy to know what was permitted and not permitted. This brought the king wealth [and his subjects security. Similarly the altruistic intention of Bodhisattvas on the first ground acts as a cause for everything up to the attainment of Buddhahood by sentient beings and thus allows what is of great importance to transmigrators to occur.[19]]

Some, failing to differentiate between the attributes of conventional and ultimate Bodhisattvas, claim that if they are common beings, they cannot be fully qualified Bodhisattvas. Since this is a grave ill deed, it should be thrown out like a gob of spittle.

Question: How much merit is there in inspiring others to develop the altruistic intention of the Great Vehicle?

Answer:

107. Someone may build a precious
     Reliquary, as high as the world;
     It is said training others to generate
     The altruistic intention is more excellent.

It is said that the merit of one who builds a reliquary for the Buddha's relics, as vast as the three thousand great thousand world systems[20] and as high as the world "Beneath None,"[21] made of the seven precious substances such as gold and lapis lazuli[22] and adorned with every kind of ornament is surpassed, because it is more excellent, by the merit of one who trains others to develop the altruistic intention.

It is like the following analogy: A man died and one of his friends cremated his body, while the other looked after all his children. Just as this was best, the merit of causing others to generate the intention to attain supreme enlightenment, so that the Buddha's lineage may not be broken, is superior to cremating the body of a Buddha.

Question: How do Bodhisattvas act to benefit sentient beings?
Answer: They act according to those beings' dispositions.

> 108. **A spiritual guide who wishes to help**
> **Must be attentive toward students.**
> **They are called students because**
> **Of not knowing what will benefit.**

A spiritual guide who wishes to help must be physically and verbally attentive to students in keeping with their dispositions. They are called students because they do not know what actions are of benefit and need someone else's advice. [An elephant is made submissive by first giving it sweets and sugar cane. The training hooks are used on it later.[23]] It is like the following analogy: Through miraculous feats the Teacher gradually took care of Uruvilvā-Kāśyapa.[24]

Even if students are recalcitrant, one must endeavor to overcome their disturbing emotions.

> 109. **Just as a physician is not upset with**
> **Someone who rages while possessed by a demon,**
> **Subduers see disturbing emotions as**
> **The enemy, not the person who has them.**

Though a possessed patient rages at him, a physician will not be upset with this sick person of whom a demon has taken hold. Similarly, Subduers see that because they make sentient beings unruly, the disturbing emotions in a trainee's mindstream are at fault and not the person who has them. Those who wish to take care of trainees must learn to act like this.

It is like the analogy of a lion who attacks the one who throws the weapon, not the weapon that is thrown.

110. That for which someone has
     Liking should first be assessed.
     Those who are disinclined will not
     Be vessels for the excellent teaching.

A spiritual guide teaching students should discuss whatever practice, such as giving, appeals to a particular trainee. Having first taught this properly, an assessment should be made. One should only discuss the profound later, after initial and subsequent instruction has been given. Those whose minds are disinclined because of being deterred by discussion of the profound at the outset will not be receptive vessels for the ultimate teaching. The miserly dislike talk of generosity. [The angry do not like to hear about patience, nor those with loose morality about ethical conduct.²⁵] Therefore those who desire resources should be told to give. [Those who want high status will like to hear about ethics and those who desire a good appearance will enjoy hearing about patience.²⁶] It is like the following analogy: The Bodhisattva Keśava gradually guided a merchant's daughter according to her disposition.

A merchant's daughter, crazed by attachment, carried her husband's corpse on her shoulders. To relieve her suffering, the Bodhisattva Keśava, who was a doctor, carried a woman's corpse on his shoulders for six months.²⁷

A Bodhisattva is particularly compassionate to one who, despite having been stopped from doing wrong a hundred times, again and again engages in improper actions.

111. Just as a mother is especially
     Anxious about a sick child,
     Bodhisattvas are especially
     Compassionate toward the unwise.

A mother, for instance, feels especially anxious about a sick child. Similarly, Bodhisattvas are especially compassionate toward the unwise. It is like the following analogy: A Caṇḍala woman greatly feared that the king would put her sixth son to death because of his wrong deeds.

A Caṇḍala woman, five of whose sons were Exalted ones, was not anxious when the king threatened to put them to death if they did wrong, for she had no fear of them doing so. However she was worried when he threatened the sixth son, because he was an ordinary person and she feared he might do wrong.²⁸

112. They become students of some
     And become teachers of others,
     Through skillful means and knowledge
     Giving understanding to those who do not under-
        stand.

Since people's dispositions, interests and capacities differ, when Bodhisattvas act for their good, they teach some what is of benefit after first becoming their students. They act as spiritual guides to those who feel inferior and teach them by pointing out their special attributes. Through all kinds of skillful means and knowledge in training, they make sentient beings who do not understand the suchness of phenomena understand it.

It is like the following analogy: A good physician will prescribe different diets to his patients, such as rich food or bland food.

113. Just as for an experienced physician
     A sickness that cannot be cured is rare,
     Once Bodhisattvas have found their strength,
     Those they cannot train are extremely few.

A Bodhisattva with a well-developed capacity for maturing sentient beings is like an experienced physician who only rarely finds a disease incurable and beyond treatment. Similarly, one should understand that when Bodhisattvas who are able to discern superior and inferior aptitudes and are skilled in the four ways of gathering students[29] have found their strength, those they cannot train are extremely few.

It is like the following analogy: While all the other physicians did not realize it, the Master Nāgārjuna recognized that desire for a woman had caused the mental illness of a king's son and was able to pacify it.

114. If some within a Bodhisattva's sphere,
     Lacking encouragement, go
     To bad rebirths, that one will be
     Criticized by others with intelligence.

If a Bodhisattva possessing the special ability to train sentient beings encourages trainees within his or her sphere of influence, they will not go to bad transmigrations. If some, lacking encouragement, go to bad rebirths, the promise to help all sentient beings will have been impaired. Therefore that Bodhisattva will be criticized by others with intelligence. Thus one should encourage people by teaching them appropriate practices. It is like the following analogy: A leader who does not assist those in his care will be criticized.

115. How can one unwilling to say
That compassion for the oppressed is good,
Later out of compassion
Give to the protectorless?

If out of jealousy a Bodhisattva who is a beginner is unwilling to admit that it is good to act compassionately toward other sentient beings who are oppressed by suffering and its causes, how could that Bodhisattva later, out of compassion, give protectorless beings his or her body, possessions and root-virtues? It is like stealing a blind man's things or killing for a pair of boots. Thus one should endeavor to increase the strength of one's compassion.

Question: What are the faults of hating a Bodhisattva who is governed by compassion?
Answer:

116. When those [beings] suffer loss
Who are indifferent toward
One who stays in the world to help transmigrators,
What doubt about those who are hostile?

It is a great loss for those who, through indifference, do not appreciate and render service to one who is motivated by the wish for all sentient beings without exception to attain the final state of nirvāṇa in which the aggregates do not remain,[30] and who, to help transmigrators, has the power to stay in worldly existence while it lasts for others' benefit. This being so, what doubt can there be that hostility toward one like that is an ill deed? The *Miraculous Feat of Ascertaining Thorough Pacification Sūtra*[31] and the *Seal of Engagement in Augmenting the Strength of Faith Sūtra*[32] say that one will definitely experience the misfortune of suffering in bad rebirths more than a hundred times.

It is like the following analogy: Someone begged some men in charge of many elephants to look after his cattle and sheep. Later when he asked the men if they were well, they replied, "How can we be well? The rain caused a flood which carried all the elephants away." Hearing this he knew about the other animals and did not inquire further.

It is also like the analogies of sweets fried in oil and the walking stick.

A man left a walking stick in a bag at a friend's house. When he went there later and asked about his health, his friend replied, "How could I be well? The rats have been causing so much damage, they even ate the walking stick you left here." The man went away without asking about the bag.[33]

Seeing some old men eating the flowers of the spider wisp plant,[34] another person said:

> When old men who can eat a lot
> Eat flowers of the spider wisp,
> Know that also they will eat
> Sweets and pastries fried in oil.[35]

It is proper to rid oneself of animosity toward Bodhisattvas and develop strong appreciation for them, since they do what is most difficult.

117. **One who in all lives has the five**
     Super-knowledges [appears] as inferior
     With a nature like the inferior—
     This is extremely hard to do.

A Bodhisattva who has attained forbearance[36] as well as the five kinds of super-knowledge[37] which will not decline throughout all future lives, may, in order to help sentient beings in the form of an inferior transmigrator in a bad rebirth, completely assume a body whose nature is like that of inferior beings such as worms, butterflies, buffalo and dogs with their appearance and voice. The feat of thus maturing sentient beings is extremely hard to perform. It is like the Bodhisattva who saw that many dogs would be harmed in the future and took rebirth as a dog to prevent it.

As soon as he was born he looked for a lonely place to live and always stayed at the edge of the wilderness with the other dogs. One day the dogs ate the leather cover of the king's favorite chariot. The king was furious and ordered all the dogs to be rounded up and killed. Without being seen by anyone, the Bodhisattva crept under the king's lion-throne, which was set in the center of his court, but the king caught sight of him and declared, "The one that ate the leather cover of the king's horse-chariot is here. Now that you're here, we will not let you go."

To this the Bodhisattva replied, "If I fail to dissuade you, of course I should be punished."

"How can you do anything but fail, when you ate the leather cover?" said the king.

The Bodhisattva replied, "It's the palace attendants' fault. Animals don't know what they should or shouldn't eat. For a start, even if I did eat it myself, the guards are still in the wrong and not I. In that case how can all the dogs living in this district, this town and this country be guilty? If one ate it, all of them didn't do it. The king's order that they should all be punished is therefore unjust. Do humans receive the same treatment? I think not. And if they don't, it is ridiculously unfair." The king was moved and delighted by these amazingly human words. He prevented the dogs from being harmed and became involved in religious practices.[38]

When a king was abroad, he stayed with a serving woman who bore him a child. The other children said to him, "Serving woman's brat, be off! You don't even know whose son you are!" He went to his mother and when he asked who had fathered him, she said it was the king. He told her, "Offer me to the king and tell him to accept his son." She replied that the king would not accept him and that she would be beaten. He began to cry and his longing pained her heart. She went to see the king who was surrounded by his courtiers and pointed to her son, but the king looked the other way. Urged on by the child, she walked over to the other side, but when she showed him the boy, the king just did the same again. The boy told his mother, "Why are you gesturing? Speak to him!" Because of her son's misery, she spoke to the king in a loud voice: "Your Highness, recognize your son. Till now I have brought him up." The king was embarrassed and ordered his men to beat the serving woman who, he said, was a liar. As they approached her with whips in their hands, the Bodhisattva, like the king of geese spreading his wings, flew up from his mother's lap and hovering in the sky asked the king, "Are you not pleased that I am the king's son?" The king, with tearful eyes and gooseflesh, rose from his golden throne and stretching out his arms said in a barely audible voice, "Please come down, holy being. If you take care of Indra, king of the gods, my son, surely you must take care of such as me." Having said this, he made offerings to him and his mother as was befitting.[39]

One should develop faith in Bodhisattvas by considering their boundless qualities.

118. The Tathāgata said that the merit
Gathered constantly through skillful means
For a very long time is immeasurable
Even for the omniscient.

Through their ability effortlessly to accomplish difficult feats for sentient beings, the merit created constantly by their three doors and accumulated over an extremely long period of countless aeons is as limitless as space. It is said to be immeasurable even for the omniscient. The Tathāgata said:

The ocean may be [measured] in drops,
[Mount Meru in mustard seeds,
The earth in tiny quantities —
Who can measure a Bodhisattva's qualities?][40]

The analogy can be understood completely from the above.

The life stories of the Buddha and so forth say that talk of ethical conduct does not interest Bodhisattvas to the same extent as talk of giving.

119. The word "giving" indicates
Death, practice and other existences.
That is why the word "giving" always
Is of interest to Bodhisattvas.

When the Sanskrit word for giving, *dāna*,[41] is explained in terms of etymologies that repeat the syllable of the root, it indicates dying, which is consistent with aversion. It sometimes indicates practices included within the six perfections by way of the divisions of giving,[42] and sometimes the attainment of desired rebirths by guarding the purity of the three doors. Thus since the word "giving" denotes death, practices and other existences, it is always of interest to Bodhisattvas who therefore take special delight in giving. It is like a man who was condemned to death hearing he is to be spared. No other words are as sweet.

Question: Is only a Bodhisattva's generosity and not that of others boundless?
Answer:

120. When one thinks that by giving gifts now
     There will be a great result,
     Receiving and giving are like trade
     For profit, which will be criticized.

To receive and give away things thinking that giving gifts in this life
will result in great prosperity is like trade for profit and will therefore be criticized by the excellent. It is like the profit from selling all
one's goods.

When a merchant sells all his goods he makes a profit but not
merit. Similarly one who gives, desiring the results of giving, will gain
prosperity but not liberation, because of still being bound in the
prison of cyclic existence.[43]

121. For such a one, even previously
     Performed ill deeds will have no [effect].
     There is nothing one with virtue
     Considers should not be accomplished.

Though Bodhisattvas who create limitless merit may even have performed a few ill deeds previously, these will not be able to produce
an effect. It is said:

> A few grams of salt can change the taste
> Of a little water, but not of the Ganges.
> Understand it is likewise with small ill deeds
> And expansive roots of virtue.

There is nothing that Bodhisattvas, whose virtuous activity is powerful, consider should not be done for others' benefit. They therefore fulfill all the needs of sentient beings. The analogy is as in the
cited stanza.

Question: Since Exalted Bodhisattvas are entirely virtuous and do not
take birth in cyclic existence through the force of contaminated actions and disturbing attitudes, why do they not remain absorbed in
the sphere of peace?
Answer:

122. Even here nothing harms
     One with a powerful mind, and thus
     For such a one, worldly existence
     And nirvāṇa are no different.

Bodhisattvas whose minds hold a powerful special wish, and who
do not create even the slightest ill deed though remaining in cyclic
existence, are not tainted by its faults. Since even in cyclic existence
nothing harms them, there is no difference, in terms of harm,
whether they remain in worldly existence or enter nirvāṇa. Thus they
do not prefer one kind of peace to another. It is like the following
analogy: A mother does not feel discouraged caring for her only child
who is ill. [Similarly, Bodhisattvas are never discouraged in their efforts to free sentient beings from all the sicknesses of the disturbing
emotions.][44]

Question: Why do they have mastery of most Bodhisattva activities
from the time they generate the first ultimate altruistic intention?
   Answer:

123. **Why should anyone who takes birth**
     Through constant control of the mind
     Not become a ruler
     Of the entire world?

Bodhisattvas who have attained the grounds can, through their constant mental control, take rebirth in worldly existence as they wish.
Why then would they not become rulers of the entire world with
dominion over the welfare of sentient beings? By taking birth as lords
of the four continents and so forth, they accomplish the well-being
of others. They are like a wish-granting jewel, a wish-fulfilling tree,
and a fine pot of treasure.

Question: What is the result of doing Bodhisattva deeds?
   Answer: The inconceivable features of a peerless supramundane
Buddha's power.

124. **Even in this world among excellent things**
     Some are seen to be most excellent.
     Thus realize that certainly also
     Inconceivable power exists.

The Mīmāṃsakas[45] and others, who lack conviction with regard
to this, say the Tathāgata is not omniscient because of being a person, like any common man on the road. This is inappropriate. Are
the subject[46] and predicate[47] to which your reason is applied one or
different? In the first case, the Tathāgata is unsuitable as the subject, because subject and predicate are one, just as a pot cannot be
its own attribute. In the second case the Tathāgata is also unsuit-

able as such, because subject and predicate are different and resemble in all respects a pot and a woollen cloth.[48] Similarly, because of being asserted as inherently existent, if the reason[49] and thesis[50] are inherently one, they should be inseparably one, and if they are inherently different, they should be unrelated. Thus in both cases they will not be that which is to be understood and that which enables understanding.

Furthermore, the subject, the sound of the Vedas, is not permanent, non-produced, self-created or valid because of being sound like a madman's utterances. Also you are not Brahmins because of having hands like fishermen. There will be many such unwanted entailments for you.

Therefore, just as the excellent features of an effect are seen to arise through the special features of its cause, the existence of omniscience, too, can certainly be accepted. Among exceptional and excellent things, some which are particularly excellent are seen even in this world. The Brahmin caste is seen to be the most excellent caste; the Peak of Existence,[51] the most excellent state of rebirth; Mount Meru, the most excellent mountain; and a universal monarch, the most excellent of kings. Thus you should realize that superlative awareness, the inconceivable power of Tathāgatas, definitely exists, because of the stores of merit accumulated by Bodhisattvas over three countless aeons.[52] Moreover you should accept this proof of omniscience established by reasoning without depending on scriptural citations.

The assertion that the Buddha's body is not the Buddha, being a contention of the Mīmāṃsakas, should be thrown out like a gob of spittle.

The analogy of how a hundred jars of oil were acquired with the help of a monk is as in Candrakīrti's commentary.

A learned monk put up in a poor man's house. The poor man provided bedding and oil to massage his feet. Hearing of the monk's presence, the administrator of the district visited him and respectfully asked if there was anything he could do. The monk told him to give the man in whose house he had spent the night one hundred jars of oil.[53]

Question: Why are most people afraid of the Great Vehicle and uninterested in attaining Buddhahood?
Answer: It is because of their weak conviction.

125. Just as the ignorant feel afraid
     Of the extremely profound teaching,
     So the weak feel afraid
     Of the marvelous teaching.

The ignorant, whose minds are untrained, feel afraid of the very profound teaching of dependent arising free from inherent production with the feasibility of all actions and agents. Similarly those whose conviction is weak feel afraid of the marvelous, profound and extensive teaching of the Great Vehicle and of the superlative power of a Buddha. It is like King *Surūpa who had no faith in monks.

King *Surūpa, a householder, saw an ascetic who lived like a deer copulating with a doe, which made him lose faith in monks. He thought that if ascetics who endure suffering had not stopped the urge for sexual intercourse, how could the Śākya monks, living in great comfort, have done so? He was afraid to let monks into the women's quarters and prevented them from being part of the queen's retinue. His elder brother, the wise King Aśoka, subdued him by threatening to have him put to death.[54]

The summarizing stanza:

> Having considered the faults of cyclic existence well,
> Enter this profound and extensive Great Vehicle
> Of which those with poor intelligence feel afraid,
> And make Bodhisattva deeds your quintessential practice.

This is the fifth chapter of the *Four Hundred on the Yogic Deeds*, showing Bodhisattva deeds.

This concludes the commentary on the fifth chapter, showing Bodhisattva deeds, from *Essence of Good Explanations, Explanation of the "Four Hundred on the Yogic Deeds of Bodhisattvas"*.

COMMENTARY TO CHAPTER V
BY GESHE SONAM RINCHEN

The inconceivable activities of Bodhisattvas, who are motivated by love, compassion and the altruistic intention in all they do, are distinguished by six excellent features. If we bear these in mind and try to integrate them as far as possible, the quality of our own everyday actions will be transformed. Bodhisattvas' actions have an excellent basis (*rten dam pa*) in that they are motivated by the wish to attain enlightenment in order to help others with total efficacy. They are performed with the excellent objective (*ched du bya ba dam pa*) of impartially helping all sentient beings to find temporary and ultimate happiness. Whatever Bodhisattvas do is intended as an excellent purification (*dag pa dam pa*) of the obstructions to liberation and omniscience by counteracting them. The excellent means (*thabs dam pa*) accompanying whatever they do is the understanding of emptiness. In each activity they employ the excellent conduct (*spyod pa dam pa*) of incorporating the practice of all the perfections and conclude by making an excellent dedication (*bngo ba dam pa*) for the happiness and unsurpassable enlightenment of all sentient beings.

By cultivating unselfishness and the wish to benefit others as fully as possible, while recalling and trying to practise these excellent features which alter our normal perspective, we prepare to become Bodhisattvas ourselves. Since the mind plays a pivotal role, the ultimate value of our activities depends on the attitude with which they are performed. Intelligent action based on a good intention increases our store of positive energy and has a beneficial effect on others.

Bodhisattvas can act unselfishly without difficulty, but when we attempt to emulate them, we should at first be prudent, taking into account our own capacities and circumstances. In this way we avoid the possibility of regretting a positive action performed impulsively, for such regret is very detrimental. Instead, what we do should be based on a realistic assessment of our capabilities. Meanwhile we should inspire ourselves to become more courageous and unselfish by imagining that we are doing for others what we find too demanding at present. If practised continuously this kind of mental training can have a profound transformative effect.

When helping others, their inclinations and aptitudes must be taken into consideration, since we can only hope to benefit them if what we do or say is attuned to their needs and personalities. Thus intelligence and empathy are essential to establish what is relevant.

Since Bodhisattvas are willing to take any form, no matter how humble, to help others, we should also be prepared to adopt an inferior position when necessary. Willingness, a cheerful expression and gentle speech lend grace to our actions and make others feel valued. We should avoid actions that we find disturbing and upsetting when done by others, and behave in ways that from our own experience we know give joy and happiness. By doing what we can at present and making heartfelt prayers to be capable of more ambitious actions for others' sake in the future, we grow stronger and more courageous.

Chapter VI

Abandoning Disturbing Emotions

Since the source of all trouble lies in cyclic existence, which is caused by contaminated actions and disturbing emotions, Bodhisattvas who act as close friends to transmigrators encourage trainees to put an end to such actions and emotions.

Assertion: If that is so, it is unreasonable to give the ordained buildings five hundred masonry courses high and food of a hundred flavors. Since these are pleasurable, they increase desire. From the outset, one should therefore avoid things like visual form that arouse desire. Those who undergo overt suffering by mortifying their bodies with heat and cold, letting their hair become matted and so forth are called ascetics, overcoming contaminated actions and disturbing emotions.

Answer:

> 126. If desire increases through pleasure
>   And anger[1] increases through pain,
>   Why are those with pleasure not ascetics?
>   Why are the ascetics those with pain?

If pleasure from one's body and possessions increases desire, and pleasure as well as its causes should be avoided, physical and mental pain which increase anger should be avoided too. Why are those who have pleasure not ascetics and why are the ascetics those who fast and experience the pain that sun and wind inflict on their bodies? Those who overcome contaminated actions and disturbing emotions are called ascetics, not those who torment the body.

The Supramundane Victor gave certain individuals twelve rules of training to prevent desire. To prevent anger he gave the angry fine food, clothing and so forth. Therefore only the Śākyas who conquer disturbing emotions should be called ascetics. Just as one gets sugar and so forth by crushing sugar cane, all kinds of happiness in this life and in the future are gained by crushing the disturbing emotions.

Having understood how the disturbing emotions function, one must get rid of them.

> 127. Desire's activity is acquisition;
>   Anger's activity is conflict.
>   As wind is to all the elements,
>   Confusion's activity is nurture.

Desire's activity is to acquire both the animate and inanimate. Its antidote is to meditate on repulsiveness and to give up one's circle of friends and one's possessions. Anger's activity is strife and conflict. Cultivating love and using houses and so forth that one likes are its antidote. Just as wind increases the strength of fire and the other elements, confusion's activity is to nurture both desire and anger. Its antidote is meditation on dependent arising and so forth. It is like killing a sea monster with fire.

A sea monster cannot be intimidated by impartiality, hostility or by generous gifts but only by punishment. Since its flesh is very sensitive, fire alone is effective. Similarly desire, anger and confusion cannot be stopped by acquisition, conflict and indifference but only by the fire of wisdom.[2]

Swimming around in the water, a sea monster got what he needed for survival. Then one day two fishermen arrived. The sea monster turned himself into a human and asked them who they were and what they wanted. They told him they were fishermen and had come to fish. He said, "One of you make the fire and the other can do the cooking. I'll provide the fish, and that way we'll have a good meal without any bother." They agreed and each did his work enthusiastically. Just as the sea monster's task was to catch the fish, desire's activity is to acquire things. One man's task was to cook; similarly anger creates conflict and when there is conflict, unpleasant and abusive words make others boil. Just as the third person's task was to stoke the fire, confusion's function is to feed desire and anger.[3]

Assertion: Though there are antidotes to the three poisons, why should one get rid of them?

Answer: Because they produce suffering.

128. Desire is painful because of not getting,
     Anger is painful through lack of might,
     And confusion through not understanding.
     Because of this, these are not recognized.

Desire produces suffering when one does not encounter what one badly wants. Anger produces suffering when one lacks might to crush the strong. Confusion induces suffering when one fails to understand a subtle matter thoroughly. The inability to recognize these forms of suffering when one is overwhelmed by desire and so forth is great suffering indeed. Therefore, persevere in getting rid of the disturbing emotions. It is like a poor man's son who suffered because he wanted a queen.

A certain poor man wanted a queen, but kings keep their queens heavily guarded, and because he could not get her, his desire made him suffer. He felt anger toward the king for guarding his queens well, and since he could not do the slightest harm to the king, he suffered acutely on account of his anger. Blinded by desire and anger his confusion grew, and unable to understand the situation properly, he was tormented by the suffering it caused him.[4]

Question: Do anger and desire occur together the way confusion occurs with both of them?

Answer:

129. Just as it is seen that bile
     Does not occur with phlegm,
     One sees that desire, too,
     Does not occur with anger.

Just as it is seen that bile and phlegm do not occur together,[5] one sees that desire and anger too, do not occur simultaneously in manifest form in one mental continuum. Since one has the aspect of longing and the other of aversion, the two must be treated individually. It is like putting fire into a water-pot.

A fool thought he would mix fire and water and dropped some fire into a water-pot. Since they are incompatible, the two cannot co-exist.[6]

130. Desire should be driven like a slave
     Because severity is its cure,
     And anger looked upon as a lord
     Because indulgence is its cure.

Understanding the characteristics of desire and anger and how they function, a spiritual teacher engaged in forming students makes those with desire work like slaves. This is because severity and lack of deference cure desire. The angry should be looked upon as lords. By treating them with indulgence and serving them respectfully their anger will not arise; thus indulgence cures it. It is like the order in which a washerman trains his donkey.

A washerman curbs his donkey's spirit and keeps him busy. Anything capricious the donkey does he considers a fault and beats him hard. Similarly, the wise deliberately keep those habituated to desire busy, and when they do something wrong, make them go on working. When the washerman takes his donkey home, he treats him like a lord and gives him a nose-bag of fodder and other things, one after another. Likewise, spiritual guides should treat those habituated to anger like lords.[7]

The antidotes should be applied with an understanding of when disturbing emotions arise.

> 131. First there is confusion,
>   In the middle there is anger,
>   And later there is desire,
>   In three stages during the day.

At night sleep and lethargy increase and because phlegm predominates, first in the morning there is confusion. In the middle of the day one rides on the wheel of suffering caused by the frustrations of making a living, and anger arises because one is plagued by hunger and thirst. Later, in the evening, when one has recovered from exhaustion and so forth, desire arises. Thus, associated with different forms of physical weakness, the disturbing emotions arise in three successive stages during the day, and one must apply their antidotes accordingly with care.

It is like the following analogy: When King *Jentaka asked a Brahmin questions, the Brahmin felt hostile, but when he was given pots of oil, his greed was aroused.

Desire masquerading as a friend deceives ordinary people.

> 132. Desire is no friend, but seems like one,
>   Which is why you do not fear it.
>   But shouldn't people particularly
>   Rid themselves of a harmful friend?

Since desire is hard to recognize, you must pay special attention to getting rid of it. Ultimately it produces suffering, so it is not a friend, but looks like one because it seems benevolent. Therefore you do not fear it. Shouldn't people make a particular effort to rid themselves of a harmful friend? Similarly one should get rid of desire. It is like the following analogy: King Pāṇḍu shot an arrow at a sage copulating with a doe and, disregarding his curse, died as soon as he had intercourse with a woman.

When King Pāṇḍu was out hunting, he heard a sage, who had turned himself into a deer, copulating with a doe. He shot an arrow and hit the sage, who cursed him, saying, "When you have sexual intercourse you will die." Wishing to practise sexual continence the king gave up his kingdom and went into the forest. One day he saw his queen standing naked, facing the setting sun. He thought, "My queen is so beautiful, she could seduce even the gods." Out of desire he had intercourse with her and died.[8]

> 133. Desire arises from causes and
>   Also arises through circumstance.
>   Desire arising through circumstance
>   Is easy to deal with; not the other.

Never give desire a chance to arise! It arises in two ways: some forms of desire arise from a cause of a similar type created by repeated familiarity in the past. Some arise adventitiously through the circumstance provided by the proximity of an object. Of these two, desire caused by circumstance is easier to counteract: one can get rid of it by getting rid of the object. The other is not like that, since a strong antidote is needed to get rid of it. The kind that arises through circumstance is like the following: a bird cannot fly without one of its wings. The kind that is difficult to discard is like a pigeon's instinctive desire.

Anger is a fault more grave than desire, and therefore one should strive to get rid of it.

> 134. Anger is lasting and certainly
>   Makes one do grave non-virtue.
>   Thus constant awareness of their distinctions
>   Will bring to an end disturbing emotions.

Since anger, which is made to last and held fast by resentment,[9] certainly burns one's own and others' mindstreams and causes others harm, it is totally non-virtuous. It makes one do serious misdeeds such as the five heinous crimes.[10] Through constant awareness of their different faults, disadvantages, causes and the means to eliminate them, disturbing emotions will be brought to an end. Thus, once their specific antidotes are known, one must get rid of them. It is like the following analogy: Dharmaruci was born ninety-one times as an animal because of anger, but became a Foe Destroyer within the Teacher's spiritual tradition.

Seeing the Buddha Dīpamkara place his feet on the Bodhisattva Sumati's hair while making a prediction to him, Dharmaruci was incensed and performed a verbal misdeed by saying, "He's like an animal standing on the hair with both feet." He was born as an animal ninety-one times because of this action. As a fish he wrecked a boat and heard the Supramundane Victor Śākyamuni's name. He thought, "Why should I just continue comfortably in an animal's rebirth?" and destroyed his body. He took rebirth as a human being and became ordained in the Buddha Śākyamuni's spiritual tradition. Through aversion to cyclic existence while walking outside his door, he actualized the state of a Foe Destroyer.[11]

Question: The different characteristics of desire and anger have been described, but what are the various characteristics of confusion?
Answer:

135. As the tactile sense [pervades] the body
     Confusion is present in them all.
     By overcoming confusion one will also
     Overcome all disturbing emotions.

In the body the tactile sense organ pervades all other sense organs such as the eye and acts as a basis without which none of the others could exist. Confusion, which is the disturbing attitude ignorance,[12] misconceives dependent arising free from inherent existence as truly existent. It similarly is present in and pervades all disturbing emotions such as desire and anger. Misconceiving things distorted by confusion as inherently pleasant or unpleasant, one thinks of them as desirable or repugnant. Thus one must understand how the mode of apprehension entailed in the conception of true existence is present in the modes of apprehension of anger and desire. All other disturbing attitudes and emotions depend on the disturbing attitude ignorance, which is principal. By overcoming confusion through meditation on dependent arising empty of inherent existence, all other disturbing attitudes and emotions will be overcome as well. Therefore make effort to understand emptiness as the meaning of dependent arising. For instance, by cutting down a poisonous tree, everything useless associated with it ceases.

Question: What are the means to get rid of confusion, which is the root of futility?
Answer:

> 136. When dependent arising is seen
>   Confusion will not occur.
>   Thus every effort has been made here
>   To explain precisely this subject.

If a sprout, action[13] and so forth existed by way of their own entities, they would not depend on the seed nor on ignorance, but they do. With the help of many different kinds of reasoning one must understand that the existence of a sprout and so forth is exclusively a dependent existence and not an existence by way of its own entity. When dependent arising free from existence by way of its own entity is seen by direct valid perception, confusion will not arise, and because confusion has ended, all other disturbing attitudes and emotions too will end. Thus here in the *Treatise of Four Hundred* every effort is made specifically to explain how emptiness means dependent arising.[14] By merely understanding the dependent arising of a sprout, one does not understand its emptiness of true existence; if one did it would not be a reason establishing emptiness of true existence. When one discovers that existence by way of a thing's own entity is invalidated in many ways, one discovers how phenomena exist. Understanding that they only exist dependently means one should thereby understand they do not exist by way of their own entities. This resembles what appears in the expression of worship in the text and commentary on the *Sixty Stanzas of Reasoning.*[15] Just as the full moon dispels darkness, [seeing dependent arising makes the moon of wisdom shine, dispelling confusion.[16]]

Question: How does one recognize people in whom desire is a strong habit?
Answer:

> 137. They always like "Claiming the Earth,"[17]
>   Are extravagant, greedy and fastidious.
>   Characteristics such as these
>   Are seen in people with desire.

They always like dances such as "Claiming the Earth," fun, flirtation, flowers, perfume, garlands, jewelry, color and so forth. They are extravagant to others, greedy, fastidious, clever, alert and speak frankly. Characteristics such as these are seen in people with desire and their opposite in people habitually inclined toward anger. Those whose behavior is a mixture are inclined to confusion. It is like a wealth-creating spirit that makes a variety of goods appear and disappear.

While one has a wealth-creating spirit various kinds of goods accumulate, but if one gets rid of him, they all disperse.[18]

Question: How does one train someone in whom desire is a strong habit?
Answer:

138. Buddhas told those with desire
That food, clothes and dwellings are all
To be avoided and to remain
Close to their spiritual guides.

Buddhas told those with desire that objects of beauty and quality which stimulate desire such as fine food, clothes and dwellings are all to be avoided, and that they should always remain close to their spiritual guides. Being made to work constantly by their spiritual guide will curb their desire and through instruction in training,[19] they will be able to rid themselves of their incorrect mental approach. Those with desire were taught twelve rules of training[20] to counteract attachment to dwelling places, beds, food and clothing. Those habituated to anger should make use of dwellings and so forth that are contrary to these. It is like the following analogy. If someone captured by a Brahmin ogre gives him unclean things, he will go away.

If one wants to get rid of anger, one should think about its disadvantages.

139. Through anger, those who are powerless
Only make themselves look ugly;
But one who has power and is merciless
Is said to be the worst.

Anger toward those one is powerless to harm makes one's face turn dark, while angry frowns and the like just make one look ugly. However the merciless anger of those who have the power and ability to harm is said to be the worst, since it is detrimental both to themselves and others. It is like a Brahmin contravening the rules of his caste, which harms others too.

It is foolish to feel angry when one hears harsh words.

> 140. **It is said unpleasant words**
> **End previously done ill deeds.**
> **The ignorant and unwise do not**
> **Want to purify themselves.**

Hearing unpleasant words is said to rid one of the effects of previously done ill deeds by bringing them to an end. Not to feel glad but angry at the circumstances that end these effects is simply to be ignorant regarding actions and their effects and unwise in not wanting to purify ill deeds. It is like an old bull killing the cowherd who gives him medicine.

For the following reason, too, it is inappropriate to be angry about harsh words:

> 141. **Though unpleasant to hear**
> **They are not intrinsically harmful.**
> **Thus it is fantasy to think that**
> **What comes from preconception comes from else-**
> **where.**

Though hearing harsh words is unpleasant, they are not intrinsically harmful, otherwise the speaker would also be harmed. Thus, when the damage done by anger comes from one's own preconception that one has been insulted, it is just fantasy to suppose it comes from elsewhere. When one's own ideas have done the harm, it is unreasonable to be angry with others. It is like the following analogy: When a herdswoman heard someone eating in the dark, thinking it was the junior wife's daughter she said, "What are you eating, you cow?" Then, realizing it was her own daughter, she said, "My pet is eating something."

Assertion: Treatises on social conventions state that those who are abusive should be punished.
   Answer:

> 142. **Just as it plainly says**
> **The abuser should be punished,**
> **Likewise why should one who speaks**
> **Pleasantly not be rewarded?**

Just as it plainly says those who are abusive should be punished, like-wise why should those who speak pleasingly not be rewarded? It would be reasonable to reward them, but since these treatises do not mention that, they are misleading. It is like the people of Dravira who consider killing because of a mere disagreement, but do not reward those who speak pleasantly.

Assertion: Anger is reasonable because abuse reveals one's faults to others.
   Answer:

> 143. **If that for which you are reviled**
>   **Is known to others though they are not told,**
>   **And anger at the speaker is unreasonable,**
>   **How much more so toward those who lie.**

If those things for which you are reviled, such as your blindness or lameness, are known to others even when they have not been told, it is unreasonable to be angry with the one who mentions them, for even unmentioned they are self-evident to others. If that is unrea-sonable, how much more so is anger toward those who speak untruly when one does not possess a fault. Thus anger is always inappro-priate. It is wrong for a king to punish both someone who calls the blind "blind" as well as someone who calls those who are not blind "blind."

It is unreasonable to be angry at hearing abuse from one's inferiors.

> 144. **Abuse from inferiors**
>   **Does not ensure escape.**
>   **Abuse from inferiors thus should be**
>   **Seen as isolated and trivial.**

Merely some abusive words from inferiors, who like what is profane and constantly do ill deeds, taking a delight in others' suffering, do not ensure one's escape, since they may beat or kill one. Therefore regarding mere abuse from one's inferiors as an isolated and trivial error, it is appropriate to feel glad. It is like the following analogy: When the Exalted Pūrṇa promised to bear whatever the people on the other side of the River Sona[21] did, the Teacher gave him permis-sion to train them.
   The Exalted Pūrṇa wanted to train the people of the country on the other side of the River Sona. The Supramundane Victor told him, "Those people are wild and fierce. If you live there, you'll experience

suffering." He answered, "If they abuse me I will think, how wonderful they didn't beat me. They are kind. If they take my life I will think, how wonderful that they have put an end to this rotten body. They have helped me." Then the Supramundane Victor agreed.

Assertion: It is not wrong to punish those who slander the innocent.
  Answer:

145. **If harming others is not even**
     Of the slightest use to you,
     Your approval of useless aggression
     Is just an addiction.

Retaliation by hurting others like the slanderer is not of the slightest use to you in reversing what has already been done and so forth. In that case your approval of aggression, which has nothing but drawbacks and no advantages, is just an addiction to something wrong. It is like testing a weapon to see whether it is sharp or not.

Someone wondered whether a weapon was sharp or not and tested it on the body of the very man who had made it. Testing the weapon in that way was a waste of his work and of no benefit; it only created an ill deed.[22]

Question: What wise person tolerates others' worthless abuse?
  Answer:

146. **If through patience enormous merit**
     Is acquired effortlessly,
     Who is as foolish as
     One who obstructs this?

If through patience one gives anger no opportunity and does not harm others, one will acquire the fragrance and adornment [of virtue], a flowing river [of tranquillity] undisturbed by ill will, and a pleasing appearance. Then who is as foolish as one who obstructs this supreme path, for he assiduously destroys his good qualities. Therefore only those who bear abuse should be called wise. It is like a woman who killed her husband when he had only a little life left.

A woman's husband wanted to die and had only a little life-force left. She thought, "He's going to die in pain. I should kill him," and exerted herself to perform an ill deed.[23]

For the following reason, too, one should get rid of anger:

147. Aggression especially
     Does not arise toward the powerful.
     Why then do you approve of
     Aggression which defeats the weak?

Aggression especially does not arise toward the strong because one is powerless to harm them. For what reason then do you approve of aggressive anger toward the wretched, which defeats only the weak? Such approval is improper. It is like bravery in defeating women.

A certain king wanted to take a city and called his soldiers together to ask what they would do when they besieged it. One said, "My Lord, I will stop anyone from entering or leaving the city." Some said they would advance as far as the moat, while others said they would climb the walls. Another said he would do what would give the king great pleasure and at the same time protect himself. The king expressed his approval. Then one of them said, "While they are thoroughly defeating the king, I shall make him watch me beat the women of the queen's retinue with a cudgel." When he heard this, the king said, "This perverted fellow intends to vanquish the weak," and taking a dislike to the soldier, treated him with contempt.[24]

Assertion: It is reasonable to get angry, since if one is patient, others may think one is incapable of retaliating and despise one.
    Answer: It is not reasonable.

148. Whoever is patient with the source
     Of anger develops meditation.
     Saying you fear the source of
     Good qualities is just foolish of you.

Whoever patiently tolerates a cause for anger will develop meditative stabilization on love and other kinds of meditation. Even cultivating love for as short a time as it takes to milk a cow brings eight benefits. The *Precious Garland* says:

> Gods and humans will be friendly,
> Even non-humans will protect you,
> You will have pleasures of the mind and many
> [Of the body], poison and weapons will not harm you,
> Effortlessly will you attain your aims
> And be reborn in the world of Brahma,
> Though [through love] you are not liberated
> You will attain the eight virtues of love.[25]

It is just foolish of you to claim you fear patience and give up the source of the above-mentioned virtues because of contempt regarding your ability to retaliate, for you destroy an excellent source of good qualities. It is like someone who was embarrassed about abstaining from misdeeds.

A young man, born in a good family, met someone holy and gave up killing and so forth. His stupid friends taunted him: "You don't hunt deer and if people with weapons came to fight with you, you'd run away. You've become a girl. Do you still have the marks of a man?" Being foolish, he felt embarrassed.[26]

Assertion: Since it is difficult for the powerful to bear being disparaged by inferiors, it is proper to punish them.
Answer:

> 149. Who has gone to the next world
> Having ended all disparagement?
> Therefore consider contempt
> Preferable to ill deeds.

Who goes or has gone to the next world having completely put an end to his enemies by defeat and humiliation? Not even a few have done so. By retaliating one creates ill deeds and will go to bad rebirths. Therefore one should endure contempt, thinking it is preferable to the ill deeds created by subjugating one's enemies. Through doing the former one will not go to bad rebirths but by doing ill deeds one will. Just as there is no end to a water-wheel, there is none to disparagement either.

Since consciousness is produced in dependence on causes, it is a product. Since products change from moment to moment, they do not have inherent duration. Their production and disintegration are therefore not inherently existent either.

> 150. Disturbing emotions will never
> Remain in the mind of one
> Who understands the reality of
> The abiding and so forth of consciousness.

One must abandon all disturbing emotions, understanding that the three realms are like an illusion, since production, disintegration, abiding and so forth do not have inherent existence. Disturbing emotions will never remain in the mind of any adept who understands that the production, disintegration, abiding and so forth of consciousness do not have even an atom of real or inherent existence and who gains familiarity with this. It is like uprooting a poisonous tree.

Thus by first gaining familiarity with the antidotes that overcome manifest disturbing emotions and eventually understanding dependent arising as devoid of inherent existence, one should rid oneself of all the seeds of disturbing emotions.

The summarizing stanza:

> Transmigrators governed by disturbing emotions
>   like desire,
> Which prevent activities for the attainment of
>   enlightenment,
> Are conveyed to the happiness of liberation by
>   teaching them
> To become familiar with love and repulsiveness
>   and by teaching them suchness.

This is the sixth chapter from the *Four Hundred on the Yogic Deeds*, showing the means to abandon disturbing emotions.

This concludes the commentary on the sixth chapter, showing the means to abandon disturbing emotions, from the *Essence of Good Explanations, Explanation of the "Four Hundred on the Yogic Deeds of Bodhisattvas"*.

COMMENTARY TO CHAPTER VI
BY GESHE SONAM RINCHEN

Disturbing emotions make the mind unruly. When it is turbulent, perception is unclear, distortion occurs, and all kinds of problems follow. When water is disturbed, nothing is reflected in it clearly and only a distorted image appears. All disturbing emotions can be subsumed under the three poisons, which cover a diversity of feeling tones: desire/attachment, hostility/anger, and confusion/ignorance. Unless we can free ourselves of even their latencies, they may arise again at any time even though they appear to be under control and are temporarily dormant. Thus we must seek the means to eradicate them completely. This is like distilling water and removing all impurities. No matter how clear the water looks, if a sediment of mud remains, it will make the water cloudy as soon as it is disturbed.

Meanwhile, however, we must become skilled at recognizing different disturbing states and at counteracting them. Anger and hostility are easy to identify as negative since they are accompanied by unpleasant feelings, but attachment and desire are initially often accompanied by pleasurable feelings and do not seem harmful. When trying to counteract them we need to consider the unattractive aspects of the object on which they focus, but we feel reluctant to do this. We should begin working with whichever disturbing emotion we find predominates. By watching the kind of stimulus required, whether weak or strong, and the strength and duration of our response, we can determine how habitual a disturbing attitude is. If a small stimulus creates a disproportionate reaction, we may infer prolonged familiarity with this response in past lives. When we recognize the detrimental effects of these emotions, we will want to control them instead of allowing them to control us.

Just as there are many forms of attachment and desire, there are many antidotes. We must discover what is effective in our own case. Where attachment to our body is concerned, we may find thinking about its unclean nature useful. We may also try a meditation which begins by imagining a small spot in the center of the forehead which is bare to the bone. Gradually we enlarge this, stripping away skin, flesh, muscle, sinew, etc., baring our bones until our whole skeleton is exposed. We then imagine this growing larger and larger until it fills the whole world and nothing but our skeleton remains. The process is then reversed.

To counteract an excessive preoccupation with food we may try to regard it as medicine. A sick person takes medicine and follows a specific diet not because it tastes good but in the hope of getting well. Similarly we should think of food merely as sustenance for the body so that we can use it for others' well-being and happiness. To help overcome a preoccupation with clothing, we should think of it as a means to cover the body and protect it from the elements, like the dressing on a wound which is applied for protection and not for the sake of appearance.

Thinking about the imminence of death and its unpredictability is one of the most effective ways to loosen the grip of attachment and desire. Enjoyment and pleasure are not in themselves harmful, but we must be alert to the craving and discontent that tend to follow. Cultivating a sense of contentment and considering the instability and dissatisfactoriness of the things for which our greed and desire reach out are valuable as antidotes.

The unhappiness and anger we frequently experience when something we own is lost or damaged is proportionate to our attachment. Our acquisitiveness leads to many difficulties. For instance, if we are building up a collection, we go to much trouble and expense to acquire the specific items we wish to include. We then protect the collection from the detrimental effects of the climate and ensure it against theft. What was intended as a pleasurable pursuit becomes an expensive, time-consuming and tiring chore. We end up the servant of our possessions.

Anger is like a fire that first makes us burn inside. Then our palms and armpits turn damp and beads of sweat appear. No matter how fine our clothes and jewelry, no one finds us attractive when our face is contorted with rage. Anger destroys our own physical and mental peace and upsets others, inciting them to respond aggressively, which makes the fire grow. Even animals feel uncomfortable in our presence and try to escape when we are in a bad temper.

Realizing how disturbing anger is and how good it feels to remain calm, we will want to prevent anger rather than suppress it. The aim is not to hold anger inside but to stop its arising. When we feel unhappy and anxious, either for specific reasons or for no specific cause, irritation and anger arise easily. Therefore we must attempt to relieve the unhappiness and anxiety which are characterized by tightness. If there are specific causes, we should direct our energy toward trying to resolve the problem. If it is not possible to do so, letting go and accepting the difficulties is a more positive approach than dwelling on the seeming injustice of the situation which reinforces the unhappiness and helplessness. It is useful to think of the experience as a maturation and ending of past negative actions, allowing it to show us the unsatisfactory nature of cyclic existence.

There are many situations in which we already know we are vulnerable to anger. This knowledge gives us the opportunity to remain calm and apply antidotes effectively to prevent anger altogether. If it does arise we should ensure it is short-lived and does not breed aggression, resentment, spite and other negative feelings. When the mind is under the influence of anger it is hard to arouse feelings of love and compassion for the other or to consider how one has set oneself up as a target through past actions or through present intentional or unintentional provocative behavior. Since it is essential to train ourselves to think in these ways and gain familiarity with them, meditation on these themes when we are calm is encouraged. It is also valuable to imagine provocative circumstances and rehearse an appropriate and constructive response.

We should not confuse anger which is based on a wish to harm with the need to act sternly at certain times arising from a positive beneficial intention. When positive states of mind are operating the negative ones cannot assume an overt form. Thus, the cultivation of constructive states of mind provides us with a way to deal with difficult circumstances.

Only our eventual understanding of reality, of how everything arises dependently without inherent existence, will enable us to deal with the confusion and ignorance that lie at the root of all other disturbing attitudes and emotions. However, even without a full understanding of this, thinking how we, our emotions, situations and others do not exist as they appear and how our hard delineation of them is a superimposition which does not correspond to reality, may help to decrease the intensity and duration of feelings which disturb and trouble us.

Chapter VII

Abandoning Attachment to Sense Objects

One must first think about the disadvantages of cyclic existence in order to give up the contaminated actions which are its cause.

> 151. **When there is no end at all**
> **To this ocean of suffering,**
> **Why are you childish people**
> **Not afraid of drowning in it?**

The beginningless cycle of rebirths is an ocean of suffering without any end at all, infested by thirty-six sea snake fetters[1] of ignorance, pride and craving of worldly existence.[2] It is churned by sea monsters of the sixty-two wrong views[3] and fraught with whirlpools of birth and death. Why are you ordinary childish people, drowning in it since beginningless time, not afraid? If one should fear to drown in a sea whose depth and breadth are apparent, how much more so in this one! It is like the following analogy: A sage who had five kinds of super-knowledge wanted to go beyond worldly existence. With miraculous speed he placed his foot on the summit of Mount Meru but died before he could reach the other side. After his death he was reborn as a god [and came before the Buddha who told him, "I will show you the world, the source of the world, cessation of the world, and the path that leads to the world's cessation in relation to your body which is just four cubits high." When taught the four noble truths in this way, the sage understood them.[4]]

Assertion: Though cyclic existence has many disadvantages, those who are proud of their youth and so forth are not afraid.

Answer:

> 152. Youth lies behind and then
>   Once more it is ahead.
>   Though [one imagines] it will last,
>   In this world it is like a race.

Since youth and the like do not last, pride on that account is unreasonable. In this life youth lies behind old age; after death it is once more ahead and then again it is behind old age. Though one imagines one can remain young, in this world youth, old age and death compete as if in a race, claiming, "I'm ahead, I'm ahead!" Since none can always remain ahead, it is unreasonable to feel proud because of that. It is like the following analogy: The shadow of the wheel which crushes sesame seeds [sometimes falls in front and sometimes behind.[5]]

Assertion: Though one must go on to another life, it is not frightening.
   Answer:

> 153. In worldly existence there is never
>   Rebirth of one's own free will.
>   Being under others' control,
>   Who with intelligence would be fearless?

In worldly existence childish beings like you do not have the power to will their own rebirth in good rebirths as gods, humans and so forth, but are under the control of other factors—contaminated actions and disturbing emotions. While in such a frightening situation, what intelligent person would be fearless? One should feel repugnance at being controlled by contaminated actions and disturbing emotions. One is like a piece of wood swept along by the current.

   The words *gzhan yang* which appear in some versions of the text refer to time and mean "never."[6]

Assertion: Though unable to cut through worldly existence in this life because of being enthralled by pleasure, one will try to do so in a future rebirth.
   Answer:

> 154. The future is endless and
>   You were always a common being.
>   Act so that it will never again
>   Be as it was in the past.

Future rebirths are endless and the past is beginningless. Throughout the past you were always only a common being. Act so that the present and future will not be as meaningless as the past during which you failed to free yourself from worldly existence.

Some versions of the text read "again," which should be taken to mean "again in the future."[7]

It is like the following analogy: Though the friends of a man who was going with someone else's woman tried to stop him, he did it again later. The *Array of Tree Trunks Sūtra*[8] says:

> Think of the past bodies you have meaninglessly wasted
> Because of your desires.
> From today engage in the discipline of seeking enlightenment
> And through that discipline destroy desire.

You must break the continuity of rebirths in worldly existence.

Question: Does the cycle of rebirths have an end or not? If it does one will gain freedom without the need for effort. If it does not, effort to cut through the cycle of birth and death is senseless, since despite effort one will not gain freedom.

Answer:

155. **The conjunction of a listener,**
     What is to be heard and an exponent
     Is very rare. In brief, the cycle of
     Rebirths neither has nor has not an end.

A listener is one who has attained a special life of leisure and fortune and is ready to generate spiritual paths. What is to be heard refers to discourses teaching suchness, and their exponents are the Tathāgatas. These three occur in the world simultaneously as rarely as the udumbara flower.[9]

Tathāgatas are rare because they depend on stores of merit and insight accumulated over three countless aeons. The other two depend on Tathāgatas. Thus, in brief, for a person who has these three rare and supreme prerequisites for the growth of spiritual paths, the cycle of rebirths is not without an end, since the causes and conditions for stopping it are assembled. In the case of a person for whom they are not assembled, it does not have an end because one cannot determine precisely when the cycle of rebirths will cease. With regard also to its final mode of existence, it is not specified as either having or not having an end in terms of ultimate existence. The three are like the udumbara flower.

Assertion: As long as scriptural texts exist, there will be spiritual friends and oral transmissions of them. One may therefore try to end worldly existence in other rebirths.

Answer:

> 156. Most people cling to
> An unwholesome direction.
> Thus most common beings
> Certainly go to bad rebirths.

Though the texts and the other two may exist, it is difficult to be a proper listener for the following reason: Most people cling to the ten non-virtuous paths of action, which is an unwholesome direction, and thus through the power of their actions they are reborn in different states. Since most common beings therefore go to bad rebirths, one should make effort to hear the teaching while the two prerequisites are assembled. Not to strive for liberation as if one's head were on fire is like crowning an idiot as king. It is like the analogy of carrying hemp in Candrakīrti's commentary.

Two men went to fetch hemp and as they were returning, they saw two loads of cotton. One of them put down his load of hemp and took the load of cotton. He arrived home carrying a load of gold. The other thought, "I've carried this load such a long way, how can I carry the other?" and he continued carrying the load of hemp.[10] Similarly the rich and powerful are attached to their own viewpoint and do not appreciate Buddha's words, which are supported by the reasoning of an unbiased mind. They say, "How can we give up these views to which we've been accustomed for a long time?"[11]

Assertion: Although bad rebirths must be avoided because they are states without freedom, full of many kinds of suffering, one need not feel aversion toward good rebirths since they are happy states.

Answer: It is proper to feel aversion toward good rebirths just as one does toward bad ones.

> 157. On earth the maturation of ill deeds
> Is seen to be only deleterious.
> Thus to the wise the world appears
> Similar to a slaughterhouse.

The remains of previous contaminated actions are seen only to debilitate even those in a good rebirth—deformed limbs and members, defective senses, poverty and so forth are the unwanted maturation of the ill deeds of human beings living on earth. Thus to the wise Exalted, worldly existence seems like a slaughterhouse where living beings are killed. It is like the following analogy: A cherished minister was not afraid of the king and was punished later because of this.

A certain king favored a minister by giving him the highest honors. Later, because the minister did not fear him, the king had his hands, feet, ears and nose cut off. Similarly, those who are rich and do not think about future lives but heedlessly do ill deeds first experience their maturation after death in the hells and so forth. They experience the remaining maturation as misfortunes, when they are eventually reborn as humans.[12]

Question: If the wise see worldly existence like a slaughterhouse, why do ordinary people feel no horror?
Answer: They are as insane as a mad elephant.
Question: Insane in what way?
Answer:

> 158. If "insane" means
>   That one's mind is unstable,
>   What wise person would say that those
>   In worldly existence are not insane?

In the world someone whose mind does not function with normal stability due to an imbalance of physical constituents is called insane. If that is insanity, what intelligent person would claim that those in worldly existence are not insane? Ordinary people who want many outrageous things and speak impulsively do not have sound minds. It is like the following analogy: A king had a beloved son but got the idea, because his mind was unsound, that he did not want to see the boy.

A certain king had a son who was very accomplished and dear to his father's heart. When the king did not see his son, he ached with longing, and whenever he saw the boy he put him on his lap and hugged and held him tight. Then one day just the sight of his son upset him terribly, and he said, "You wicked boy, go away and don't stay in my presence. The sight of you burns me like fire." The boy got down on his knees and placed his palms together. Crying and trembling he asked the king in a faltering voice what he had done wrong. The king answered, "You have done nothing wrong, but I feel displeasure at seeing you." Recognizing this change, a skilled physician secretly told one of the ministers, "This loss of affection is a bad sign and indicates that the king's mind undoubtedly is unstable. It may cause insanity. Try to treat him before this illness becomes serious. If you don't and the illness is neglected, it will be difficult to cure." The minister then thought about the situation carefully and it was so, but being preoccupied with the king's business, he abused the physician. He called him a vile mischief-maker and said, "May not even the great man's enemies go mad! Do not speak to anyone else in this way and leave the country!" Nothing was done about the king's illness until after some time it got the better of him, making him laugh, cry, dance and sing for no apparent reason. Ordinary people are insane like the king who lost affection for his son because his mind was unstable. They act perversely because of their mental instability.[13]

The wise rid themselves of rebirth in cyclic existence which is governed by the force of contaminated actions. Moreover they do so by stopping the process of contaminated action.

> 159. The pain of walking, one sees,
> Decreases when doing the opposite.
> Thus the intelligent generate
> The intention to end all action.

One sees that the pain caused by actions like walking, strolling, lying down and so forth decreases and gradually loses its former intensity when doing the opposite kind of action such as sitting. By breaking the continuity of all contaminated actions, all suffering stops. Thus the intelligent expand their minds to encompass the means to attain the state of nirvāṇa in which all contaminated actions projecting worldly existence have ceased. Childish beings in cyclic existence are like someone on a long journey who suffers because of exhaustion and the depletion of his provisions. [They suffer from weariness travelling along the roads of cyclic existence and they suffer because their store of virtuous actions is depleted.[14]]

The intelligent rid themselves of cyclic existence by stopping the process of contaminated action.

> 160. When a single effect's original cause
> Is not seen, and one sees the extensiveness
> Regarding even a single effect,
> Who would not be afraid?

No one can perceive the original cause of even a single effect, such as an element, an elemental derivative,[15] the mind and so forth, which are the outcome of a beginningless continuity. When one realizes that even a single effect has a limitless multitude of causes, what childish person would not be afraid? Therefore one should always feel aversion toward, and strive for the means to gain liberation from, this vast wilderness of cyclic existence, made difficult to cross by the thickets of ignorance failing to comprehend its continuity. For instance, even a single clay pot requires a limitless variety of causes.

161. Since all results will not definitely
     Be achieved, and those that are
     Will certainly come to an end,
     Why exhaust yourself for their sake?

Effort would be appropriate if the results of actions for a specific purpose, motivated by attachment, could definitely be achieved. It is however not certain that you will achieve all the results such as perfect happiness. Moreover whatever is achieved is sure to perish in the end. Why exhaust yourself physically, verbally and mentally to achieve mistaken objectives? Make effort to give up actions projecting cyclic existence. It is like the following analogy: When a potter fires his pots, it is not certain whether they will turn out well, and those that do will certainly disintegrate.

Since actions themselves, like their results, are bound to perish, do not exert yourself for no purpose.

162. Once it is done, work done with effort
     Effortlessly disintegrates.
     Though this is so, still you are not
     At all free from attachment to actions.

Work, like building a wall, requires effort, but when it is finished it disintegrates effortlessly. This being so, since you still do such things, your utter lack of freedom from attachment to actions shows how foolish you are. It takes effort to set up a stone on a mountain top but it will fall down of its own accord.

Assertion: Though actions which require exertion do perish, one cannot free oneself from attachment to them, because they are a source of pleasure.

Answer:

> 163. There is no pleasure in relation to
>   Either the past or the future.
>   That which occurs now, too, is passing.
>   Why do you weary yourself?

There can be no real pleasure in relation to past consciousness, since it has already ceased, nor in relation to future consciousness, since it is not yet produced. Moreover consciousness which is occurring now disintegrates moment by moment and passes. Since there is no reliable happiness, why do you weary yourself? To strive for a non-existent effect is unreasonable and like building a house on the bank of a river.

Someone built a house on the bank of a river but the land subsided. He then rebuilt it on another similar part of the riverbank. That too subsided, and so it went on indefinitely. The man who was building the house only wore himself out but did not achieve the result he desired. Worldly endeavors are like that.[16]

Assertion: One should perform virtuous actions for the sake of a high rebirth.
Answer:

> 164. The wise feel the same fear for even
>   A high rebirth as for the hells.
>   It is rare indeed for a worldly state
>   Not to produce fear in them.

Even high rebirths as gods and so forth, ablaze with the fire of rampant disturbing emotions and shrouded in the darkness of ignorance like the hells, produce fear in the wise with direct perception of suchness. As it is rare indeed for any worldly state not to inspire the Exalted with fear, the intelligent should consider the disadvantages of cyclic existence. The accumulation of actions out of craving based on seeing a high rebirth as something attractive in itself, without cultivating aversion to worldly existence, is rejected. However, it is completely wrong to prevent and give up the accumulation of causes for life as a god or human for the purpose of liberation. It is like the following analogy: After being released from King Bāla's jail, one had to follow a single pattern of behavior till the end of one's life and therefore was not freed from bondage.

165. If childish people ever perceived
     The suffering of cyclic existence,
     At that moment both their mind
     [And body] would completely fail.

If childish people ever directly perceived the suffering of cyclic existence as do the Exalted, their mind or heart and body would both completely fail, but because they do not realize it, they continue as if they were happy. It is like *Indrabāla, who sacrificed his life out of desire to be chief [and was a chief again in his next life. If ordinary people realized the suffering of the cycle of rebirths they would give up worldly existence for fear of it, and by destroying it completely would become free.[17]]

Though belonging to the best caste and having the finest possessions is known as happiness, aversion even toward that is appropriate.

166. People without pride are rare,
     And the proud have no compassion.
     Thus it is said to be very rare
     To go from light to light.

People of good caste and so forth who are not inflated with pride are rare. Moreover, since those who are conceited think themselves best and out of envy want to crush their equals and betters, they lack compassion. Thus the *Topics of Instruction*[18] and so forth say that it is very rare to go from light to light. It is like *Jamadagni's son, who did away with members of the royal caste twenty-one times [because he was proud of his strength and lacked compassion.[19]]

Assertion: Though the proud are deprecable because they perform ill deeds, it is appropriate for those without pride to strive for a high rebirth.
Answer:

167. Whoever renounces them now
     Will, it is said, obtain sense objects.
     For what reason would such perverse
     Practice be considered correct?

It is said that those who promise to be chaste in this life for the sake of a high rebirth in future and who renounce sense objects, having cultivated antipathy toward them, will, as a result of their practices, have whatever attractive objects they desire when they take a high rebirth. If, accordingly, out of aversion one gives up the things one has, it is a perverse practice to seek them again. Why would the wise consider such a pursuit correct? It is unreasonable to seek what one has deliberately renounced. It is like the following analogy: When rams want to butt, though they first recoil, it is perverse [because they do so in order to charge.]

168. Wealth, the result of merit,
    Must be thoroughly protected from others.
    How can that which must be constantly
    Protected from others be one's own?

Even those with large resources should not be attached to them, for wealth, the result of meritorious actions like giving, must constantly be protected from other factors such as robbers, thieves, fire, water and so forth. How can anything needing constant and diligent protection from other factors be one's own exclusive property over which one has control? Though the effects have been accomplished, they cannot benefit one as desired. The need to expend effort constantly on their account is like [the sustained effort required in cultivating[20]] a spiritual guide.

Assertion: If practices like giving are wrong, one should follow conventionally accepted practices.
    Answer: Adherence to those is also improper.

169. Different social customs
    Are termed "religious practices."
    Thus it seems as if society has
    More influence than religious practices.

The term "religious practice" is applied to different social customs like giving away and taking a bride. Such conventions are called religion but they change according to place and time. It is therefore improper to be attached to society which, though it appears more influential than religion, does not remain stable. It is like taking one's daughter as bride in a particular country.

A certain man visited Yawana and watched a local man light a fire. By means of a spell, the fire uttered the words, "You may take your daughter as wife." The visitor, who was very lustful, had an attractive young daughter at home. He approached the man from Yawana and offered him a lot of money for the spell. When he got home he wanted to marry his daughter and asked the fire to speak. The fire said, "The customs are different."

Assertion: Pleasure does not occur without attractive sense objects. Since these are the result of merit, it is permissible to perform meritorious actions out of attachment to attractive objects in order to have pleasure.
   Answer:

> 170. Through virtue there are attractive objects,
>   But such objects too are considered bad.
>   By giving them up, one will be happy.
>   What need is there to acquire them?

Though attractive visual forms, sounds and other objects are obtained through virtues like giving, those who desire liberation disparage and consider even such sense objects bad, since they are the root of futility and are constantly affected by suffering and impermanence. If one becomes happy and virtuous by giving up a source of faults, what need is there to acquire it? No need at all! It is like the following analogy from Candrakīrti's commentary: When a certain monk went to beg alms in Cambodia, a trickster told him not to speak in that country.

A monk went to beg from the people of Cambodia. For his own purposes, a trickster told him, "It is the custom in this country not to speak when going for alms, otherwise people will make fun of you." The monk believed him and acted accordingly. The people thought that the fellow had made and sent a mechanical man to dupe them. They marvelled at the way he opened and closed his eyes just like a real man and they discussed all his parts. Then they made a similar mechanical man and sent him to the trickster who told the monk that it was time to speak to people. He did so, which amazed them, and they said that the trickster had clearly outwitted them by doing what they could not do. When the monk discovered the trickster's true nature, he considered him bad.[21]

Assertion: Though sense objects should be disparaged, one ought to create merit for the sake of kingship, a source of superlative pleasure.
   Answer: It is inappropriate to do so.

171. For one not in need of authority,
     Practices for that [end] are meaningless.
     Whoever strives for authority
     Is called a fool among men.

For adepts who have gained mental control and can effortlessly accomplish whatever they desire, practices such as giving for the sake
of attaining worldly authority are senseless. Whoever strives for the
authority of mere verbal domination is a fool among men, because
he seeks kingship, a source of great futility. It is like the following
analogy: An astrologer had a lovable son whom he killed when he
knew the boy would die after six days. [His authority to make astro-
logical predictions caused him to act in a futile way.]

Assertion: One should do meritorious actions, since one wants their
effects (such as wealth) in future lives.
   Answer:

172. With a view to future effects
     You grasp at practices out of greed.
     When you see the future outcome
     Why are you not afraid?

If, on realizing that there will be future effects such as wealth, one
grasps at practices like giving, out of greed and attachment, one will
have to experience many bad rebirths as a result of that attachment.
When you see that the future outcome of such attachment is a bad
rebirth, aren't you afraid? What use is attachment? Just as you do
not grasp at bad rebirth, do not grasp at practices either. It is like an
unwise person who buys a place that gives rise to suffering.

173. Merit is in every way
     Just like a wage for a wage earner.
     How could those who do not want
     [Even] virtue do what is non-virtuous?

Just like a wage earned by a worker, merit will come to resemble a
payment. Therefore the wise do not do even meritorious actions
motivated by attachment. When the wise do not want even the virtue that produces worldly existence, because of seeing it as a cause
for the cycle of rebirths, how could they do demeritorious actions
which are non-virtuous? They always avoid them. It is like the fol-

lowing analogy: When a dog ate *Raṅgaṭa's food, *Raṅgaṭa accused a prince who was fasting nearby of having eaten it.

*Raṅgaṭa, a destitute beggar, found some badly cooked food and wrapped it in a stinking pus-stained rag. When he wasn't looking, a dog stole it. Not far away a prince was fasting in the service of his deity. The beggar accused him of breaking his fast by stealing and eating the food. When the prince would not eat even his own well-prepared food, why would he have eaten food like that?[22]

174. Whoever sees phenomena as like
     A collection of mechanical devices
     And like illusory beings,
     Most clearly reaches the excellent state.

Only childish people like cyclic existence. The wise who directly perceive dependent arising as lacking inherent existence see external and internal phenomena as like a collection of mechanical devices made of wood that look like men and women. Those who see phenomena as empty of inherent existence, yet appearing like illusory people, traverse cyclic existence and most clearly reach the excellent states of liberation and omniscience. It is like the mechanic who shamed a painter by means of a mechanical woman. The painter caused him suffering in return.

A painter was staying in the home of a master mechanic who, as a joke, sent a mechanical woman to him. Thinking that she was a maid who had been sent for him to enjoy and with whom he could do as he pleased, he took her hand only to find it was hard wood. He felt mortified and to take revenge painted himself committing suicide on the wall. When the master mechanic saw it, he felt remorse and thought the painter had killed himself in shame after touching the mechanical device.[23]

175. For those who do not enjoy
     Any objects in cyclic existence
     It is altogether impossible
     To take pleasure in this [world].

When those who are wise with regard to the meaning of reality do not enjoy or crave even those objects in cyclic existence which are normally enjoyable, how could they enjoy the source of birth, aging and so forth which normally cause aversion? Thus for them there is never any joy out of attachment to cyclic existence. It is like the following analogy: in the city of Kuśīnagar, Mahāsudarśana gave up eighty-four thousand queens because he saw the faults of sense objects, and developed the four concentrations.[24]

Thus as has been explained previously, after considering the disadvantages of sense objects, one should become wise with regard to the meaning of reality and strive to attain unsurpassable enlightenment.

The summarizing stanza:

> Thinking thoroughly about impermanence and
>   suffering
> Give up craving for objects such as visual form,
> The cause for this bottomless boundless ocean of
>   suffering,
> And strive to attain unsurpassable enlightenment.

This is the seventh chapter from the *Four Hundred on the Yogic Deeds*, showing the means to give up clinging to objects of enjoyment which humans desire.

This concludes the commentary on the seventh chapter, showing the means to give up clinging to objects of enjoyment which humans desire, from *Essence of Good Explanations, Explanation of the "Four Hundred on the Yogic Deeds of Bodhisattvas"*.

COMMENTARY TO CHAPTER VII
BY GESHE SONAM RINCHEN

The famous Ga-dam-ba master Ge-shay Bo-da-wa's *Precious Heap of Analogies for the Teaching*[25] elaborates an analogy by Vasubandhu:

When a fisherman is catching fish, he puts some meat on the end of the hook and throws it down into the depths of the water. Since fish have a great liking for fresh meat, they swallow the bait and the hook catches in their throats. Then they are brought on to dry land and killed. Taste is the fish's undoing. Similarly our tongue pursues tastes and, caught on the hook of disturbing emotions, we are fried in the pan of bad rebirths.

The moth sees the butterlamp as a celestial mansion and with delight at once flies toward it. Burnt by the flame, it falls into the melted butter. Appearance is the moth's undoing. Similarly we see the suffering nature of deceptive appearances as pleasurable. Through our attachment we fall into the ocean of cyclic existence and are burnt by the fires of bad rebirths.

It is said that an elephant likes to be touched. It enjoys having its body gently scratched and remains perfectly still. An iron hook is then attached to the crown of its head, and it can be led wherever one wishes. Touch is the elephant's undoing. Similarly we enjoy physical contact and are caught by the hook of suffering.

A fly enjoys bad smells and circling around falls into the cesspool, only to be carried off by a large or small bird. Smell is the fly's undoing. Similarly we circle around the smell of sensual pleasure, drown in a morass of disturbing emotions and are carried away by demons.

Hunters in the south hide in remote forests and play the flute and vina. Deer love sweet sounds, so the hunters lie in wait till they come near to listen to the music. Then they shoot arrows and kill them. Sound is the deer's undoing. Similarly we run after fame and are killed by the hunters of desire and anger.

Vasubandhu says:

Sound is the deer's perdition;
For the elephant it is touch.
Appearance is the moth's perdition
And for the fish it is taste.
The fly is attracted to smells —

For them there is but a single cause.
Among humans, each individual
Both day and night is constantly
Destroyed by all five of these.
How can they attain a happy state?

Normally we do not recognize just how much sense objects preoccupy us. Not only do we constantly and often automatically seek to satisfy the senses, but the aesthetic criteria of our society or segment of society and our own innate and acquired preferences with regard to sense objects influence our response to others and our judgments.

This preoccupation with sense objects and our craving for new and stimulating sensory experiences is continually exploited and reinforced. The compulsive quality of our attention indicates the presence of attachment, which frequently robs us of expected pleasure and accounts for an underlying anxiety. The more intense the grasping, the greater the anxiety and the more vulnerable we are to frustration which may express itself as anger. Despite repeated disappointments, we continue to pursue the elusive pleasure which these objects seem to promise. Though we may realize that the pursuit of sensual gratification is futile and gives rise to sickness, problems and all kinds of misfortunes, we remain addicted to the hope of finding happiness in this way. Our enthrallment is not superficial but fundamental to us as beings of the Desire Realm, so called because of our preoccupation with sense stimuli. We must therefore reflect again and again on the true nature of sense objects and their inability to provide lasting happiness. This will help to diminish our obsession with them, which blinds us to the unsatisfactoriness and misery of cyclic existence.

Chapter VIII

Thoroughly Preparing the Student

Question: How do we escape from the bondage of desire to which we have been accustomed since beginningless time?
Answer:

> 176. Just as friendship between people
> Who disagree does not last long,
> Desire does not last long
> When all things' faults are recognized.

A friendship motivated by desire between people who are not amicable and who disagree does not last long. Similarly desire does not last long for an adept who recognizes the faults in all external and internal things[1] which give rise to many unwanted consequences. When properly investigated, its root is found to be unstable and thus one can get rid of it.

It is like the following analogy: When a Brahmin called Gyu was getting married, he wanted to hold his young bride's hand. The Teacher said, "Brahmin boy, relationship is bondage, separation is freedom." Hearing this, Gyu analyzed the four noble truths, through which he became a Foe Destroyer. ["Relationship" indicated true sources of suffering; "bondage," true sufferings; "separation," true paths; and "freedom," true cessations.[2]]

Disturbing emotions can be abandoned not only through seeing the faults in objects, but also because those objects, the basis of these faults, lack true existence.

177. Some are attracted to it,
     Some are averse to it,
     Some feel confused by it:
     Thus desire has no object.

Desire depends on and operates in relation to a desired thing which, moreover, does not exist by way of its own entity, for some are attracted to that object, some have an aversion to it, and some are confused by it. If the desired object existed by way of its own entity, only desire should arise toward it. Since this is not inevitable, focal objects are only imputed by conceptuality, and that which is desired does not exist by way of its own entity. Therefore, from the point of view of the basis too, disturbing emotions can be abandoned.

It is like the following analogy: A man had two wives. When the one who was a mother saw her daughter, she felt happy. When the younger wife [who had no children[3]] saw the daughter, she suffered. Their servant remained indifferent.

Not only can disturbing emotions be abandoned because their focal objects lack true existence, but also because their causes do not have true existence.

178. Apart from conceptuality,
     Desire and so forth have no existence.
     Who with intelligence would hold [that there are]
     Real things [imputed by] conceptuality?

It says:

Desire, anger and confusion are explained
To arise through conceptuality.

The existence of disturbing emotions such as desire cannot be found apart from the conceptualizations of an incorrect mental approach and imputation by conceptuality, as a snake is imputed to a mottled rope. Their existence is simply a reliant existence, and they do not exist by way of their own entity. If they did, who with intelligence would hold they are imputed by conceptuality, which means the opposite of existence in terms of their own reality? Imputation by conceptuality and existence by way of a thing's own entity are contradictory.

When a snake is imputed to a rope, neither the parts of the rope, that which possesses the parts, its continuum, nor that which possesses the continuum appropriately illustrate a snake. Similarly, neither the collection of the aggregates, that which makes up the collection, its continuum, nor that which possesses the continuum is appropriate as the person.[4] You should understand that because of being imputed in dependence on the aggregates, the person does not exist by way of its own entity, and that this, furthermore, applies to all phenomena.

An instance of mistaken and wrong perception is when a practitioner of concentration mistakenly imagines there to be a skull on top of his head. If someone else shows him a skull and says, "This fell from your head," the idea will be dispelled.

The meaning of the text and of Candrakīrti's commentary at this point may be understood by a thorough comprehension of what the *Sixty Stanzas of Reasoning* says:

> The world is caused by ignorance —
> The Fully Enlightened One said so.
> Therefore why is it not feasible
> To say the world is conceptuality?[5]

Assertion: Since men and women are bound together by mutual desire, one cannot give up women and thus cannot give up desire.
Answer:

179. **None is, as it were,**
     Bound to another.
     It is unfeasible to separate
     That which is bound together.

No man is intrinsically bound to a woman. Since anything inherent is irrevocable, whatever is intrinsically bound together should not be separable. Yet in the case of that which should not be separable, separation is seen.

It is like the following analogy: Though a black and a white ox are not intrinsically bound together, they are bound by means of a yoke and harness. Similarly, craving binds objects and sense organs together.

Assertion: If disturbing emotions are stopped by analyzing in this way, why do most people appear not to have abandoned them?
Answer: It is because they lack a strong belief in the profound teaching.

180. Those with little merit
      Do not even doubt this teaching.
      Entertaining just a doubt
      Tears to tatters worldly existence.

Those with little merit do not even have a doubt regarding the two
truths as asserted by Nāgārjuna: that while dependent arising is
empty of inherent existence, actions and agents are feasible. Since
they do not wonder whether this is so or not, how can they attain
the liberation of having abandoned all disturbing attitudes and emotions? When emptiness is taught, simply entertaining the positive
doubt that it might be so tears worldly existence to tatters, since to
some extent the fundamental nature of existence has become the
mind's object. Someone who has such a positive doubt will seek
certainty, and by ascertaining the correct view through scriptural citations and reasoning, will attain liberation when disturbing attitudes
and emotions come to an end.

It is like the following analogy: A captain was captured by an ogress
who told him not to look toward the south. Feeling suspicious, he
went that way and met the king of horses, Balāhaka, escaped from
the ogress and crossed the ocean. [Had he not been suspicious, he
would not have escaped from the ogress nor reached the other
shore.⁶] This shows that even to attain just liberation it is essential
to understand the meaning of reality.

181. The Subduer said of this teaching
      There will be increase until liberation.
      Anyone who lacks interest in it
      Clearly has no sense.

The Subduer said that from the first moment of the path of seeing
until liberation there will be no decline, only increase in the direct
perception of emptiness, concerning which even a doubt tears
worldly existence to tatters. The practice of giving and so forth, conjoined with it, will also only increase. Anyone who lacks interest in
the meaning of emptiness clearly has no sense and shows how very
foolish he or she is.

[A certain man had become accomplished in the use of two mantras. One mantra said over a spoon pacified people's sicknesses. The
second acted likewise when accompanied by a hand gesture. He
advised a close friend to acquire the two mantras from him because

they would help him, but the friend did not do so. After the man's death his friend contracted a serious illness which was incurable and he died.[7]

The wise should take an interest in contemplating emptiness. Worldly practices come to an end once they have yielded their fruit, but the understanding of emptiness leads the practices of giving and so forth to the city of omniscience.[8] The contemplation of emptiness is like a sugar-candy—it should always be savored.

Question: Does one meditate on emptiness, although things are not empty, to free oneself from desire, or does one view them that way because they actually are empty of true existence?

Answer:

> 182. One does not regard that which is not empty
> As empty, thinking [thereby] to gain nirvāṇa.
> Tathāgatas say that nirvāṇa
> Will not be attained through wrong views.

Once one has an understanding of that which is empty as empty, one familiarizes oneself with it. It is not the case that things, which are actually not empty, are simply regarded as empty, with the thought that nirvāṇa will be attained by meditating on emptiness. One who holds this view does not understand the emptiness of the person and aggregates but thinks of them as truly existent. Tathāgatas say one will not reach nirvāṇa by means of wrong views misconceiving the fundamental nature of existence. The Teacher said, "All phenomena are empty in that they do not exist inherently." No matter which of the three states of nirvāṇa one enters, one must become learned in the meaning of emptiness.

It is like a novice monk sent to fetch a prohibited drink at night.

A novice's teacher insisted he fetch a prohibited drink at night. The novice asked him, "If this is unsuitable for monks, why do you drink it?" His teacher replied, "I imagine it's water." Another day the novice brought water and his teacher asked him why he had brought something different. The novice answered, "If you imagine it's water when you drink it, how is it different from this?"[9]

Question: If things are empty of inherent existence, it is appropriate to teach suchness. What is the use of teaching how the world of sentient beings and environments comes into existence?

Answer: Emptiness cannot be understood without an explanation of how the world comes into being. Therefore explaining it is essential as a means for understanding suchness.

183. Whatever contains teaching
      About the world speaks of engagement.
      Whatever contains elucidation
      Of the ultimate speaks of disengagement.

Scriptures teaching about action caused by ignorance and so forth, the world of sentient beings and environments describe the stages by which one engages in cyclic existence. Their purpose is to refute belief in causeless production or production from incompatible causes, which is based on conceptions of true existence. They are thus a means for understanding suchness. Those scriptures elucidating the ultimate, the emptiness of inherent existence of phenomena, describe the stages by which one disengages from cyclic existence.

It is like the following analogy: When entering a deep narrow passage, any equipment one has must be discarded, [since it is useless. Similarly the wise abandon futile involvement in worldly existence.[10]]

Objection: If all things are empty there are many unwanted consequences, since by denying the existence of objects, actions and agents, even liberation will not exist.

Answer:

184. Thinking, "Nothing exists, what is the use?"
      You may be afraid.
      But if actions did exist,
      This teaching would not be a prevention.

You who fear emptiness may be frightened by thinking, "What is the use of striving for liberation, since things do not exist if they are empty of inherent existence?" But if actions existed ultimately, it would not be possible for anyone to prevent cyclic existence by understanding the teaching of emptiness, since actions and agents are not feasible in a context of inherent existence. Thinking the aggregates are truly existent is like thinking a mirage is water.

185. While attached to your own position
      And disliking others' positions
      You will not approach nirvāṇa.
      Neither [kind of] conduct will bring peace.

Thinking the thesis of emptiness which stops cyclic existence is supreme and others are wrong, you may be strongly attached to your own position and antagonistic to others'. You will not approach the liberation of nirvāṇa until you discard this strong attachment to your own thesis, emptiness, and your dislike for and antagonism toward others' theses. Peace can never be attained through conduct based on the idea that both adopting and discarding are truly existent.

It is like the following analogy: A certain ascetic was told by the Exalted Saṅghasena to hold layperson's vows. When he saw Brahmins, he felt the urge to kill them. [Some days later he said, "Venerable One, I now hold layperson's vows because when I see a Brahmin I feel like killing him."[11]]

Assertion: We cannot attain the perfect happiness of nirvāṇa, because it is extremely difficult to do so, but we enter cyclic existence because it is easy to acquire without effort.

Answer:

> 186. Not acting brings about nirvāṇa;
> Acting again brings worldly existence.
> Thus, without complication, nirvāṇa
> Is easy to attain, but not the latter.

Understanding about not doing actions, whether they are virtuous or non-virtuous activities, brings about nirvāṇa. Worldly existence is brought about by doing various virtuous and non-virtuous actions. Thus by giving up the performance of all actions, nirvāṇa is easy to attain without complication.[12] On the other hand, the pleasures of cyclic existence are not easy to gain. Therefore it is unreasonable for the wise to give up striving for nirvāṇa, which is attained without the need for tiring exertion, and instead strive for cyclic existence, which is acquired through all kinds of tiring exertion. It is like the following analogy: There are many factors through which immunity to sickness can be acquired, but if one does not want that, one will not seek them.[13]

Question: If not doing any actions at all in a context of ultimate existence brings about nirvāṇa, why are impermanence, suffering and so forth taught in this treatise?

Answer: It is done to produce aversion to the cycle of birth and death, so that one will attain nirvāṇa free from all the activities of cyclic existence.

> 187. How can anyone who has no aversion
> To this take an interest in pacification?
> Like [leaving] home, it is also hard
> To leave worldly existence behind.

How could anyone who has no aversion to cyclic existence take an interest in liberation, which is the pacification of the suffering it entails? If one isn't suffering from thirst, one will not feel a strong urge to drink in order to relieve the discomfort. It is like the following analogy: Though one's home may contain little of worth, one cannot completely give up attachment to it. Similarly, it is difficult for those of limited intelligence completely to leave worldly existence behind because they are bound by attachment, like someone about to be killed who has not stopped craving things and wants a drink.

The rich and powerful, who are attached to the pleasure they derive from things, may not be able to give up their homes and strive in seclusion to attain liberation. However, it is surely fitting for those afflicted by sickness and poverty to give up their attraction to cyclic existence.

188. **One sees that some who are overwhelmed**
By suffering long for death,
Yet entirely due to their confusion
They will not reach the excellent state.

Some people who are overwhelmed by the suffering of poverty, of being separated from what is dear to them and the like, long to die by leaping into fire, water, or into an abyss and so forth in order to gain release. In exactly the same way, by gaining certainty concerning the suffering of cyclic existence and abandoning attachment to the self, they could quickly attain the happiness of liberation, but entirely due to their extreme confusion about what to adopt and discard, they will not reach the excellent state of nirvāṇa. It is like the following analogy: Without taking the medicine a patient will not be cured of his illness. Similarly, even if one suppresses manifest disturbing emotions to some extent, one will not gain liberation from cyclic existence except by employing the antidote which completely eradicates them.

Question: If one is to strive for liberation which ends cyclic existence, advice only about meditation on suchness would be appropriate. Why did the Teacher also give advice on giving and ethics?
Answer: There is no fault in this.

189. Giving is taught to the lowest
   And ethics to the middling.
   Pacification is taught to the best;
   Therefore, always do the best!

One must lead others gradually, distinguishing between those of least, intermediate and best ability. Advice about giving is for those who at first are capable only of generosity but cannot give up killing and so forth. Thus advice on giving is directed to those of least ability who, for the time being, are not ready to practise ethics and meditation. Those of intermediate ability already practising generosity are taught about ethics, since they are ready to take birth as gods or humans. Those with the best ability are principally instructed in meditation on suchness, the means to pacify cyclic existence. Thus one should always endeavor to do the best and think, "Why shouldn't I attain liberation?"

It is like the following analogy: According to their ages, one of a king's three sons is taught to recite the alphabet, the second to recite a treatise on grammar and the third a treatise on the use of weapons. This is what it means to be knowledgeable about the stages by which trainees are led, since one person must be taught everything gradually.

If reality is explained to someone as yet unready for such an explanation, that person will deny actions and agents, thinking there is no difference between virtue and ill deeds, and will go to bad rebirths.

190. First prevent the demeritorious,
   Next prevent [ideas of a coarse] self.
   Later prevent views of all kinds.
   Whoever knows of this is wise.

Initially, therefore, they should be taught about virtuous and non-virtuous actions and about cause and effect since that is easy to understand. As it is the proper time, they should thus be prevented from engaging in demeritorious misdeeds. Next the coarse self should be repudiated by refuting the referent object of twenty views of the transitory collection[14] by means of a five-fold analysis of the aggregates.[15] Later, when the mindstream has become receptive, selflessness of persons is taught, and by showing that even selflessness does not exist truly, all views conceiving extremes are prevented. Whoever knows these stages of teaching is wise regarding the sequence in which trainees are led. It is like a skilled physician who prescribes a bland or oily diet to specific patients.

Question: By what path is liberation attained?
   Answer: By understanding that all phenomena are empty of inherent existence.
   Qualm: Since there are limitless things, their realities are also limitless. Who could know them all? Moreover, it is said that one cannot attain liberation while there is a single phenomenon one does not know and has not abandoned.
   Answer: There is no fault.

   191. **Whoever sees one thing**
        Is said to see all.
        That which is the emptiness of one
        Is the emptiness of all.

Whoever sees one thing's fundamental mode of existence which is its emptiness of inherent existence is said to see the reality of all things. The *King of Meditative Stabilizations* says:

   Through one all are known
   And through one all are seen.[16]

The *Meditative Stabilization of Gaganagañja* says:

   Whoever through one phenomenon knows
   All phenomena are like illusions, mirages, and are
        inapprehensible,
   [Hollow, deceptive and ephemeral,
   Will before long reach the essence of enlightenment.[17]]

   It is like the following analogy: By drinking one drop of sea-water you know the rest is salty. "That which is the emptiness of one thing is the emptiness of all" means this very emptiness of true existence is the fundamental mode of existence of all phenomena. It does not appear in different ways as do blue and yellow. However, one should not assert in relation to an inferential cognition that the awareness cognizing the pot's emptiness of true existence cognizes the woollen cloth's emptiness of true existence.[18] It is like the space in different receptacles.

Question: If everything is to be given up because of being empty, why does sūtra say that one should show respect and create merit?
   Answer: There is no contradiction.

192. Tathāgatas speak of attachment to practices
To those who want a high rebirth.
That is disparaged for those who want freedom—
What need to mention other [attachments]?

To those who fear bad rebirths and want a high rebirth, and who are incapable of meditating on subtle production, disintegration and so forth, Tathāgatas speak of attachment to practices like giving and leave aside the understanding of suchness. If such an aspiration for merely a high rebirth is disparaged in those who seek liberation, what need is there to mention attachment to wrongdoing? It says, "If all practices must be abandoned in the sphere of nirvāṇa, how much more so malpractices!" It is like the following analogy: When the advent of a universal monarch called Śaṅkha was being predicted, a monk prayed to be that monarch, for which the Teacher criticized him.

In Varanasi the Supramundane Victor Śākyamuni predicted to the Bodhisattva Ajita: "In the future you will be the Tathāgata Foe Destroyer, the fully enlightened Buddha Maitreya. At that time there will be a universal monarch called Śaṅkha. In this very city, while you are alive and when you die, he will make great offerings and will die as a Foe Destroyer." In that gathering there was a monk called Ajita who prayed, "How wonderful if I could be that universal monarch Śaṅkha and rule the four continents." The Supramundane Victor criticized him, saying, "You became ordained to stop suffering. Having become ordained you are foolish to seek this suffering." Having said this the Supramundane Victor added, "I do not praise the actualization of even a moment's cyclic existence. If you ask why, monks, it is because the actualization of worldly existence is suffering. For instance if a small lump of excrement smells foul, how much more so a large one!"[19]

Assertion: If all suffering is stopped by understanding emptiness, it would be appropriate to teach only suchness.
Answer: That is not so.

193. Those who want merit should not
Always speak of emptiness.
Doesn't a medicinal compound
Turn to poison in the wrong case?

It depends upon differences in receptivity. If emptiness is explained to those who are not receptive, it will cause misfortune: either they will reject emptiness, or, misunderstanding emptiness to mean that everything is non-existent, they will go to bad transmigrations. Therefore those with compassion who want the merit of caring for others should never speak about emptiness without first examining the recipient. Doesn't even an appetizing and potent medicinal compound turn to poison when given to the wrong patient? It is like giving someone who has not been poisoned an antidote to poison and thereby killing them. Mātṛceṭa says:

> [Only] unstained cloth [is good for] dyeing.
> [Likewise] the mind must be properly developed
> By first speaking of giving and so forth.
> Then one should meditate on the teaching.

One must examine the recipient.

At the outset one should teach in accordance with how ordinary people accept that things exist.

> 194. Just as a barbarian cannot be
>   Guided in a foreign language,
>   Ordinary people cannot be guided
>   Except by way of the ordinary.

Just as a barbarian cannot be guided in a foreign language but must be taught in his own, teaching initially should be in keeping with conventionally accepted things like generosity. Ordinary people cannot be guided to an understanding of ultimate truth unless they understand the ordinary, namely the explanation of how conventional things exist. [Candrakīrti's] *Supplement* says:

> Conventional truth is the means;
> Ultimate truth, the outcome of the means.[20]

One should teach ultimate truth based on an acceptance of conventional existence in one's own system. It is like the following analogy: One cannot make a child understand in a foreign language.

> 195. Teaching existence, non-existence,
>   Both existence and non-existence, and neither
>   Surely are medicines for all
>   That are influenced by the sickness.

As a means of guiding the world, to eliminate views of non-existence, the Teacher told trainees that everything exists, and to eliminate conceptions of true existence, he taught that there is no true existence. In relation to conventional awareness and analytical awareness he taught existence and non-existence[21] and to eliminate the two extreme views of existence and non-existence, he taught that both things and non-things[22] are not truly existent. Surely these are simply medicines to remove all views influenced by the sickness of wrong thinking. Therefore everything the Teacher said is a means to attain nirvāṇa, taking into consideration individual trainees. It is like the following analogy: There were three brothers of whom one became ordained, the second became a harmful spirit with supernatural powers, and the third a hungry ghost. The meaning of the analogy is as in Candrakīrti's commentary.

These two went to their brother the monk, who explained the benefits of giving to the harmful spirit, so that he would know what causes prosperity. He also taught him about the faults of unethical conduct. Having given the hungry ghost a drink to relieve his fiery torment, he told him about the faults of miserliness, to make him understand his suffering.[23]

Showing how things are free from the extremes of existence and non-existence by teaching that they exist, do not exist and so forth is teaching on the ultimate.

> 196. Correct perception [leads to] the supreme state,
> Some perception to good rebirths.
> The wise thus always expand their intelligence
> To think about the inner nature.

Correctly perceiving the ultimate with supramundane wisdom leads to the attainment of the supreme state of liberation. Perceiving it to some extent with the mundane wisdom arising from meditation or from hearing and thinking leads to good rebirths. Thus the wise constantly expand their intelligence to think about the inner nature, emptiness. It is like the analogy of a thief in the king's palace who was solicited by an immoral woman.

A thief kept visiting a temple where some monks said, "Please accept a gift from us." When he asked what kind of gift, they answered that it was a religious one: the precepts of basic training. However, he said that he could not abstain from killing, stealing, lying or drinking liquor but would give up sexual misconduct. So, promising to give that up, he took one precept. At night he crept into the king's palace to steal, and there an immoral woman solicited him but he did not accept. When he heard about it, the king decked him out in the queen's jewels and honored him.

197. Through knowing reality, even if now
     One does not attain nirvāṇa,
     One will certainly gain it effortlessly
     In a later life, as it is with actions.

Even if one does not attain nirvāṇa in this life by knowing the reality of dependent arising free from extremes of elaboration, through familiarity with the understanding of suchness, one will certainly attain it effortlessly in a later life, merely by virtue of remaining in seclusion. It is like an action performed out of ignorance, the effect of which will be experienced upon taking rebirth. What intelligent person would not strive to understand suchness? It is like the following analogy: After eating a ripe mango, if you plant its stone, you'll get fruit later.

The *Fundamental Treatise Called Wisdom* says:

> When consummate Buddhas do not appear
> And Hearers too have come to an end,
> The wisdom of Solitary Realizers
> Manifests independently.[24]

Question: If there are many who understand suchness why does one not see people who are released from worldly existence?

Answer: Though one does see some, mere intention does not create results. The coming together of causes and conditions does, yet this is very rare.

198. Accomplishment of all intended
     Actions is extremely uncommon.
     It is not that nirvāṇa is absent here
     But conjunction and the released are rare.

The accomplishment, merely through intention, of actions that result as intended is extremely uncommon not only in the case of liberation but in all cases. It is not that no one aspires to attain nirvāṇa in the Buddha's teaching, but that causes and conditions — external conditions such as a spiritual friend, and internal ones such as the correct mental approach — very seldom combine and come together, which is why the released are rare. The analogy of the Caṇḍala woman licking iron is as in Candrakīrti's commentary.

Although a Caṇḍala woman was innocent of the theft of which she was accused, she said, "Because I am a Caṇḍala, I am low caste and must lick the iron by the temple," but she could not bear to do so.[25] Had she done it, she would have been cleared of the suspicion that she had done wrong. Similarly, some childish people consider themselves inferior and lack the patience to apply themselves to attaining Buddhahood. If they applied themselves in the correct way they would undoubtedly attain enlightenment.[26]

Question: How can one be sure there is an end to this multitude of disturbing attitudes and emotions which have continued to occur for so long, since beginningless time?
Answer:

> 199. **On hearing that the body lacks good qualities,**
> **Attachment does not last long.**
> **Will not all disturbing attitudes**
> **End by means of this very path?**

When the intelligent, who know how to think analytically, hear that the body lacks good qualities in that its nature is to disintegrate no matter how long it is cared for with all kinds of things, that it is ungrateful and difficult to nurture, their attachment to the body does not last long. Similarly why should it not be possible to end all disturbing attitudes and emotions through the path that consists of meditating on dependent arising free from extremes of elaboration? Since one can certainly put an end to them, one will attain liberation.

It is like the following analogy: When Canaka made a little gold with the gold-producing elixir, he knew he could make a lot of gold this way and threw away the small piece. On hearing that the body lacks good qualities the wise should discard attachment to it [and realizing that by means of this path they can stop all disturbing attitudes and emotions, they should gain familiarity with it.[27]]

Question: How can the continuity of rebirths occurring since beginningless time come to an end?
Answer:

> 200. **Just as the end of a seed is seen**
> **Though it has no beginning,**
> **When the causes are incomplete**
> **Birth, too, will not occur.**

Although a seed, such as a barley seed, has no beginning, its end is seen when it is burnt by fire and the like. Similarly the causes for birth in worldly existence are made incomplete by eliminating all conceptions of a personal self. Thus through the strength of the antidote, rebirth in worldly existence due to contaminated actions and disturbing attitudes and emotions will not occur again. It is like the following analogy: Once a butterlamp's fuel is exhausted it will not burn.

The Master Buddhapālita says:

> Though seeing transmigrators as empty,
> Since you wish to remove their suffering
> You have toiled for a long time.
> This is most amazing!

The deeds of Bodhisattvas, who are concerned with the welfare of sentient beings though they see that transmigrators do not exist inherently, are most amazing. Therefore, one should emulate them.

The summarizing stanza:

> Develop recognition that through contaminated action,
> Even to attain the best states as gods and humans is
>   imprisonment.
> Through familiarity with meditation on dependent arising
>   free from extremes,
> Make yourself a suitable vessel for the Great Vehicle.

This is the eighth chapter from the *Four Hundred on the Yogic Deeds*, on training the student.

This concludes the commentary on the eighth chapter, about thoroughly training the student, from *Essence of Good Explanations, Explanation of the "Four Hundred on the Yogic Deeds of Bodhisattvas"*.

COMMENTARY TO CHAPTER VIII
BY GESHE SONAM RINCHEN

Whenever one is teaching students of different aptitudes or is in a position to guide and encourage a particular student's gradual development, choosing appropriate topics and practices is of vital importance. Ge-tsang (*ke'u tshang*),[28] in his *Channel for the Sea of the Clear Minded, Notes on the Short Exposition of the Stages of the Path to Enlightenment*,[29] mentions a story the great Atīśa told when he came to Tibet which illustrates this.

Long ago in India the carcass of an elephant had been picked clean by big and small birds. Only the skeleton covered by the hide remained, and inside this tent-like shelter a meditator gained insight into emptiness. He became known as the Elephant-hide Meditator, and his fame spread. One of India's religious kings invited him to his court. Soon after his arrival, he began to teach the king about emptiness. The king, however, thought he was denying the existence of ordinary self-evident things and decided he was a nihilist masquerading as a great Buddhist teacher. Fearing that the laws he had enacted based on the ten virtues would not flourish among his subjects if he allowed such a teacher to remain there, he had him beheaded.

He then invited another teacher who at once informed him that he did not like sensual pleasures and doubted whether he and the king would see eye to eye, since the king indulged in them a great deal. He began by explaining the faults in sense objects and gradually led the king toward higher insights. Eventually he taught him about emptiness and the king understood the nature of reality. Having done so, he felt enormous remorse for having killed his former teacher and made great efforts to purify this ill deed. One night the Elephant-hide Meditator appeared in a dream. He told the king to go to where the hide still was and to paint a picture of him on it. He was then to acknowledge his wrongdoing until he received signs of purification.

Both teachers had understood emptiness but one was a competent teacher while the other was not. The skillful one was able to help while the other, who lacked skill, caused harm.

It is equally important to try to understand our own disposition and aptitudes as well as possible, and to seek teaching and choose practices for which we have a natural inclination. If we do not assess our abilities and our stage of development honestly, we may embark on practices that are too advanced. Then, when we do not achieve the insights and experiences that these practices are intended to induce, we will feel disappointed and give up. When we undertake a practice, it should not be out of competitiveness or the wish to do what others are doing, but from a sense of personal conviction. In order to experience the benefits of any practice, we should approach it in a relaxed and gentle way, without forcing it. Regular and moderate practice is more valuable than sporadic bursts of intense practice, which are often followed by apathy or even antipathy. When we throw a pile of dry twigs on the fire, it flares and burns brightly for a short time and then dies down. A log does not ignite quickly, but once it does the fire grows hotter gradually and keeps burning for a long time.

Chapter IX

Refuting Permanent Functional Phenomena

Explaining the stages of the paths dependent on ultimate truth has two parts. The first is an extensive explanation of ultimate truth. The second shows the purpose of writing these chapters and how to meditate on settling [the procedure between] teachers and students by way of eliminating remaining counter-arguments. The extensive explanation of ultimate truth begins with a general refutation of true existence by refuting permanent functional phenomena. This is followed by refuting truly existent functional phenomena individually. Finally the inherent existence of production, duration and disintegration, the characteristics of products, is refuted.

GENERAL REFUTATION OF TRUE EXISTENCE

By cleansing the mindstream with the flowing water of means by which to understand suchness, the previous chapters have made it a vessel fit for the nectar of suchness. The remaining chapters will explain how products which arise and disintegrate do not have even the slightest essence of inherent existence.

> 201. All are produced for their effect,
> Thus none are permanent.
> There are no Tathāgatas other than
> Subduers [who know] things as they are.

In the world it is accepted that when a laborer works hard for his wage, it is for the result and not because it is his nature to do so. Similarly all external and internal functional phenomena[1] do not arise of their own accord. Since they are produced solely through a multifarious aggregation of factors consisting of interrelated causes and effects, functional things are produced for their effects.[2] They therefore are not permanent, inherently produced or truly existent. They do not have an essence able to sustain analysis, nor do they exist as things in and of themselves.

Only Subduers, because they have the abilities of perfected body, speech and mind, directly know impermanence, emptiness and all things without exception as they are. Since no one else does, there are no other Tathāgatas. Moreover the Teacher said, "Whatever is produced inevitably ceases, for aging and death are conditioned by birth." Thus, since production is for the sake of disintegration, nothing endures by way of its own entity.

Some refute permanence and true existence by virtue of autonomous reasons.[3] The unfeasibility of this is explained in Candrakīrti's commentary.[4] There is no commonly appearing subject, such as a sprout, posited by tenets, in relation to which a direct valid cognition perceiving it is valid, since all except Prāsaṅgikas assert that it is valid in relation to a sprout existing by way of its own character. Prāsaṅgikas assert this is impossible.[5]

Vaiśeṣika assertion: Although things that are produced for their effect are not permanent, functional things—from space to the mind,[6] which lack both the feature of being produced and that of being producers; and the smallest particles, which, though they are producers, are not produced—are permanent and truly existent.
Answer:

> 202. There is not anywhere anything
>   That ever exists without depending.
>   Thus never is there anywhere
>   Anything that is permanent.

Never, at any time or in any place, is there any chance of finding a functional thing that does not depend on relatedness. Thus never is there anywhere a permanent functional phenomenon. Since whatever exists only exists dependently, it does not have even the slightest existence by way of its own entity.

Assertion: Dependently arising phenomena like pleasure and so forth[7] exist, and the self is the cause that attracts them. Thus the self exists and, moreover, is permanent.

Answer:

> 203. There is no functional thing without a cause,
>   Nor anything permanent which has a cause.
>   Thus the one who knows suchness said what has
>   Come about causelessly does not exist.

There is no personal self since that which has no producing cause is not a functional thing, nor is there anything permanent which has a cause. [Buddha,] the one who knows suchness, said phenomena that come into being causelessly do not exist:

> Phenomena with causes and conditions are known.
> Phenomena without causes and conditions do not exist.

> 204. If the unproduced is permanent
>   Because impermanent [things] are seen to be products,
>   Seeing that the produced exists
>   Would make the permanent non-existent.

If on seeing that a pot and pleasure are impermanent and produced, one asserts that the self and so forth are by implication permanent, it would follow that because of seeing that a pot and so forth are produced and exist, whatever is permanent like the self should be non-existent like a sky flower.

Assertion: The treatises of knowledge say space, individual analytical cessations,[8] and non-analytical cessations[9] are permanent and substantially existent. Any refutation of this is invalidated by your own assertions.

Answer: That is not so.

> 205. That space and so forth are permanent
>   Is a conception of common beings.
>   For the wise they are not objects perceived
>   Even by conventional [valid cognition].

Not understanding the significance of applying the term "space" to a mere absence of obstructive contact and so forth, common people think that uncompounded space and so on are permanent [functional phenomena]. Those who are wise concerning the suchness of functional phenomena, far from thinking they exist ultimately, do not regard permanent functional phenomena even as objects perceived by conventional valid cognition. Only that which does not change is termed permanent. What sūtra says is not primarily stated to establish [substantial existence, but to refute the existence of permanent functional things].

Assertion: Space is permanent because it is omnipresent. Whatever is impermanent like a pot is not omnipresent.

Answer: The following refutes permanence by refuting omnipresence. It is contradictory to assert that space is omnipresent but partless.

> 206. **A single direction is not present**
> **Wherever there is that which has directions.**
> **That with directions therefore clearly**
> **Also has other directional parts.**

The part of space contiguous to an eastern pot is not present wherever there is space which has directions, such as where there is a western pot. If it were, the western pot would be in the east and the eastern pot in the west. If to guard against such a fallacy one asserts that the part of space which is in the east is not in the west, directional space very clearly must have other parts. Therefore one should not accept permanent functional things. Sūtra says, "Kāśyapa, permanence is one extreme, so-called impermanence is the other extreme."[10] The belief that ultimate truths are permanent functional phenomena is foreign to this teaching.[11]

Assertion of Vaidāntikas and others:

> 207ab. **Since time exists, functional things**
> **Are seen to start and stop.**

Since permanent time exists the beginning and growth of things like a sprout are seen, while in winter and so forth, although other conditions are present, this is seen to stop. One can thereby infer the existence of time which, moreover, is permanent because of not depending on a cause.

Answer: Then it follows that sprouts and so forth are constantly produced and there is never a time when they are not produced, because of being produced by a permanent cause.

Assertion: Their production depends on other factors.

Answer:

207cd. It is governed by other factors;
Thus it is also an effect.

Then it follows that time, too, is an effect, for the intermittent production of sprouts is governed by other factors, being dependent on conditions like heat and moisture.[12] We do not assert that time is non-existent, for it says:

> The actions of the embodied do not
> Go to waste even in a hundred aeons.
> When conditions assemble and the time is ripe
> Their fruit will mature.

If proponents of time as a cause accept it as such, they should also accept it as an effect.

208. Any cause without an effect
Has no existence as a cause.
Therefore it follows that
Causes must be effects.

Without the effect it produces, a cause lacks that which establishes it as a cause, for the establishment of a cause depends on its effect. Thus since it follows that all causes must be effects, one should not accept causes that lack effects.[13] Anything accepted as a cause should be accepted as facilitating an effect.

209. When a cause undergoes change
It becomes the cause of something else.
Anything that undergoes change
Should not be called permanent.

A cause such as a seed acts as the cause of something else such as a sprout, through a change from before in its potency. Any functional thing which changes so that its former and later moments are unalike should not be called permanent. Thus one should not accept permanent time and so forth as causes.

210. A thing with a permanent cause is produced
By that which has not come into being.
Whatever happens by itself
Cannot have a cause.

If one does not accept that time, too, changes, it follows that a functional thing, such as a sprout whose cause is unchanging permanent time, has come about of its own accord because of being produced by a cause that has not come into being. Whatever happens by itself cannot have a producing cause, since its dependence on a cause is inadmissible.

> 211. How can that which is produced
>   By a permanent thing be impermanent?
>   Never are the two, cause and effect,
>   Seen to have incongruent characteristics.

How can functional things such as sprouts be impermanent? It follows that they are not, because of being produced by that which is permanent. This entailment follows because cause and effect are never seen to have incongruent characteristics in that one is permanent and the other impermanent.

Vaiśeṣika assertion: Permanent particles of the four elements activated by the force of karma form the substantial entity of a composite, producing the environmental world and so forth.

   Answer: That is incorrect, for it follows that when particles coalesce and form a composite, an increase in size is impossible if there is total interpenetration. If some parts coalesce, those that do are causes while those that do not are not causes.

> 212. That of which some sides are causes
>   While other sides are not is thereby
>   Multifarious. How can that
>   Which is multifarious be permanent?

It therefore follows that the smallest particle has parts, because some of its sides are causes while others are not. Being multifarious,[14] it follows that it cannot be a permanent functional thing because of having diverse parts.

Assertion: Although particles interpenetrate completely because they are partless, a separate accretion of coalesced particles forms, which produces the composite.

   Answer: It follows that it is not feasible for particles to interpenetrate completely when composites form. If they merge completely there will be no gradual increase in size from the first to the second composite and so forth.

213. The cause which is spherical
    Is not present in the effect.
    Thus complete interpenetration
    Of particles is not feasible.

Also the causative sphere with the characteristic of appearing to the mind as partless and spherical is not present in the resultant substantial entity, the composite.

214. One particle's position is not
    Asserted as also that of another.
    Thus it is not asserted that
    Cause and effect are the same size.

Where complete interpenetration does not occur, one particle's position will not be asserted as also that of another. Thus since the causal particles and resultant composite are not asserted to be equal in size, the absurd consequence that the composite is not an object of the senses is avoided. Nevertheless since particles have parts, their consequent unfeasibility as permanent functional things remains.[15]

Assertion: The problem of their having parts occurs when the resultant substantial entity is forming, but prior to that the smallest particles do not have parts.
Answer: That is incorrect. If a particle has no sides, it cannot be surrounded by particles on its four sides.

215. Whatever has an eastern side
    Also has an eastern part.
    Those whose particles have sides admit
    That they are not [partless] particles.

If it has sides, such as an eastern one, it definitely must have parts, since any particle with an eastern side must also have an eastern part. For that reason any opponent who holds that particles have sides prior to the formation of a composite admits those particles are not partless ones, because of accepting that they are located within the ten boundless directions.

216. The front takes up, the back relinquishes —
    Whatever does not have
    Both of these [motions]
    Is not something which moves.

It follows that such particles would not move from one place to another. When a thing moves from one place to another, its front takes
up a position ahead while its rear relinquishes the rearward position, but partless particles neither take up nor relinquish a position.
If it is asserted that they do not move, it is contradictory for partless
particles to form the substantial entity of a composite. Thus truly existent particles should never be accepted.

Assertion: Permanent particles do exist because adepts perceive them
by virtue of the divine eye.[16]
    Answer: What adept sees such a permanent particle?

217.   **That which does not have a front,**
       Nor any middle,
       And which does not have a rear,
       Being invisible, who will see it?

Seeing it is not feasible because such a form — a particle which firstly
has no front, nor any middle, and finally does not have a rear portion — is not evident to any kind of perception.

Assertion: Since coarse things would have no cause if particles did
not exist, particles do exist and, moreover, are permanent because
of being causeless functional things.
    Answer:

218ab. **The effect destroys the cause;**
       Therefore the cause is not permanent.

It follows that causal particles are not permanent, for just as the seed
changes and disintegrates when the sprout is produced, the causal
particles are destroyed by the production of the resultant composite.
    Objection: This is not established, for they produce a separate ef-
fect without giving up their causal identity.
    Answer:

218cd. **Alternatively, where the cause**
       Exists the effect does not.

Alternatively, since the presence of the causal particles in a place
precludes that of the resultant composite, it follows that they are not
cause and effect because of being simultaneous and occupying individual positions, like a pot and a woollen cloth in their respective
places.

For the following reason, too, particles are not permanent: particles are obstructive in that they cannot be penetrated completely by other particles. That which is obstructive cannot be permanent.

219. **A permanent thing that is obstructive**
Is not seen anywhere.
Therefore Buddhas never say
That particles are permanent.

The reason why Buddhas never say that permanent particles exist is because they do not perceive obstructive permanent things.

Cittamātrins, who refute the existence of particles by applying the reasoning of ultimate analysis but assert that consciousness is truly existent, should accept objects and consciousnesses as they are conventionally accepted, since exactly the same reasoning applies.[17]

Assertion of our own sectarians[18] *who do not understand uncompounded phenomena as merely nominal:* Although it is true that Buddhas do not mention permanent particles, they say uncompounded phenomena are permanent. Thus there is substantially existent cessation, which is like a dam. If this were not so it would be inappropriate to speak of the third noble truth.

Answer:

220. **If liberation, which is other than**
What binds, is bound and the means existed,
It should not be called liberation
Since nothing is produced from it.

True sources bind to cyclic existence, true sufferings are that which is bound and true paths are the means which liberate one from sufferings and their sources. If liberation which is other than these were a functional phenomenon it should facilitate an effect, but it does not produce any effect and not the slightest facilitation occurs. Thus it is inappropriate to call such a substantially existent cessation "liberation." It contradicts what the Teacher said: "Monks, these five are only names—past time, future time, space, nirvāṇa and the person." One should therefore accept liberation as a mere term, a mere imputation and not as substantially existent.

221ab. **In nirvāṇa there are no aggregates**
And there cannot be a person.

The Subduer said, "That which is the complete abandonment, removal, and extinction of this suffering ... the abandonment of all the aggregates, the end of worldly existence and separation from attachment, is cessation and nirvāṇa." According to proponents of functional things as truly existent, this citation means the aggregates are entirely non-existent in the sphere of nirvāṇa. Nor can there be a person imputed in dependence upon them, for neither the reliance nor reliant exist.

221cd. What nirvāṇa is there for one
Who is not seen in nirvāṇa?

Neither the aggregates nor the person are seen as a truly existent reliance which reaches nirvāṇa through the ending of disturbing attitudes and rebirth. What truly existent nirvāṇa reliant upon that is there? Not the slightest, thus one should accept liberation, too, as a mere imputation.

Sāṃkhya assertion: According to us there is no flaw that nirvāṇa is not liberation because of lacking a reliance. When an adept understands that the principal and person are different the process of involvement in cyclic existence such as the great one and so forth stops.[19] When everything subsides into the latent state of the principal, the conscious person remains alone. Thus there is a liberated self.

Answer:

222ab. When free from attachment at [the time of]
liberation
What good is the existence of consciousness?

It follows that it is illogical to accept the existence of a conscious person at the time of liberation when there is freedom from attachment to objects, because you assert that the intellect makes known to the person objects to which there is attraction. You also assert that it is the person's nature to be conscious and that this is permanent and immutable. What is the value of accepting the existence of consciousness during liberation? There is not the slightest value, because while accepting the conscious person as an experiencer of objects, the transformations which are experienced no longer exist, having subsided into a latent state.

Question: What if the person remains without consciousness at liberation?

Answer:

222cd. Also to exist without consciousness
Is clearly the same as not existing.

It follows that to accept the existence of a liberated person without consciousness clearly amounts to accepting the person's non-existence, because of accepting that the person and consciousness are of one nature, being either equally existent or non-existent.

Assertion: There is a self during liberation, for though there is no actual consciousness, the potential to be conscious of objects exists.
Answer: That too is illogical.

223ab. If at liberation a self existed
There could be a seed of consciousness.

If at liberation a self existed, there could be such a potential or seed of consciousness, but at that time there is no consciousness.
Objection: If there is no liberated self, there is no liberation and thus cyclic existence is indestructible. Many such unwanted entailments arise.
Answer:

223cd. Without it there is no speculation
With regard to worldly existence.[20]

It is irrelevant to speculate whether, because there is consciousness, [people would or would not enter liberation] or whether, because its seed is truly existent, people would or would not enter worldly existence. It would be relevant if a self as reliance existed but there is no liberated self.

224. It is certain that those liberated
From suffering have no other [self].
Therefore the end of the self
Should always be affirmed as good.

It is certain that in the state of nirvāṇa, people who have gained liberation from suffering by completely abandoning the contaminated aggregates through the total elimination of disturbing attitudes and emotions have no other causeless permanent self which does not depend on the aggregates. Therefore people who aspire to become free should always affirm that the complete ending forever of conceptions of a self is good and should never assert the existence of such a useless liberated self.

Assertion:

> 225. The conventional is preferable
>   But the ultimate never is.
>   Ordinary people have some [belief in this]
>   But none in the ultimate.

If during liberation there is no liberated self, and nirvāṇa which is termed the ultimate is said to be the mere ending of conceptions of a self through the non-recurrence of that which is composite, what is the purpose of striving for such an ultimate? It is preferable[21] for those interested in their own good to accept conventionalities like eyes, sprouts and so forth but not to assert any ultimate,[22] for ordinary people have some belief in virtuous and non-virtuous actions, their homes, forests and so forth but none whatsoever in the ultimate.

This stanza was written in connection with the extensive refutation of the self in the following chapter. Since it is interpreted as a controversial contention in Candrakīrti's commentary, it should not be accepted as our own contention.[23]

The summarizing stanza:

> Discovering that external and internal dependently arising
> Phenomena exist in reliance, and understanding
> Their emptiness of existence by way of their own entities,
> Grow wise in the meaning of the middle way free from
>   extremes.

This is the ninth chapter from the *Four Hundred on the Yogic Deeds*, showing how to meditate on the refutation of permanent functional phenomena.

This concludes the commentary on the ninth chapter, showing how to meditate on the refutation of permanent functional phenomena, from *Essence of Good Explanations, Explanation of the "Four Hundred on the Yogic Deeds of Bodhisattvas"*.

Chapter X

Refuting Misconceptions of the Self

If the so-called self existed by way of its own entity, [it should be seen in the state of nirvāṇa.] Fearing its discontinuation because it is not seen during nirvāṇa, they say, "The conventional is preferable," and so forth.[1] However the self does not exist by way of its own entity for if it did, it should be male, female or neuter,[2] but that is inappropriate.

> 226. When the inner self is not
> Female, male or neuter,
> It is only out of ignorance
> That you think your own self male.

The Forders[3] assert two selves, an inner self and an outer self. The first is inside the body, and this inner agent which makes the various sense organs engage with objects is the focus of the conception "I." The second is a combination of the body and sense organs which assists the first.

It follows that the inner self does not exist by way of its own entity. If it did a woman should in future lives too only ever be a woman, yet change is observed. Femaleness and so forth are also not attributes[4] of the self. Thus it follows that the inner agential person does not exist by way of its own entity, for when the inner self is neither female, male or neuter, it is just out of ignorant confusion that you imagine your own self male. It is a fabrication like mistaking a mottled rope for a snake. Sūtra says:

> An attitude of doubt foments poison,
> And though it has not entered one, one faints.

Assertion: Male gender, female gender and so forth are marks of the outer self. Through its connection with this the inner self is male and so forth.

Answer: It follows that because of their connection with the outer self, the four great external elements would also be a male self and so forth. If that were so, all the elements would be the person, since for truly existent functional things there can be no differences between what is and is not male and so forth.

> 227. When all the elements are not
>   Male, female or neuter,
>   How is that which depends on them
>   Male, female or neuter?

When all the elements do not have male, female or neuter gender, how can the inner self which relies upon the outer self—those elements—feasibly be male, female or neuter? It cannot. If all the elements were male, female or neuter, it would follow that even during the early stages of the fetus,[5] maleness and so forth should be observable.

Objection: The same error is entailed for you.

Answer: Since we impute gender in dependence upon elements which lack inherent existence, there is no error.

It follows that the personal self is not established by way of its own entity. If it were, just as the thought "blue" arises universally in relation to blue, the thought "I" should arise in Yajñā when he observes Devadatta's self, but it does not.

> 228. Your self is not my self and thus there is
>   No such self, since it is not ascertained.
>   Does the conception not arise
>   In relation to impermanent things?

Since that which is your self is not my own self, it follows that the object of your conception of "I" is not a self existing by way of its own entity, because it is not ascertained as the object of my conception of "I" or my attachment to the self. Therefore doesn't the thought "I" arise in relation to impermanent things called form and so forth? The self is only imputed.

Assertion: The self is permanent because of being the one that enters and leaves cyclic existence. If there were no self, who would be

in cyclic existence because of accumulating actions? Who would gain freedom from cyclic existence? Thus the self exists.
Answer:

229. **From one rebirth to another**
      The person changes like the body.
      It is illogical for yours to be
      Separate from the body and permanent.

It follows that it is illogical for the self you assert to be permanent and a separate entity from the body, because the person, like the body, changes from one rebirth as a god, human and so forth to another.

Assertion: Without a self there would be no physical movements such as stretching or flexing because the body would lack an activator. Thus an inner agential person exists who activates the body just as Devadatta drives his chariot.
Answer: That is illogical. It follows that your life force or self is not the instigator of physical movement because the self is not tangible.

230. **Intangible things do not**
      Produce so-called motility.
      Thus the life force is not
      Agent of the body's movements.

It is so because, just as a chariot can only be moved by something tangible and not by anything intangible, an intangible functional thing cannot actually move that which has form from one place to another. Though Vaiśeṣikas assert that the self has form, they do not accept that it has external tangibility and so forth.

231. **Why [teach] non-violence and wonder about**
      Conditions for a permanent self?
      A diamond never has to be
      Protected against woodworm.

It follows that if the self is permanent, it is contradictory to teach non-violence as a practice to protect it from dangers such as a bad re-birth or to wonder what conditions are not unfavorable to it, because nothing can harm a permanent functional thing, just as a diamond which is not in danger of harm is never protected against woodworm, nor does it need to be.

Assertion: The self is permanent because there is memory of previous rebirths. Memory of other lives is not feasible for a composite thing whose nature is to disintegrate as soon as it is produced.
   Answer:

> **232. If your self is permanent**
> **Because of remembering other lives,**
> **How can your body be impermanent**
> **When you see a scar previously formed?**

You may consider the self permanent because there is memory of past lives, like thinking, "I was human in my last rebirth." Then how could your body be impermanent? It should be permanent because in a past life you saw the scar of a wound inflicted on the body and now, when you see a birthmark which resembles that previously inflicted wound, you say, "That is the scar of the wound inflicted in the past." According to us the object of the thought "I" is co-extensive with both the self of the past and of this life.[6] Since it is merely imputed, memory of past rebirths is feasible.

There is a bowl of curd in a house. The footprint of a pale-colored pigeon perched on the thick thatch is visible on it, even though its foot has not touched the curd and so forth. Similarly, all actions and agents are feasible for that which arises dependently.

It follows that the self cannot remember past rebirths because it is asserted as mindless matter. It is also unreasonable to assert that it remembers past lives by virtue of having mind, because by first lacking memory and later possessing memory, it has given up its entity.

> **233. If the self when possessing that**
> **Which has mind is a knower,**
> **By that [same argument] that which has mind would be**
> **Mindless and the person permanent.**

If the self, despite being matter, is a knower of the past because of possessing that which has mind, by that [same argument] the attribute, that which has mind, should be mindless and matter because of possessing a self which is classified as matter.[7] It follows that the self is also not permanent because first it does not remember but later newly develops memory of past lives.

234. A life force which has pleasure and so forth
     Appears as various as pleasure and so forth.
     Thus like pleasure it is not
     Suitable as something permanent.

If the life force or self has mind because of having attributes like intelligence, then because of having attributes like pleasure and pain, it should appear as different as pleasure and so forth while experiencing satisfaction and affliction. Thus like pleasure and so forth it cannot be permanent either.

Sāṃkhya assertion: If the self is asserted as matter these inconsistencies apply, but since, according to us, the person's nature is to be conscious, there is not the least unwanted entailment.

Answer: Sāṃkhyas define twenty-five categories of phenomena of which twenty-four are matter and the twenty-fifth is asserted as the knower, person and self. They assert that the person experiences objects which the intellect makes it crave. This is explained extensively elsewhere.[8]

235. If consciousness is permanent
     An agent is superfluous.
     If fire is permanent
     Fuel is unnecessary.

If the conscious person is asserted as permanent, it follows that agents such as the eyes and so forth which permit experience of objects are superfluous and useless because the person that experiences objects exists as a permanent functional thing. Fuel is needed to make a fire but if fire is permanent, fuel is unnecessary.

Assertion: The person whose nature is potential consciousness is the experiencer of objects, and being conscious is the activity of experiencing. Since this depends on agents like the eye, there is no flaw.

Answer: Movement does not occur unless, for instance, a tree is agitated by the wind, but those fallacies[9] would entail movement until the substantial entity disintegrates. The phenomenon of activity depends on the substantial entity and is motion.

236. A substantial entity, unlike an action,
     Does not alter until it disintegrates.
     Thus it is improper to claim
     The person exists but consciousness does not.

The activity of moving depends on the substantial entity and may cease even though the substantial entity has not disintegrated. The nature of the substantial entity does not likewise change between its production and its disintegration. By contrast, consciousness and the person are an indifferentiable permanent entity. Thus it is improper to claim that the person but not consciousness exists prior[10] to experiencing an object.

Assertion: Although there is no consciousness prior to experiencing objects, its potential and thus the person exists.
   Answer:

237. **At times one sees potential consciousness,**
      At others consciousness itself.
      Because of being like molten iron
      The person undergoes change.

On occasions other than when objects are being experienced one sees potential consciousness, and when objects are being experienced, consciousness itself. In that case, like molten iron which later becomes a solid mass, former potential consciousness later becomes actual consciousness. It therefore follows that the person undergoes change because consciousness and the person are accepted as one entity.

Naiyāyika assertion: Our person is not a conscious entity. Since a part of the self the mere size of a particle has mind, there is consciousness of objects. It depends on just this part with mind. A person that is conscious and not separate from mind is produced through this association. The person is permanent and very extensive like space.
   Answer:

238. **Merely [a small part with] mind is conscious**
      But the person is as vast as space.
      Therefore it would seem as though
      Its nature is not to be conscious.

Since except for a part as small as a particle the rest of this permanent and extensive self is not associated with consciousness, that self's nature does not seem to have consciousness of objects. Just as it cannot be said that the water of the Ganges is salty because of contact with a grain of salt, it is inappropriate to assert that which is not conscious as the person.

239. If the self is in everyone then why
Does another not think of this one as "I"?
It is unacceptable to say that
It is obscured by itself.

If there is a partless permanent self which is omnipresent like space
and in each individual sentient being, why would another person
not think "I" in relation to my own self? It follows that they should
think of it as "I" because the two selves are one. It cannot be omnipresent if the object of someone else's conception of the self is not
my own self.

Assertion: It is not perceived because it has been obscured by the
other's self.

Answer: It is unacceptable to say that the self obscures itself for
there is no duality of that which obscures and that which is obscured.

Sāṃkhya assertion: The great one, a synonym for the intellect, evolves
from the principal which is matter and a balance of pleasure, pain
and equanimity. The three I-principles evolve from the great one.
Eleven faculties evolve from the I-principle associated with lightness:
five mental faculties, five faculties for action and the speculative faculty.[11] From the I-principle associated with motility come the five
mere objects[12] from which the five elements evolve. The I-principle
of darkness acts as the basis for the other two I-principles.

240. There is no difference between
The insane and those for whom
The attributes are the creator
But are never conscious.

It follows that it is contradictory to assert, as do the Sāṃkhyas, that
the principal which is a balance of the three attributes is the creator
of all manifestations but is never conscious. There is not the least
difference between those who assert the like and the insane whose
perception is distorted.

241. What is more illogical
Than that the attributes should always
Know how to construct homes and so forth
But not know how to experience them?

Since such a contention contradicts reason and conflicts with worldly
convention, it is utterly incorrect. What is more illogical than to claim

that the attributes whose nature is pleasure, pain and equanimity know how to construct homes and so forth but do not know how to experience these amenities? It contradicts both reason and convention.

Vaiśeṣika assertion: The self alone is the doer of actions and the experiencer of their maturation.
   Answer: If that is so, the self cannot be permanent.

242ab. The active is not permanent.
   The ubiquitous is actionless.

If the self is an agent it must be accepted as causing action. If it does not perform actions it is unsuitable as an agent. That which performs actions like coming and going is not permanent since one must admit that it differs from before. Something the whole of which is everywhere all the time does not perform activities such as coming and going, since there is no place or time it does not occupy.
   Assertion: Well then, an actionless self exists.
   Answer:

242cd. The actionless is like the non-existent.
   Why do you not prefer selflessness?

Since an actionless self is as non-existent as a sky flower, why do you not prefer selflessness? It is worth doing so, for understanding it frees one from all fears.

It follows that the conception of a personal self is erroneous. Since the self, if it existed, would do so by way of its own entity, it should appear without differences.

243. Some see it as ubiquitous and for some
   The person is the mere [size of the] body.
   Some see it as a mere particle.
   The wise see it as non-existent.

Some such as Vaiśeṣikas and Sāṃkhyas see the self as existing in each body and as being ubiquitous like space. Others such as Nirgranthas see that which has a body as proportionate to the size of that body, such as an ant's or an elephant's.
   Nirgranthas assert the life force is
   Large or small like the size of the body.
   Others, unable to accept this, see it as a mere particle. Those with the wisdom that perceives the suchness of functional things with-

out distortion see the self as non-existent. Indeed, if the self existed by way of its own entity, the Forders' views would not differ.

244. How can what is permanent be harmed,
Or the unharmed be liberated?
Liberation is irrelevant
For one whose self is permanent.

For an opponent who asserts a permanent self, attaining liberation is irrelevant. How can that which is permanent be harmed by dangers and so forth in cyclic existence, and how can that which is unharmed in cyclic existence be liberated by subsequent meditation on the paths? It cannot for these very reasons.

245. If the self exists it is inappropriate
To think there is no self
And false to claim one attains nirvāṇa
Through certain knowledge of reality.

If the self exists by way of its own entity, it follows that thinking there is no self is inappropriate and that attainment of liberation is not feasible, since the basis for conceptions of a self is intact. Moreover the contention of these amazing people [who assert that the self exists but claim] that through ascertaining knowledge of suchness one abandons conceptions of a self and thereby attains nirvāṇa would be false. Therefore those who seek liberation should accept selflessness.

Fearing the absurd consequence that conceptions of a self would occur in the liberated state if the self exists, one might assert that though there is no self, there is a truly existent liberated person.

246. If it exists at liberation
It should not be non-existent before.
It is explained that what is seen
Without anything is its nature.

It follows that there must be such a truly existent liberated person previously too during cyclic existence, because its entity, isolated from any associated factors, as perceived by unmistaken awareness, is said to be its nature. If there is no self during liberation, it should not be asserted as existing during the cycle of rebirths either.

Assertion: If there is no self, composite things whose nature is to disintegrate moment by moment would discontinue because of disintegrating as soon as they are produced.
   Answer:

247.   If the impermanent discontinues
        How could there be grass at present?
        If, indeed, this were true,
        No one would have ignorance either.

Understanding impermanence to mean discontinuation is unacceptable. If it did, how could there today be fields and grass whose continuity is beginningless? There should not be any, for if impermanence meant discontinuation, then whatever is impermanent would have the defect of discontinuing. If the view that whatever is impermanent discontinues were true, it follows that no one would have ignorance because it is impermanent. It also follows that pleasure and desire would not occur either.

248.   Even if the self exists
        Form is seen to arise from other [causes],
        To continue by virtue of others
        And to disintegrate through others.

It follows that even if the self exists, it is not acceptable as the initiating cause of things which are seen to arise exclusively from other causes. Fire arises from the contact between sunlight and a fire-crystal, water from the contact between moonlight and a water-crystal, the sprout from the seed, and forms such as the sense organs from an earlier stage of the fetus. They continue because of other factors: fire keeps burning because of fuel and so forth and just as it does not burn when there is insufficient fuel, they disintegrate through other factors. The self cannot exist for if it did, it alone should produce all effects.

249.   Just as the sprout which is a product
        Is produced from a product, the seed,
        Similarly all that is impermanent
        Comes from the impermanent.

An effect cannot arise from something permanent and thus, just as the sprout, a product, arises from the seed which is a product, all that is impermanent comes from impermanent causes. Therefore composite things, undergoing production and disintegration moment by moment, can never be permanent nor discontinue. The thunderbolts of permanence and annihilation which strike and destroy the relationship of cause and effect between composite things are driven off to a distance by the wise with the mantra of dependent arising.

> 250. Since functional things arise
>   There is no discontinuation
>   And because they cease
>   There is no permanence.

Since resultant things like sprouts arise and are produced, the cause's continuum is not in danger of being annihilated. Since the seed ceases once the sprout has been produced, the cause is not in danger of being permanent. The *Fundamental [Treatise Called] Wisdom* says:

> Whatever has arisen depending on something
> Is firstly not [one with] it

and so forth.[13] In brief this shows how permanence and annihilation are avoided in relation to the conventional.

The summarizing stanza:

> Through familiarity with meditating on
> The impermanence, suffering and uncleanness
>   of cyclic existence,
> Abandon the limitless views of the self,
> Both innate and those imputed by tenets.

> **This is the tenth chapter from the *Four Hundred on the Yogic Deeds*, showing how to meditate on refuting the self.**

This concludes the commentary on the tenth chapter, showing how to meditate on refuting the self, from *Essence of Good Explanations, Explanation of the "Four Hundred on the Yogic Deeds of Bodhisattvas"*.

Chapter XI

Refuting Truly Existent Time

Assertion of Vaidāntikas and other proponents of permanent time:
Though it is correct to admit that a permanent self does not exist
since it is not established by either direct or inferential cognition,
permanent functional things are not non-existent since there is permanent time. Though water, manure, seeds and so forth are present,
one observes that sprouts, flowers and the like are not produced at
certain times but are produced at others. From this one can infer the
presence of another cause which is time. Though it is a permanent
entity different from the functional things which exist in the three
times, it is revealed in terms of instants, moments, brief spans, and
so forth.

Answer: This is unacceptable, for if time were an entity different
from functional things it should be perceived but it is not perceived.
That has already been refuted.[1] In this context the refutation is made
taking a future pot to represent future time. The same should be
understood with respect to the other two times.[2]

> 251. The present pot and the past one
>   Do not exist in the future pot.
>   Since both would be future,
>   The future would not exist.

It follows that the present pot does not exist in the future pot, nor
does the past pot exist at that time, for if they both existed at that
time, time would be disrupted, since things which are to occur later
would already exist at an earlier time. Also at any one time another
cannot exist. For these reasons, since both the past and present
would be future if they existed at the time of the future pot, they do

not already exist at that time. If the future of the future[3] existed by way of its own entity, it should be future. In that case since all three times would have to be future, there could not be any past or present. If that were so, the future itself would not exist, since it could not be posited as future in relation to anything.

Assertion: The past pot is not altogether non-existent in the future pot. Since there is a part of it which has not yet come into existence as an entity that has occurred, there is no error.
   Answer:

> **252. If a disintegrated thing exists as**
> **A future entity in the future,**
> **How can what is future in nature**
> **Become that which is past?**

If at the time of the future pot, the disintegrated pot existed in the future as an entity which had not yet come into existence, it would follow that the past pot was future because of being, by way of its own entity, that which had not yet occurred at the time of the future pot. If this is accepted, it follows that there would be no past. This would necessarily be so, for how could anything that truly existed as future in nature become past? It is contradictory. Moreover by virtue of this reasoning, if the future in relation to the pot is asserted as truly existent it must be accepted as being only future, which undermines the contention.

> **253. Because of being future in nature**
> **A future functional thing**
> **Is thus present**
> **And cannot be future.**

If, according to proponents of permanent time, future things exist, it follows that the future pot is present because of already being in the nature of a future substantially existent thing. If something exists as a substantially established entity, it must be present since it has been produced and has not disintegrated. If this is accepted, it follows that it cannot be future.

254. If the future, past and present exist,
     What does not exist?
     How can there be impermanence
     For one for whom all times exist?

If, as asserted by Vaiśeṣikas, Vaibhāṣikas and so forth, things existent by way of their own character exist in the future, exist in the past and exist in the present, what part of a thing could ever not exist? How can there be impermanence for a proponent of substantially existent time? It follows that there cannot be any impermanent things, for if all three times are substantially existent, whatever exists at an earlier time must be accepted as existing later and whatever exists at a later time must be accepted as existing earlier.

The future is not substantially existent since future time cannot exist in the future. Similarly has the past passed beyond its own nature as the past or not?

255. If it has passed beyond the past
     Why is it the past?
     If it has not passed beyond the past
     Why is it the past?

In the first case, why is it the past? It follows that it is not the past because of having passed beyond and gone from the past [just as curd which is no longer milk cannot be called milk and a youth who has left childhood behind cannot be called a child.]⁴ In the second case, for what reason is it the past? It follows that it is not the past for it has not passed beyond being a past substantial entity but continues to exist as a substantial entity performing a function.

Regarding Vaibhāṣikas and so forth who assert that there is a common locus⁵ of a pot and the future:

256. If the future is produced
     Why is it not present?
     If it is unproduced
     Is the future permanent or what?

If a produced future pot exists, why is it not present? It follows that it should be, because it has been produced and has not ceased. If it is not produced, is the future pot permanent or what? It follows that it should be permanent because of being an unproduced thing.

Assertion: Although the future is unproduced, causes and conditions make it become the present, thus it is not permanent.
   Answer:

   257. **If the future is impermanent because**
        Though not produced it disintegrates,
        Since the past does not disintegrate
        Why not consider it permanent?

If even though the future is not produced, the future pot is impermanent because it subsequently disintegrates [in that it undergoes change[6]], why not consider the past pot permanent since it does not disintegrate? It follows that it is permanent because of being a thing which does not disintegrate.

Alternatively, what is impermanent according to you?

   258. **If the past and present**
        Are not impermanent,
        The third which is different
        From these is also not.

The past and present are not impermanent because the past cannot disintegrate. If the present is impermanent by way of its own entity, through its subsequent connection with disintegration it follows that disintegration, too, is impermanent [or that the present is permanent because of its connection with disintegration which is permanent.[7]] Since the third which is different from both the past and present, namely the future, also is not impermanent, there is nothing impermanent for proponents of inherently existent things. Thus it is inappropriate for them to assert the existence of time.

Assertion: Future things exist because they are produced later when the conditions obtain. That which is previously non-existent, like a barren woman's child, will not be produced later.
   Answer:

   259. **If a thing which will be produced**
        Later exists beforehand,
        The contention of Niyativādins
        Is not erroneous.

If a thing to be produced later is substantially existent prior to its production, the contention that things are inherently established as causeless held by Niyativādins[8] and those asserting that things are not created by peoples' activity and are without cause is not erroneous. Yet their assertions are wrong for they contradict everything that is both seen and unseen.[9]

260. **To say something which will be made to occur**
Already exists is unreasonable.
If that which exists is produced,
What has been produced will arise again.

Moreover even if the future were substantially existent, it would be unreasonable to say that a thing which will be made to occur later is substantially existent prior to its production. If that which already exists is produced later, what has already been produced will come into existence again, which is purposeless. As a consequence the effect would find no opportunity for production, since the cause must reproduce itself until the end.

Assertion: The future exists because there is yogic perception of wished-for objects which focuses on future things, and because predictions concerning the future are later seen to turn out just as predicted. This is impossible in relation to a barren woman's child.
   Answer:

261ab. **If future things are seen,**
   Why is the non-existent not seen?

If future things are directly perceived by way of their own entity in the period before their production, why are non-existent things not seen? It follows that they would be seen, for it is not feasible to make distinctions between what is seen and not seen with regard to the non-existent. Such fallacies arise for those who assert that the past and future exist by way of their own entity, but no fallacies accrue to us who assert the three times as arising dependently without inherent existence.

Buddhas directly perceive in the present even those things which will occur after ten million aeons. Though they are future at the time of the consciousness perceiving them, they are neither non-functional nor permanent for they will not remain for a second moment[10] after their formation. There is no need for a Buddha to cognize the present explicitly and the past and future implicitly,[11] for though the latter do not exist at that time, they are in general directly perceived. Similarly it is not contradictory for objects of aspiration, though they

232 The Yogic Deeds of Bodhisattvas

do not exist at that time, to appear clearly to yogic perception of that which is wished for, just as a dream appears to be real.

Even though the barley seed exists, the sprout which has not yet come into existence may be called future but the sprout itself must not be called future. An understanding of the other two times should be inferred from this. In our own system we accept that Buddhas perceive all three times directly and do not at all assert to trainees that they merely appear to do so.

261cd. **For one for whom the future exists**
        There can be no distant [time].

Moreover there cannot be a distant time for a protagonist for whom the future exists by way of its own entity because the future exists in terms of its own entity.[12]

262. **If virtue exists though nothing is done,**
     Resolute restraint is meaningless.
     If even a little is done
     The effect cannot exist.

If, because the future is substantially existent, virtue exists without actions such as safeguarding one's ethical conduct once one's faculties have become mature through meeting a spiritual friend and listening to teaching, resolute restraint from unethical conduct and so forth for the sake of future results [such as a high rebirth] is meaningless, for virtue will exist even if that has not been done. If even the slightest thing is done to enhance one's capability, future effects cannot be substantially existent. It is impossible!

In accordance with the assertion that all composite things are impermanent, all functional things are impermanent.

263. **If they are impermanent**
     How can it be said effects exist?
     That which has a beginning and end
     Is called impermanent in the world.

How can it be said then that an effect exists prior to its production? It is unreasonable since impermanence and existence prior to production are contradictory. Anything which has a beginning, in that it is newly produced, and an end, in that it does not last for a second moment after the time of its formation, is called impermanent in the world.

264. Liberation will occur without exertion.
For the liberated there is no future,
Or otherwise, if this were so,
Desire would arise without attachment.

According to Sautrāntikas and so forth who assert that future functional things do not have the slightest existence, liberation will occur without any exertion to generate the paths of the Exalted in order to prevent future disturbing emotions and suffering, because future things do not exist. This would be like liberated Foe Destroyers for whom there are no future disturbing emotions and so forth and who thus do not need to exert themselves because of them. If the future were non-existent and desire were to arise without there being a person, consciousness and so forth or predispositions for attachment as a basis, it follows that desire would arise in a Foe Destroyer too.[13]

The words "or otherwise" imply "or otherwise the future is not non-existent."

265. For those who assert effects exist,
And for those who assert they do not exist,
Adornments like pillars and so forth
For a home are purposeless.

Sāṃkhyas say that since what is non-existent cannot be produced, and since the effect is present in the cause in a potential form, the fallacy that anything arises from anything does not occur. Some Vaibhāṣikas assert that the three times are substantially existent and that effects exist prior to their production. Sautrāntikas and so forth assert that although things are truly existent, future effects are non-existent. It follows that for all of these, adornments such as pillars for a resultant home are purposeless, since according to some it exists from the outset, while according to others the future home is non-existent, like a barren woman's child. For proponents of dependent arising free from inherent existence, there is no possibility of error and thus everything is properly established.

In meditative equipoise the Exalted who are still learning do not perceive dependently arising phenomena as existent. Failure to distinguish between this non-perception and the perception of phenomena as non-existent, as well as inability to posit conventional valid cognition in one's own system, seem to give rise to numerous errors. One must therefore master the meaning of the establishment of the two truths by valid cognition in our own system.

Assertion: Although existence of the past and future are being refuted, the present exists. Since it does, the future exists too, for the principal, giving up its state of futurity, assumes the state of present curd. Thus the present exists.
  Answer:

> 266. The transformation of things also
>   Is not perceived even by the mind.
>   Those who lack wisdom nevertheless
>   Think that the present exists.

It is not feasible for the principal, which is matter and permanent by nature, also to undergo temporary changes into things like milk and curd. Such transformations are not perceived even by mental consciousness that engages with extremely subtle objects, let alone observed by the five kinds of sense consciousness. Although transformation with respect to the present and its causes is not observed, those who lack wisdom and are ignorant about the meaning of suchness consider the present truly existent.

Assertion: Time exists because functional things which act as the basis for imputing time exist. Since time may be investigated by considering functional things but not on its own, time is truly existent.
  Answer:

> 267. How can there be things with no duration?
>   Being impermanent, how can they endure?
>   If they had duration first,
>   They would not grow old in the end.

How can functional things, the basis for time, be truly existent? It follows that they are not because of not having inherent duration. How could they have inherent duration, since they are continually consumed by impermanence? Moreover, if they had inherent duration at the start, they would not grow old in the end, because that which is inherently existent cannot cease.

> 268. Just as a single consciousness
>   Cannot apprehend two objects,
>   Similarly two consciousnesses
>   Cannot apprehend one object.

Furthermore there is no inherent duration, for just as a single moment of consciousness does not apprehend two consecutive objects actually presenting their own likenesses, two consecutive moments of consciousness do not apprehend a single object simultaneously, for they undergo momentary production and disintegration.

Objection: Well, that contradicts the assertion in the sūtras of knowledge that the five objects such as visual form are each apprehended by two kinds of consciousness.[14]

Answer: If one does not accept momentary disintegration, one is not a Buddhist.[15] If one does, the object of observation of a visual consciousness cannot act as object of observation for a subsequently arising consciousness. The sūtra passage means that the visual consciousness cognizes the form clearly and the mental consciousness which is produced subsequently cognizes it in an unclear way.[16]

Assertion: Duration has inherent existence because of being the characteristic of present time.

Answer: If time and duration are different and have an inherently established relationship, they must act as basis and that which is based upon it.

> 269. **If time has duration**
> **Duration is not time.**
> **If it has not, without duration**
> **There will also be no end.**

If duration relies on time as something separate, duration is not time because they are mutually exclusive. If time does not have duration, then without duration there cannot finally be disintegration. Therefore since time does not have inherent duration, the latter is unsuitable as the present's characteristic.

Assertion: Duration exists because there are impermanent things that have duration.

Answer:

> 270. **If impermanence and things are separate**
> **Things are not impermanent.**
> **If they are one, since things are precisely that**
> **which is**
> **Impermanent, how can they have duration?**

If impermanence and functional things are separate in nature, it follows that things are not impermanent. If this is accepted, they must be permanent. If things and impermanence are one, since precisely that which is impermanent is a functional thing, how can they have inherent duration? Duration is impossible.

Assertion: While things continue to exist, duration is stronger and impermanence weaker, but it is not impossible for the weak to overcome the strong.
  Answer:

271. If duration is not weak
     Because impermanence is weak,
     Why should a reversal
     Afterwards be seen?

How can such a reversal be seen when things later finally become impermanent? It follows that it is unfeasible. If duration is not weaker because impermanence is weaker while things continue to exist, nothing can harm what has inherent strength.

272. If impermanence is not weaker
     And is present in all things,
     None of them will have duration
     Or not all are impermanent.

If impermanence is not weaker and is present in functional things at all times, it follows that all functional things do not have inherent duration, for impermanence, which overrides it, is always present. Alternatively, if not all things are impermanent, it follows that those which are not are permanent, because impermanence is weaker and duration has inherent strength.

Furthermore, does impermanence arise together with the products it characterizes or does it arise later?

273. If there is always impermanence
     There cannot always be duration,
     Or else that which was permanent
     Later becomes impermanent.

If there is always impermanence because that which is characterized and its characteristic are inevitably concomitant, it follows that duration is not inherently existent. Alternatively, having been permanent, a thing would later become impermanent, and if it remained for a second moment, it would be permanent. Yet one thing cannot be both permanent and impermanent.

274. **If things have duration**
     And impermanence together,
     Either it is wrong that things are impermanent,
     Or duration is a fallacy.

The characteristics of products are concomitant with one another. Thus if one accepts that the duration of a thing's existence and the impermanence of its existence are simultaneously of one nature with a thing, either it is wrong that things are impermanent or else inherent duration is a fallacy. These two can exist together in false products [which do not exist as they appear] but cannot have a common locus in truly existent functional things.

Assertion: Time exists because there is past time depending on past products. If that were not so, it would be impossible to remember past rebirths, thinking that one was this or that in the past.

Answer: This proof of time's true existence is also without the slightest substance. Memory focuses on an object which one has experienced.

275. **Things seen do not reappear,**
     Nor does awareness arise again.
     Thus memory is in fact deceived
     With regard to a deceptive object.

Though things seen previously do not reappear later, and though awareness observing objects belonging to a past rebirth does not occur again, memory[17] arises with a sense of seeing as one sees present objects. Memory which is in fact mistaken and deceived arises in relation to a so-called remembered object which is false and deceptive like an optical illusion. However, we do not deny that memory focusing on past objects arises dependently. This is certainly accepted in our own system.

The summarizing stanza:

> Not knowing how to posit continuity and transitoriness,
> They say time is permanent and the three times
>   exist substantially.

238 *The Yogic Deeds of Bodhisattvas*

Having understood that phenomena are like
   optical illusions,
Learn how the three times are perceived.

**This is the eleventh chapter from the *Four
Hundred on the Yogic Deeds*, showing how to
meditate on refuting time.**

This concludes the commentary on the eleventh chapter, showing
how to meditate on refuting time, from *Essence of Good Explanations,
Explanation of the "Four Hundred on the Yogic Deeds of Bodhisattvas"*.

Chapter XII

Refuting Wrong Views

Question: Even though you have explained selflessness very clearly and extensively and the Tathāgata fully understood and gave instruction on it, why do most people not follow this teaching?

Answer: Although the one who formulated it and those who elucidate it may be the perfect embodiment of greatness, a listener with great qualities is extremely hard to find.

Question: What qualities does one need?
Answer:

> 276. An unprejudiced, intelligent and interested
> Listener is called a vessel.
> Neither the teacher's nor the student's
> Good qualities will be taken as faults.

One should be unprejudiced, without attachment to one's own position or aversion to others' positions. *Heart of the Middle Way* says:

> One will never know peace
> While prejudice afflicts the mind.[1]

If one is not unprejudiced one will fail to understand a good explanation because of thinking it is someone else's. One must have the intelligence to distinguish between good and bad explanations, otherwise one may reject correct explanations and adopt incorrect ones. A keen interest in good explanations is needed, for without that one will make no effort and simply be like the lifeless picture of a human being. One should appreciate and be attentive to the teaching and the teacher. A listener with these five qualities[2] is said to be a vessel for the teaching. Someone with all these attributes will recognize the teacher's good qualities[3] and fully understand the clarity and orderliness of the teaching, as well as the good intentions of other listeners. The teacher's lack of self-interest and the like will not be seen as faults and other than as they are, but only as virtues. Nor will the good qualities of the listeners be construed as faults.[4]

Although the teacher may be perfect, if the listeners lack the prerequisite qualities, they will not recognize their own faults but will consider faults as virtues and virtues as faults.

> 277. He explained existence and its causes,
>   The means to peace and peace itself.
>   What people do not understand
>   Is seen as the Subduer's [fault].

The Subduer taught about worldly existence in the form of the five contaminated and suffering aggregates and about true sources, the cause of worldly existence. He taught about true paths, the means to peace, such as the eightfold path of the Exalted,[5] and also about peace, liberation and nirvāṇa. He taught the four noble truths for those who seek liberation, but ordinary people who make no effort to hear, think and meditate are unaware that they do not possess all the qualities of a suitable vessel. Whatever they fail to understand correctly, they see as the Subduer's fault, saying he did not explain it in sufficient detail. However, merely that does not mean the Teacher is to blame. A blind person's inability to see is not the sun's fault.

Assertion: Although the Subduer's discussion of high rebirth is extremely clear, we do not understand or approve of his discussion of definite goodness, since the teaching that everything is without inherent existence refutes the very nature of things.
   Answer:

> 278. These strange people all agree that by
>   Giving up everything one attains nirvāṇa.
>   For what reason do they dislike
>   That which puts an end to all?

These strange Sāṃkhyas, Vaiśeṣikas and the like, who believe in liberation, all agree that one attains nirvāṇa by giving up attachment to everything associated with disturbing emotions, such as pleasure, pain and so forth. Why do they dislike it when the person and aggregates are said to be empty of existence by way of their own entities? The understanding of this destroys all that is associated with disturbing emotions. Therefore they should be glad. Sūtra says:

> In nirvāṇa there are no phenomena.
> Whatever does not exist then never existed.
> The suffering of those with ideas of existence
>   and non-existence
> Who act accordingly will not be pacified.[6]

Since only the Buddha's words contain undistorted statements about suchness, and Sāmkhyas and so forth do not make even the slightest mention of it, one should recognize it as a unique teaching.

Question: If these strange people all agree that one attains nirvāṇa by giving up everything, what difference is there between you and the Forders?

Answer: They are different in that they merely have the wish to give everything up but do not know how to do so.

> 279. How will one who does not know
>   The means to give it up, do so?
>   Certainly, therefore, the Subduer said
>   There is no peace in any other [teaching].

How can those belonging to other systems give up cyclic existence while they cling to the wrong methods? They do not know that the means to give it up is to understand that all phenomena are empty of inherent existence. Therefore certainly with this in mind the Subduer said, "The first practitioner of virtue has come about thus. The second and third have come about thus. The fourth has come about thus. Others' doctrines lack such practitioners of virtue."[7] On account of this he said, "There is no peace in any teaching other than this."

Question: If he is omniscient, he must have super-knowledge of hidden things such as the size of Mount Meru and the continents, but how can one be sure of that?

Answer: One can ascertain it with the help of inference.

> 280. Whoever doubts what the Buddha said
>   About that which is hidden
>   Should rely on emptiness
>   And gain conviction in him alone.

One might wonder whether what the Buddha has said is true or not regarding the size of the abodes, bodies and lifespans of the six kinds of gods of the Desire Realm and so forth from whom one is separated by time and place, and regarding the size of the human physical world and so on, all of which are hidden to common beings. To dispel such doubts one should take as example the fact that the features of the two truths which are very subtle and difficult to understand—the teaching that all phenomena are empty of inherent existence together with the feasibility of all actions and agents—are actually as he explained. Understanding through this that the extremely hidden things he taught are just as he described, one should gain conviction that he alone is omniscient. Having ascertained dependent arising free from fabricated extremes through correct reasoning without relying on scriptural citations as proof, one should ascertain extremely hidden things relying on the Buddha's words as reason. Regarding the general presentation of this, the explanations of Dignāga and his spiritual son are like those of the great trailblazers.[8] In this context objects can be understood through the presentation of four kinds of valid cognition.[9]

> 281. Those who find it hard to see
>   This world are ignorant of others.
>   Those who follow them will be
>   Misled for a very long time.

Non-Buddhist teachers who have difficulty in discerning even the way coarse cause and effect operate in relation to the physical environment and inhabitants of this world are ignorant regarding other subtle matters. People who follow them will thus come under the influence of innate and intellectually formed attitudes which must be given up, and they will be misled for a very long time. Those interested in their own good should leave false teachers. They should trust and value the true one.

Question: Why do those who seek liberation follow the Forders?
Answer: Because they are afraid to listen to teaching on emptiness. It is as follows:

> 282. The unwise take no delight in letting
>   Their mind follow a guide
>   Who has done that which is
>   Most difficult—attained nirvāṇa.

To be taken care of by a spiritual friend and go to the city of Nirvāṇa, having rid oneself of the stains of conceiving things as truly existent, is very difficult. Though one with great compassion who did what was difficult to do has come to guide them, unwise people take no delight in letting their minds follow this guide because they fear emptiness.

Question: Who is afraid?
Answer:

> 283. **When it is not seen, fear does not begin.**
> **When seen, it stops completely.**
> **Thus one can say with certainty:**
> **Those who know a little are afraid.**

People like cowherds, who see neither virtues nor faults in it, can hear about emptiness a hundred times without beginning to feel afraid, because they do not regard it as either beneficial or harmful. When one perceives emptiness directly through a gradual process of hearing, thinking and meditating, fear stops completely because one is free from conceptions of a self which are the cause of fear. Thus one can say with certainty that fear arises in people who have only a little knowledge of emptiness. It is like the following analogy: A well-trained person is not afraid to mount a mad elephant, nor is an extremely stupid person. Yet someone who knows a little about the dangers and benefits involved feels frightened.

Question: Why do they fear emptiness?
Answer: Because of a lack of familiarity.

> 284. **Childish beings are certainly only**
> **Familiar with that which involves them.**
> **Because of unfamiliarity**
> **They fear that which extricates them.**

Childish beings are certainly only familiar with innate and intellectually formed conceptions of a self which involve them in cyclic existence. Since such childish beings have no previous familiarity with a teaching that extricates one from the cycle of birth and death, they fear emptiness. One should therefore give up doctrines that are wrong and unwholesome.

Emptiness should be taught to those who, because they feel grateful to the Tathāgata, are suitable vessels, but who, because of their great fear, are tempted to reject it.

285. If someone who is shrouded in
     Complete ignorance and impedes suchness
     Will not even attain good fortune,
     What need to mention liberation?

Someone who not only has a total disregard for emptiness but is completely shrouded in ignorance and impedes teaching, hearing and thinking about suchness out of jealousy, meanness and the like will not even attain the good fortune of a high rebirth. This being so, what chance is there of such a person attaining liberation, since such actions are grave ill deeds? Rejecting dependent arising free from fabricated extremes is a more serious ill deed than killing a hundred million people, so one must take care in this matter to avoid deceiving oneself.

286. Lapsing from ethics is preferable
     To lapsing from the view.
     Through ethics one gains a high rebirth;
     The supreme state is reached by means of the view.

Since denying emptiness is most detrimental to oneself and others, a lapse in ethical conduct is preferable. One should never lapse from the view of emptiness, for while the result of ethical conduct is a high rebirth, the view that understands emptiness takes one to the supreme states of liberation and enlightenment. Sūtra says:

> A lapse in ethics is preferable;
> A lapse in view is not.

The wise only teach the view of suchness after carefully examining the vessel. It is also said:

> Taught to fools, it confuses them
> And does not further peace.
> When snakes drink milk
> Their poison only increases.

287. For the unreceptive, conceptions of a self are best;
     To teach them selflessness is not.
     They would go to bad rebirths,
     While the extraordinary attain peace.

It is best to teach the uneducated and unreceptive that there is a self in accordance with their conceptions of a self, for their attachment to the self will cause them to give up harmful behavior, making it easier for them to find a happy rebirth. It is not good to teach them emptiness, for they will ruin their three doors by rejecting or misunderstanding it. Thus teaching emptiness has a disadvantageous as well as an advantageous aspect. On the one hand, rejecting it through lack of appreciation or denying cause and effect because of taking non-existence to be the meaning of emptiness leads to a bad rebirth. On the other hand, the extraordinary who have mastered suchness attain peace.

One must definitely understand suchness to reach enlightenment in any of the three vehicles.

> 288. There is no other door to peace,
>   And it destroys wrong views.
>   That which is the object of
>   All Buddhas is called selflessness.

Since the root of worldly existence cannot be cut without understanding emptiness, there is no other door to peace. Dependent arising's lack of inherent existence is called the fundamental mode of existence, ultimate truth, emptiness and selflessness,[10] and is the object of Hearer and Solitary Realizer Exalted ones and of all Exalted Buddhas. Understanding it destroys wrong views holding to extremes.

> 289. The unreceptive are terrified
>   Just by its very name.
>   What so-called strong man is seen
>   Who does not frighten the weak?

Selflessness must not be taught to the weak-minded for the very word "emptiness" terrifies the unreceptive. Does one see any so-called strong man who does not frighten the weak? For instance, just the sight of a lion or tiger frightens small animals.

Assertion: Since this teaching destroys all wrong views, it should be taught to the unreceptive in order to defeat its opponents.
Answer:

> 290. This principle is not taught
>   By Tathāgatas for the sake of debate,
>   Yet it burns up others' contentions
>   As fire does its fuel.

Tathāgatas do not teach this principle only to outshine opponents in debate but as the door to liberation. Nonetheless this teaching of emptiness burns up others' wrong contentions just as fire consumes its fuel without formulating the intention to burn. The Master also says:

> Like the dew on the tip of the grass
> When it meets with the rays of the sun,
> Opponents' arguments and errors
> Evaporate when they meet you.[11]

Question: How does this teaching burn up others' contentions, when understanding of it arises in the mind of someone with interest in it?

   Answer:

291. Whoever knows this teaching
     Will not relish others.
     Thus to me this teaching seems
     Like the door to destruction.

Whoever comes to know the nectar-like taste of this teaching, the emptiness of inherent existence, through hearing, thinking and meditating will not relish views adhering to the true existence of things. The Master Āryadeva therefore says that this teaching of emptiness seems to him like the door and means to the destruction of wrong views. Alternatively he says it with texts on emptiness in mind, in that the words of the Buddha that teach emptiness also seem like this to the Master.

Question: Why does emptiness not cause the Exalted fear?

   Answer: Because they have destroyed the seed of attachment to the self.

292. For those who think there is
     In reality no self and abide in this thought,
     How will existence cause pleasure
     Or non-existence cause fear?

Since they have no attachment to views of a self or hostility toward selflessness, how will those who think that external and internal phenomena are in reality selfless and who abide in a direct understanding of this be pleased by the existence of the self or frightened by selflessness? Fear therefore does not arise in those who have direct understanding of selflessness because they have eliminated the cause of fear.

> 293. Seeing the many Forders
> Who are seeds of futility,
> Who would not feel pity
> For people who long for a teaching?

The Forders' many venomous snakes drive their students into thorny thickets of wrong views holding things to be truly existent, the seed of uninterrupted futile suffering in cyclic existence, daily killing their life force of virtue consistent with liberation. Seeing this and knowing the nature of these teachings, who with a Bodhisattva's disposition would not feel pity for those who long for a teaching that will liberate them from cyclic existence? Therefore one must show sentient beings the path of non-inherent existence so that they will not be ravaged by the Forders' snakes.

Question: Why, despite their inclination toward virtue, do people mostly follow Forders' systems and not the Buddha's teaching?
Answer: Because it is subtle and hard to understand.

> 294. The teaching of the Śākyas,
> Nirgranthas and Brahmins are perceived
> By the mind, the eyes and the ears.
> Thus the Subduer's teaching is subtle.

Since the teaching of the Śākyas, the Nirgranthas and Brahmins is understood by the mind, the eyes and the ears respectively, the Subduer's textual system is more subtle and thus most people do not follow it. The sun-like view, the understanding of non-inherent existence, is said to illuminate one's mindstream. It destroys all the thickets of unwholesome views. Seeing all products as being like dreams makes one's mindstream stainless. All this must be understood through meditative equipoise, and thus the Śākyas' teaching is subtle. Since the practices of Nirgranthas consist of a lack of hygiene and physical pain caused by the sun and wind, they can be understood by merely seeing them, and since Brahmins take recitation alone as the essence of their practice, it can be understood by hearing it. These are therefore easier to comprehend.

Assertion: If ordinary people engage in outsiders' practices because they may be perceived by coarse forms of awareness, it is right for you to do so too.

Answer: It is not right.

> 295. Brahmin practices are said
> Mainly to be an outward show.
> The practices of Nirgranthas
> Are said to be mainly stultifying.

Since most Brahmin practices such as recitation, burnt offerings, auspicious incantation, repentance, confession and so forth are mainly an outward show for the sake of reward and respect, it is said that they should not be performed by those who seek liberation. Similarly it is said that most of the Nirgranthas' practices, such as allowing their hair to become matted and employing the five fires, are stultifying. Therefore those who seek liberation should avoid them completely.

> 296. Brahmins are revered
> Because they adopt the orthodox.
> Nirgranthas are pitied
> Because they adopt the deluded.

Brahmin practices are mainly for outward show. Thus some unintelligent people revere Brahmins because they adopt orthodox practices such as reciting the Vedas and so forth. They revere and pity Nirgranthas because they adopt painful and deluded forms of behavior such as mortifying the body through sun and wind.

> 297. Suffering is a maturation
> And thus is not virtuous.
> Similarly, birth too is not virtuous,
> Being a maturation of actions.

Painful sensations such as mortification of the body are not virtuous but are instead, like the suffering in the hells, the maturation of non-virtuous actions. Similarly, because it is a maturation of past actions as are eyes and so forth, birth as a Brahmin is not something virtuous enabling the attainment of liberation.

Question: If birth and suffering are not virtuous, what is?

Answer: Harmful thoughts toward others as well as physical and verbal actions thus motivated constitute violence toward others.

Non-violence is the opposite of this, namely the ten virtuous paths of action.

298. **In brief Tathāgatas explain**
Virtue as non-violence
And emptiness as nirvāṇa—
Here there are only these two.

In brief Tathāgatas say that the principle through which one attains a high rebirth is non-violence. The principle through which liberation is attained is natural nirvāṇa, the emptiness of inherent existence of all phenomena. By directly experiencing this and recognizing that suffering will never arise again, there is separation from adventitious stains—the nirvāṇa of separation from adventitious stains.[12] Here [in this system] there are only these two. *Sixty Stanzas of Reasoning* says:

When reality is seen
Nirvāṇa is attained; the task is accomplished.[13]

It is posited that having reached the path of seeing one attains mere nirvāṇa. To attain this, all the aggregates do not have to cease.[14] The reason for explaining this here is to show that one definitely needs to understand emptiness to attain liberation.

Question: When outsiders are aware of the Subduer's teaching, why do they not appreciate these two principles?
Answer: Because they are attached to their own mistaken positions.

299. **To ordinary people their own position,**
Like their birthplace, is attractive.
Why would you find attractive
That which precludes it?

Attachment to their own position is something ordinary people have been accustomed to since beginningless time. Like their birthplace they find it attractive and do not want to give it up because of their attachment. Why would you outsiders find attractive these two principles which preclude and are contrary to your own position? You do not follow the Buddha's teaching because you cling to your own wrong views.

300. The intelligent who seek what is good
     Adopt what is worthwhile even from others.
     Does the sun not belong to all
     On earth who have sight?

Wise people, who see their birthplace as a reason for their difficulties, leave and settle in a prosperous place. Likewise, intelligent people seek what is good and therefore adopt those points which facilitate the attainment of a high rebirth or liberation once familiarity with them has been gained, even though they are from others' texts. The sun is unbiased and thus provides light for all on earth who have sight. Does it not belong equally to all? Similarly, the practice of these two principles can only be of benefit to everyone. Thus it is fitting to practise them with a sense of appreciation.

The summarizing stanza:

> Become a proper vessel for good explanation
> And learned in the non-inherent existence of
>   dependent arising,
> The final object of the path that severs worldly
>   existence,
> The understanding of which frees from attachment
>   to extreme views.

This is the twelfth chapter from the *Four Hundred on the Yogic Deeds*, showing how to meditate on refuting views.

This concludes the commentary on the twelfth chapter, showing how to meditate on refuting views, from *Essence of Good Explanations, Explanation of the "Four Hundred on the Yogic Deeds of Bodhisattvas"*.

Chapter XIII

Refuting Truly Existent Sense Organs and Objects

Question: When it says [in stanza 300]:

> The intelligent who seek what is good
> Adopt what is worthwhile even from others,

what is this good explanation?

Answer: It is about seeing that all phenomena have no inherent existence.

Assertion: It is impossible to cognize that all phenomena have no inherent existence, for if they did they would be totally non-existent like the horns of a donkey and so forth, and would not be directly perceptible. However, since a pot and blue are directly perceptible, all functional things are in fact inherently existent.

Answer:

> 301. When seeing its form, one does not in fact
> See the whole pot. Who that knows
> Reality would claim that the pot
> Is directly perceptible also?

It follows that direct perception of a pot which exists by way of its own entity is not feasible. If it were, the awareness perceiving the visible form[1] of the pot should perceive all its parts. Yet when visual consciousness perceives the pot's form, it does not in fact perceive every single part of the pot. Who that knows the reality of things would claim that the pot is directly perceptible? "Also" refers to also blue existent by way of its own character.[2]

The pot is imputed in dependence on eight substances[3] and therefore cannot exist by way of its own character, nor by seeing one part can one see all its parts. Similarly, if fire existed by way of its own entity, the fallacy that it should always keep burning would arise, since it would not require fuel.

Dialecticians contradict both reasoning and common knowledge when they call awareness arising in dependence upon individual sense organs direct perception, and assert that an awareness free from conceptuality in which a sound image and a generic image may be apprehended as merged[4] is direct perception. Each individual moment of consciousness cannot be a direct perceiver.[5] In the world objects like the waxing moon, which are directly perceived by many people, are commonly held to be directly perceptible, whereas that which perceives these objects is not. Furthermore since they assert that sense consciousness is a direct perceiver, it is inconsistent to think that it is also a valid perceiver.[6] An extensive explanation of this may be found in Candrakīrti's commentary.[7] It has not been included here for fear that it would be too long.

302. **By means of this very analysis**
   Those with superior intelligence
   Should refute individually
   All that is fragrant, sweet and soft.

By means of this very analysis using the reasoning which refutes the assertion that sense consciousness is a direct perceiver in relation to a pot, blue and so forth, existent by way of their own entity, the wise with superior intelligence refute separately in each case the contention that sense consciousnesses are direct perceivers in relation to fragrances such as the fragrance of jasmine flowers, sweet tastes and that which is soft to touch, all existent by way of their own entity. Since one cannot make distinctions such as seeing one part but not seeing others, or distinctions with regard to what touches and what does not, or with regard to closeness and distance in relation to truly existent functional things, such fallacies ensue.

Assertion: All parts of the pot are seen when its visual form is seen, for the pot is not a separate entity from its visual form.
Answer:

303. If because the form is seen
     Everything is seen,
     Why because of what is not seen
     Would the form not be unseen?

If on the grounds that visual consciousness sees the pot's form one can posit that all parts of the pot are seen, why on the grounds that visual consciousness does not perceive the pot's smell would even the visible form, which is accepted as seen, not be unseen? If one posits that all parts are seen because one part is seen, even that which is accepted as seen cannot be posited as seen if one part is not perceived.

Assertion: Though the pot is not a directly perceptible object of comprehension, its visible form is established by direct perception and thus, indirectly, the pot existing by way of its own entity is also directly perceptible.
  Answer:

304. There is no direct perception
     Of just the form alone,
     Because it has a close and distant
     As well as a central part.

It follows that there is no direct perception of just the visible form alone existent by way of its own entity, because the visible form too has many parts, such as close, distant and central parts, and is thus imputed in dependence upon many parts. There is not the slightest thing existent by way of its own entity that is directly perceptible to any kind of awareness.

305. This also applies when one examines
     Whether particles have parts or not.
     Thus to prove a thesis by that
     Which must be proved is not feasible.

When all the parts are separated, that form is finally reduced to the smallest particles. An investigation of whether particles have parts or not applies to those particles too. If they have parts like a front and a back, they are, like the pot, imputed in dependence upon many parts, in which case they no longer are the smallest particles. If they do not have parts, they cannot exist because of being inapprehensible. Thus it is not feasible to prove that the pot exists by way of its entity as a directly perceptible object of comprehension by means of that which must be proved, for things do not exist by way of their own character.

> 306. Everything too is a component
>   As well as being a composite.
>   Thus even a spoken syllable
>   Does not have existence here.

Moreover when objects apprehended by the physical sense organs are examined, all are components in relation to their composites as well as composites in relation to their components and are therefore merely imputed in dependence upon their parts. As with the analysis of the smallest particle, names, which are ultimately reduced to spoken syllables such as "a," are also just conventions in this world and do not exist by way of their own entity. Thus you must recognize all dependently arising phenomena as mere names and terms.

Assertion: The pot is directly perceptible since visual consciousness sees the pot's visible form existent by way of its own character, consisting of color and shape.
Answer:

> 307. If shape is distinct from color
>   How is shape apprehended?
>   If not distinct, why would the body
>   Not also apprehend color?

Are color and shape inherently one or distinct? If shape such as length and so forth is inherently distinct from color, how can a visual consciousness take shape as its object of apprehension? It follows that it cannot because shape is an entity distinct from color. Alternatively, if they are not distinct but inherently one, why does touch not apprehend color in the dark just as it apprehends shape? It follows that it should because they are one.

Assertion: The visible form source[8] exists because the four great elements which are causal forms exist.
Answer:

308ab. Only the form is visible
      But the form's causes are not seen.

Only the resultant form is visible but the form's causes such as the earth element are not seen. Since causal form is imputed in dependence upon resultant form, they cannot be inherently different. If they are inherently one, they must be one.

308cde. If indeed it is thus,
       Why are both not also
       Perceived by just the eyes?[9]

In that case why does just visual consciousness itself not apprehend both the causal and resultant forms? It follows that it should because they are one.

309. Earth is seen as firm and stable
     And is apprehended by the body.
     Only that which is tangible
     Is referred to as earth.

Earth is seen as firm and stable and furthermore is apprehended by tactile consciousness. Thus only that which is tangible is referred to as earth. Therefore since visible forms are objects apprehended by visual consciousness and the four elements are objects apprehended by tactile consciousness, they are different. If one accepts them as truly existent, they are unrelated. It would thereby follow that visible form is causeless.

Vaiśeṣika assertion: A pot is not a visible object by way of its own entity but neither is it not a visible object, since it is directly perceptible by virtue of possessing visibility, a separate generality.[10]
   Answer: This too is unacceptable.

310ab. Since it was produced as something visible,
       It is of no use at all to the pot.

Has the pot come into existence as something visible through its own causes or not? In the first case it would follow that an association with the separate generality of visibility is of no use in making the pot directly perceptible, because it has come into existence as something visible through its own causes. For this reason the generality of visibility is not produced in relation to the pot.

310cd. As with the production of visibility,
        It lacks even the entity of existence.

Further, a pot that has no connection with visibility and is not something visible lacks any inherently established entity of existence.
Therefore the pot could not be either actually or imputedly directly
perceptible as you contend.

Assertion: Because sense organs exist—such as the eyes, which are
instruments of perception—directly perceptible objects such as visible form exist.
  Answer:

311ab. The eye, like the ear, is an outcome of
        The elements. The eyes see while the others do not.

Regarding the subject, the eye organ: since the eye perceives visual
stimuli while other senses do not, it does not perceive visible form
by way of its own entity, for like the nose sense organ it is an outcome of the elements. A demonstration of the valid reasons which
invalidate the entailment is given below.[11]
  Objection: If the eye and so forth do not exist it contradicts explanations concerning the maturation of actions.
  Answer: But even we do not refute that.
  Question: Why is that not refuted?
  Answer: We refute that things exist by way of their own entity but
far from refuting the existence of all that is dependent arising, we
affirm it in our own system.

311cd. Certainly therefore the Subduer said
        The fruition of actions is inconceivable.

Although it cannot sustain investigation by the reasoning which
analyzes suchness and though it is not established by way of its own
entity, it is undeniable that the eye sees visible form and does not
hear sound. Thus recognizing that the maturation of actions is inconceivable, one should accept it without applying analysis by reasoning. Certainly therefore the Subduer said that the fruition of actions is inconceivable. Sūtra says:

  The maturation of sentient beings' actions is inconceivable.
  Thus this whole world comes into existence through causes.

Assertion: The eye and so forth are inherently existent because one experiences consciousness, their effect.
   Answer:

312. **Because the conditions are incomplete**
     There is no awareness before looking,
     While afterwards awareness is of no use.
     The instrument is of no use in the third case.

A visual consciousness does not exist before looking at a form, for prior to that the conditions which produce it are incomplete. Alternatively if it exists after looking at the form, it follows that the eye consciousness is of no use in looking at the form, because looking takes place before it exists. As a third possibility one might think that that which looks and consciousness are simultaneous. It would then follow that the instrument of looking would be of no use in the production of that visual consciousness because the two would exist simultaneously and would be unrelated.

Assertion: The eye is the instrument of looking.
   Answer:

313. **If the eye travels, that which is**
     Distant would take long to see.
     Why are extremely close
     And very distant forms not clear?

When the eye looks at a form, does it look after travelling to the object or without doing so? In the first case, if when the eye looked at a form there were motion of travelling toward the object, it should take longer to see distant objects. If the eye perceived through contact, why would the eye ointment and spatula, which are extremely close, and very distant forms not be equally clear? It follows that they would be because of being perceived through contact.

314. **If the eye travels when the form is seen**
     Its movement is of no benefit.
     Alternatively it is false to say
     What it intends to view is ascertained.

If the eye travelled to the form after seeing it, its movement would be of no benefit, for though it does so to view the form, that form has already been seen. Alternatively, if it approached without seeing the form which it intended to view, it would be false to say it had definitely been seen, for it approaches what is to be viewed without seeing it, like a blind man.

315. If the eye perceives without travelling
       It would see all these phenomena.
       For that which does not travel there is
       Neither distance nor obscuration.

To avoid these errors one might assert that it perceives form by way of its own entity without travelling. In that case the eye which stays here would see all of these phenomena: the close and distant, as well as the obscured and unobscured. For an eye which does not approach the object there should be no difference between close or distant, obscured or unobscured objects.

316. If the nature of all things
       First appears in themselves,
       Why would the eye not
       Be perceived by the eye itself?

Just as the fragrance of the magnolia or blue lotus is first found at its source and afterwards, through contact, on a sesame seed and so forth, it is the way of all things that their nature first appears in themselves. Since it cannot relinquish its nature even in relation to itself, if it is an instrument of looking by way of its own entity, why does the eye not perceive itself? It follows that it should since the eye organ even with the eye as its object cannot give up its nature as an instrument of looking. Yet valid cognition negates that the eye perceives itself. Thus the subject, the eye, is not an instrument of looking at form by way of its own entity, because it does not look at itself.

Assertion: The eye alone does not have the ability to view form. The form is seen in dependence upon a combination of three factors.
   Answer:

317. The eye does not have consciousness
       And consciousness lacks that which looks.
       If form has neither of these,
       How can they see form?

Since the eye is matter it is not conscious of the object. Consciousness is not that which looks at the object. The form, the objective condition, is neither that which looks nor consciousness. How can form be seen by way of its own entity through a combination of these three factors? It follows that it is not feasible because visible form which is one of them has no ability to see.

Just as form cannot be looked at in terms of its own suchness, sound too cannot be listened to in this way.

> 318. If sound makes a noise as it travels
> Why should it not be a speaker?
> Yet if it travels noiselessly, how could
> Awareness arise in relation to it?

When sound is heard, does hearing occur because it approaches as an object of that which listens or not? In the first case, if it approaches as an object of auditory consciousness, does it do so emitting sound or silently? If it travels toward auditory consciousness making a noise as it travels, why is it not a speaker, since like Devadatta it travels, emitting sounds? If this is accepted, it follows that it would not be sound. Alternatively, if it travels toward auditory consciousness noiselessly, how could awareness focusing on the sound be produced, since no sound is emitted?

> 319. If sound is apprehended through contact,
> What apprehends the beginning of sound?
> If sound does not come alone,
> How can it be apprehended in isolation?

Furthermore, if sound is apprehended through contact with the ear organ, what apprehends the beginning of sound before contact occurs? It follows that there is nothing with which to apprehend it, since neither the ear organ nor any other does so. If this is accepted, it follows that it would not be sound. Sound consists of nine substances and thus since it does not come alone, how can sound in isolation be apprehended? It follows that smell and so forth which are inseparably combined with it would also be apprehended, for according to you they must, like the sound, have contact with the ear organ.

Question: What is wrong if the beginning of sound is not apprehended?

Answer: It would fail to be sound.

320. **While sound is not heard, it is not sound.**
It is impossible
For that which is not sound
Finally to turn into sound.

Until it is heard it is not sound because, like smell, it is not the ear's object. It becomes sound when it is heard. If initially it was not sound but later became sound, it would follow that smell and so forth could do so too, but this is unacceptable with regard to permanent functional things. Sūtra says:

For instance, in dependence upon the strings and wood
And the hand's effort—through these three together—
Sound is produced and issues from
Instruments like the vina and flute.
When the wise investigate and think
From where it has come and where it has gone,
Searching in the main and intermediate directions,
They find no coming nor going of sound.

Assertion: The mind apprehends objects after travelling to them.

Answer: That is incorrect. Auditory consciousness does not travel to the object along with the ear organ, for the organs always remain in the body.

321. **Without the sense organs what will mind**
Do after it has gone?
If it were so, why would that which lives
Not always be without mind?

Even if mind, such as an auditory consciousness, approached its object without the sense organs, how could it perform the functions of listening, looking and so forth, since like a blind person it would lack the ability to perceive its object? If it were so, why would that which lives, i.e. the self, not always be without mind? When one investigates in this way by means of reasoning, neither sense organs nor consciousnesses have by way of their own entity the ability to apprehend objects.

Objection: If sense organs and their objects do not exist inherently, the aggregate of recognition which discerns what is exclusive to them will be non-existent.

Answer: Although they do not exist when analyzed by reasoning, they are not conventionally non-existent, for mental consciousness apprehends the exclusive aspects of an object such as a visible form which has already been perceived.

> 322. An object already seen
> Is perceived by mind like a mirage.
> That which posits all phenomena
> Is called the aggregate of recognition.

For instance, though a mirage does not contain even a drop of water, a recognition of water occurs. Likewise that which perceives the exclusive aspects of an object, a mental factor positing the exclusive signs of all phenomena, is called the aggregate of recognition. Phenomena are simply posited by recognition and do not exist by way of their own entity.

Objection: If the aggregate of recognition does not exist inherently, it is impossible to posit phenomena.

Answer: There is no such error.

> 323. In dependence upon the eye and form
> Mind arises like an illusion.
> It is not reasonable to call
> Illusory that which has existence.

Even though it does not exist by way of its own entity, mind arises like a magical illusion in dependence upon the eye and visible form. Any phenomenon whose existence is existence by way of its own entity cannot be called illusory, just as women who exist in the world are not called illusory.

Assertion: It is amazing to claim that the sense organs can in no way whatever apprehend objects and that visual consciousness is produced in dependence upon the eye and visible form.

Answer: That alone is no cause for amazement.

> 324. When there is nothing on earth
> That does not amaze the wise,
> Why think cognition by the senses
> And suchlike are amazing.

Although when analyzed by reasoning a sprout and so forth neither comes into existence from a seed which has ceased nor from one which has not ceased, [sprouts are produced in dependence upon seeds[12]]. When to the wise there is nothing on earth which is not as amazing as magic, why should one think that cognition of objects by sense consciousnesses which do not have true existence and such-like are amazing, for this applies equally to everything.

> 325. The firebrand's ring and magical creations,
> Dreams, illusions, and the moon in water,
> Mists, echoes, mirages, clouds
> And worldly existence are alike.

Thus all dependently arising phenomena are like the ring formed by a firebrand which is whirled quickly. Though the woman created through meditative stabilization and the dream body do not have true existence, they act as causes for erroneous attachment to the self. Although the illusory maiden conjured by a magician does not have true existence, she confuses the mind. Similarly the moon in the water, mists and echoes resounding from mountain clefts and caves give rise to a distorted perception of them as they appear to be. A mirage causes mistaken perception, and clouds in the distance seem like mountains. Worldly existence consisting of environments and living beings, while empty of inherent existence, is able to function. Understand that it is like these analogies. Sūtra says:

1. In a young girl's dream she sees
   A youth arrive then die, and feels
   Happy when he arrives, unhappy when he dies.
   Understand all phenomena are like this.

2. Those who conjure illusions create forms
   Of various kinds—horses, elephants and chariots.
   They are not at all as they appear.
   Understand all phenomena are like this.

3. The reflection of the moon shining
   In the sky appears in a clear pool,
   Yet the moon does not enter the water.
   Understand the nature of all phenomena is like this.

4. Echoes arise in dependence upon
   Caves, mountains, forts and river gorges.

Understand all products are like this.
Phenomena are all like illusions and mirages.

5. A person who is tormented by thirst
In summer at noon—that transmigrator
Sees mirages as a body of water.
Understand all phenomena are like this.

6. Although a mirage contains no water
Confused beings want to drink it.
Unreal water cannot be drunk.
Understand all phenomena are like this.

7. Instantaneously in a cloudless sky
A circle of clouds appears,
But try to find from where they came—
Understand all phenomena are like this.

8. Like mirages and smell-eaters' cities,[13]
Like magical illusions and like dreams,
Objects of meditation are empty of a real entity.
Understand all phenomena are like this.[14]

The summarizing stanza:

Thus in the illusory city of the three false worlds
Manipulated by the puppeteer of karmic action
The smell-eater maiden performs her illusory dance.
Amazing that desire should chase a mirage!

This is the thirteenth chapter of the *Four Hundred*
on the *Yogic Deeds,* **showing how to meditate on**
the refutation of sense organs and objects.

This concludes the commentary on the thirteenth chapter, showing
how to meditate on the refutation of sense organs and objects, from
*Essence of Good Explanations, Explanation of the "Four Hundred on the
Yogic Deeds of Bodhisattvas".*

Chapter XIV

Refuting Extreme Conceptions

Question: If, like the ring formed by a firebrand and so forth, worldly existence, because of being a dependent arising, does not exist inherently, what has inherent existence?

Answer: Not the slightest thing has inherent existence.

> 326. **If a thing did not depend**
> **On anything else at all**
> **It would be self-established,**
> **But such a thing exists nowhere.**

Anything existing by way of its own entity would not rely on anything else at all, but not the least thing is independent or exists without relying on something else. If anything existed inherently, independence would be established as its nature when examined by the reasoning which investigates the ultimate, yet this does not exist anywhere. A mode of existence of phenomena not merely posited by nominal convention is known as independent existence, existence by way of their entity, existence by way of their character, inherent existence and true existence. This clearly indicates the object of negation through whose refutation there is no focus for conceptions of true existence. Since Candrakīrti's commentary repeatedly mentions qualifying the object of negation[1] when refuting fabrications of true existence, one should not deprecate the Mādhyamika view.

If the composite known as "pot" exists by way of its own entity, are the visible form and the pot one or different?

327. "The form is a pot"—they are not one.
     The pot that has form is not separate.
     The pot does not have form,
     Nor does the form have a pot.

In the first case it follows that the form and the pot in the statement "The form is a pot" are not inherently one, otherwise there would be a pot wherever there was a visible form. One might think that the pot which is something distinct from visible form possessed form the way Devadatta possesses a cow, as something separate. However it follows that the pot which has form is not inherently separate from the form, otherwise it would be apprehensible independently of its form. The pot does not have form as something apart which depends upon it, nor does the form have a pot dependent upon it, like a dish and its contents, because neither exists inherently.

Vaiśeṣika assertion: Though the pot and its form are not different substantial entities, existence and the pot are. The pot is a substantial entity and is said to exist through its connection with the great generality "existence," which is something separate from it.
  Answer:

328. Since the two are seen to have dissimilar
     Characteristics, if the pot is separate
     From existence, why would existence
     Not also be separate from the pot?

Existence and the pot are seen to have the dissimilar characteristics of a generality and of a specific. It is not feasible for the pot to be a substantial entity which is separate from existence, for if it were, why would existence not be a separate entity from the pot? It follows that it would be. If this is accepted, the pot is non-existent.

Assertion: The substantial entity, the pot, exists because it acts as a basis for attributes, such as one and two, which are distinct from it.
  Answer: "Attribute" and "substantial entity" are different words and have different meanings.

329ab. If one is not accepted as the pot
       The pot also is not one.

If the number one is not accepted as the pot, the pot is not one either because, like two and so forth, these are different words and have different meanings. If this is accepted, the term and thought "one" do not validly apply to the pot.

Assertion: The pot is one by virtue of possessing the attribute one, but one is not the pot.
Answer:

329cd. Moreover possession is not reciprocal,
Therefore also it is not one.

Possession occurs between two similar things, as in the case of consciousness,[2] and not between dissimilar things. Moreover there is no reciprocal possession between the pot and one, since the pot possesses one, but one does not possess the pot. The pot is also not one because of being a separate entity from one.

Furthermore, your contention that attributes qualify substantial entities but that one attribute does not qualify another is contradictory.

330ab. If the form is the size of the substance,
Why is the form not large?

If the size of the substantial entity, the pot, and the size of its visible form are the same, why is the attribute form not large just as the substantial entity is large? One must accept that the form has a separate attribute "large."
Objection: Small and large cannot qualify form, for according to our textual system, one attribute does not qualify another.
Answer:

330cd. If the opponent were not different
Scriptural sources could be cited.

If your opponents were not from a school other than your own, you could cite your textual system to fault their argument, but it is inappropriate here, since we are engaged in rejecting these very tenets.

Assertion: Even if distinct attributes like separateness are refuted, the pot which they characterize is not refuted and thus exists by way of its own entity.
Answer:

331. By virtue of its characteristic
The characterized does not exist.
Such a thing has no existence
As something different from number and so forth.

If one contends that existence and so forth have the characteristic of accompanying things while the pot has the opposite characteristic, then by virtue of this opposite characteristic the pot it characterizes does not exist anywhere by way of its own entity. Such a thing, distinct from numbers like one, two and so forth, has no existence as a pot established by way of its own entity. In brief, something characterized which is a different entity from its characteristics and characteristics which are different entities from that which they characterize cannot be found.

Sautrāntika assertion: The pot and its eight substantial particles are one truly existent entity.
   Answer:

   332ab. Because the pot is not separate
   From its characteristics, it is not one.

It follows that the pot would not be a truly single unit, because it is, by way of its own entity, one with and not separate from its eight substantial particles which have diverse characteristics.
   Assertion: The pot is a plurality.
   Answer: In that case there should be a pot for each of the eight substantial particles.

   332cd. If there is not a pot for each,
   Plurality is not feasible.

Since there is no pot for each, the pot is not feasible as a plurality.

Assertion: The pot is a single unit through the coming together of the eight substantial particles.
   Answer:

   333. The tangible and the intangible
   Cannot be said to coalesce.
   Thus it is in no way feasible
   For these forms to coalesce.

The pot's composite can in no way be a truly existent single unit due to the coalescence of the eight substantial particles such as visible form and so forth, because the four elements which are tangible, and visible form, smell and so forth which are intangible cannot touch and coalesce.

Assertion: Even though there is no mutual contact, their combination is the "truly existent" pot.
   Answer:

334ab. Form is a component of the pot
And thus, for a start, is not the pot.

The pot's visible form is a component or part of the pot and thus, for a start, is not the pot, just as smell and so forth are not.

Assertion: Since a compound reliant upon its components exists, that is the pot.

Answer:

334cd. Since the compound does not exist,
Neither do the components.

Since visible form, smell and so forth do not each have a pot, the compound pot does not exist by way of its own entity. The components, too, therefore do not exist by way of their own entity, because they have parts.

Why are some things that have form pots and other things that have form not pots?

335. If the definition of form
Applies without incongruity
To all forms, for what reason
Is one a pot and not all others?

It follows that all should equally be pots, for if the definition that form is simply that which is appropriate as form applies without any incongruity to all forms such as smell, taste and so forth as well as pots and woollen cloth, truly existent things with form should be the same in all respects.

It follows that form, smell and so forth would also be one, because of being one with the pot.

Objection: Form, smell and so forth are different.

Answer:

336. If you assert that form is distinct from
Taste and so forth but not from the pot,
How can that which does not exist
Without these not be distinct from form?

You assert that smell, taste, and so forth are distinct from visible form because they are objects apprehended by different senses, but that visible form is not distinct from the pot. Yet how can the pot that cannot be posited without taste and so forth, which are distinct from form, not be distinct from form? It follows that it should be, because the pot is different from form, smell and so forth by way of its own entity.

> 337. The pot has no causes
> And is itself not an effect.
> Thus there is no pot at all
> Apart from form and so forth.

Since form and so forth are not the pot's causes by way of their own entity, the pot is not an effect existent by way of its own entity. Thus there is nowhere a pot that exists by way of its own entity apart from its components like visible form and so forth. Since a pot cannot be found isolated from its components, a pot which is a different entity from them does not exist.

Assertion: The pot is the effect of its components, such as clay, and they are its causes.
  Answer:

> 338. If the pot exists by virtue of its causes
> And those causes by virtue of others,
> How can that which does not exist
> By virtue of itself produce something disparate?

If the pot exists by virtue of its causes, and those causes exist by virtue of other causes, how can that which does not exist by virtue of its own entity produce a disparate effect? Anything, therefore, that needs to rely on causes does not exist by way of its own entity. If it existed by way of its own entity, it follows that it would be causeless. This reasoning which refutes the existence of a pot by way of its own entity should be applied to all effects.

Assertion: Though it has many components, the pot is a truly existent single unit.
  Answer:

> 339. Though they meet and come together
> Form cannot be smell.
> Therefore like the pot
> The composite cannot be one.

Though visible form, smell and so forth meet and combine, form cannot be smell, for the things that create the composite do not give up their different characteristics. Though form, smell and so forth combine they do not have one nature. Thus just as the pot as a truly existent single unit was refuted by the words [in stanza 332],

> Because the pot is not separate from
> Its characteristics, it is not one,

the composite too cannot be a truly existent single unit.

340. **Just as the pot does not exist**
     Apart from form and so forth,
     Likewise form does not exist
     Apart from air and so forth.

Just as the previously explained reasoning shows that there is no truly existent pot apart from form, smell and so forth, there is no truly existent component visible form apart from the great elements such as air, for it is imputed in dependence upon these.

Just as visible form, smell and the like cannot exist without air and so forth, the great elements too do not exist by way of their own entity without relying on each other. Thus fire is that which burns and the other three elements that which is burnt.

341. **That which is hot is fire but how**
     Can that burn which is not hot?
     Thus so-called fuel does not exist,
     And without it fire too does not.

Fire burns only fuel whose nature is the other three elements, yet hot fuel is fire and no longer fuel to be burnt. If it is not hot, since it is unrelated to fire how will it burn? Thus fuel independent of fire does not exist by way of its own entity and because of this, fire independent of fuel does not exist by way of its own entity either.

Assertion: Fuel is hard and so forth but not hot by nature. When it is overpowered by fire, it grows hot and is that which is burnt.
  Answer:

342. **Even if it is hot only when**
     Overpowered, why is it not fire?
     Yet if not hot, to say fire contains
     Something else is not plausible.

Even if fuel grows hot only when overpowered by fire, why is it not fire? It follows that it should be fire because it is hot and burns.[3] Yet if fuel is not hot at that time, it is implausible to claim that something else which is not hot is present in fire. In that case just heat divorced from the other three elements would be fire, but if one of the great elements does not exist the others cannot exist either. Moreover it contradicts the statement, "Things that arise simultaneously are reciprocal effects like the elements."[4]

Assertion: Since the other three elements are not present in the smallest substantial fire particle, there is fire even without fuel.
   Answer:

343. If the particle has no fuel
     Fire without fuel exists.
     If even it has fuel, a single-natured
     Particle does not exist.

Fire without fuel exists if the smallest fire particle does not have fuel. Since it therefore would follow that uncaused fire exists, one should not assert a smallest substantial particle as do the Vaiśeṣikas. If one admits that even the fire particle has fuel, for fear of the conclusion that it would otherwise be causeless, it follows that there is no single-natured particle since the other elements are certainly present in each particle.

344. When different things are examined
     None of them have singleness.
     Because there is no singleness
     There is no plurality either.

When functional things like pots and woollen cloth are examined as to whether they are or are not truly existent, these various things, because they have parts, do not have truly existent singleness. Nor do they have truly existent plurality for the very reason by which they are not truly single, since plurality comes about through an accumulation of single units. External and internal phenomena are not truly existent because they are neither one nor many. They are like reflections.

345. Though they assert that where there are none
     Of those things there is singleness,
     Singleness does not exist
     Since everything is threefold.

One may think this refutation applies to our own sectarians who assert that the elements and elemental derivatives occur simultaneously, but not to outsiders who assert that a small permanent earth particle which is a single unit exists where there are no functional things apart from the smallest particles such as earth particles and so forth. Yet even in their system the smallest earth particle is threefold in that it has substantial entity, singleness and existence. Attributes have attributiveness, singleness and existence. By virtue of the fact that everything is threefold even in their system, just unaccompanied singleness does not exist. Thus precisely the same fallacies apply to them.

> 346. The approach of existence, non-existence,
>   Both existence and non-existence, and neither,
>   Should always be applied by those
>   With mastery to oneness and so forth.

Those who have mastered the art of employing the meaning of suchness always refute oneness, otherness, both and neither by applying the kinds of reasoning which refute the assertions of those like the Sāṃkhyas who claim the effect exists at the time of the cause; of the Sautrāntikas who assert that cause and effect truly exist but that the effect does not exist at the time of the cause; of the Nirgranthas who assert both existence and non-existence in that a thing is permanent in nature yet temporarily impermanent; and of those who assert that though things are substantially existent, they neither exist nor do not exist since they cannot be said to be this nor that. They apply the reasons previously explained in [stanza 265], "For those who assert effects exist ...": the reason of dependent arising, the lack of being one or many, the diamond fragments reason and so forth.[5]

Question: If things therefore do not have the slightest inherent existence, for what reason do those opponents hold that they are truly existent?
Answer:

> 347. When the continuum is misapprehended,
>   Things are said to be permanent.
>   Similarly when composites are
>   Misapprehended, things are said to exist.

Though there is no valid reason, in the case of a thing which lasts three days, they feel compelled to assert that whatever existed before must exist later. Functional things are said to be permanent when the continuum which is posited through imputation upon former, intermediate and later moments is misapprehended. Similarly when the composite is misapprehended, it is said that there are truly existent functional things. There seem to be even many adherents to the *Seven Treatises on Valid Cognition*[6] who, through not knowing how to posit the composite and the continuum, follow outsiders.

Objection: Even if our view that things exist were wrong, your view is that things do not exist, since you do not accept functional things. It is unreasonable because it contradicts both what is seen and unseen.

Answer: We make no claim that things do not exist for we are proponents of dependent arising.

Question: Do you assert that things are truly existent?

Answer: No, because we are proponents of dependent arising.

Question: What does that mean?

Answer: It means that while things are empty of inherent existence, like magical creations and mirages, they can produce effects.

> 348. Anything that has dependent arising
>   Is not independent.
>   All these are not independent,
>   Therefore there is no self.

Any relative thing which is found to arise and exist dependently is not found to exist independently. All these phenomena lack an independent mode of existence and thus there is no self of persons or of phenomena. The person and the aggregates do not exist inherently because they arise dependently.

Question: We too accept that effects are not independent, so what is the difference?

Answer: The difference is that you do not understand that dependent arising means mutual reliance.

> 349. Things do not assemble
>   Unless there is an effect.
>   Aggregation for an effect
>   Is not included for the Exalted.

Since nothing is produced by way of its own entity, things do not assemble and come together to produce an effect unless there is an effect to produce. Since anything inherently existent would be permanent, it could not rely on an effect. Aggregation for the sake of an effect is not included within the perception of the Exalted during meditative equipoise which sees suchness, because it directly perceives the lack of inherent existence of things.

One gains release from cyclic existence when deluded ignorance which conceives things as truly existent ends. This depends on understanding emptiness of inherent existence.

> 350. The awareness that is the seed of existence
> Has objects as its sphere of activity.
> When selflessness is seen in objects,
> The seed of existence is destroyed.

The seed of worldly existence is the conception that phenomena are truly existent. Objects such as form are its sphere of activity. The seed of worldly existence is destroyed and one attains liberation by seeing that these objects lack an inherently existent self and by gaining familiarity with this. On becoming a Hearer or Solitary Realizer Foe Destroyer or on reaching the eighth ground, one achieves the complete elimination of conceptions of true existence.

The summarizing stanza:

> All who have gained a free and fortunate human body,
> Following the reasoning of Nāgārjuna and his son,
> Should understand emptiness to mean dependent arising.
> Who would not make effort to achieve this end?

This is the fourteenth chapter of the *Four Hundred on the Yogic Deeds*, showing how to meditate on the refutation of extreme conceptions.

This concludes the commentary on the fourteenth chapter, showing how to meditate on the refutation of extreme conceptions, from *Essence of Good Explanations, Explanation of the "Four Hundred on the Yogic Deeds of Bodhisattvas"*.

Chapter XV

Refuting Truly Existent Characteristics

Assertion: Products exist inherently because their characteristics such as production exist.

Answer: Products would exist if their characteristics existed, but these do not exist inherently. If production is asserted to produce products,[1] then according to those who propound the non-existence of the effect, the sprout which does not exist at the time of the seed is produced after the final moment of a seed for which the necessary causes and conditions are assembled.

> 351. How can the non-existent be produced,
> If what does not exist at the last is produced?
> How can that which exists be produced,
> If what exists from the outset is produced?

A sprout which does not exist during the last moment of the seed cannot be produced by way of its own entity, otherwise it follows that donkeys' horns and ao forth would also be produced. Thus how can anything which does not exist at the time of its cause be produced by way of its own entity? It cannot. How can anything which exists at the time of its cause be produced? It follows that it will not be produced, since anything existing at the time of its cause was produced from the outset, prior to being itself. The subject, a sprout, is not produced by way of its own entity, for neither that which exists at the time of its cause nor that which does not exist at the time of its cause is produced by way of its own entity.

352ab. Since the effect destroys the cause,
That which does not exist will not be produced.

Since the sprout cannot be produced unless the seed undergoes change, the process which produces the resultant sprout destroys the causal seed. Thus something which does not exist at the time of the seed will not be produced by way of its own entity. In general, even though a sprout which is non-existent at the time of the seed is produced, it is incorrect to accept truly existent production, for then one must also accept the production of rabbits' horns.

352cd. Nor will that which exists be produced
Since what is established needs no establisher.

Since something which is established at the time of its cause does not need anything to establish it, that which exists at the time of its cause will not be produced.

353. There is no production at that time,
Nor is there production at another.
If not produced at that time nor another,
When will there ever be production?

At a time when the sprout itself exists there is no production, since it does not need to be produced. Other than that, when it does not exist there is no production, since it cannot be produced. If it is not produced at that time nor at the other, when will there ever be production? There cannot be a time of production.

Assertion: Milk turning into something which is curd constitutes production.
Answer: That is incorrect.

354. Just as there is no production
Of that as the thing it is,
Neither is it produced
As something else.

Since something which exists as milk does not need to become milk, there is no production. Neither is that milk produced as something else, i.e. curd, for the two are different entities.

There is no inherent production for the following reason too:

355ab. The first, intermediate and last
Are not possible prior to production.

First production, then duration and lastly disintegration are not possible prior to production, because that which is unproduced cannot have production, duration and disintegration.

Assertion: Production while a thing is being produced, duration while it lasts and disintegration when it disintegrates exist consecutively by way of their own entity.[2]

Answer:

355cd. How can each begin
Without the other two?

How could each at its particular time begin without the other two? Duration and disintegration are impossible without production. The same applies to the other two. Moreover a product is not feasible without any one of these characteristics.

For this reason too products cannot be inherently produced:

356. The thing itself does not occur
Without other things.
Thus there is no coming into existence
Either from self or from other.

The thing itself, such as a clay pot, does not occur without other things, such as clay, since it depends upon clay. The clay does not exist by way of its own entity either, since it depends on pebbles. Thus the pot does not come into existence either from self or from other, for since neither self nor other exist by way of their own entity, there is no inherent production.

357. It cannot be said to exist
Before, after or simultaneously.
Therefore production does not occur
Simultaneously with the pot.

Moreover there is no inherent production, since it is impossible to say that production and so forth exist before, after or simultaneously with the pot. Therefore the pot's production does not occur simultaneously with the pot by way of its own entity. If it did, since the basis and that which is based upon it would be co-existent,[3] it would follow that the pot had been produced, for it must exist even as it is approaching production.

Assertion: The pot's production exists, for without it there could be no oldness and so forth, but there is oldness characterized by cessation.
   Answer: That is incorrect.

> 358. That which was previously produced
>   Was not old when first produced.
>   Also that which afterwards has been
>   Constantly produced is not old.

The previously produced pot was not old when first produced because at that time it was new. A previously produced thing does not grow old by way of its own entity. Nor is that old which afterwards has constantly been produced, for also at that time it is new. Since afterwards it is newly produced, it will not become old by way of its own entity. Furthermore, by refuting production existent by way of its own entity, oldness existent by way of its own entity is refuted, but mere [conventional] oldness is accepted in our system too.

Since there is no inherent production in any of the three times, production does not truly exist.

> 359. A present thing does not
>   Come into existence from itself,
>   Nor come into existence from the future,
>   And also not from the past.

Since cause and effect are not simultaneous, a present thing does not come into existence from its present self. Nor does it come into existence from the future, nor from the past. Moreover, since there is no inherent production in any of the three times, one must accept that production is false and like a magician's illusion.
   Sūtra says: "Monks, it is as follows: when the eye is produced, it does not come from anywhere, and when it ceases, it does not go anywhere." Thus if there were inherent production, a thing should come from somewhere when it is produced, like the rising moon, and go somewhere when it ceases, like the setting moon. In that case it would be permanent, but since production and cessation are mere nominal imputations, one must accept that they are like magical illusions.

360. There is no coming of the produced,
Likewise no going of that which has ceased.
Since it is thus, why should existence
Not be like a magician's illusions?

Since things do not come from anywhere when they are produced nor go anywhere when they cease, why should external and internal existence not be like a magician's illusions? When dependent arising is seen as it is, it is like a created illusion and not like a barren woman's child.[4]

At this point Candrakīrti's commentary says that if mere production is negated, it is the kind of object of comprehension that a barren woman's child is and thus a denial of dependent arising.[5] Inability to assert production in one's own system and placing hope in a system which claims production neither exists [nor does not exist][6] destroys the Mādhyamika view. Since adherence to such an interpretation creates causes for bad rebirths, it should be discarded like a gob of spittle!

361. Production, duration and disintegration
Do not occur simultaneously.
If they are not consecutive either,
When can they ever occur?

Since production, duration and disintegration, the characteristics of products, do not occur simultaneously by way of their own entity nor consecutively by way of their own entity, when do they occur by way of their own entity? The subjects—production, duration and disintegration—do not exist inherently because of not being inherently simultaneous or consecutive.

362. If for production and all the others,
All of these occurred again,
Disintegration would seem like production
And duration like disintegration.

Since production, duration and disintegration would all require the production of production and so forth, disintegration, like production, would have another disintegration, and duration too would seem like disintegration in that one would have to assert that it has another duration. Thus there would be infinite regress. In that case the basic characteristics would not be established. Therefore there is not even an atom of inherent existence.

Question: Are the characteristics and that which they characterize one or different in nature?
Assertion: That which is characterized, namely a product such as a pot, is different in nature from its three characteristics—production, duration and disintegration.
Answer:

> 363. **If that which is characterized is said to be**
> **Different from its characteristics,**
> **How can the characterized be impermanent?**
> **Alternatively, existence of all four is unclear.**

How can that which is characterized, namely a product such as a pot, be impermanent? It follows that it is not, for impermanence and the pot are inherently different. Alternatively, if they are inherently not different, the four, i.e. the three characteristics and that which they characterize, do not clearly have the entity of existing as functional things. It follows that the characteristics are not characteristics because of being one with that which they characterize, and that which they characterize is not what is characterized because of being one with the characteristics. One should therefore not assert that they are inherently one or different.

Assertion: Production and so forth exist inherently because the agent of production exists inherently.
Answer:

> 364. **A thing is not produced from a thing**
> **Nor is a thing produced from a non-thing.**
> **A non-thing is not produced from a non-thing**
> **Nor is a non-thing produced from a thing.**

The sprout, as an already existing functional thing, is not produced again while the seed as a functional thing exists, because a sprout is not produced unless the seed undergoes change. Also a sprout that has already been produced cannot be produced again. The sprout as a functional thing is not produced from a non-functional seed, because a non-functional thing does not have the ability to produce an effect. Furthermore a non-functional effect is not produced from a non-functional cause: a burnt seed does not produce a burnt sprout.

A non-functional effect is not produced from a functional cause since the fallacies already explained apply.[7] Since inherent production is impossible, causes and conditions giving rise to it are meaningless.

Moreover, should one consider that production and disintegration pertain to that which has the nature of a functional thing or a non-functional thing? Both are inappropriate.

365. A thing does not become a thing,
    Nor does a non-thing become a thing.
    A non-thing does not become a non-thing,
    Nor does a thing become a non-thing.

Something already produced does not again become a thing being produced, since it is senseless for it to be produced again. A non-functional thing is not produced again as a thing, otherwise it follows that even a barren woman's child could be born. Thus there is no inherent production of either functional or non-functional things. A totally disintegrated non-functional thing does not again become a disintegrating non-functional thing, for something non-existent like a barren woman's child does not disintegrate. A functional thing that is already produced does not become a non-functional thing, because the two are contradictory. Sūtra says: "All products and non-products are free [from inherent existence]. Those sages who do not have conceptions [of inherent existence] understand that which is a non-product with regard to all phenomena and are free from views of an [inherent] self."[8]

Assertion: Neither that which has been produced nor that which is unproduced is being produced. That which is in the process of production is being produced.
  Answer:

366. A thing in the process of production
    Since half-produced, is not being produced.
    Alternatively it follows that everything
    Is in the process of being produced.

It follows that a sprout in the process of production is not being produced by way of its own entity, because that which is in the process of production must be posited as half produced and half unproduced. The produced part belongs to what has already been produced and the unproduced part to what is unproduced. There is nothing in the process of production with parts other than these existent by way of its own entity. If the produced and the unproduced are both considered to be that which is presently being produced, both past and future are also in the process of being produced. Alternatively, it follows that all three times are presently being produced, since all produced and unproduced things are in the process of production.

If that which is presently being produced exists by way of its entity, is it considered to have its own nature or not? Both are unacceptable.[9] It follows that it could not be in the process of production.

367. **That which has the nature of presently being pro-**
    duced
    Is not in the process of production,
    Nor is that in the process of production
    Which lacks the nature of presently being produced.

It follows that anything which has the nature of presently being produced does not have the nature of being in the process of production. It follows that whatever does not have the nature of presently being produced is also not in the process of production, because that which is not presently being produced is contrary to that which is.

Assertion: That which is in the process of production exists, since it is located between the past and future. These two times may be posited in relation to what is presently being produced.
    Answer:

368. **For anyone to whom the two are**
    Impossible without an intermediate,
    There is nothing in the process of production,
    For it too would have an intermediate.

In any opponent's system in which there is definitely an intermediate stage without which the past and future cannot exist, that which is presently being produced could not exist by way of its own entity, since there would be infinite regress, in that anything in the process of production would require another intermediate stage and that one yet another and so on.

Question: If the half-produced is not in the process of production, what is?
    Assertion:

369. Since the process of production is the arising
     Of the produced through cessation,
     That which is presently being produced
     Appears to be a different entity.

Since the process of production is, for example, the sprout's being produced through cessation of the seed, something in a state where its production has begun is said to be in the process of production. Thus what is presently being produced appears to be a different entity from that which is half produced and half unproduced.

Answer: If one could point to anything and say, "This thing has been produced from this thing which is in the process of production," one could identify something in the process of production existent by way of its own entity in relation to the thing produced from it.

370ab. When a thing is produced there cannot be
       Anything in the process of production.

However when a thing has been produced, there cannot be anything in the process of production which exists by way of its own entity, for what was in the process of production has ceased. A produced thing which has arisen from such a process of production and which would permit its inference does not exist.

Assertion: The produced is in the process of production.
Answer:

370cd. If the produced is in the process
       Of production, why is it being produced?

If the produced is in the process of production, why is it being produced again? This is unfeasible because it has already been produced.

Assertion: A thing which is presently being produced is said to be produced, for although unproduced, it is approaching production.
Answer:

371. A thing in the process of production is said
     To be the entirely unproduced arising.
     Since there is no difference, why should the pot
     Not be considered as non-existent?

If a thing that is in the process of being produced is said to be produced because, even though it is entirely unproduced, it is approaching production, why should a pot while performing its function not

be considered a non-functional thing? It follows that this is a reasonable assertion, since there is no difference between the produced
and the unproduced.

Assertion: There is a difference between that which is in the process
of being produced and the unproduced. That which is in the process of production is said to be associated with the activity of production, whereas the unproduced is not necessarily associated with
the activity of production.
Answer:

> 372. That which is presently being produced,
>   Though incomplete, is other than unproduced.
>   Yet also since other than produced,
>   The unproduced is being produced.

Since a thing in the process of being produced is associated with the
activity of production, you assert that even though it has not completed that activity, it is other than unproduced and future. Yet in
that case, since a thing in the process of being produced is other than
something produced, you are saying that the unproduced is being
produced.

> 373. That which is presently being produced,
>   Though not yet existent, is later said to exist.
>   The unproduced is thus being produced—
>   But the non-existent does not arise.

Since that which is presently being produced is other than something produced, you must accept that it is unproduced. You might
claim that anything in the process of being produced exists as a thing,
because, even though it did not exist previously, it has afterwards
become associated with the activity of production. If on this account
you say that an entirely unproduced thing associated with the activity of production is being produced, that too is incorrect. An
unproduced thing, referred to as non-existent, has not attained its
entity. It does not undergo production, because it is not engaged in
that activity.

> 374. The completed is called existent.
>   The uncompleted is called non-existent.
>   When there is nothing in the process of production
>   What is being referred to as such?

That which has completed the activity of production is said to exist as a thing, and that which has not performed the activity of production is said not to exist as a thing. If neither that which has nor that which has not completed the activity of production is in the process of being produced, what is being referred to as presently being produced? Anything in the process of being produced does not have the least existence by way of its own entity.

> 375. Since without a cause
> There is no effect,
> Both starting and stopping
> Are not feasible.

Investigation by reasoning shows that there is no effect without a cause. Since cause and effect, then, do not truly exist and since the bases therefore do not truly exist, the sprout's starting to be produced and the seed's stopping to exist are not feasible by way of their own entity. Sūtra says:

> Sentient beings, humans, those born from power whoever they may be,
> None that were born and died here were born [inherently].
> The nature of all things is empty like magicians' illusions,
> But the Forders are unable to recognize it.[10]

For instance, the men and women conjured by an illusionist cause the spectators of the magic, who think of them as men and women, to feel attraction and aversion. Though they also appear to the magician, he does not think of them in this way. They do not even appear to those who are unaffected by the spell. You must understand that these analogies apply respectively to the perception of common beings who have not understood dependent arising's emptiness of inherent existence, to the wisdom of subsequent attainment of the Exalted, and to the meditative equipoise of the Exalted.[11] You should learn how conventional phenomena are established by conventional valid cognition and ultimate truth by conceptual and non-conceptual reasoning consciousness from the presentation in [*Gateway for Conqueror Children*], *Explanation of [Śantideva's] "Engaging in the Bodhisattva Deeds"*[12] and so forth.

The summarizing stanza:

Production and disintegration of composite things
Are like dreams and like illusion.
When they are mere terms and mere imputation,
How could non-products be truly existent?

This is the fifteenth chapter from the *Four Hundred on the Yogic Deeds*, showing how to meditate on the refutation of that which constitutes products.

This concludes the commentary on the fifteenth chapter, showing how to meditate on refuting [the inherent existence of] that which constitutes products, from *Essence of Good Explanations, Explanation of the "Four Hundred on the Yogic Deeds of Bodhisattvas"*.

Chapter XVI

Refuting Remaining Counter-Arguments

These chapters were written so that trainees may enter the state of liberation through giving up attachment to cyclic existence. Without ascertaining the meaning of emptiness as it actually is, one cannot develop enthusiasm for omniscience or even for liberation through the giving up of attachment to cyclic existence. The emptiness of inherent existence of all phenomena frightens those who have not heard sufficient teaching and are bound by the noose of clinging to a self. As already described, the path leading to freedom from worldly existence should therefore only be explained after first making the mind ready, in the way that the death of a king's beloved queen was conveyed to him.[1]

> 376. For various reasons, that which is empty
> Appears nonetheless as if not empty.
> These are refuted individually
> By all the chapters.

Even though things are empty of inherent existence, they appear not to be empty and are thought of in this way for various reasons, such as considering them truly existent. All of the preceding fifteen chapters refute these reasons individually.

Assertion:

> 377ab. When the author and subject also exist
> It is incorrect to call them empty.

If the chapters were written for these purposes, things are established as not being empty, since the author and the subject matter explained by the fifteen chapters exist. "Also" indicates the words that express the meaning of emptiness. Therefore it is incorrect to speak of the emptiness of inherent existence of things.

Answer:

> **377cd. Also with regard to these three, whatever**
> **Arises in dependence does not exist.**

According to us, the words, subject matter and author are imputations dependent on one another and do not exist independently. Whatever arises in dependence does not exist inherently. Since the author, subject matter and words are all dependently imputed, these three also do not have inherent existence. Thus emptiness is well established.

Assertion: If all of these were empty, the senses and their objects would be like donkeys' horns! But since they exist, things do exist inherently.

Answer:

> **378. If through flaws concerning emptiness**
> **[Things] were established as not empty,**
> **Why would emptiness not be established**
> **Through flaws concerning lack of emptiness?**

If on account of the [presumed] flaws concerning proof of emptiness, the words and so forth were not empty because one has to accept their existence, why would emptiness not be established through flaws concerning your proof that things are not empty? It follows that you should certainly accept emptiness because you accept the interdependence of the words and so forth.

You cannot establish your own thesis merely by dismissing the proponents of emptiness.

> **379. In refuting the thesis of others**
> **And in proving your own thesis,**
> **If on the one hand you like to disprove,**
> **Why do you not like to prove?**

Opponents asserting that things exist truly must refute the others' thesis of emptiness as well as prove their own thesis that things are truly existent. You, however, are simply engaged in dismissing the proponents of emptiness. If on the one hand you like disproving the thesis of others, why do you not like proving your own? You should! To proponents of emptiness whatever proofs you adduce to validate your own thesis remain as unestablished as that which is to be proved. You should therefore give up adherence to the thesis that things are inherently existent.

Assertion:

> **380ab. When thoroughly investigated,**
> **The non-existent is not a thesis.**

The thesis put forward by proponents of emptiness is not feasible since when thoroughly investigated, it is illogical. Something which does not exist as a knowable object[2] is not an assertable thesis. Therefore the thesis put forward by proponents of true existence is established.

Answer: No thesis is feasible when investigated by the reasoning that analyzes the ultimate.

> **380cd. Then all three, such as oneness,**
> **Also are not theses.**

Since negated by this reasoning, truly existent oneness, otherness and ineffability asserted by any opponent are also not theses. Therefore one should not assert even the slightest true existence.

Assertion:

> **381ab. Where a pot is directly perceptible,**
> **The argument of emptiness is meaningless.**

The reason proving the pot empty of true existence is meaningless and ineffectual, for wherever there is a directly perceptible pot, that truly existent pot is, according to us, established by direct perception.

Answer:

> **381cd. Here reasons appearing in textual systems**
> **Are not [acceptable]; elsewhere they are.**

In relation to the thesis of proponents establishing emptiness of true existence through reasoning, reasons appearing in their opponents' textual systems are unacceptable, because they are engaged in rejecting them.

Question: Then are reasons from these textual systems inappropriate in all cases?

Answer: Elsewhere there is no incompatibility, since they pertain where both protagonists' tenets are similar.

Assertion: You proponents of emptiness accept the entity of emptiness, and since emptiness is not feasible unless it relies on non-emptiness, things are truly existent.

Answer: It follows that the existence of emptiness does not establish its opposite, that there is true existence.

> 382. When there is nothing that is not empty,
>   How can emptiness be so?
>   When the one does not exist,
>   Why should the antidote exist?

If emptiness were truly existent, truly existent things as its basis would be feasible, but as there is nothing that is not empty of true existence, how can emptiness be truly existent? Its basis cannot possibly be truly existent. Why, when the basis does not have true existence, would the antidote negating it be truly existent? For emptiness to be truly existent, its basis would have to have a truly existent nature. *Fundamental Wisdom* says:

> If the slightest thing were not empty
> Emptiness would have some existence

and so forth.[3] *The Two Truths* says:

> Since the object of negation is non-existent,
> The negation clearly does not exist as [its own] reality.[4]

Assertion: Since there is not even the slightest emptiness, it cannot constitute one's thesis. Nevertheless by accepting the absence of a system of one's own as one's system, one is asserting a thesis. Since there is no thesis which does not depend on a counter-thesis, truly existent things—the counter-thesis—exist.

Answer:

> 383. If there were a thesis, absence of the thesis
>   Would in entity be a thesis,
>   But where there is no thesis
>   What can be the counter-thesis?

If we had any thesis of existence by way of a thing's own entity, the absence of a thesis would in entity be a thesis existent by way of its own entity. However since we do not have any thesis of existence by way of a thing's own entity, a counter-thesis dependent upon that is also impossible. Moreover all theses concerning truly existent things have already been refuted above. Thus if the absence of a thesis does not exist by way of its own entity, what truly existent thing could constitute the counter-thesis? Neither thesis nor counter-thesis have even an atom of true existence. By this we refute truly existent emptiness as our system, which should not, however, be interpreted as showing that we have no system.[5]

Assertion: There are truly existent things, because specific things like fire and so forth exist.
　Answer:

> **384. How can fire be hot,**
> **When things do not exist?**
> **This was refuted above: it was said**
> **That even hot fire does not exist.**

How can fire be hot by way of its own entity? It cannot, for there are no truly existent things. Above it was said that even hot fire does not exist inherently. [Stanza 341] says:

> That which is hot is fire but how
> Can that burn which is not hot?
> Thus so-called fuel does not exist,
> And without it fire too does not.

This point has already been refuted.

> **385. If through seeing things one could refute**
> **The statement that things do not exist,**
> **Who then sees the elimination**
> **Of fallacies regarding all four theses?**

Moreover, even if, on seeing the thing which is fire, it were appropriate to refute the statement that fire does not exist truly, who sees the elimination of fallacies associated with the true existence of oneness and difference and of all four theses such as existence and non-existence and so forth exposed by the reasoning of dependent arising?[6] Since all four theses are seen to be flawed, one should not accept any thesis of true existence.

For the following reason, too, it is incorrect to assert true existence:

386. When there is nowhere, even in particles,
     A truly existent entity, how can it occur?
     Even for Buddhas, it does not exist.
     Thus it is irrelevant.

As explained in the context of [stanza 305],

> This also applies when one examines
> Whether particles have parts.

If there were a truly existent entity, it should be observable even in extremely small things such as particles, but it is not observable. How can truly existent production occur for that which does not exist anywhere? It is totally incorrect to accept as existent that which is non-existent to the perception of Buddhas, the sun-like radiance of whose consummate understanding of the suchness of things dispels all darkness of ignorance. Asserting true existence is thus unrelated to any feasible thesis.

387. If they are not twofold, how can
     Anything have an existent entity?
     If that is reasonable to you also,
     Why raise further arguments?

If there is no twofold division of phenomena into truly existent and not truly existent, what, such as particles and so forth, could have a truly existent entity, since all forms of true existence have been precluded? If for the very reasons we have explained, it is appropriate for you too to accept the system which has eliminated the two extremes, why do you cling to the thesis of true existence and raise further arguments against us?

If any reasoning could disprove the thesis concerning emptiness of true existence, we would be convinced, but since things cannot be proved truly existent, you should accept only our thesis.

388. Regarding the non-functional [aspect] of all things,
     Differentiations are inappropriate.
     That which is seen in all substantial entities
     Is not differentiable.

If the nature of internal and external things were truly existent, they would not depend on causes and conditions. Also differentiations of truly existent and not truly existent are inappropriate with regard to the absence of truly existent things. There are no differences in the entity of space, because it is a mere absence of obstructing form. Similarly regarding emptiness of true existence, the nature seen in all substantial entities, [stanza 191] says:

> Whoever sees one thing,
> Is said to see all.
> That which is the emptiness of one
> Is the emptiness of all.

Sūtra says, "Whoever has come to know the non-functional with regard to functional things has no attachment to functional things."[7] There are no distinctions of truly existent and not truly existent with regard to any phenomenon whatsoever.

Challenge: After first analyzing, you should either accept emptiness or make a reply.

Objection: It would be appropriate to make a reply if the slightest thing were accepted as truly existent, but since according to you everything is non-existent, how can any reply be made?

Answer:

389. **If owing to non-existence you claim**
    No reply is made to the other's thesis,
    Why should you not also prove
    Your own thesis which is refuted by reasons?

If you claim that no reply is made to the Mādhyamika thesis because everything is non-existent, why should it not also be proper to prove your own thesis which is refuted by the reasons that prove emptiness? Since one cannot refute another's thesis without proving one's own, yours has become non-existent.

Assertion: Even if one is unable to prove one's thesis, it is said and well known in the world that reasons which refute others' theses are easy to find.

Answer:

390. **Though the world says it is easy**
    To find reasons with which to refute,
    Why can the errors regarding
    The others' thesis not be stated?

Since in that case you too must be in possession of those easily found reasons with which to refute, why are even you unable to fault the others' thesis, that of the Mādhyamikas? Thus as you are unable to fault the others' thesis, reasons refuting emptiness are not easy to find.

> 391. If just by saying "They exist"
> Things really did exist,
> Why should they not also be non-existent
> Just by saying "They do not exist"?

If even without reasoning, but merely by saying the words "They exist," things existed as their own suchness, why should their emptiness of true existence not also be established merely by our saying the words "They do not exist truly"? The reasoning is the same in all respects. Therefore, rejecting assertions regarding the two extremes, we both should firmly establish the textual system free from all fabrications which asserts non-existence of the two extremes.

Assertion: If things do not exist ultimately, the designation "things exist" is incorrect and as unreasonable as terming a barren woman's child existent.
  Answer:

> 392. If a thing is not non-existent
> Because the term "existent" is ascribed,
> Neither is it existent
> Because the term "existent" is applied.

If things do not lack true existence because the designation "they are and exist" is ascribed, neither are they truly existent because the designation "they exist truly" is applied. Calling someone with good eyesight blind or someone with a short life long-lived does not make them so. Besides, if things could be accomplished by words alone, it would be just as reasonable to accept that they lack true existence as to think they are truly existent.

Another's assertion: Words do not reveal an object's entity.[8] If they did, one's mouth would burn when saying "fire" or be full when saying "pot." Therefore we assert that ordinary people all have means of expression and terms for that which is being expressed which do not touch an object's own entity.
  Answer:

393. If everything is a convention
Because expressed by ordinary people,
How can anything which exists
As [its own] suchness be a convention?

Supposedly things all exist inherently and as conventions[9] because ordinary people speak of them by means of words which do not touch their entity. But how can anything that exists inherently, existing as its own suchness, be a convention? It could only be ultimately existent.[10]

Assertion: Since you deny that things have true existence, things are non-existent.
Answer:

394. If things are non-existent because
Things all do not exist,
In that case it is incorrect that all theses
Concern the non-existence of things.

If even the slightest thing is non-existent because things are not truly existent, it is incorrect that all Mādhyamika theses concern the non-existence of things through refutation of previously existent truly established things, for there has never been any true existence.[11]

395. Since a thing does not exist
A non-thing cannot exist.
Without a thing's existence,
How can a non-thing be established?

Since truly existent functional things, the object of negation, do not exist, their non-functional negation cannot be truly existent. In the world a completely disintegrated thing is said to be non-functional.[12] In keeping with this, a completely disintegrated pot would not be feasible if the pot had never existed. Thus how could the non-functional be truly existent, when there are no truly existent functional things? The existence of a dependent thing is not feasible without that on which it depends.

Assertion: In order to prove emptiness you must adduce reasons. Thus since the reasons exist, things are not empty, for like the reasons everything else is also truly existent.
Answer:

396. If things are not empty because
They are empty by virtue of reasons,
The thesis would not be distinct from the reasons,
And thus the reasons would not exist.

If things were not empty because emptiness of true existence is established through reasons, and the thesis and reasons were inherently distinct, they would be unrelated. If the thesis were not inherently distinct from the reason but inherently one with it, they would have to be one and therefore what is to be proved could not be understood by depending on the reason. Then it follows that there are no correct reasons, since the fallacy of there being no reasons arises when one asserts truly existent things. Therefore all phenomena are established as lacking inherent existence.

Assertion: Since there are analogies for emptiness of inherent existence, such as the reflection and so forth, everything else, like those analogies, exists and is not empty.
Answer:

397. If things are not empty because
There are analogies for emptiness,
Can one say, "Just like the crow,
So too the self is black"?

Is the analogy related or unrelated to the reason's meaning? The first has already been precluded by the reasoning which refutes truly existent reasons. In the second case, if the meaning is established through an analogy unrelated to the reason, is one able to say, "Just as the crow is black, so too is the self," because they are alike in being functional things? One should be able to do so. Yet an analogy, merely by virtue of its existence, is not suitable as an analogy for true existence.

Question: If analogies, reasons and all things do not exist, what is the purpose of writing all the chapters of your treatise?
Answer: It is for the attainment of liberation and omniscience through understanding the meaning of suchness.

398. If things exist inherently
What good is it to perceive emptiness?
Perception by way of conceptions binds.
This is refuted here.

If things existed inherently, what good would there be in perceiving emptiness, since it would be erroneous? Thinking of things as truly existent causes one to accumulate actions and thereby wander in cyclic existence, but through fully understanding that all phenomena lack inherent existence, one gains release from worldly existence. Thus as long as one sees things as truly existent, because of conceptions which cling to their true existence, one is bound to cyclic existence. In this treatise, therefore, the truly existent person and aggregates, which are the referent objects of conceptions of true existence, are refuted by an extensive collection of reasoning. Sūtra says, "All phenomena are empty in that they do not exist inherently" and so forth. Accordingly, this was written to teach lack of inherent existence, which does not contradict the acceptance in our system of all dependently arising phenomena.

Among our own sectarians, Vijñaptivādins and all those who have not understood the actual meaning of the scriptures assert that consciousness is truly existent, and that external objects do not even exist conventionally. This is therefore shown to be wrong, for both are alike in existing conventionally but not ultimately.

> 399. To say one exists and the other does not
> Is neither reality nor the conventional.
> Therefore it cannot be said
> That this exists but that does not.

To say that one exists and the other does not is not a presentation of reality, since both do not exist ultimately and are not ultimate truths. Nor is it a presentation of the conventional, since both exist conventionally and are conventional truths. Therefore all five aggregates exist conventionally but not ultimately, and so it cannot be said that mind and mental factors exist truly while external objects do not even exist conventionally. Thus Mādhyamikas, too, accept both external objects and consciousness as they are known in the world.

When assertions regarding true existence of things and so forth have been thoroughly refuted in this way, it is impossible to state any refutation of the assertions regarding emptiness.

Assertion: Even though we are unable to answer you at present, you will receive an answer—there will be those who make great effort on behalf of the Tathāgata's teaching.

Answer: That is a futile hope! If we held a faulty thesis, it could be refuted by proving its converse.

400. Against one who holds no thesis that [things]
    Exist, do not, or do and do not exist,
    Counter-arguments cannot be raised
    No matter how long [one tries].

No Mādhyamikas hold the erroneous theses that things are inherently existent, that even the slightest thing is non-existent, that non-things are inherently both existent and non-existent, or neither. No matter how long one tries, no counter-arguments can be raised. You should understand that refuting skilled proponents of emptiness is as impossible as drawing pictures in space or causing space pain by beating it with an iron bar.

The Master Dharmadāsa[13] gave one analogy for each stanza of the first eight chapters. Fearing an excess of words, they have merely been cited but not elaborated in detail.

The summarizing stanza:

The sun's light dispels all darkness.
Darkness has no power to destroy the sun's light.
The correct view destroys all extreme conceptions,
Banishing any opportunity for controversy.

This is the sixteenth chapter from the *Four Hundred on the Yogic Deeds*, showing how to meditate on settling [the procedure between] spiritual guides and students.

This concludes the commentary on the sixteenth chapter, showing how to meditate on settling [the procedure between] spiritual guides and students, from *Essence of Good Explanations, Explanation of the "Four Hundred on the Yogic Deeds of Bodhisattvas"*.

Colophon

This concludes the *Treatise of Four Hundred Stanzas on the Yogic Deeds of Bodhisattvas* from the mouth of Āryadeva, the spiritual son at the Exalted Nāga's feet. He was born miraculously from the heart of a lotus on the island of Siṅhala. Having crossed the ocean of our own and others' tenets himself, he made the Middle Way most clear by distinguishing between correct and incorrect views.

It was translated and [the meaning] settled in the temple of Ratnaguptavihāra in the center of the glorious Kaśmīri city of Anupamapura by the Indian abbot Sūkṣmajana and the Tibetan translator Ba-tsap Nyi-ma-drak.

This concludes the explanation both of the great trailblazer and Bodhisattva, the Master Āryadeva's work *Four Hundred Stanzas on the Yogic Deeds of Bodhisattvas* and of its commentary by the Master Candrakīrti.

It was translated from the Indian into the Tibetan language in the temple of Ratnaguptavihāra[1] in the center of the glorious Kaśmīri city of Anupamapura[2] by the Indian abbot Sūkṣmajana,[3] son of the Brahmin Sajjana from the paternal line of the Brahmin Ratnavajra[4] and by the Tibetan translator Ba-tsap Nyi-ma-drak (*pa tshab nyi ma grags*)[5] who had consummate understanding of all texts on sūtra and tantra. The meaning of the text was properly settled by explaining and listening to it.

May the one predicted[6] by the Conqueror who attained the
   supreme state,
As well as Āryadeva and the glorious Candrakīrti,
Who most clearly elucidated Nāgārjuna's good system,
Rest victoriously on the crown of our heads.

May the one predicted[6] by the Conqueror who attained the
supreme state,
As well as Āryadeva and the glorious Candrakīrti,
Who most clearly elucidated Nāgārjuna's good system,
Rest victoriously on the crown of our heads.

Unable to bear misinterpretations of this system
Through the misconceptions of those who follow their own
presuppositions,
Who lack the flawless eye of reasoning
And ignore the textual systems of the great trailblazers,

I have explained the words and meaning of this text simply,
Commenting in a clear, unconfused and complete way
On the paths that mature the mind and bring about release
For all people with a Mahāyāna disposition.

Since Āryadeva's thought is hard to ascertain
And my mind is poor, my acquired knowledge weak,
May my spiritual guides and deities
Forgive whatever errors there may be.

Through any immaculate virtue created by my efforts
To illuminate the good Mādhyamika path free from extremes,
May all transmigrators, bound in the prison of worldly
existence,
Attain the peerless happiness of liberation.

May I, too, in all future lives never be separated
From a spiritual guide of the supreme vehicle,
And through fully entering this path by listening, thinking and
meditating,
May I obtain the state of an omniscient Conqueror.

This *Essence of Good Explanations, Explanation of the "Four Hundred"*
was written at the insistence of La-ma Nam-ka-sang-bo-wa (*bla ma
nam mkha' bzang po ba*) who cherishes his precious precepts and holds
the three sets of vows, and of La-ma Drak-seng-wa (*bla ma grags
seng ba*), exceptionally tireless in bearing the responsibility of spreading the Subduer's teaching—they urged me again and again from
Upper Do-Kam[7] (*mdo khams*) with lavish and repeated flower-like
offerings. It was written also at the insistence of Kun-ga Seng-ge (*kun
dga' seng ge*) of Dzay-tang[8] (*rtse thang*), a great holder of the three
sets of teachings who has heard the texts of sūtra and tantra many

times, and at the insistence of numerous other holders of the three sets of teaching.

It was written at Drok-ri-wo-che Gan-den-nam-bar-gyel-way-ling[9] (*'brog ri bo che dga' ldan rnam par rgyal ba'i gling*) by the logician and fully ordained monk Dar-ma-rin-chen (*dar ma rin chen*). This was made possible by the kind explanations received directly from the noble, venerable and holy Ren-da-wa Shon-nu-lo-dro (*red mda' ba gzhon nu blo gros*), great follower of the Conqueror, with consummate understanding especially that all external and internal dependently arising things are like the reflection of the moon in water, and from the great omniscient one in this time of degeneration, whose prayer to hold the excellent teaching of the Conquerors is perfectly accomplished, the glorious and good foremost precious Lo-sang-drak-ba (*blo bzang grags pa*). They are the father and son, the dust beneath whose feet I have long and respectfully venerated.

The scribe was Rin-chen-cho-gyel (*rin chen chos gyal*), holder of the three sets of teaching and observant of his vows.

By virtue also of this, may the precious teaching of the Conquerors spread and flourish in all ways, in all directions, and endure for a long time.

May any merit resulting from this work
help to keep alive the flame of the Buddha's teaching,
protected and nourished for many centuries
by the people of Tibet.
May it act as a cause for all living beings
to enjoy peace and enlightenment.

Appendix

GYEL-TSAP'S TOPICAL OUTLINE

Each point of the outline is keyed to a stanza number as well as to two page and line numbers that indicate the beginning of the section of commentary relevant to the stanza.

"Var." refers to the Varanasi edition (Pleasure of Elegant Sayings Printing Press, 1971) of Gyel-tsap's *Essence of Good Explanations, Explanation of the "Four Hundred"*.

"C.W." refers to Vol. *ka* of the Dharamsala edition (Shes rig par khang, 1981) of the same work in Gyel-tsap's *Collected Works (rgyal tshab rje'i gsung 'bum)*.

PART I
EXPLAINING THE STAGES OF THE PATHS
DEPENDENT ON CONVENTIONAL TRUTHS

Section A: Showing how the aspiring altruistic intention is generated after training in the attitudes of a person of intermediate capacity by explaining elimination of the four errors.

Chapter I

Explaining how to abandon erroneous belief in permanence by thinking extensively about being mindful of death

	Var.	C. W.	St.
I. Brief explanation urging conscientious effort on the path to liberation by being mindful of death	10.4	514.4	1
II. Extensively explaining how to meditate on impermanence			
A. How to cultivate awareness of one's own death			
1. Meditation on coarse impermanence			

Chapter II

Explaining how to abandon erroneous belief in pleasure by meditating on the contaminated body as suffering

3. Refuting the existence of real pleasure

Chapter III

Explaining the means to abandon erroneous belief in cleanness by considering the unclean nature of cyclic existence

* Since the title of this section was omitted from the editions of Gyel-tsap's commentary which were examined, the title included here is hypothetical and deduced from the content of the section.

Section B: Explaining how to train in the deeds, having generated the practical altruistic intention

Chapter V

The actual meaning

Chapter VI

Explaining the means to abandon disturbing attitudes and emotions which prevent the deeds

Chapter VIII

Showing the methods of fully training the student's mindstream making it receptive to the development of spiritual paths.

Var. C.W. St.

PART II
EXPLAINING THE STAGES OF THE PATHS
DEPENDENT ON ULTIMATE TRUTH

Section A: Extensively explaining ultimate truth

Chapter IX

General refutation of true existence by refuting permanent functional phenomena

Chapter X

Individual refutation of truly existent functional phenomena: Refuting the self

Chapter XI

Individual refutation of truly existent functional phenomena: Refuting truly existent time

Chapter XII

Refuting the true existence of that which is viewed

Chapter XIII

Refuting the true existence of sense organs and objects

Chapter XV

Refuting the inherent existence of production, duration and disintegration, the characteristics of products

I. Extensively establishing dependent arisings which are not inherently produced as existing in the manner of a magician's illusions

  A. Specific refutation of inherent production

    1. Extensive explanation

      a. Refutation by examining whether that which exists or does not exist is produced

Section B: Showing how to meditate on settling [the procedure between] spiritual guides and students by way of [explaining] the purpose of the chapters and eliminating remaining counter-arguments by misguided opponents

Chapter XVI

Settling [the Procedure Between] Spiritual Guides and Students by way of [Explaining] the Purpose of the Chapters and Eliminating Remaining Counter-Arguments by Misguided Opponents

Notes

ABBREVIATIONS

Can. Peking edition of Candrakīrti's *Commentary on the "Four Hundred Stanzas on the Yogic Deeds of Bodhisattvas"*, P5266, Vol.98.

D. Can. Candrakīrti's *Commentary on the "Four Hundred Stanzas on the Yogic Deeds of Bodhisattvas"*, No.3865 of the *sDe dge Tibetan Tripiṭaka - bsTan hgyur preserved at the Faculty of Letters, University of Tokyo* (Tokyo: Tokyo University Press, 1977-82).

Bö. bod sprul bstan pa'i nyi ma, *Naga King's Ornament for Thought, Explanation of the "Four Hundred on the Middle Way"* (Varanasi: Pleasure of Elegant Sayings Printing Press, 1987).

Gah. kah thog mkhan po ngag dbang dpal bzang, *Sea Spray, Explanation of the "Four Hundred on the Middle Way"* (Bylakuppe: Nyingmapa Monastery, 1984).

Gyel. rgyal tsab dar ma rin chen, *Essence of Good Explanations* (Varanasi: Pleasure of Elegant Sayings Printing Press, 1971).

Ren. red mda' ba gzhon nu blo gros, *Commentary to Āryadeva's "Four Hundred Verses"* (Varanasi: Pleasure of Elegant Sayings Printing Press, 1974).

Since work on this translation was carried out entirely in Dharamsala, India, most books on Mādhyamika philosophy by modern western scholars were not available. It is therefore not out of a lack of respect or appreciation that no reference is made to these works. On the other hand the writing of Tibetan scholars on this subject was easily accessible and relevant passages which serve to clarify issues arising in Gyel-tsap's commentary have therefore been translated from the works of Dzong-ka-ba and others.

334   *The Yogic Deeds of Bodhisattvas*

Notes to the Introduction

[1]Lama Chimpa and Alaka Chattopadhyaya, trans., *Tāranātha's History of Buddhism in India* (Calcutta: K.P. Bagchi & Company, rpt.1980), pp.123-26. E. Obermiller, *History of Buddhism by Bu-ston* (Heidelberg: Otto Harrassowitz, 1931), pp.130-31.

[2]Tsultrim Kalsang Khangkar, *On the History of the Buddhist Doctrine in India* (Kyoto: Tibetan Buddhist Culture Assoc., 1988), Part II, pp.61-62. *Tibetan Chronicle of Padma dKarpo* (New Delhi: International Academy of Indian Culture, 1968), pp.71-79. mKhan po blo gros bzang po, *Biography of the Six Ornaments and Two Supreme Ones and a Synopsis of their Views (rgyan drug mchog gnyis kyi rnam thar dang lta ba mdor bdus pa)* (Delhi: Jamyang Samten & Trayan, 1979), p.40. *Jewel Garland: Notes on History (chos 'byung zin bris nor bu'i phreng ba)* (Dharamsala: Shes rig par khang, 1970). *Six Ornaments and Two Supreme Ones (rgyan drug mchog gnyis)* (Gangtok: Namgyal Institute of Tibetology, 1962).

[3]Can. 184.1.3.

[4]Gyel. Ch. I, 3.12 ff.

[5]For instance, Acharya Abhayadatta Śrī, *Biography of Eighty-Four Saints*, trans. Acharya Sempa Dorge, Bibliotheca-Indo-Tibetica 4 (Varanasi: Central Institute of Higher Tibetan Studies, 1979), p.85.

[6]*Tāranātha's History*, pp.131-32.

[7]Maheśvara.

[8]Bu ston, *Collected Works* (New Delhi: International Academy of Indian Culture, 1967), Part XXIV, p.834.4.

[9]Chandra Das, *Tibetan-English Dictionary*, p.214, says: "A piece of thick plank measuring about 6 feet by 12 inches either of white sandal wood or deodar, which when struck with a hammer or another piece of thick hard wood, produces a kind of ringing sound which is heard from a great distance. It is used on special occasions to summon the monks of a monastery to attend any special service." It is still used today for the confession rite in the Tibetan tradition.

[10]Some accounts read "sister" (*sring mo*); others read "ogress" (*srin mo*).

[11]According to some versions rotting hide had been placed on Mātṛceṭa's parasol. When he looked up in the hope that Śiva would come, he caught sight of it and at once removed it. This allowed Śiva to enter him, thereby enabling him to continue debating with Āryadeva without suffering defeat for much longer than he could otherwise have done.

[12]*Fundamental Tantra of Mañjuśrī (mañjuśrīmūlatantra, 'jam dpal gyi rtsa ba'i rgyud)*, P162, Vol.6, 259.3.6 ff.

[13]Āryadeva, *Compendium of Quintessential Wisdom (jñānasārasamuccayanāma, ye shes snying po kun las btus pa zhes bya ba)*, P5251, Vol.95. Bodhibhadra, *Explanation of the Compendium of Quintessential Wisdom (jñānasārasamuccaya-nāmanibandhana, ye shes snying po kun las btus pa'i bshad sbyar)*, P5252, Vol.95, 146.3.3.

[14]*Fundamental Tantra of Mañjuśrī*, P162, Vol.6, 266.2.8. The Sanskrit word *ārya* refers to an Exalted one, namely one who has attained direct understanding of emptiness.

[15]See Karen Lang, *Āryadeva's Catuḥśataka, On the Bodhisattva's Cultivation of Merit and Knowledge*, Indiske Studier VII (Copenhagen: Akademisk Forlag, 1986), p.8, for a discussion of Āryadeva's dates.

[16]*Tibetan Tripiṭaka* (Tokyo-Kyoto: Tibetan Tripiṭaka Research Foundation, 1956).

[17]*Śataka* (Taisho 1569).

[18]*akṣaraśataka, yi ge brgya pa*, P5234, Vol.95.

[19]*caryāmelāpakapradīpa, spyod pa bsdus pa'i sgron ma*, P2668, Vol.61.

[20]The late Professor J. Upadyaya, founder of the Institute of Higher Tibetan Studies, Sarnath, and director of the Rare Buddhist Manuscripts Project, discovered a version in Newari of *The Hundred on the Essence Facilitating Understanding (pratipattisāraśataka, go bar byed pa snying po brgya pa*, P4695, Vol.82), which is attributed to Āryadeva. On account of certain stylistic similarities with *The Four Hundred*, he was prepared to attribute it to Āryadeva. It is a Vajrayāna work dealing with the wisdom of bliss and emptiness in the context of the Hevajra Tantra. The expression of worship is made to Heruka.

[21]For a list of the topics covered by the translated portion of *The Hundred* and how they correspond to those treated in the second half of *The Four Hundred* and for further correlations, see Lang, *Āryadeva's Catuḥśataka*, Introduction, pp.11-13. For a translation into English of *The Hundred*, see G. Tucci, *Pre-Diṅnāga Buddhist Texts on Logic from Chinese Sources* (Madras: Vesta Publications, 1984).

[22]Can. 184.1.5 ff. Gyel-tsap cites this passage in his preface and discusses it.

[23]*Clear Words, Commentary on the "Treatise on the Middle Way" (mūlamadhyamakavṛttiprasannapadā, dbu ma rtsa ba'i 'grel pa tshig gsal ba)*, P5260, Vol.98, 92.2.3.

[24]T.R.V. Murti, *The Central Philosophy of Buddhism* (London: Unwin Paperbacks, 1980), p.93, expresses the opinion that *The Hundred* is a rearranged version of *The Four Hundred*. He suggests that Āryadeva wrote *The Four Hundred* first, then *The Hundred* and then *The Hundred Syllables*.

[25]See V.V. Gokhale's translation, *Akṣara-śatakam, The Hundred Letters* (Heidelberg: 1930).

[26]The following is drawn from Jik-may-dam-chö-gya-tso's (*'jigs med dam chos rgya mtsho*, 1898-1946) *Gateway to (Dzong-ka-ba's) "Essence of Good Explanations" (drang nges legs bshad snying po'i 'jug ngogs)* (Dharamsala: Shes rig par khang, 1988), Part II, fol. 30a-b.

[27]Gyel. Ch. I, 7.15 ff.

[28]Can. 183.4.5

[29]Gyel. Ch. I, 17.16 ff.

[30] *Supplement to (Nāgārjuna's)* "Treatise on the Middle Way" *(madhyam-akāvatāra, dbu ma la 'jug pa),* P5261, P5262, Vol.98, 100.2.5 ff.

[31]Can. 194.4.7 ff.

[32]George N. Roerich, *Blue Annals* (Delhi: Motilal Banarsidass, 1976), p.341.

[33]See Karen Lang's "sPa tshab Nyi ma grags and the Introduction of Prāsaṅgika Madhyamaka into Tibet," in *Reflections on Tibetan Culture: Essays in Memory of Turrell V. Wylie,* edited by Lawrence Epstein and Richard Sherburne (Lewiston, NY: Edwin Mellen Press, 1990), pp.13-14.

[34]*yuktiṣaṣṭikākarikā, rigs pa drug cu pa'i tshig le'ur byas pa,* P5225, Vol.95, translated with Muditasri.

[35]*prajñānāmamūlamadhyamakakārikā, dbu ma rtsa ba'i tshig le'ur byas pa shes rab ces bya ba,* P5224, Vol.95, revised with Hasumati.

[36]*rājaparikathāratnāvalī, rgyal po la gtam bya ba rin po che'i phreng ba,* P5658, Vol.129, revised with Kanakavarman.

[37]*madyamakāvatāra, dbu ma la 'jug pa,* P5261, P5262, Vol.98.

[38]*madhyamakāvatārabhāṣya, dbu ma la 'jug pa'i bshad pa,* P5263, Vol.98.

[39]*mūlamadhyamakavṛttiprasannapadā, dbu ma rtsa ba'i 'grel pa tshig gsal ba,* P5260, Vol.98.

[40]He is also known as Shar-wa-ba *(shar ba pa). The Blue Annals* gives his name in this form.

[41]Tang-ba Sar-bo *(gtang pa sar sbos),* Ma-ja Jang-chup-dzon-dru *(rma bya byang chub brtson 'grus),* Ngar Yon-ten-drak *(ngar yon tan grags),* Tang-sak-ba *(thang sag pa).*

[42]*Twenty Rituals of the Guhyasamāja Mandala (śrīguhyasamājamaṇḍalo-pāyikāvimśatividhi, dpal gsang ba 'dus pa'i dkyil 'khor gyi cho ga nyi shu pa),* P2675, Vol.62.

[43]*Following Definitions, an Explanation of the Commentary on the* "Treasury of Knowledge *(abhidharmakoṣaṭīkālakṣaṇānusāriṇī, chos mngon pa'i mdzod kyi 'grel bshad mtshan nyid kyi rjes su 'brang ba),* P5594, Vol.117.

[44]*bodhicittavivaraṇa, byang chub sems kyi 'grel pa,* P2665, P2666, Vol.61.

[45]*mahāsūtrasamuccaya, mdo kun las btus pa chen po,* P5358, Vol.103.

[46]Can. 183.5.7 - 184.1.5.

[47]Can. 184.2.4. *Tāranātha's History of Buddhism in India,* p.186, says, "Born in Bhaṅgala in the east, he [Dharmadāsa] was a disciple of Asaṅga and his brother. He went round the countries all around and built in each direction a temple of Ārya Mañjuśrī. He is said to have prepared a commentary on the entire *yogacaryā-bhūmi."*

[48]*dbu ma bzhi brgya pa'i 'grel pa* (Varanasi: Pleasure of Elegant Sayings Printing Press, 1974), abbreviated hereafter as Ren.

[49]Ren. 156.14 ff.

[50]*dbu ma bzhi brgya pa'i rnam bshad klu dbang dgongs rgyan* (Varanasi: Pleasure of Elegant Sayings Printing Press, 1987), abbreviated hereafter as Bö.

[51]Bö. 65, commentary on stanza 136 (chapter VII).

[52]Bö. 85.19 ff., commentary on stanza 190 (chapter VIII).

[53]Bö. 81-82, commentary on stanzas 178 and 179 (chapter VIII).

[54]Bö. 90.11, commentary on stanza 191 (chapter VIII).

[55]Commentary on stanza 191 (chapter VIII).

[56]Bö. 70, commentary on stanza 150.

[57]*dbu ma bzhi brgya pa'i rnam par bshad pa rgya mtsho'i zeg ma* (Bylakuppe, India: Nyingmapa Monastery, 1984), abbreviated hereafter as Gah.

[58]Gah. 246.

[59]Gah. 258 ff.

[60]Gah. 397.

[61]Gah. 518-519.

[62]*bstan bcos bzhi brgya pa zhes bya ba'i tshig le'ur byas pa'i mchan 'grel*, Vol. 6 of *gzhung chen bcu gsum gyi mchan 'grel* (Dehra Dun: Nyingmapa Lamas' College, 1978).

[63]*byang chub sems dpa'i spyod pa la 'jug pa'i rnam bshad rgyal sras 'jug ngogs* (Varanasi: Pleasure of Elegant Sayings Printing Press, 1973), p.280.6 ff.

Notes to Prologue, Preface and Chapter One

[1]This stanza of the prologue incorporates the names of Ren-da-wa (*red mda ba gzhon nu blo gros*, 1349-1412) and of Dzong-ka-ba (*tsong kha pa blo bzang grags pa*, 1357-1419) by including the words *gzhon nu blo gros* and *blo bzang grags pa*. The device of weaving a name into the text is frequently found in prayers recited for the long life of a spiritual teacher.

[2]*shing rta chen po*, literally "great chariots," because they broke new ground and opened the way for others to follow.

[3]*bstan bcos*. Fol. 59a 1, Vol. *ka* of the first part of *General Meaning (spyi don)/ Ocean of Enjoyment (legs bshad skal bzang klu dbang gi rol mtsho)* (Buxaduor: Nang bstan shes rig 'dzin skyong slob gnyer khang, ca. 1963), the text book of Se-ra Jay (*se rva byes*) College of Se-ra (*se rva*) Monastery by Jay-dzun-ba (*rje btsun chos kyi rgyal mtshan*, 1469-1546), clarifying difficult points in the commentaries on the *Ornament for Clear Realization*, defines *bstan bcos* as "pure speech possessing the two qualities of correcting and protecting" (*'chos skyob kyi yon ten gnyis dang ldan pai ngag rnam dag*). Further explanation (fol. 60a, 7 ff.) says, "qualities of correcting and protecting in that it corrects the trainee's mind of disturbing emotions, the enemy, and protects from the suffering of cyclic existence and bad transmigrations" (*gdul bya'i shes rgyud nyon mongs pa'i dgra las 'chos shing 'kor ba dang ngan song gi sdug bsngal skyob par byed pa'i 'chos skyob kyi yon ten*). The text quotes Vasubandhu's description in *Science of Exegesis (vyākhyāyukti, rnam bar bshad pa'i rigs pa*, P5562, Vol. 113), "that which cor-

rects the enemy, all disturbing emotions without exception, and protects from
existence in bad transmigrations is a [Buddhist] treatise, because of the qualities of correcting and protecting" *(nyon mongs dgra rnams ma lus 'chos pa dang /
ngan 'gro'i srid las skyob byed gang yin pa / 'chos skyob yon ten phyir na bstan bcos
te)*.

[4]The custom of inserting a translator's homage at the beginning of the text
was instituted by the great religious kings of Tibet to facilitate identification of
its subject matter. The three categories under which texts were classified are
knowledge, sūtra and discipline. Since texts belonging to the category of knowledge deal primarily with training in wisdom, the homage is made to Mañjuśrī,
the deity embodying perfect wisdom. Texts belonging to the sūtra category deal
primarily with training in meditative stabilization. Since Buddhas and
Bodhisattvas are its foremost practitioners, homage is made to them. Texts
belonging to the category of discipline are mainly about karma, i.e. actions and
their effects, and since only an omniscient mind can know all its subtleties,
homage is made to the Omniscient Ones.

[5]*dmigs pa.*

[6]*klu sgrub*, first to second century C.E. For a short traditional biography, see
Jeffrey Hopkins, *Meditation on Emptiness* (London: Wisdom Publications, 1983),
pp. 356-59.

[7]Can. 184.1.2 ff.

[8]*caryāmelāpakapradīpa (spyod pa bsdus pa'i sgron ma)*, P2668, Vol. 61, 361.4.55
ff., says, "Birth is known as conventional truth / And that named death as ultimate truth. / I, who have attained these two stages / Through the master's kindness, am a future Buddha." In tantra the arising of the illusory body is associated with appearances, i.e. conventional truths. The clear light is associated with
emptiness, i.e. ultimate truth.

[9]Although Gyel. Ch. I, 4.5 names this text as *ye shes rdo rje kun las btus pa'i
'grel pa*, it must refer to Bodhibhadra's commentary on Āryadeva's *Compendium
of Quintessential Wisdom (jñānasārasamuccayanāma, ye shes snying po kun las btus
pa)*, P5251, Vol. 95. Commenting on Āryadeva's name in his *Explanation of the
"Compendium of Quintessential Wisdom" (jñānasārasamuccayanāmanibandhana,
ye shes snying po kun las btus pa'i bshad sbyar)*, P5252, Vol. 95, 146.3.3,
Bodhibhadra says that he is called "Ārya" because of having attained the eighth
Bodhisattva ground, the Immovable, and "deva" because of being very beautiful like a god.

[10]*chos skyong*: Lama Chimpa and Alaka Chattopadhyaya's translation of
Tāranātha's History of Buddhism in India (Calcutta: Bagchi, 1970), p.197, mentions that Candrakīrti and Dharmapāla were contemporaries. P.213 says,
"[Dharmapāla] received ordination under Ācārya Dharmadāsa and listened to
Vinaya from him. ... He preached the Doctrine at Vajrāsana, for over thirty years
and succeeded Śrī Candrakīrti as the upādhyāya of Śrī Nalendra. ... He composed a commentary on the *Madhyamakacatuhśatikā* from the Vijñānavada
standpoint. This commentary was composed at Vajrāsana and was clearly
enough earlier than Candrakīrti's *Catuhśatakatīkā*." This account also mentions

that he was renowned as a bard, which accounts for the appellation *snyan dngags mkhan*.

[11]*rnam rigs pa*, also *sems tsam pa*, Cittamātra.

[12]Can. 184.1.4 ff. states that because Āryadeva was Nāgārjuna's close disciple, "the suchness [explained] in the *Treatise of Four Hundred* does not have a different character from that explained in the *Treatise on the Middle Way*."

[13]This refers to Buddhist and non-Buddhist contentions.

[14]Can. 183.4.6.

[15]*smon sems*.

[16]*'jug sems*. Gyel-tsap's *Gateway for Conqueror Children, Explanation of Engaging in the Bodhisattva Deeds (byang chub sems dpa'i spyod pa la 'jug pa'i rnam bshad rgyal sras 'jug ngogs)* (Varanasi: Pleasure of Elegant Sayings Printing Press, 1973), p.16.19 ff., says, "While the intention of going to a particular place is the same, the difference [between the aspiration and implementation] lies in whether that intention is accompanied by the action of going or not. The wise understand that the difference between the aspiring and practical altruistic intention is like this. The intention to attain Buddhahood for the sake of others is the same, but the one does not depend upon being accompanied by practice of the six perfections, such as giving, while the other does."

[17]*nyon sgrib*, obstructions preventing liberation.

[18]*shes sgrib*, obstructions preventing the omniscient state in which a single awareness directly cognizes the two truths simultaneously.

[19]*'phags lam*. When the paths of the Exalted, beginning with the path of seeing, are attained, the end of cyclic existence is in sight and no further actions are created under the influence of ignorance. A Bodhisattva who has reached the path of seeing of the Great Vehicle is no longer subject to involuntary death brought about by contaminated actions and disturbing attitudes and emotions. Vasubandhu's *Treasury of Knowledge (abhidharmakośakārikā, chos mngon pa'i mdzod kyi tshig le'ur byas pa*, P5590, Vol.115) says, "for one who has seen the truth there is no projecting [activity]" *(bden pa mthong la 'phen pa med)*. Maitreya's *Sublime Continuum of the Great Vehicle (mahāyānottaratantraśāstra, theg pa chen po rgyud bla ma'i bstan bcos*, P5525, Vol.108) says, "The Exalted have completely eliminated / Suffering of aging, sickness and death" *('phags pas rga dang na ba dang / 'chi ba'i sdug bsngal rtsad nas spangs)*.

[20]*dal 'byor*, the condition of not merely being human, but enjoying certain freedoms and conducive circumstances which allow one to practise. The majority of human beings are not in the fortunate situation of enjoying all the eighteen features which constitute a human rebirth of leisure and fortune.

[21]*kun tu rgu mo*, an itinerant female ascetic.

[22]Nāgārjuna and the Seventh Dalai Lama, *Precious Garland and the Four Mindfulnesses* (London: George Allen & Unwin, 1975), trans. Jeffrey Hopkins, p.58, stanza 278.

[23]*bcud len*. According to Dr. Losang Tenzin of the Tibetan Medical Institute, Dharamsala, India, the preparation and administration of essential nutrients

is described in the medical tantras. The purpose of taking these nutrients is to restore and preserve physical vitality and postpone the effects of aging. Maintaining physical strength and not permitting it to decline results in longevity. Different kinds of essential nutrients exist such as essential mineral extracts, flower extracts and meat extracts.

[24]Gyel-tsap here refers to Can. 185.4.5 ff.

[25]The citation of Āryadeva's text in Can. 186.1.7 ff. reads, "What wise person would call loving ...?" *(byams zhes mkhas pa su zhig smra),* to which Gyel-tsap refers here.

[26]Can. 186.3.3 ff.

[27]Can. 186.3.8 - 186.4.2.

[28]Can. 186.4.1 ff.

[29]Ren. 12.10-11.

[30]Can. 187.4.2.

[31]A concreted resinous gum, with a strong alliaceous odor procured from *Narthex asafoetida,* used in cookery and as an antispasmodic medicine. *(Oxford English Dictionary).*

[32]Can. 187.4.4 ff.

[33]Can. 187.5.4.

[34]Can. 188.5.4 ff.

[35]Can. 189.3.1 ff.

[36]Ibid.

[37]Can. 189.3.8 - 189.4.1.

[38]Ibid. *nges legs,* "definite goodness," refers to liberation.

[39]The text cited in Can. 189.3.5 says, "whoever certainly has" *(gang la nges par yod gyur pa).*

[40]*dge shes po to ba,* 1027-1105, one of the foremost masters of the Ga-dam-ba *(bka' gdams pa)* tradition.

Notes to Chapter Two

[1]Can. 189.5.2 ff.

[2]Can. 190.3.6.

[3]Can. 190.5.2.

[4]Can. 190.5.8 - 191.1.1.

[5]Can. 191.3.7 ff.

[6]Can. 192.3.3.

[7]Ren. 14.15. All further interpolations in the commentary to stanza 41 are from Can. 192.4.5 ff.

[8]Gyel-tsap's interpretation seems at variance with Candrakīrti's, but since the former's commentary is very terse at this point, it is difficult to determine what he means by *gnod byed kyi brlag bzhin pa ni*. Candrakīrti (193.1.3 ff.) says that clothing, soft seats, cooling sandalwood paste and so forth are used to alleviate and prevent suffering and not for pleasure. If they were innate causes of pleasure, they should always produce it, but they do not. Thus antidotes to suffering and decreased suffering are mistaken for pleasure. He makes the point that the process of overcoming suffering by means of antidotes should not be mistaken for pleasure. Accordingly *gnod byed kyi brlag bzhin pa ni*, words which do not appear in Candrakīrti's commentary, would refer to the process of overcoming suffering by that which counteracts it.

[9]Can. 193.1.6 ff.

[10]Can. 193.2.2 ff.

[11]Can. 193.2.4 ff.

[12]*rtags kyi dgag bya'i chos* refers to inherent existence.

[13]Can. 193.4.8

[14]*ka ta ya na la gdams pa'i mdo* is part of the *Topics of Detailed Discipline Sūtra* (*vinayaksudrakavastusūtra, 'dul ba phran tshegs kyi gzhi*, also known as *lung gzhi*), P1035, Vol. 44, 108.5.6 ff.

[15]*dga' bo mngal 'jug* is also part of the above-mentioned sūtra (50.2.3 - 60.5.6) and describes the suffering of birth, etc. in detail.

[16]Can. 194.2.4 ff.

[17]Gyel-tsap (Ch. II, 15.19) uses the plural *de bzhin gshegs pa rnams*, but follows it with a very specifically addressed statement. Candrakīrti (194.3.2) uses the singular, "the Supramundane Victor" (*bcom ldan 'das*), to refer to the one who has made the statement. Ren. 27.12 ff. quotes it and does not make a specific attribution, but follows it with the words, "the Tathāgatas have said confusion is the worst of all obstructions" (*de bzhin gshegs pa rnams kyis gti mug sgrib pa kun gyi tha mar gsungs so*).

[18]*chos mgon pa'i bstan bcos*, referring to *rnam pa sde bdun* (see below), are not accepted by Sautrāntikas as the Buddha's words.

[19]Vasubandhu's *Treasury of Knowledge*, P5590, Vol.115, 117.2.3.

[20]Ibid. 124.1.8. The order of the lines is not as quoted. The last two lines quoted stand before the first two in Vasubandhu's text, i.e. *yid 'ong yid du mi 'ong dang / de las gshen zag bcas rnams nyid / sdug bsngal nyid gsum ldan pa'i phyir / ci rigs ma lus sdug bsngal lo.*

[21]*rnam pa sde bdun*: Chim-jam-bay-yang (*chim 'jam pa'i dbyangs*, twelfth century), in his *Commentary on the Treasury of Knowledge (chos mngon mdzod kyi tshig le'ur byas pa'i 'grel pa mngon pa'i rgyen)* (Buxaduor: Nang bstan shes rig 'dzin skyong slob gnyer khang; no date), 11a, 4, lists the seven as: *ye shes la 'jug ka tya'i bus / rab tu byed pa dbyig bshes kyis / rnam shes tsogs ni lha skyid kyis / chos kyi phung po sha' ri'i bus / gdags pa'i bstan bcos mo'u gal bus / 'gros ba'i rnam grangs gsus po ches / khams kyi tsogs ni gang pos byas*—*Engaging in Exalted Wisdom (jñānaprasthāna)* by Kātyāyana; *Classification (prakaraṇapāda)* by Vasumitra;

Collection of Consciousnesses (vijñānakāya) by Devaśarman; *Aggregate of Phenomena (dharmaskandha)* by Śāriputra; *Treatise of Attributions (prajñāptiśāstra)* by Maudgalyāyana; *Enumeration of Transmigrators (saṃgītiparyāpa)* by Mahākausthila; *Collection of Constituents (dhātukāya)* by Pūrṇa. Thus he attributes authorship of these texts to Foe Destroyers, but some Sautrāntikas do not accept even this.

[22]*Explanation of the "Treasury of Knowledge" (abhidharmakośabhāṣya, chos mgon pa'i mdzod kyi bshad pa,* P5591, Vol.115), 242.3.2 ff.

[23]Can. 195.3.4 ff.

[24]*samādhirajasūtra, ting nge 'dzin rgyal po'i mdo,* P795, Vol.31, 283.4.7 ff.

Notes to Chapter Three

[1]Can. 197.3.2.

[2]Ren. 30.11.

[3]Ren. 30.16.

[4]Can. 197.3.8.

[5]Can. 197.4.1 ff.

[6]Regarding the emphasis on women's bodies throughout this chapter, see the introduction, page 32-33.

[7]Can. 198.1.2 ff.

[8]Ibid.

[9]Ren. 31.11 ff.

[10]Can. 198.2.2 ff.

[11]Can. 198.5.7 - 199.1.2.

[12]Bö. 32.12.

[13]Can. 199.3.8.

[14]Can. 199.5.3.

[15]Can. 199.5.7 ff.

[16]Ren. 35.1 ff.

[17]Ibid.

[18]Can. 200.2.2 ff.

[19]Bö. 30.14.

[20]Can. 200.5.2.

[21]Ren. 37.1 ff.

[22]Gyel-tsap comments on the version of Āryadeva's text which reads, "when all except people" *(mi rnams ma gtogs).* Both Can. 204.1.4 and D.Can 36.23 read "people do not realize" *(mi rnams ma rtogs).* Candrakīrti says, "How would anyone sensible consider clean that from which a mass of filth constantly is-

sues," implying that all, except those not in their right mind, would find it objectionable, since he adds, "Therefore, it is wrong to say that women's bodies are not objectionable." Gyel-tsap cites Ren-da-wa's interpretation, which he finds does not accord with Candrakīrti's.

[23]Can. 201.1.6 ff.

[24]Can. 201.3.3.

[25]Ren. 38.6.

[26]Ren. 38.6 ff.

[27]Chandra Das, *Tibetan-English Dictionary* (Delhi: Motilal Banarsidass, 1976 reprint of 1902 edition), p.777 under the entry *pa la sha* notes that this tree is *Butea frondosa;* p.1226, under the entry *sha 'gugs*, reads "lit. curled flesh or body [the flower of the tree *Butea frondosa*]."

[28]Can. 202.1.3 ff.

[29]There seems to have been a fashion in artificial noses in the past. Tycho Brahe (1546-1601), a Danish astronomer, is said to have had a golden fake nose, the original having been lost in a student duel.

[30]Ren. 39.1 ff.

[31]Can. 202.2.8 ff.

[32]Ren. 39.10 ff.

[33]Can. 202.4.1 ff.

[34]Ren. 40.1.

[35]Can. 202.5.2.

Notes to Chapter Four

[1]Can. 203.1.6 ff.

[2]Can. 203.2.5 ff.

[3]Can. 203.5.3 ff.

[4]*skye rgu / skye dgu* also can mean "all beings" *(skye bo kun)*. It may refer to those with five aggregates and four elements, thus excluding those who belong to the Formless Realm. It may also refer to nine kinds of beings: those born into the Desire Realm from the Desire, Form and Formless Realms; those born into the Form Realm from the Desire, Form and Formless Realms; and those born into the Formless Realm from the Desire, Form and Formless Realms.

[5]*snyigs ma lnga:* (1) Degenerate times, *dus snyigs ma*. First there was a time of fullness without killing, stealing, sexual misconduct and strife. A gradual deterioration then occurred. The era in which the Buddha Śākyamuni came to this world and in which we live today is known as a time of strife *(rtsod dus)*, in which war, famine, epidemics, droughts, floods and other calamities abound. (2) Degenerate beings, *sems can snyigs ma*. Those who were easy to teach and

guide because of their maturity and receptivity have gained realizations and are on the way to or have already attained liberation. The majority of those who live now are obstinate and difficult to guide. (3) Degenerate life span, *tshe snyigs ma*. Originally beings had extremely long lives. A gradual decrease in life span has occurred and now people rarely live for much more than eighty years. Untimely death is frequent. (4) Degenerate disturbing attitudes, *nyon mongs snyigs ma*. These are present in a crude form, leading to many unwholesome physical, verbal and mental activities. (5) Degenerate views, *lta ba snyigs ma*. Harmful and misleading views are prevalent and views such as the correct understanding of reality and of the connection between actions and their effects are unpopular.

[6]Can. 204.1.4.

[7]Can. 204.3.2 ff.

[8]Ren. 44.3.

[9]Can. 204.4.5.

[10]Can. 204.4.6.

[11]Gyel-tsap uses a version of the text which employs a double negative: *rgyu ni gang du med mi 'gyur* (see the first line of the stanza). The version of the text cited in Can. 204.5.1 reads *rgyu ni gang du yod min 'gyur*.

[12]Can. 205.1.2 ff.

[13]Can. 205.3.3 ff.

[14]Can. 205.4.6 ff.

[15]Can. 206.3.2 ff.

[16]Can. 206.3.8 ff.

[17]Can. 206.4.3 - 207.1.6.

[18]Āryadeva's text reads *ma btang*, past tense. Gyel. Ch.IV, 11.12 introduces *mi gtong*, present and future tenses.

[19]Can. 207.2.6; Can. 208.1.3.

[20]The third chapter of Vasubandhu's *Explanation of the "Treasury of Knowledge"* (abhidharmakośabhāṣya, chos mngon pa'i mdzod kyi bshad pa, P5591, Vol.115) contains a description of this devolution.

[21]Can. 208.1.3.

[22]Can. 208.2.1 ff.

[23]Can. 208.4.7 ff.

[24]Can. 208.5.6 ff.

Notes to Chapter Five

[1]Any activity, virtuous or non-virtuous, is performed through one or more of the three doors: body, speech, and mind.

[2]P795, Vol.31, 289.2.3 ff.

[3]Ibid., 287.3.3 ff.

[4]For a list of the thirty-two major and eighty minor marks of a Buddha's supreme Emanation Body, see chapter VIII of Maitreya's *Ornament for Clear Realization (abhisamayālamkāra, mngon par rtogs pa'i rgyan,* P5184, Vol. 88). For the causes which give rise to the thirty-two major marks, similitudes of which are also said to adorn universal monarchs, see *The Precious Garland* (trans. Jeffrey Hopkins and Lati Rinbochay with Anne Klein; New York: Harper and Row, 1975), stanzas 176-196, pp.43-46.

[5]Can. 209.3.7 ff.

[6]Hearer Vehicle, Solitary Realizer Vehicle and Great Vehicle. Extensive discussion of the three vehicles can be found in Hopkins, *Meditation on Emptiness* (London: Wisdom Publications, 1983).

[7]Can. 209.5.2 ff.

[8]A rabbit's horn does not exist, thus discussion about its size is irrelevant. Similarly, since there is no truly existent self, discussion as to whether such a self is impermanent or permanent is not apposite.

[9]*The Precious Garland,* stanzas 73-74, based on Hopkins' translation, p.27.

[10]Can. 210.4.1 ff.

[11]The Buddha prescribed that monks should wear robes made of small pieces of cloth stitched together. This was intended to counter attachment to clothing. The Buddha's cousin Devadatta, who failed to recognize his extraordinary qualities, habitually did the opposite of what the Buddha recommended to express his dissent. The "bait" refers to Devadatta's ill deeds, such as causing schism in the spiritual community, which would bring him suffering in the future.

[12]Ren. 55.7 ff.

[13]Although Āryadeva's text reads "without cognition" *(sems ma rtogs par),* referring here to the intention, both Gyel-tsap and Ren-da-wa use "except for the intention" *(sems ma gtogs par).* Thus Ren. 55.8 ff. reads, "Unless established as a virtuous or ill deed through the motivation of the mind, actions such as coming, going, standing or walking are not in themselves seen as meritorious or demeritorious."

[14]*gcer bu pa.* At times this refers to a Nirgrantha (Jaina) ascetic, whose nakedness is intended to symbolize non-attachment and the total renunciation of possessions.

[15]Can. 210.5.5 ff. says, "Such faults arise for those according to whom merit [and its converse] may be gained without mental cognition and without mind [i.e. intention]. Thus meritorious action and so forth cannot be posited without mental cognition." In both Candrakīrti's and Gyel-tsap's commentaries the naked ascetic's intentions are not mentioned. Gyel-tsap's conclusion that he created both virtuous and non-virtuous karma seems to contradict Candrakīrti's emphasis on the importance of motivation in determining the nature of actions.

346 The Yogic Deeds of Bodhisattvas

[16]Can. 211.1.6 ff.

[17]This is a frequently cited story about the Buddha Śākyamuni in a former life.

[18]Attainment of the Mahāyāna path of seeing is simultaneous with the attainment of the first of the ten Bodhisattva grounds, each of which is conjoined with the altruistic intention, dedication (bsngo ba), and direct realization of emptiness. The ten perfections—giving, ethics, patience, effort, concentration, wisdom, method, aspiration, power, and exalted wisdom—are practised on every ground, but on each ground one of the perfections is developed completely. Thus on the first ground the emphasis is on the complete development of giving.

[19]Can. 211.5.4 ff.

[20]stong gsum gyi stong chen po 'jig rten gyi khams. From this world to the Brahma Abode of the Form Realm is counted as one world system. A thousand such world systems constitute the first set of a thousand. A thousand of the first set constitute the second set of a thousand and a thousand of the second set constitutes the third, the great thousand world systems, consisting of three sets of thousands, i.e. 10 to the ninth power world systems. The term bye ba phrag brgya also refers to this number—bye ba being 10 to the seventh power; phrag brgya, a hundred times. The three thousand great thousand world systems are referred to in the third chapter of Vasubandhu's Treasury of Knowledge.

[21]'og min here refers to the highest of the seventeen abodes of the Form Realm and is thus a state within cyclic existence. It can also refer to one's own pure land produced by limitless stores of merit and wisdom, in which one attains enlightenment.

[22]rin po che sna bdun. One version gives ruby, sapphire, emerald, diamond, pearl, coral and lapis lazuli. Another gives lapis lazuli, gold, silver, crystal, red pearl, the essence of stone (rdo'i snying po) and a substance referred to as spug. According to Dr. Losang Tenzin of the Tibetan Medical Institute, Dharamsala, India, spug refers to a kind of gold obtained from animal horns. An indication of its presence is that the horns glow at night. Dr. Dorje Gyalpo, also of the Tibetan Medical Institute, describes the essence of stone as ice which has petrified under perpetual snow to form "water crystal." When placed in water, the crystal is said to be indistinguishable from the water. Traditionally these substances were used in the preparation of Tibetan medicines and are described in the medical tantras. Bai dur ya, mostly translated as lapis lazuli, may refer to beryl, which the Oxford English Dictionary describes as "a transparent precious stone of pale green color passing into light blue, yellow and white." The medical tantras speak of three kinds of bai dur ya: blue, yellow and white. Only blue lapis lazuli is known, the word "lazuli" being derived from the Persian word meaning "azure."

[23]Ren. 58.18 ff.

[24]Aśvaghoṣa's Buddhakarita, Book XVII, stanza 8 in Buddhist Mahāyāna Texts, edited by E.B. Cowell (New York: Dover Publications, 1969).

[25]Ren. 59.13 ff.

[26]Ibid.

[27]Can. 212.4.8 ff.

[28]Can. 213.1.2 ff.

[29]*bsdu ba'i dngos po bzhi.* These four skillful means are employed to gain others' trust and to make others become mentally mature and receptive to increasingly profound teaching. The first is giving (*sbyin pa*). Since most ordinary people are attracted by material generosity, Bodhisattvas first give gifts and act generously towards those they intend to help, in order to establish a positive relationship. When a suitable occasion arises they teach in an informal, interesting and pleasant way (*snyan par smra ba*) adapted to the other person's capacities and inclinations. They then encourage the person to apply in practice (*don spyod pa*) what was explained. At the same time Bodhisattvas must conduct themselves accordingly (*don thun pa*) to validate the advice through their personal example.

[30]*phung po lhag ma med pa'i mya ngan las 'das pa'i mthar thug pa.* The final state of nirvāṇa here refers to Buddhahood which is known as non-abiding nirvāṇa (*mi gnas pa'i myang 'das*), constituting separation from obstructions to liberation and omniscience, and not abiding in the extremes of worldly existence or solitary peace. In this context the term "without remainder" can be taken to refer to the two Truth Bodies of a Buddha—the Wisdom Truth Body and the Nature Body. The term "with remainder" then refers to the two Form Bodies—the Enjoyment Body and the Emanation Body. For further explanation of what is meant by nirvāṇa with and without remainder in the different Buddhist systems of tenets, see Geshe Lhundup Sopa and Jeffrey Hopkins, *Practice and Theory in Tibetan Buddhism* (London: Rider and Co., 1976), p.142; revised edition, Geshe Lhundup Sopa and Jeffrey Hopkins, *Cutting Through Appearances* (Ithaca: Snow Lion Publications, 1989), p. 316 ff.

[31]*praśāntaviniścayaprātihāryasāmadhisūtra, rab tu zhi ba rnam par nges pa cho 'phrul gyi mdo,* P797, Vol.32.

[32]*śraddhābalādhānāvataramudrasūtra, dad pa'i stobs bskyed pa la 'jug pa phyag rgya'i mdo,* P867, Vol.34.

[33]Can. 214.1.6 ff.

[34]*ar ka me tog;* in Sanskrit, *surjavarta* or *arkapuśpika.* Its botanical name is *Gyandropsis gynandra* or *pentaphylla.* According to information from the Royal Botanic Gardens, Kew, England, this is an annual found throughout much of the tropics, called "bastard mustard" in English works and "spider wisp" in American ones. Since this plant is mentioned as an unsuitable offering in some texts, it is probably unpalatable or malodorous.

[35]Can. 214.2.1 ff.

[36]*bzod pa thob.* It is not quite clear to what this refers. Bodhisattvas, once they have attained the first ground, have no fear of emptiness and thus have gained forbearance or tolerance with regard to it. They also have the ability to take any rebirth they wish and will never again be born in cyclic existence through the force of contaminated actions and disturbing attitudes. Bodhisattvas on the forbearance stage of the path of preparation have certainty that they will never

again be born in a bad transmigration but do not yet have the complete control which ensures they can take rebirth as they wish.

[37]*mngon shes nga.* By attaining the divine ear (*lha'i rna ba*) it is possible to perceive the most subtle sounds of the universe. By accomplishing the divine eye (*lha'i mig*) it is possible to perceive the most subtle forms in the universe. Knowledge of others' minds (*gshan gyi sems shes pa*) means one can, for instance, tell which disturbing emotions affect a particular person most. Memory of former abodes (*sngon gyi gnas dran pa*) refers to the ability to remember one's own and others' past lives. Super-knowledge of miraculous feats (*rdzu 'phrul gyi mngon shes*) refers to the ability to perform miraculous feats like shaking the ground, making one become many and many become one.

[38]Can. 214.4.4 ff.

[39]Can. 214.3.2 ff.

[40]Can. 215.1.6 ff.

[41]Can. 215.2.1 ff. mentions the Sanskrit verbal roots *do*, to cut or divide, in relation to death; *da*, to give, in relation to practices such as giving; *de*, to guard; and *da*, to purify, in relation to safeguarding body, speech and mind.

[42]Giving the teaching (*chos kyi sbyin pa*), giving fearlessness (*mi 'jigs pa'i sbyin pa*), giving material things (*zang zing gi sbyin pa*). According to Gah. p.182, the first is associated with concentration and wisdom, the second with ethical conduct and patience and the third with generosity in the most common sense. Effort is associated with all three.

[43]Can. 215.3.5 ff.

[44]Can. 215.5.2.

[45]*spyod pa ba*, who believe that only the words of the Vedas are true and that the words of persons are always false. See *Practice and Theory of Tibetan Buddhism*, p. 62 or *Cutting Through Appearances*, p.166; also Radhakrishnan, *Indian Philosophy* (George Allen & Unwin; reprint in India: Bombay: Blackie & Son Pvt. Ltd., 1977), Vol.2, pp.375-429.

[46]*rtsod gzhi*, basis of debate.

[47]*bsgrub bya'i chos.*

[48]The similarity lies in the fact that the pot and woollen cloth are unrelated.

[49]*rtags.*

[50]*dam bca'.*

[51]*srid rtse*, the highest abode of the Formless Realm and thus of all the abodes within cyclic existence.

[52]Before a world system comes into existence there are twenty intermediate aeons (*bar bskal*) of vacuity, followed by twenty during which the world system is forming. It then lasts for twenty and disintegrates for twenty. Eighty such intermediate aeons form a great aeon (*bskal pa chen po*). When counting in sequence 1, 10, 100, 1000, 10,000, 100,000, etc. the sixty-first number is referred to as "countless" (*grangs med*). Asanga's *Bodhisattva Grounds* (*yogacaryā-bhūmaubodhisattvabhumi, rnal 'byor spyod pa'i sa las byang chub sems dpa'i sa,*

P5538, Vol.110) explains that when the term "three countless aeons" is used regarding the length of time spent accumulating merit for the attainment of enlightenment, it refers to a finite number of great aeons as described above. When the words "many countless aeons" are used, countless means that we cannot count the years, months and days involved. For the names of the sixty numerals, see Chandra Das, *Tibetan-English Dictionary*, p.241.

[53]Can. 216.4.6.

[54]Can.216.5.8 - 217.1.5.

Notes to Chapter Six

[1]*khro ba*. Throughout this chapter *khro ba* is used in the sense of *khong khro*, one of the six basic disturbing emotions, and not, except possibly in stanzas 145 and 147, in the sense of aggression or belligerence, which is a secondary disturbing emotion stemming from anger. *Zhe sdang* has also been rendered as anger, since *zhe sdang* and *khong khro* are used interchangeably in Tibetan. The common translation of *zhe sdang* as hatred limits the meaning to an extreme state of bitter animosity, whereas the term clearly refers to a far more common range of emotions such as aversion, hostility, vindictiveness and anger. Hopkins, *Meditation on Emptiness*, p.256, defines anger as "an intention to harm sentient beings, to harm sufferings in one's own continuum, or to harm phenomena that are sources of suffering." Ibid., p. 261 reads, "Belligerence is an extremely disturbed state of mind which, upon a great increase in anger, is a wish to inflict harm on another such as by physically striking that person when he is in one's presence." Definitions such as these of the fifty-one mental factors are found in Tibetan monastic textbooks currently in use.

[2]Can. 218.1.1 ff.

[3]Can. 218.1.5 ff.

[4]Can. 218.3.2 ff.

[5]In Tibetan medicine, phlegm (*bad kan*) is associated with an imbalance of the earth and water elements, and bile (*mkris pa*) with an imbalance of the fire element.

[6]Can. 218.4.3 ff.

[7]Can. 218.5.2 ff.

[8]Can. 219.2.7 ff.

[9]Hopkins, *Meditation on Emptiness*, p.263, defines resentment ('*khon 'dzin*) as "a wish to harm or to answer harm, involving non-release of a continuum of anger. It has the function of serving as a basis for impatience."

[10]*mtshams med lnga*: murdering one's father, mother or a Foe Destroyer, causing schism within the spiritual community, and with bad intent drawing blood from a Buddha. Unless these actions are purified, their consequences cannot be deferred and rebirth in one of the hell realms will follow in the very next life.

[11]Can. 219.5.5 ff.

[12]*nyon mongs can gyi ma rig pa.* Ignorance is nescience, involving confusion with respect to the nature of phenomena. It refers to active misconception rather than a mere absence of knowledge. Its two principal forms are confusion with respect to the connection between actions and their effects, and confusion with regard to the fundamental nature of phenomena.

[13]*'du byed kyi las,* the second of the twelve members of dependent arising of cyclic existence. For a succinct explanation of the dependent arising of cyclic existence, see Hopkins, *Meditation on Emptiness,* pp.275-83 and Appendix 2.

[14]Dzong-ka-pa's *Ocean of Reasoning, Explanation of (Nāgārjuna's) "Treatise on the Middle Way" (rtsa shes ṭik chen rigs pa'i rgya mtsho;* Varanasi: Pleasure of Elegant Sayings Printing Press, 1973), p.430, says, "Emptiness comes to mean dependent arising for Mādhyamikas who have refuted inherent existence through valid cognition, not for others. When such Mādhyamikas explicitly *(dngos su)* ascertain that external and internal things arise dependently reliant on causes, they ascertain the meaning of emptiness of inherent existence through the force of that very awareness."

Through explicitly ascertaining that phenomena arise dependently, those who have discovered the correct view of reality will immediately and explicitly ascertain their emptiness of true existence, for by understanding that true existence implies lack of dependence, they know validly that this and dependent arising are contradictory.

Dependent arising comprises three aspects: dependence on causes and conditions, dependence on parts and dependence on imputation by conceptuality. The first applies only to products while the other two describe how all phenomena exist. Dependence on causes and conditions and on parts are easier to understand than dependence on imputation. Understanding the former serves as a means to bring about understanding of emptiness. To understand dependence on imputation by conceptuality fully one must understand emptiness. Through the force of explicitly understanding emptiness, this subtle level of dependent arising is ascertained without the need for further reasons.

For further discussion of how dependent arising can both function as the reason for emptiness and be the meaning of emptiness, see Donald S. Lopez, "On the Relationships of Emptiness and Dependent Arising: Some dGe-lugs-pa Views," *Tibet Journal,* Vol.XIV, No.1 (Dharamsala, Library of Tibetan Works and Archives, 1989).

[15]The expression of worship in Nāgārjuna's *Sixty Stanzas of Reasoning (yuktiṣaṣṭikākārikānāma, rigs pa drug cu pa'i tshig le'ur byas pa,* P5225, Vol.95, 11.2.2) reads:

> Homage to the King of Subduers
> Who taught dependent arising,
> Eliminating [inherent] production
> And disintegration in this way.
>
> *gang gi skye dang 'jig pa dag*
> *tshul 'di yis ni spangs gyur pa*
> *rten cing 'byung ba gsungs pa yi*
> *tub dbang de la phyag 'tsal lo*

Gyel-tsap also refers to Candrakīrti's *Commentary on the "Sixty Stanzas of Reasoning"* *(yuktiṣaṣṭikāvṛtti, rigs pa drug cu pa'i 'grel pa,* P5265, Vol.98), which explains why among all the supreme qualities for which the Buddha may be praised, his explaining emptiness of inherent existence as meaning dependent arising is singled out for praise by Nāgārjuna. Since the Buddha has direct ultimate perception of emptiness of inherent existence as dependent arising and therefore possesses complete personal authority to teach this, he is called the King of Subduers and is superior to other teachers. Sūtra passages explaining emptiness of inherent existence as meaning dependent arising are the essence of the scriptural doctrine, and realization of it constitutes the principal doctrine of insight. Without such insight one cannot become free from the seeds of obstructions and thus cannot attain liberation or omniscience. The emptiness of inherent existence of dependent arising is a non-affirming negative. ("A negative which is such that the term expressing it does not suggest in place of the negation of its own object of negation another, positive phenomenon which is its own object of suggestion." For further explanation of this definition see Hopkins, *Meditation on Emptiness*, p.725). It is also ultimate truth, but as such should not be looked upon as truly existent, since this is a wrong view referred to by Nāgārjuna as incurable.

[16]Can. 220.3.2 ff.

[17]*sa 'dzin. The Great Tibetan-Chinese Dictionary (bod rgya tshig mdzod chen mo* [Beijing: Mi rigs dpe skrun khang, 1985] Vol.3, p.2905) defines *sa 'dzin pa,* the "earth claimant," as a theatrical role. It is reported that this refers to an actor in certain forms of Tibetan drama who has charge of the stage which he symbolically demarcates and cleans by performing a dance at the beginning. It is possible that a similar custom obtained in ancient Indian drama.

[18]Can. 220.3.8 ff.

[19]*bslab pa* here refers to the three kinds of training, which include all practices: training in ethical conduct *(tshul khrims kyi bslab pa),* training in meditative stabilization *(ting nge 'dzin gyi bslab pa)* and training in wisdom *(she rab kyi bslab pa).* Without a foundation of ethical conduct, the mind is too turbulent to permit sufficiently steady concentration for the development of special insight which, when practised in relation to emptiness, becomes the antidote to incorrect mental engagement and misconceptions of reality.

[20]*yon ten bcu gnyis.* One should live in seclusion at least five hundred armspans from the nearest settlement, under trees, in a roofless shelter or in a cemetery, depending wholly or partly on what is found there by way of food, clothing and utensils. These four rules counteract attachment to one's dwelling place. Two rules pertain to behavior: one should use a pallet of grass or leaves which must not be renewed and one should never sleep lying down. To overcome attachment to food there are three rules: one should live on alms, begging food from the same people daily or calling at three doors in line without making any distinction, and in both cases accept whatever is given. Food should be eaten in a single sitting each day and nothing more taken after rising from one's place, swallowing the last mouthful or after rinsing one's mouth at the end of the meal. One should not go for alms a second time in the day but should col-

lect as much as is needed and not begin eating before that amount has been received. There are three rules to counteract attachment to clothing: one should possess only the bare essentials (three robes if one is ordained), wear clothing made from felt or discarded rags and only use clothes worn by others for at least four months.

[21]This possibly refers to the River Son which rises in the modern Indian state of Madhya Pradesh and flows through Bihar.

[22]Can. 222.2.1 ff.

[23]Can. 222.3.1 ff.

[24]Can. 222.3.7 ff.

[25]*The Precious Garland* (trans. Hopkins), p.59, stanzas 284-285. Lines 7, 8, 1, and 2 of Gyel-tsap's citation constitute stanza 284, and lines 3-6, stanza 285.

[26]Can. 222.5.7 ff.

Notes to Chapter Seven

[1]*kun sbyor*. Nine primary fetters are mentioned in sūtra and in Asanga's *Compendium of Knowledge* (*abhidharmasammuccaya, mngon pa kun btus*, P5550, Vol.112). These are the six basic disturbing attitudes and emotions: desire (*'dod chags*), anger (*khong khro*), pride (*nga rgyal*), ignorance (*ma rig pa*), doubt (*the tshom*), deluded view (*lta ba nyon mongs can*), as well as miserliness (*ser sna*), envy (*phrag dog*) and the fetter of holding erroneous conceptions as supreme (*mchog tu 'dzin pa'i kun sbyor*). The latter comprises holding bad views as supreme (*lta ba mchog 'dzin*) and holding bad ethics and modes of conduct as supreme (*tshul khrims dang brtul zhugs mchog 'dzin*). The fetter of deluded views comprises views of the transitory collection as real "I" and "mine" (*'jig tshogs la lta ba*), views holding to an extreme (*mthar 'dzin pa'i lta ba*), and wrong views (*log lta*). Anger, miserliness and jealousy only occur in the Desire Realm.

Vasubandhu's *Treasury* also mentions five fetters concordant with the lowest realm, i.e. the Desire Realm (*tha ma'i cha mthun lnga*): views of the transitory collection, holding bad ethics and modes of conduct as supreme, doubt, the wish for sense objects (*'dod pa la 'dun pa*), and harmfulness (*gnod sems*). Five fetters concordant with the upper realms (*gong ma'i cha mthun lnga*) are desire of the Form Realm, desire of the Formless Realm, excitement (*rgod pa*), pride and ignorance.

[2]*srid pa las byung ba'i sred pa*. This refers to desire of the upper realms and is an inwardly directed form of attachment to meditative equipoise. It is referred to as desire of worldly existence (*srid pa'i 'dod chags*) to preclude misconceptions of the two upper realms as liberated states.

[3]*lta ngan*. There are limitless bad views which can be classified as views of permanence, of annihilation, and of both. They may be divided into three groups, each consisting of one hundred and twenty, yielding a total of three hundred and sixty. The *Brahma Net Sūtra* (*brahmajālasūtra, tshangs pa'i dra ba'i mdo*, P1021, Vol.40), p.286.2.8 ff., extensively discusses these views and their

origins. The *Condensed Perfection of Wisdom Sūtra (sañcayagāthāprajñā-pāramitāsūtra, shes rab kyi pha rol tu phyin pa sdud pa*, P735, Vol.21), p.193.1.2, says, "...just as the sixty-two views are subsumed under the view of the transitory collection" *('jig tshogs lta bar lta ba drug bcu gnyis 'dus ltar)*. This refers to the sixty-two bad views and indicates their connection with the view of the transitory collection as real "I" and "mine".

[4]Can. 223.5.1 ff.

[5]Can. 224.1.4.

[6]The text cited in Can. 224.1.7, D.Can. 61.1.7, and the Varanasi edition, p.115.13, reads *'gro ba gzhar yang yod min na. gzhar yang* with a negative means "never." *gzhan yang* appears in place of *gzhar yang* in only one edition that was inspected.

[7]All examined versions of the text read *de yang mi 'gyur de ltar byos*.

[8]*sdong po bkod pa'i mdo*. This sūtra is not extant in present versions of the *bka' 'gyur*, however the volume of contents of the *sde dge mtshal par bka' 'gyur* (Delhi: Karmapae Chodhey Gyalwae Sungrab Partun Khang, 1976-1979), pp.238-39, says, "Volume eleven, the forty-fifth: the *Chapter Ornamented by Tree Trunks* from the *Array of Tree Trunks* and its elaborated meaning" *(pam po bcu gcig zhe nga pa sdong po dkod pa 'phros don dang bcas pa las sdong pos rgyan pa'i le'u)*.

[9]The *Explanation of the Guhyasamāja Maṇḍala Ritual (gsang 'dus dkyil 'khor cho ga'i rnam bshad)*, by the Seventh Dalai Lama, Gel-sang-gya-tso (*bskal bzang rgya mtsho*, 1708-1757) (Delhi; no further publication data available), fol. 3.14, reads:

> The *King of Ascertainments Sūtra (rnam par gtan la dbab pa rgyal po'i mdo)* says: "Ānanda, it is like this: the udumbara flower appears when a Buddha is born. It is colorful, bright, and has a fine aura. Its fragrance pervades a radius of one mile. This flower removes dimness and clears the memory. It even pacifies sickness. It also removes bad smells, illuminates, and gives off a sweet fragrance which purifies the four elements. If it does not appear even for universal monarchs, how could such a flower, whose occurrence is as rare as Buddhas, appear for unethical sentient beings?" An *Account of Realizations (rtogs brjod)* describes other features of the flower: "To the north, beyond the great lake Manasarowar and over the five mountain peaks, is an udumbara garden. When Supramundane Victors descend from their existence as gods in the Joyous Land (*dga' ldan*) and enter their mother's womb, the garden begins to bud. When they are born from their mother's womb the flowers begin to open. When they attain the full awakening of complete unsurpassable enlightenment, the flowers bloom. When they are about to pass away, they wither, and when they pass into the state of parinirvāṇa, the garden's leaves, flowers, petals and fruit fall. An udumbara flower is the size of a chariot wheel. When Supramundane Victorious Buddhas appear in the royal caste, the color of the flower is white. When they appear in the Brahmin caste the color of the flower is white." Regarding the latter, incorrupt versions read "...is red." This analogy illustrates the rarity of a Buddha's advent.

[10]Only coarse fabrics like canvas can be produced from hemp. Cotton is of greater value because it can be used for a wide range of fabrics, including extremely fine ones such as muslin.

[11]Can. 225.1.6 ff.

[12]Can. 225.2.8 ff.

[13]Can. 225.4.2 ff.

[14]Can. 226.1.3 ff.

[15]*'byung 'gyur*. The particles that constitute physical objects consist of eight substances—earth, water, fire, wind, visible form, smell, taste and that which is tangible. The latter four are elemental derivatives or evolutes. See Hopkins, *Meditation on Emptiness*, pp. 230-31.

[16]Can. 226.4.6 ff.

[17]Can. 227.2.4 ff.

[18]*lung gzhi*, also referred to as *Topics of Discipline* (*vinayavastu, 'dul ba gzhi*, P1030, Vol.41). This explains in 37.1.4 ff. how rare it is for beings to go from one good rebirth to another, or from a bad one to a good one. Compared to those who go to bad rebirths, they are as few as the particles of earth that adhere to one's fingertip when compared to the number of particles of earth in the world.

[19]Can. 227.3.4.

[20]Can. 227.4.8 ff.

[21]Can. 228.1.7 ff.

[22]Can. 228.4.8 ff.

[23]Can. 229.1.3 ff.

[24]Can. 229.2.3 ff.

[25]*dpe chos rin chen spungs pa* (no publication data), pp.105-07.2

Notes to Chapter Eight

[1]This division of sense objects is made on the basis of whether or not they are conjoined with the mindstream of a living being. When appearance, sound, smell, taste and tactile quality are features of a being with consciousness, they are referred to as internal sense objects, because of their association with consciousness. When they are not features of a living being and therefore are not associated with consciousness, they are referred to as external sense objects. For example, the appearance, smell, taste, etc. of a stone are external sense objects.

[2]Can. 229.3.6 ff.

[3]Can. 229.5.1.

[4]The snake in the analogy and the person are similar in being merely imputed to a basis of imputation and unfindable under analysis. However,

unfindability in the case of the snake denotes non-existence, for even when no analysis is made, a rope-snake cannot perform the functions of a snake. In the case of the person, unfindability implies not non-existence but lack of true existence, for when no analysis is made, the person attributed to the collection of the aggregates functions satisfactorily as such, and statements regarding it such as "John is eating" are not invalidated by conventional valid cognition. All phenomena are imputed by conceptuality, but not everything imputed by conceptuality exists.

[5]The statement that disturbing attitudes and emotions arise through conceptuality indicates two aspects of dependent arising: dependence on imputation by conceptuality and dependence on causes among which an incorrect mental approach is mentioned. The citation from the *Sixty Stanzas of Reasoning* (P5225, Vol.95, 11.5.5) first emphasizes the causal aspect by saying the world is caused by ignorance, a fact which is confirmed by the Buddha. This can be taken to refer to his description of how the contaminated aggregates arise in dependence on a twelve-membered process. The statement that the world is conceptuality includes the causal aspect, in that the conceptuality of an incorrect mental approach causes disturbing attitudes and emotions, giving rise to contaminated actions through which the environment and living beings come into existence. It also indicates the dependent nature of all phenomena in being mere designations dependent upon the conceptual consciousnesses that designate them. For an extensive discussion of the dependent arising of cyclic existence, see Hopkins, *Emptiness Yoga* (Ithaca, New York: Snow Lion Publications, 1987), pp. 303-29.

[6]Can. 230.3.6.

[7]Can. 230.4.5 ff.

[8]A group of blind people will not reach their destination unless they have a sighted guide. Wisdom is frequently compared to the guide and the other perfections to the blind people.

[9]Can. 230.5.6 ff.

[10]Can. 231.2.2.

[11]Can. 331.4.1 ff.

[12]In the outline provided by Gyel-tsap, this section is entitled, "With effort, liberation is easy to attain." One may thus conclude that according to Gyel-tsap's interpretation, not doing actions does not imply total inactivity, but rather restraint from contaminated virtuous and non-virtuous actions which produce cyclic existence and, as the question at the beginning of the next section indicates, restraint from actions based on a conception of true or ultimate existence. "Without complication" *(bsam khral med pa)* may sometimes be interpreted as "without the focus of conceptions of true existence" *(bden 'dzin gyi dmigs gtad med par)*. The focus here refers to true existence, the referent object of such conceptions. Thus "without complication" may also be taken to mean without fabrications of true existence.

[13]Immunity to sickness *(nad med pa'i stobs)* seems somewhat infelicitously to denote cyclic existence in the analogy.

[14]*'jig tshogs la lta ba nyi shu*. These are speculative misconceptions concerning the relationship between the self and the aggregates. There are four pertaining to each aggregate. Thus in relation to the aggregate of form they are as follows: the misconceptions that the self is form, that it inherently possesses form, that form has an inherently existent self, and that the self has inherently existent form.

[15]The self and aggregates are examined in the following five-fold way as to whether they are inherently one, inherently different, whether the self inherently depends on the aggregates or the aggregates inherently depend on the self, and whether the self inherently possesses the aggregates.

[16]P795, Vol.31, 290.1.3 says, "Through just one all are known, / Through just one all are seen" (*gcig gis kyang nyid thams cas shes / gcig gis kyang nyid thams cas mthong*). Although Gyel-tsap's version drawn from Candrakīrti's commentary differs slightly, the sense does not: *gcig gis thams cas shes 'gyur zhing / gcig gis thams cas mthong bar 'gyur*.

[17]Gyel. Ch. VIII 12.19 ff. and Ren. 95.19 read *gang gis chos gcig sgo nas chos rnams kun* for the first line which is the version translated here. Both Can. 232.5.2 and D.Can. 70.2.3 say, "Whoever by meditating on one phenomenon ..." (*gang gis chos gcig bsgoms nas chos rnams kun*). The *Meditative Stabilization of Gaganagañja*, listed as the *Sūtra Requested by Gaganagañja* (*gaganagañjapariprcchasūtra, 'phags pa nam mkha'i mdzod kyis shus pa'i mdo*, P815, Vol.33, 16.3.2) says, *gang zhig chos gcig kis ni chos rnams kun / sgyu ma smig rgyu 'dra bar bzung med dang / gsog dang rdzun dang rtag pa med par shes / de ni byang chub snying por nyur du 'gro*. In both versions of Candrakīrti's commentary the third line reads *gsob brdzun ther zug min par shes pa de*.

[18]Jay-dzun-ba, commenting on the citation from the *King of Meditative Stabilizations Sūtra* in his *General Meaning of the Middle Way* (*dbu ma'i spyi don*) (Buxaduor: Nang bstan shes rig 'dzin skyong slob gnyer khang, 1963) says, "It does not follow that when one cognizes the emptiness of one phenomenon one cognizes the emptiness of other phenomena. These citations mean that when a valid cognition ascertains lack of true existence with respect to one established base, the lack of true existence of another base can be cognized merely by directing the mind to it with the question whether or not it is truly existent" (fol.52b). This implies that the whole process of reasoning which induced the initial cognition does not need to be repeated.

[19]Can. 233.1.4 ff.

[20]*Supplement to (Nāgārjuna's) "Treatise on the Middle Way"* (*madhyamakāvatāra, dbu ma la 'jug pa*, P5261, P5262, Vol.98, 103.1.5): *tha snyad bden pa thabs su gyur pa dang / don dam bden pa thabs byung gyur pa ste*.

[21]Things are not totally non-existent but are validly ascertained to exist by a consciousness verifying conventionalities. However, these same things are not found under investigation by a consciousness analyzing their final and fundamental mode of existence.

[22]"Things" (*dngos po*) refers to functional things, such as a pot, produced from causes and conditions. "Non-things" (*dngos med*) refers to non-functional

phenomena which are not produced by causes and conditions, such as a pot's emptiness of true existence.

[23]Can. 233.5.4 ff.

[24]P5224, Vol.95, 1.3.7 reads *rdzogs sangs rgyas rnams ma byung zhing / nyan thos rnams ni zad pa na / rang sangs rgyas kyi ye shes ni / brten pa med par rab tu skyes.* The versions cited in Candrakīrti's commentary and by Gyel-tsap all differ slightly but convey the same sense.

[25] This refers to a trial by ordeal in which the suspect's innocence is established if he or she survives unscathed the ordeal of licking hot iron.

[26]D.Can. 72.2.2 ff.

[27]Can. 234.5.3 ff.

[28]*Ke'u tshang sprul sku, blo bzang 'jam dbyangs smon lam,* late eighteenth century.

[29]*byang chub lam gyi rim pa chung ngu'i zin bris blo gsal rgya mtsho'i 'jug ngogs* (Dharamsala: Library of Tibetan Works and Archives, 1984), p.472.1 ff.

Notes to Chapter Nine

[1]*dngos po,* also translated as "functional thing" and "thing," usually connotes something impermanent which is able to perform a function. It may also connote any existent phenomenon, either permanent or impermanent, and sometimes refers to true existence, as in the phrase *dngos por smra ba,* "proponents of true existence."

[2]Functional things are produced through a process and are themselves part of a process, giving rise to their own effects and undergoing constant change and disintegration.

[3]*rang rgyud kyi gtan tshigs* refers to the reason of an autonomous syllogism (*rang rgyud kyi sbyor ba*) in which the three criteria (*tshul gsum*), i.e. the presence of the reason in the subject, the pervasion and counter-pervasion, are established from their own side. Since Prāsaṅgikas assert that nothing is established from its own side or has autonomous existence, the use of such a syllogism is unacceptable.

[4]Can. 235.5.5 ff.

[5]Proponents other than Prāsaṅgikas of Buddhist systems of tenets assert that a valid cognition of a subject such as a sprout is one which is unmistaken with regard to its nature, meaning that the sprout must exist exactly as it appears to that cognition. Since the sprout appears to exist by way of its own character to such a valid cognition, asserted as unmistaken with regard to the sprout's fundamental mode of existence, that would be how the sprout actually existed. If this were so, a valid cognition of a sprout would be a valid cognition of its fundamental mode of existence. Prāsaṅgikas do not accept such a valid cognition. Since a subject is thus not asserted to be validly established or certified in a similar way in the Prāsaṅgika and other systems, there are no commonly ap-

pearing subjects. For Svātantrika-Mādhyamikas and the lower tenet systems, if a cognition is valid with respect to an object, it should be unmistaken. For Prāsaṅgikas a cognition may be both valid and mistaken with regard to its object. Unless this were so, it would be impossible for common beings to cognize things, since all perceptions of common beings are mistaken and affected by conceptions of true existence and their latencies. Thus according to Prāsaṅgikas, a direct valid cognition perceiving a pot is mistaken with respect to it in that the pot appears to exist inherently. Nevertheless that valid cognition cognizes the pot. Non-Prāsaṅgikas assert that if a perception is mistaken with respect to its object, that perception cannot cognize the object.

[6]Vaiśeṣikas (*bye brag pa*), proponents of a non-Buddhist system of tenets, assert that all phenomena are included among six categories of existents: substance, quality, activity, generality and particularity. There are nine types of substance: earth, water, fire, air, space, time, direction, self and mind.

[7]The second category of existents asserted by Vaiśeṣikas is quality, which is of twenty-five types, of which pleasure is one: form, taste, smell, touch, sound, number, dimension, separateness, conjunction, disjunction, otherness, non-otherness, consciousness, pleasure, pain, desire, hatred, effort, heaviness, moisture, heat, oiliness, momentum, merit and demerit. All qualities depend on one of the nine types of substance.

[8]*so sor rtags 'gog* is a separation from contamination, i.e. disturbing attitudes and emotions, attained through analyzing the four truths individually. Vaibhāṣikas assert that all products other than true paths are contaminated in that as focal objects or concomitants they can provoke an increase in contamination. Thus a chair, for instance, is said to be contaminated because as a focal object it can increase any of the three poisons. A disturbing emotion such as desire is contaminated because it increases contamination such as other disturbing emotions with which it is concomitant.

[9]*rtags min 'gog pa* is a cessation other than an analytical cessation, attained through the incompleteness of conditions but not through the application of an antidote. It prevents the future production of specific contaminated or uncontaminated phenomena. For instance when Bodhisattvas reach the patience stage of the path of preparation, they automatically attain a non-analytical cessation with regard to the aggregates of bad rebirths. They will never be reborn in such transmigrations again through the force of contaminated actions. These two kinds of cessation asserted by Vaibhāṣikas are described by Vasubandhu in the first chapter of the *Treasury of Knowledge*.

[10]Impermanence here denotes the extreme of total non-existence.

[11]This statement seems to target the Vaibhāṣika assertion that space is an ultimate truth and a permanent functional thing, its function being to permit movement through lack of obstructive contact. They say it is an ultimate truth because it can bear analysis in that even when reduced through the process of analysis, it can still generate an apprehension of itself in a perceiver. Other examples of such ultimate truths are partless particles and partless moments of consciousness.

[12]According to the Vaidāntikas, the fact that the sprout is not produced during certain periods when conditions for its production seem to prevail demonstrates its dependence on time. This means time is a cause since it is the key factor facilitating production. A facilitating factor (*phan 'dogs byed*) is the definition of a cause (*rgyu*). Their argument is then used to show that time is an effect because of its dependence on other factors which help it to produce the sprout.

[13]Something without an effect cannot be posited as a cause. If it has an effect and the effect facilitates its establishment as a cause, it too must be an effect. Thus to assert causes which are not effects would absurdly amount to asserting causes that lack effects.

[14]*sna tshogs pa*. The fact not merely that it has parts but that it has diverse or dissimilar parts is stressed.

[15]Permanent functional things are asserted to be truly existent, which would preclude having and depending upon parts.

[16]*lha'i mig*, a super-knowledge common to both Buddhists and non-Buddhists, attained through the practice of meditative stabilization, enabling perception of subtle forms.

[17]According to Cittamātrins, the reasoning refuting the existence of particles is that which refutes external existence. For them emptiness of external existence is the final or ultimate nature of form. Thus the existence of particles is refuted through reasoning which analyzes the ultimate. However, the reasoning that analyzes the ultimate also refutes truly existent consciousness which Cittamātrins accept. Contrary to the Cittamātra contention, both particles and consciousness are equally existent conventionally and equally non-existent ultimately.

[18]*rang gi sde pa* refers to proponents of Buddhist systems of tenets and in this context specifically to the Vaibhāṣikas.

[19]Sāmkhyas (*grangs can pa*), proponents of a non-Buddhist system of tenets, assert that the person is permanent because of not changing and is consciousness because of not being an aggregate of particles. It is the experiencer of pleasure and pain but is neither an agent of virtue or non-virtue. Nor is it the creator of manifest phenomena which evolve from the nature (*rang bzhin*) and are confused with the person until yogic perception differentiates the two and all manifestations disappear. The nature or principal (*gtso bo*) and person are truly existent because they are non-manifest. The other twenty-three of the twenty-five categories enumerated by the Sāmkhyas are manifest and therefore only exist conventionally, since they are falsities.

The great one (*chen po*), also called the intellect (*blo*), is one of the twenty-five categories. It is produced from the nature and acts like a two-sided mirror in which images of objects from the outside and of the person from the inside mingle. The intellect empowers the senses, which apprehend objects that are known by the person in this way. For a succinct account of the Sāmkhya system, see Hopkins, *Meditation on Emptiness*, pp. 321-26.

[20]Āryadeva's text, which is ambiguous, reads *de med na ni srid pa la / bsam pa'ng yod pa ma yin no*. The word *srid pa* can refer to worldly existence which is how Gyel-tsap and Ren-da-wa have interpreted it. The text has therefore been translated to accord with Gyel-tsap's interpretation. *Srid pa* can also mean "to be possible." Bö-drül's interpretation is based on this meaning; p.108.4 says, "Because in the first place the self as reliance does not exist, there too should be no speculation regarding the possibility of a reliant seed of consciousness." To accord with his interpretation, the translation of the text would read, "Without it there too is no speculation / Regarding its possible existence."

[21]Gyel. Ch.IX, 15.12 and Bö. 108.16, read *sla'i* and *sla yi* respectively, meaning simpler or easier, whereas Ren-da-wa and both versions of Candrakīrti's commentary read *bla'i* or *bla yi*, meaning preferable.

[22]The contention put forward is that from a conventional perspective certain things are accepted as real and existent such as pots, virtuous and non-virtuous actions and so on. Others are accepted as non-existent fabrications such as the water of a mirage, a mirror reflection as a real face, the principal, the permanent self and so forth, whereas the ultimate is free from assertions of any kind.

[23]Ga-tok and Bö-drül accept this stanza as an expression of the Prāsaṅgika viewpoint. It seems clear, however, from the end of chapter IX (Can. 241.1.5 ff.) and beginning of chapter X (Can. 241.2.6 ff.), that Candrakīrti regards stanza 225 as a contention raised for debate. Gyel-tsap and Ren-da-wa follow this interpretation.

Notes to Chapter Ten

[1]This refers to stanza 225.

[2]*ma ning*. Five kinds of sexually indeterminate persons are described: those with neither male nor female sexual characteristics are called *mtshan med ma ning*, without signs. Those with the sexual characteristics of both sexes are called *mtshan nyid ma ning*, with signs. Those whose sexual characteristics are changeable from birth are known as *'gyur ba ma ning*, changeable, while those who are born with male sexual characteristics but later display primarily female ones are referred to as *nyams pa ma ning*, deteriorated. Those who display male sexual characteristics during the first part and female characteristics during the later part of the lunar month are called *zla ba ma ning*. It is said that the mental instability suffered by anyone in such a condition makes them unfit to hold individual liberation vows.

[3]*mu stegs can*, "one who has a ford to the end," refers to Indian non-Buddhists who assert they have a ford or path leading to liberation from cyclic existence or to a higher rebirth.

[4]According to Jang-gya's *Presentation of Tenets* (*grub mtha'i rnam bzhag* (Varanasi: Pleasure of Elegant Sayings Printing Press, 1970), pp. 50-51, Vaiśeṣikas assert that the self has the following nine attributes: intelligence (*blo*),

pleasure (*bde ba*), pain (*bsdug bsngal*), desire (*'dod pa*), animosity (*sdang ba*), effort (*'bad pa*), virtue (*chos*), non-virtue (*chos ma yin*) and activity (*'dus byas*) which includes momentum (*shugs*), predisposition (*bag chags*), duration (*gnas pa*) and disintegration (*'jig pa*). Gender is not included as an attribute.

[5]According to accounts drawn from the second chapter of the second of the *Four Tantras of Secret Instruction on the Eight Branches of the Essence of Nectar* (*bdud rtsi snying po yan lag brgyad pa gsang ba man ngag gi rgyud bzhi*), a redacted version of which was used in Tibet since the twelfth century as the basis for medical knowledge and practice (rpt. Dharamsala: Tibetan Medical Institute, 1971), the development of the fetus takes place in three phases. The fish phase (*nya yi gnas skabs*) is from the first to the third month. The turtle phase (*rus sbal gyi gnas skabs*) when the four limbs begin to form is from the third to the fifth month. The pig phase (*phag gi gnas skabs*) when hair starts to grow is from the sixth to the ninth month.

[6]The self which is the object of the conception "I" is a generality (*spyi*) of which the self of this life and the self of one's former life are instances (*bye brag*).

[7]The argument is based on the reciprocal possession which Vaiśeṣikas assert pertains between a substance and its attributes. The different kinds of intelligence (*blo*) which are attributes of the self, such as the eye intelligence (*mig ki blo*) are not themselves cognitive (*rig pa'i ngo bo*), but act as agents of cognition (*rig byed*) or sensors for mental consciousness.

[8]Gyel-tsap's *Gateway for Conqueror Children, Explanation of "Engaging in the Bodhisattva Deeds"*, pp. 242-45, contains a longer presentation of Sāṃkhya tenets together with a refutation of them.

[9]The flaws alluded to refer to the Sāṃkhya assertion that the person and the activity of being conscious are one entity and to the consequences which this entails.

[10]Although Gyel. Ch.X, 8.6 reads, "It is improper to claim that the person but not consciousness exists at the time of experiencing an object" (*yul la longs spyod pa'i tshe skyes bu yod la shes pa yod pa med ces bya bar mi rigs so*), this should surely read, "prior to experiencing an object" (*yul la longs spyod pa'i sngar*), if the argument is to be sustained. Ren. 120.2 reads *yul la long spyod pa'i sngar*.

[11]The five mental faculties (*yid kyi dbang po*): eye (*mig*), ear (*rna ba*), nose (*sna*), tongue (*lce*), and skin (*pags pa*). The five faculties for action (*las kyi dbang po*): speech (*ngag*), arms (*lag pa*), legs (*rkang pa*), anus (*rkub*) and genitals (*'doms*).

[12]Can. 246.3.3 and Gyel. Ch.X, 14.1 mention *mer mer po*, the female fetus during the fourth week.

[13]*Fundamental Treatise on the Middle Way Called "Wisdom"* (P5224, Vol.95, 7.3.6) reads *gang la brten te gang byung ba / de ni re shig de nyid min / de las gzhan pa'ng ma yin phyir / de phyir chad min rtag ma yin*. Gyel-tsap cites only the first two lines. The last two say, "It is also not separate from that / Thus there is no discontinuation and no permanence." Dzong-ka-ba's *Ocean of Reasoning*, p.332, commenting on these lines, says, "Any effect that arises depending on a cause is firstly not one with that cause by way of its own entity, otherwise it follows that everything which is produced and everything that produces would be one.

Thus the cause is not something permanent that turns into the effect. Furthermore any effect that arises in dependence on a particular cause is not separate from that cause by way of its own entity. Since it is contradictory for it to rely on the cause if it is separate, it would arise causelessly. Thus there is no discontinuation of the cause's continuum owing to the effect not arising from the cause. Accordingly through the reasoning of dependent arising the effect is established as being neither inherently one with nor different from the cause. By virtue of this reason the cause is free from the defects of permanence and discontinuation."

Notes to Chapter Eleven

[1]Gyel-tsap refers to the refutation of permanent time as a cause in chapter IX, stanzas 207-211.

[2]A pot nearing production is a future pot. A butter lamp that has gone out, a man who has died and a house that has fallen down are a past butter lamp, a past man and a past house. These must not be confused with the charred wick, the corpse and the ruins which are present. The butter lamp, referring to one that is actually alight, the man and the house are examples of the present. Pan-chen Sö-nam-drak-ba (*pan chen bsod nams grags pa*, 1478-1554) says that the sprout's cause is the future sprout and the sprout's effect is the past sprout. Jay-dzun Cho-gyi-gyel-tsen (*rje btsun chos kyi rgyal mtshan*, 1469-1546) says the sprout which is presently being produced is the future sprout and the disintegrated sprout is the past sprout. Before a thing has come into existence it is future, and when it has disintegrated it is past. Thus there is first a future pot, i.e. a pot to be, then a pot and subsequently a past pot, namely one that has disintegrated. The future in relation to the pot will occur when the pot has disintegrated and will be the pot's effect. The past in relation to the pot occurred when the pot was not yet produced and was the pot's cause.

[3]*ma 'ongs pa'i ma 'ongs pa*, referring to the present and past.

[4]Gah. 345.5 ff.

[5]*gzhi mthun*. A common locus of a pot and the future means that which is both a pot and future.

[6]In the lower systems of Buddhist tenets it is asserted that a disintegrated pot (*bum pa zhig pa*) is non-functional, which implies that it should be causeless. In that case a butter lamp which has gone out should be uncaused, but it is quite obvious that, for instance, the burning down of the wick and running out of the butter cause the lamp to go out. The disintegration of the pot (*bum pa 'jig pa*) is its not remaining for a second moment. If its not remaining for a second moment (*dus gnyis par mi sdod pa*) is caused, its not having remained for a second moment (*dus gnyis par ma bsdad pa*) is also caused. Conversely, if its not having remained for a second moment is uncaused, its not remaining for a second moment must also be uncaused. If that were the case it could not disintegrate, since it would not be a composite thing!

[7]Gah. 351.3

[8]Dasgupta, *A History of Indian Philosophy* (Delhi: Motilal Banarsidass, 1975), Vol.5, p.170, says, "*Niyati* means the ordering of things. It stands for what we should call the natural law, such as the existence of the oil in the seed, of the grain in the husk, and all natural contingencies." In these volumes Dasgupta translates *niyati* as "destiny," over which living beings have no control.

[9]Here "seen" refers to that which is manifest or self-evident and can be cognized by direct perception. "Unseen" refers to the hidden (*lkog gyur*) and very hidden (*shin tu lkog gyur*) which can only be understood through scriptural citations and reasoning. Sometimes "seen" means that which pertains to this life and "unseen" that which pertains to other lifetimes.

[10]*rang grub pa'i dus gnyis par mi sdod pa*. This can refer to the fact that a thing only continues to exist in a specific form for a certain length of time, or to the fact that it undergoes constant change. For instance when we look at a cup that has been in constant use for five years, we can see it is no longer the brand new cup we bought in the store five years ago, and when it eventually breaks, we understand its coarse impermanence through direct personal experience. However the cup has undergone constant momentary changes from the first moment of its existence. There is constant new formation in that the cup of a moment ago has ceased to exist by the next moment, but because there is a continuity of moments of a similar type, we feel that the same cup we saw a moment ago is still there. We are thus unaware of its subtle impermanence, which initially we can only come to understand through reasoning.

[11]Explicit cognition (*dngos su rtogs pa*) means cognition of an object entailing its appearance (*snang ba sgo nas rtogs pa*). Implicit cognition (*shugs la rtogs pa*) means cognition entailing non-appearance of the object (*ma snang ba sgo nas rtogs pa*). For instance, when a conceptual consciousness explicitly cognizes sound as impermanent, it implicitly cognizes sound's lack of permanence and vice versa. It is said that omniscient mind directly cognizes all three times simultaneously. Direct cognition is necessarily explicit cognition. Past, present and future are, however, not cognized as simultaneous.

[12]Gyel. Ch.XI, 8.2 ff. reads *ma 'ongs pa rang gi ngo bo'i sgo nas yod pa'i phyir*. Ren. 133.20 says "because it has [attained] its entity" (*rang gi ngo bo yod pa'i phyir*). This is a distinguishing feature of things which exist in the present.

[13]Ren. 135.1 ff. says, "If the future did not exist, it would not be appropriate to speak of consciousness being produced, for if, because it is future, the consciousness to be produced does not exist, there will also be no process of production, since it would lack a basis. If consciousness were not produced, attachment which is the basis for desire would also not exist. In that case, if desire did not have attachment as its basis it would arise causelessly. However desire is not causeless, otherwise it would arise in Foe Destroyers too." Attachment in this context can be taken as attachment to the self (*bdag la chags pa*), in other words, the misconception of the self. Bö. 127.16 mentions "the seeds of attachment and so forth ...."

[14]This point is made in Vasubandhu's *Treasury of Knowledge* (P5590, Vol.115, 117.5.4) and in his *Explanation of the "Treasury of Knowledge"* (P5591, Vol.115, 139.1.8). See Lati Rinbochay and Elizabeth Napper, *Mind in Tibetan Buddhism*

(London: Rider and Company, 1980), pp. 18 and 86 for information on what "two consciousnesses" implies in this context.

[15]All Buddhist systems of tenets propound the four seals (*lta ba bkar btags kyi phyag rgya bzhi*): all products are impermanent, all contaminated things are miserable, all phenomena are selfless and nirvāṇa is peace. As regards view, whether one is a Buddhist or not is in general determined by whether or not one accepts the four seals. As regards conduct, it is determined by whether or not one turns to the Three Jewels as one's ultimate source of refuge.

[16]The visual consciousness cognizes its object clearly (*gsal bar dpyod*) in that the object actually appears to that visual consciousness without the presence of a generic image (*don spyi*). The subsequently arising mental consciousness cognizes it unclearly (*mi gsal ba'i tshul*) in that the object is cognized by way of its generic image.

[17]*dran pa*. If the previously experienced object on which memory focuses existed inherently, it should exist at the time of remembering. That object would not be deceptive since the way it appears and the way it exists would accord. The remembering consciousness that focuses on it would not be mistaken or deceived for it would experience the object as it actually is. However the previously experienced object is not observable when memory of it arises, yet the remembering mind perceives it as though it were present. The object is therefore false and deceptive and the perceiving consciousness deceived.

Notes to Chapter Twelve

[1]Bhāvaviveka's *madhyamakahrdayakārikā (bdu ma'i snying po'i tshig le'ur byas pa)*, P5255, Vol.96, 4.2.3.

[2]Ideal students are unprejudiced, intelligent, enthusiastic in searching for the right path to follow, respectful toward the teacher and teaching and completely attentive.

[3]Ideal teachers have the following ten qualities: They are (1) disciplined in that they practise restraint from harmful physical, verbal and mental activity and abide by the three kinds of vows; (2) calm because their practice of concentration counters distraction, thereby overcoming coarse disturbing emotions; (3) very peaceful because their practice of wisdom thoroughly pacifies disturbing emotions; (4) rich in scriptural knowledge regarding the three categories of teaching. They have (5) wisdom understanding suchness, the final mode of existence; (6) knowledge exceeding the student's in those matters in which the student seeks guidance; (7) wisdom and skill in presenting the teachings and guiding others; (8) love and compassion as their motivation for teaching. They are (9) untiring in their effort to help students, and such effort is continual. They are (10) patient in teaching and guiding students and are able to bear their ingratitude. These qualities are mentioned in Maitreya's *Ornament for the Mahāyāna Sūtras (mahāyānasūtralamkarakārikā, theg pa chen po'i mdo sde'i rgyan gyi tshig le'ur byas pa*, P5521, Vol. 108), 13.4.5.

[4]Although there is no indication of a plural in the commentaries and it is therefore unclear whether reference is being made to the student's own good qualities or those of other students, Ge-tsang's *Notes on the Stages of the Path*, p.478, elucidates this point as follows: "Not only will the good qualities of the teacher be seen as good qualities and not as faults, but the good qualities of fellow listeners will also not be seen as faults."

[5]*'phags lam yan lag brgyad*:

(1) correct view (*yang dag pa'i lta ba*): understanding through thorough investigation what was cognized during meditative equipoise.

(2) correct thought (*yang dag pa'i rtog pa*): communicating what one has cognized to others, motivated by the wish to help them understand it.

(3) correct speech (*yang dag pa'i ngag*): convincing others of the correct view and of the fact that one holds it, by speaking to them appropriately.

(4) correct action (*yang dag pa'i las kyi mtha'*): convincing others of the purity of one's ethical conduct by not performing improper actions.

(5) correct livelihood (*yang dag pa'i 'tsho ba*): convincing others that one's possessions are modest by using only the clothes, etc. which the Buddha has permitted.

(6) correct effort (*yang dag pa'i rtsol ba*): energetically cultivating the paths which counteract disturbing attitudes and emotions to be abandoned by the path of meditation.

(7) correct mindfulness (*yang dag pa'i dran pa*): counteracting laxity and excitement by not forgetting the focal object of calm abiding.

(8) correct meditative stabilization (*yang dag pa'i ting nge 'dzin*): accomplishing special forms of super-knowledge to counteract discordant factors such as obstructions to absorption, through maintaining single-pointedness by means of meditative stabilization.

The eightfold path of the Exalted is the seventh of the seven categories of yogic paths which make up the thirty-seven factors in harmony with enlightenment. Although the eightfold path is normally discussed in the context of the path of meditation, all thirty-seven factors are in fact attained when the path of seeing is reached. This is clearly stated in Maitreya's *Ornament for the Mahāyāna Sūtras* (P5521, Vol.108, 11.2.5 ff.). The quality of pure water (which is cool, has a good taste, is light, smooth, clear, odorless, not harmful to the throat, and beneficial to the stomach) is affected by the kind of vessel which holds it. Similarly, although the Exalted of all three vehicles attain this eightfold path, its quality varies depending upon which kind of Exalted one has generated it.

[6]*King of Meditative Stabilizations* (P795, Vol.31, 283.5.4). Dzong-ka-ba comments on this citation in *Ocean of Reasoning*, p.440: "In the sphere of nirvāṇa without remainder there are no actions and disturbing attitudes and emotions, nor their effects. Thus all opponents agree on their non-existence. The state-

ment that phenomena, which do not exist then, have always been non-existent indicates that even during cyclic existence they never existed in terms of their own suchness."

[7]"The four practitioners of virtue" here refers to those who abide in the fruit of a Stream Enterer, Once Returner, Never Returner and Foe Destroyer. These results are presented in the context of the Hearer Vehicle and range from abandonment of those obstructions to liberation which are eliminated by the Hīnayāna path of seeing to the complete abandonment of all obstructions caused by disturbing attitudes and emotions. The Exalted achieve these results through meditation on emptiness.

[8]Commenting on statements by Dignāga and Dharmakīrti regarding conviction in the validity of the Buddha's words in his exegesis of Dharmakīrti's *Commentary on [Dignāga's] Compendium of Valid Cognition*, Gyel-tsap's *Elucidation of the Path to Liberation (rnam 'grel thar lam gsal byed;* Varanasi: Pleasure of Elegant Sayings Printing Press, 1974, p.175 ff.) says that Buddha's statements concerning extremely hidden matters are not deceptive because they are like his statements about obvious and slightly hidden matters. The Buddha's statements that prosperity comes from giving and happiness from ethical conduct are not deceptive because, like his words concerning the four truths, they are not invalidated by any of the following three kinds of cognition used to investigate them—statements regarding what is obvious are not damaged by direct valid cognition, those regarding what is slightly hidden are not invalidated by inference through the power of the fact, and those about extremely hidden matters are not invalidated by inference through conviction. All the great trailblazers use the validity of the Buddha's statements regarding obvious and slightly hidden things to establish the validity of those about extremely hidden matters, arguing that they are all equally the Buddha's words, spoken by the same person. Moreover since his statements regarding the means to attain liberation and omniscience, the main focus of his teaching, are not deceptive, what he has taught about less important matters such as the means through which high rebirth is attained will not be deceptive either.

[9]Ren. 146.12 ff. lists the following four types of valid cognition: direct *(mngon sum)*, inferential *(rjes dpag)*, through appraisal *(nye bar 'jal ba)* and through scripture *(lung gi tsad ma)*. While all valid cognition is either direct or inferential, the latter two—which are inferential cognition—are singled out for special attention. In general there are three main types of inferential valid cognition: inference through the power of the fact *(dngos stobs rjes dpag)*; through conviction *(yid ches rjes dpag)*, which is equivalent to valid cognition through scripture; and inference through appraisal of an example *(dpe nyer 'jal gyi rjes dpag)*, sometimes replaced by inference through renown *(grags pa'i rjes dpag)*. Objects of apprehension can only be obvious or hidden, and thus valid cognitions apprehending them are only either direct or inferential. For further discussion of inference see Lati Rinbochay and Elizabeth Napper, *Mind in Tibetan Buddhism*, pp. 76-84.

[10]Can. 256.1.7 ff. succinctly formulates what is meant by self and selflessness in words that are cited in many other works. "Here 'self' is an inherent

nature of phenomena, that is, a non-dependence on another. The non-existence of this is selflessness" *(de la bdag ces bya ba ni gang zhig dngos po rnams kyi gzhan la rag ma las pa'i ngo bo rang bzhin te med pa ni bdag med pa'o).*

[11]Nāgārjuna's *Praise to the Perfection of Wisdom (prajñapāramitāstotra, shes rab kyi pha rol tu phyin ma'i bstod pa,* P2018, Vol. 46), 37.3.2.

[12]True existence is called a natural stain *(rang bzhin gyi dri ma)* because all things are naturally free from it without the need for meditation on paths. This so-called natural stain is not a stain at all because it does not exist. Natural nirvāṇa, since it is the fundamental mode of existence of all phenomena, is not actually nirvāṇa, which is a cessation of adventitious stains attained through meditation on paths.

[13]Nāgārjuna's *Sixty Stanzas of Reasoning,* P5225, Vol.95, 11.3.3.

[14]Nirvāṇa is not generally said to be attained when one reaches the path of seeing, since it is said to occur when all disturbing attitudes and emotions are eliminated. Here the meaning appears to be that one can attain nirvāṇa in the very life in which one reaches the path of seeing. Gyel-tsap's *Commentary on the Sixty Stanzas of Reasoning (rigs pa drug cu pa'i ṭikka,* from *gyal tshab rje'i gsung 'bum* [Dharamsala: Shes rig par khang, 1981], Vol. *ca,* p.411.4 ff.) says, "It is not evident in this system that the attainment of the path of seeing is posited as the attainment of nirvāṇa. Sūtra says, 'My rebirths are finished, the task is done.' The statement is made in the context of Foe Destroyers."

Notes to Chapter Thirteen

[1]*gzugs.* Since sounds, smells, tastes and tangible objects are also forms, the term *visible form* is used as a variant for *form* to denote the object of visual consciousness.

[2]*rang mtshan pa* is taken to be synonymous with *rang gi mtshan nyid kyis grub pa* in this chapter. Elsewhere it is also translated as "real." Blue is introduced here to emphasize that not only visible form but color, which along with shape constitutes visible form, does not exist by way of its own character either.

[3]*rdzas brgyas.* In the Desire Realm the five objects of the senses, when not connected with consciousness, are composed of eight substances (or nine if sound particles are present). These eight are: earth, water, fire, wind, visible form, smell, taste, and that which is tangible. The latter four derive from the elements. When the object is connected with consciousness, particles of the body sense organ are present and there are thus nine components. If particles of the other sense organs are present, there are ten components and eleven if sound particles are also present.

[4]"Dialecticians" *(rtog ge ba)* here refers to proponents of true existence *(dngos smra ba)* who assert that a direct perceiver has the three features of being a consciousness free from conceptuality, unmistaken with respect to its appearing object, a functional thing existent by way of its own entity and of both arising and engaging in its object in dependence upon a sense organ. Candrakīrti

368 The Yogic Deeds of Bodhisattvas

refutes the first of these in *Clear Words, Commentary on [Nāgārjuna's] "Treatise on the Middle Way"* (*mūlamadhyamakavṛttiprasannapadā, dbu ma rtsa ba'i 'grel pa tshig gsal ba*, P5260, Vol.98, 13.2.1 ff.) and refutes the second and third at this point in his commentary on the *Four Hundred* (259.1.5 ff.). Conceptuality usually involves perception for which a sound image (*sgra spyi*) and generic image (*don spyi*) are merged. However, someone unversed in terminology may perceive the generic image of an object without its being merged with an associated sound image. This is one explanation found in many texts for the term *sgra don 'dres rung*. Jang-gya however asserts that the sound and generic image should not be differentiated in this way.

[5]A single moment of consciousness cannot be produced and then engage with its object in dependence upon a sense organ as they assert occurs in direct perception, since moment by moment both the sense organ and consciousness cease upon production.

[6]The opponent asserts that sense consciousnesses are direct perceivers in relation to their objects of engagement, the five sense objects existent by way of their own character. However since objects merely appear to but do not actually exist in this way, these consciousnesses are mistaken and deceptive in this respect. To then refer to them as valid cognition which should be non-deceptive is inadmissible. The Prāsaṅgika definition of direct valid cognition is knowing that is not deceptive with respect to an object of comprehension which is its main object of engagement. Thus for instance, both blue and blue existent by way of its own character appear to a visual consciousness perceiving blue. However the visual consciousness is valid cognition with respect to blue, its main object of engagement, but not with respect to blue existent by way of its own character. In Gyel. Ch. XIII 3.2 ff. read *shes* for *zhes* in accordance with Can. 259.4.1 and *rtog* for *rtogs* in accordance with Can. 259.4.2.

[7]Can. 259.4.1 ff.

[8]*gzugs kyi skye mched.* The six types of objects of consciousness (forms, sounds, smells, tastes, tangible objects and phenomena) and the six organs (eye organ, ear organ, nose organ, tongue organ, body organ and mental organ) are sources in that they act as stimuli to the production and development of awareness.

[9]Stanza 308 has five lines in all versions inspected.

[10]*spyi don gzhan*, one of the six categories of existents asserted by Vaiśeṣikas—substance, quality, activity, generality, particularity and inherence. Jang-gya's *Presentation of Tenets*, p.52.10 ff., says, "A generality acts as a common cause for applying terms and the mind to phenomena which it accompanies."

[11]The entailment is that visible forms, etc. exist because the eye and the other organs that perceive them exist. Implicit in the opponent's assertion is that both the subject and object exist by way of their own entity. Stanza 316 refutes the eye as a perceiver by way of its own entity on the grounds that it does not perceive itself. Its function as a perceiver can thus not be adduced by the opponent as proof of directly perceptible objects existent by way of their own entity.

[12]Gah. 448.1

[13]Smell-eaters (*dri za*, Skt. *gandharva*) are celestial beings famed as musicians. They enjoy and gain nourishment from smells of all kinds. Although they are classed as gods in some texts and as demi-gods in others, Vasubandhu's *Treasury of Knowledge* says they are intermediate state beings (*bar srid*) and that their phantom cities are dwellings in the intermediate state.

[14]*King of Meditative Stabilizations Sūtra* (P795, Vol.31, 283.4.5 ff.) contains the stanzas in the following order: 1 (283.4.5 ff.); 2 (283.4.4 ff.); 3 (283.4.1 ff.); 4 (283.4.3: although the meaning is similar the words are not as cited by Gyeltsap); 5 (283.4.7 ff.); 6 (283.4.8); 7 (283.3.2 ff.); 8 (283.4.1 ff.).

Notes to Chapter Fourteen

[1]By qualifying existence with adjectives such as true, inherent, independent, etc. and by the use of phrases such as "by way of their own entity," "by way of their own character" and so forth, it is evident that existence in general is not being refuted, but only a particular kind of existence. Āryadeva's text often does not clearly indicate this difference. The Mādhyamika view should therefore not be misunderstood as a nihilist view.

[2]Minds (*sems*) and their accompanying mental factors (*sems byung*) possess five similarities (*mtshungs ldan lnga*). Their base (*rten*) is the same in that, for instance, both a visual consciousness and its accompanying mental factors such as feeling depend on the same uncommon empowering condition, the eye organ. They share the same focal object (*dmigs pa*) in that their object of engagement (*'jug yul*) is the same; the same aspect (*rnam pa*) in that their mode of apprehension is the same; the same time (*dus*) in that they occur simultaneously; and the same substantial entity (*rdzas*) in that a moment of visual consciousness, for example, can only be accompanied by a single substantial entity of feeling.

[3]Hot and burning (*tsha zhing bsreg pa*) is the definition of fire.

[4]Vasubandhu's *Treasury of Knowledge* (P5590, Vol.115, 118.4.4). Reference to simultaneously occurring causes and effects does not indicate the normal sequential cause and effect relationship, but a mutually supportive relationship as in the case of the four elements which occur simultaneously and cannot be isolated from one another. This relationship also pertains in the case of the four characteristics of products—production, duration, aging and disintegration—and exists between mind and the omnipresent mental factors of feeling, discrimination, intention, contact and mental engagement which accompany it.

[5]In this context refutation of the four alternatives focuses on the effect, negating the inherent production of an effect which exists or which does not exist at the time of its cause, which both does and does not exist at that time, and which neither exists nor does not exist at that time. The reasons used to refute the above, presented in somewhat more detail by Ren-da-wa in his commentary on stanza 265 (p.135.9 ff.) are then applied to refute production in terms of a cause and effect which are inherently one, inherently different, both and

370 The Yogic Deeds of Bodhisattvas

neither. This process of refutation focuses on the cause. Thus the "diamond fragments" reason is used to analyze whether an effect is produced from a cause which is the same entity, an inherently different entity, both of the former or neither of the former. Causeless production of an effect is often substituted for the last category in this analysis. Gah. 481.4 explains the Nirgrantha contention regarding the production of an effect which is both permanent and impermanent or both of one nature with yet different from its cause. An example would be a gold bracelet that does not differ in nature from the lump of gold from which it was made but is different in that the gold has temporarily taken on a new aspect. This is refuted by applying the reasons which refute cause and effect as a single entity and cause and effect as inherently different entities. The contention that cause and effect are neither one entity nor different entities can be refuted by adducing the very same reasons. If they are not one entity, they must be different entities, while if they are not different entities they must be one entity. Implicit in all these contentions is an affirmation that things have objective and inherent existence. All the reasons employed aim at refuting this underlying belief.

[6]*tshad ma sde bdun*, Dharmakīrti. See bibliography. These texts present the Cittamātra view.

Notes to Chapter Fifteen

[1]Dzong-ka-ba's *Ocean of Reasoning* (p.155.4 ff.) says, "Because of having characteristics such as production, forms and so forth are said to be products. Sautrāntikas and above [i.e. Cittamātrins and Mādhyamikas] assert that the characteristics, production and so forth are the activity of production, the activity of persisting and the activity of disintegrating of these phenomena. Vaibhāṣikas, as explained below, assert that they are agents which cause forms and so forth to be produced, disintegrate and persist. According to the latter, when something such as the form aggregate is defined as a product, it is not so defined because of being produced but because of having a separate agent of production and so forth. According to the former, it is not defined in this way. When Sautrāntikas refute that the production and so forth of forms, etc. are different substantial entities from the latter, Vaibhāṣikas object, asking how they could be characteristics of those phenomena that act as bases for characteristics. In reply [Sautrāntikas say that Vasubandhu] has explained in [his auto-] commentary on the Treasury [*Explanation of the "Treasury of Knowledge"* (P5591, Vol.115, 153.2.3)] that the combination of a hump and so forth is a characteristic of cattle and hardness a characteristic of the earth element, even though they are not different substantial entities. Production and so forth are also like this."

[2]Our normal conception of production, duration, and disintegration is in terms of a thing's complete life span from the time it is newly produced or formed until it disintegrates, is old, wears out or falls to pieces. Such a linear conception of these characteristics takes no account of the subtle changes which

take place moment by moment. Production, duration and disintegration are present at each moment, characterizing different features of an ongoing process. Thus production is the new arising of what did not exist before; duration the persisting of a previous continuum; and disintegration a thing's not lasting for a second moment after its formation.

³Dzong-ka-ba's *Ocean of Reasoning* (p.67.6 ff.) says, "If the basis and that based upon it existed ultimately, they could not undergo any change in nature. Since the activity would always require a basis, the sprout and so forth would have to exist as a basis for the activity of production even at a time when they are approaching production. Cause and effect would thereby be simultaneous. ... It is not the same with conventional production, since even if [the sprout and production] act as basis and that which is based upon it at one point, they do not always have to do so." Further, p.177.11 ff. says, "Both we and others must accept that woollen cloth to be produced is an agent and basis, and its production an activity dependent upon it; also that while the woollen cloth is approaching production, the agent and basis does not exist, but the activity of production does. However if the woollen cloth and production existed ultimately, their being basis and that which is based upon it would have an inherently existent nature and would therefore always infallibly have to exist thus. Since the woollen cloth would have to exist at that time too [when it is approaching production], that which is already existent prior to its production would have to be produced as woollen cloth again."

⁴Ibid., p.194.15 ff., says, "You should ascertain, as determined by reasoning, that production, duration and disintegration could none of them be posited if they existed by way of their own entity and their existence was not merely posited through the force of convention. Then you should train yourself to see that what is posited through the force of convention is perfectly feasible and that the appearance of all products as diverse entities, even though they are empty of existence by way of their own entity, is like a magician's illusions and like dreams." In the term *dependent arising*, "dependent" confirms the absence of independent existence, while "arising" confirms existence, precluding the total non-existence indicated by the analogy of a barren woman's child. Thus "dependent" protects from the extreme of reification and "arising" from the extreme of annihilation.

⁵Can. 272.3.8 ff.

⁶This may be aimed at the view held by Tang-sak-ba (*thang sag pa*), one of Ba-tsap Nyi-ma-drak's close disciples, and by others that Mādhyamika as propounded by Candrakīrti was a theory of neither being nor non-being (*yod min med min gyi lta ba*). See Ruegg, "The Jo naṅ pas: A School of Buddhist Ontologists According to the *Grub mtha' sel gyi me lon*," *Journal of the American Oriental Society* 83 (1963), p.89.

⁷If a functional cause could produce a non-functional effect, a seed, for instance, could produce a burnt sprout.

⁸*King of Meditative Stabilizations Sūtra* (P795, Vol.32, 24.1.4 ff.). Dzong-ka-ba's *Ocean of Reasoning* (p.194.11 ff.) cites the same lines with only very little variation. The version in Gyel. (Ch. XV, 8.19 ff.) differs somewhat but retains

the same meaning and accords with the version cited in Can. 273.3.5 ff. except for the last line. This is translated in accordance with Gyel. Ch. XV, 9.1, *bdag tu lta bar gyur pas rnam par dben*. Can. 273.3.6 reads, "are free from views of permanence" *(rtag tu lta bar gyur pas rnam par dben)*. The *King of Meditative Stabilizations* reads, "are continuously free from views" *(lta ba dag las gor mor rnam par dben)*.

⁹If things existed truly as is claimed, they ought to be findable on analysis. Here the attempt to pinpoint the thing under production focuses on whether it does or does not have the entity of being in the process of production. Both possibilities are ruled out. In the first case an entity has already been attained, while in the second, involvement in the process of production is precluded. Since experience confirms that things are produced, they must exist in a way that is different from that in which they appear to exist. Appearing to exist in one way and actually existing in another is the mark of falseness. Their existence is therefore not true but false.

¹⁰Gyel. Ch. XV, 12.16 ff. is only very slightly different from *King of Meditative Stabilizations* (P795, Vol.31, 280.4.2 ff.) and retains the same meaning.

¹¹Those under the magician's spell to whom the conjured men and women appear to be real are taken in by the appearance and think they are real. Things similarly appear to be truly existent to ordinary living beings who then assent to this appearance and act accordingly. The illusory men and women he has created appear to the magician too, but he knows they are not real. Similarly, things appear to be truly existent even to the wisdom of subsequent attainment *(rjes thob ye shes)* of the Exalted, but they do not take them to be so. Those who arrive when everything is over and who are not affected by the spell do not see any illusory men and women and thus do not mistake them for real men and women. Similarly, to the wisdom of the Exalted in meditative equipoise on emptiness *(stong nyid mnyam bzhag ye shes)* conventional phenomena do not even appear nor do they take them to be truly existent.

¹²In his *Gateway for Conqueror Children, Explanation of "Engaging in the Bodhisattva Deeds"*, p. 210.9 ff., Gyel-tsap comments on the following lines from the ninth chapter of Śāntideva's *Engaging in the Bodhisattva Deeds (bodhisattvacaryāvatāra, byang chub sems dpa'i spyod pa la 'jug pa*, P5272, Vol.99, 258.24 ff.):

> The ultimate is not [this] mind's field of activity;
> [This] mind is asserted to be conventional.

> *don dam blo yi spyod yul min*
> *blo ni kun bdzob yin par 'dod*

Gyel-tsap says, "The first line indicates the definition of ultimate truths, the second the definition of conventional truths. The former and latter [use of] mind refers not just to any mind, but to mind to which there is dualistic appearance. Also this is said from the point of view of how its object is apprehended. It should therefore be interpreted as follows: The instance, lack of inherent existence of the person and aggregates, illustrates ultimate truth. To the direct valid cognition directly cognizing this, it is not its field of activity in terms of dualistic appearance. It is that which is known by the direct valid cognition apprehending it." P. 210.17 ff. continues, "The person and aggregates as instances are said to be conventional truths because, for the direct valid cognition which explicitly cognizes them, they are that which is cognized in terms of dualistic appearance." Dualistic appearance here refers to duality of subject and object.

Notes to Chapter Sixteen

[1]Although Can. 275.3.2 ff. does not elaborate this analogy, Ge-shay Bo-do-wa's *Precious Heap of Analogies for the Doctrine* (pp.308-09) says,

> *like the dead queen*: In India a certain king went to wage war in another country. He left a capable minister in his place to look after the queens, but one of the finest queens died. If the king had been told that the queen had died, he would have been upset. This would have affected the war adversely, so his wise minister acted with diplomacy. He told a man going to see the king to say, 'The queen has a large pimple on her forehead.' The next one going to see the king was to say, 'The pimple has gotten much bigger'; then, 'It has turned into blisters'; and then, 'They have spread over her whole face and the skin has peeled off. It has turned into an open sore.' The king said, 'It would be best if she dies before I return.' Soon after, they told him she had died, but the war was not affected adversely and the king's grief was not so great. Similarly, skillful spiritual friends do not teach emptiness immediately at the outset, but gradually teach the antidotes to the four wrong conceptions. First, meditation on repulsiveness is taught as an antidote to the wrong conceptions which like a blue-bottle take what is unclean to be clean. Then meditation on all internal and external things as impermanent is taught to counteract the wrong conceptions which take what is impermanent like dew on the grass to be permanent. Next, meditation on the suffering of the whole of cyclic existence is taught as an antidote to the wrong conceptions which take suffering for happiness, like a fish and its bait. Then as an antidote to the wrong conceptions which take what is selfless and like dreams and magical illusions to have a self, one teaches and hears that all phenomena are selfless. It is said that teaching and listening by stages insures that emptiness will not be misunderstood.

This explains what is meant by the enigmatic words, "settling spiritual guides and students" *(slob dpon dang slob ma rnam par gtan la dbab pa)* in Gyel-tsap's title for this chapter and why the words "the procedure between" have been inserted in square brackets. The skillful guide leads the student step by step in a gradual progression towards an understanding of emptiness after which misconceptions regarding emptiness itself are dispelled. As part of that process the most conspicuous wrong conceptions are dealt with first. Then step by step attention is focused on increasingly subtle matters. The order described by Ge-shay Bo-do-wa of combatting these wrong conceptions differs from that of our text.

374 *The Yogic Deeds of Bodhisattvas*

[2]The opponent interprets the emptiness of a phenomenon as its non-existence. This excludes it from knowable objects, which necessarily exist. Regarding the assertion that emptiness itself is not a knowable object, the view of the great translator Ngok Lo-den-shay-rap (*ngog blo ldan shes rab*, 1059-1109) and others was that if anything is found when a reasoning consciousness investigates the ultimate mode of existence of a thing, what is found has sustained analysis and must therefore truly exist. If emptiness were found it would be truly existent. This however is unacceptable to Ngok Lo-den-shay-rap because he holds Mādhyamika tenets. He therefore asserts that nothing is cognized by a reasoning consciousness analyzing the ultimate. Since emptiness then is neither the object of a reasoning consciousness analyzing the ultimate nor of conventional valid cognition, it is not a knowable object since it is not appropriate as an object of any kind of awareness. Gyel-tsap's commentary on this stanza (380) emphasizes that under investigation nothing is findable. This means that when the final mode of existence of a pot is investigated, and one seeks to establish whether the pot is truly existent, i.e. exists as it appears, only the absence of a pot existing in this way is found, which is its emptiness of true existence. Merely being found by a reasoning consciousness does not make what is found truly existent. Only if what is sought were found would it be truly existent. Thus if the pot were found when the imputed object to which the term "pot" is attributed is sought, the pot would exist truly as something findable under analysis. An absence of such existence is found, but that absence or emptiness is not the object sought. When emptiness itself is subjected to the same scrutiny, it is not found. Only the absence or emptiness of its true existence is found. For more discussion of this topic, see Hopkins, *Meditation on Emptiness*, pp.406-11. For some of the arguments Dzong-ka-ba uses to establish that emptiness is a knowable object, see Elizabeth Napper, *Dependent Arising and Emptiness* (Boston: Wisdom Publications, 1989), pp.131-32, and Robert Thurman, *Life and Teachings of Tsong Khapa* (Dharamsala: Library of Tibetan Works and Archives, 1982), pp.162-64.

[3]Nāgārjuna's *Fundamental Wisdom* (P5224, Vol.95, 6.2.1) concludes the stanza with the following two lines:

> Since not the slightest thing is not empty
> How can emptiness exist?

Dzong-ka-ba's *Ocean of Reasoning*, p.259.18 ff. comments on the stanza in response to a contention that if one asserts emptiness, things cannot previously have been non-existent by way of their own entity. Things that are bases for emptiness must necessarily exist and do so by way of their own entity. In response Dzong-ka-ba says,

> If emptiness had the slightest existence by way of its own entity, there could be something not empty existing by way of its own entity as its basis. However here [in this system] emptiness and selflessness are asserted as the general characteristics of all phenomena. Thus when there is not even the slightest thing which is not empty of a self, how can emptiness exist by way of its own entity? It cannot. [If it did,] since the antidote [emptiness] would be without a reliance, it would be [non-existent] like a sky flower.

⁴Jñānagarbha, *Differentiation of the Two Truths (satyadvayavibaṅgakārikā, bden gnyis rnam 'byed,* Toh. 3881, Vol. *sa,* fol.2a.1-2). Nga-wang-bel-den *(ngag dbang dpal ldan,* b. 1797) in *Explanation of the Conventional and Ultimate in the Four Systems of Tenets (grup mtha' bzhi'i lugs kyi kun rdzob dang don dam pa'i don rnam par bshad pa legs bshad dpyid kyi dpal mo'i glu dbyangs* [New Delhi: Guru Deva, 1972], p. 165) comments on these lines: "The Cittamātrins assert that emptiness, the negation precluding a self of phenomena with regard to the basis of negation, exists as [its own] reality. Since the object of negation of our own system, a self of phenomena, does not exist, the negation precluding it is said not to exist as [its own] reality. Therefore the explanation that the negation of ultimate production is a conventionality means it exists conventionally and does not indicate that it is a conventional [truth]." The negation here refers to emptiness. For further discussion of this, see Lopez, *A Study of Svātantrika,* p.199.

⁵Here the argument is similar to that in stanza 382. "No thesis" or "absence of a thesis" *(phyog med)* refers to emptiness itself and the counter-thesis to the basis of emptiness. "Absence of a thesis" also refers to the absence of a thesis that exists by way of its own entity. The opponent asserts that though Mādhyamikas claim to have no system, their very contention that they have no thesis constitutes a system. Implicit in the opponent's argument is the assumption that anything which exists has inherent existence. In the commentary, stress is laid on the fact that Mādhyamikas never claim to have no system, but merely assert that emptiness, the absence of inherent existence, is not itself inherently existent. Similarly they do not deny holding views or theses, but merely deny their inherent existence. A number of contemporary scholars as well as former Mādhyamikas in India and Tibet do not accept this interpretation of the many terse statements found in the basic texts of Mādhyamika literature to the effect that Mādhyamikas hold no views or position and have no system or thesis. According to the special insight section of Dzong-ka-ba's *Great Exposition,* these statements are not to be taken literally. For an excellent discussion of this topic, see Napper, *Dependent Arising and Emptiness,* pp.116-22.

⁶Stanza 346 (chapter XIV) explains how these are refuted by the reason of dependent arising.

⁷Attachment in this context can mean clinging to the true existence of things, or attachment to the self, the self's happiness, and to that which one hopes will facilitate such happiness. This attachment is rooted in the misconception of the self as truly existent. One experiences suffering by not finding the happiness sought through the acquisition of friends, status, wealth and so forth and instead encountering unwanted situations. This suffering can be stopped by removing its cause, the underlying misconception. The understanding of selflessness apprehends the self in a way diametrically opposed to that in which the conception of true existence apprehends it. When this understanding stops attachment to the self, attachment to the other factors mentioned above also ceases.

⁸This may be identified as a Sautrāntika assertion. Nga-wang-bel-den's *Explanation of the Conventional and Ultimate in the Four Systems of Tenets,* p. 47,

says that according to Sautrāntikas Following Reasoning impermanent phenomena are "specifically characterized *(rang mtshan)* because of being phenomena that must be realized by a mind that takes them as its appearing object
through the appearance of their own uncommon characteristics [in direct per-
ception]. Due to this, they are not objects of terms since their entities cannot
fully appear to a terminologically arisen [conceptual] consciousness" (translation in Hopkins, *Meditation on Emptiness*, p. 551). According to Sautrāntikas
specifically characterized phenomena are not merely imputed by terms and
thought, but exist from their own side by way of their own exclusive mode of
being. Terms can convey this mode of being but only via the medium of generic images *(don spyi)*, and thus cannot evoke them as vividly as they are experienced by direct perception.

[9]Gyel. Ch. XVI, 11.15-16 reads *'jig rten pa la yod pa yin*, which could also mean
"...and exist to ordinary perception" *('jig rten pa'i shes ngor yod pa yin)*, i.e. an
awareness not involved in analyzing the fundamental mode of existence of a
thing.

[10]If anything existed inherently, in and of itself, it should be found by a reasoning consciousness examining whether or not it exists as a findable entity. It
would then be an ultimate truth and could not be a conventionality which is
the object of a conventional cognition.

[11]Here the opponents' argument that Mādhyamikas make things which previously existed non-existent by refuting their true existence is used against them.
If refutation of their true existence makes things non-existent, they would always have been non-existent because they have never existed truly. The *Ornament for Clear Realization* (P5184, Vol.88, 6.5.8) says:

> With regard to this there is nothing to remove,
> Nor is there anything to impose.
> By viewing reality correctly,
> When reality is seen, one is released.

Dzong-ka-ba's commentary on this passage in *Golden Rosary of Good Explanation (legs bshad gser gyi phreng ba*, P6150, Vol.155, 189.3.3 ff.) says,

> With regard to these dependently arising [phenomena], the two selves
> [a self of persons and a self of phenomena] are not at all something to be
> removed, since from the beginning the two have never existed. The two
> selflessnesses are not something to be imposed or added for they are
> perpetually present. Accordingly there is no self to remove nor selfless-
> ness to impose. When one views this reality correctly, namely without
> error, and sees the two selflessnesses which are the meaning of reality,
> one will gradually gain release from obstructions caused by disturbing
> attitudes and emotions and obstructions to omniscience.

[12]Though a pot that has disintegrated is non-functional as a pot, according
to the Prāsaṅgika system a disintegrated pot *(bum pa zhig pa)* is a functional
thing in that it has come into existence from a cause, the pot's production, and
produces an effect, the following moment of the disintegrated pot.

[13]See introduction, page 23.

Notes to the Colophon

[1]Jean Naudou, *Buddhists of Kaśmīr* (Delhi, India: Agam Kala Prakashan, 1980), p.210, says, "...the most active monastery during the eleventh century was the Ratnaguptavihara." *Tāranātha's History of Buddhism in India*, p. 185, mentions that it was founded by Saṃghadāsa, a disciple of Vasubandhu. It was thus probably more than six hundred years old when this translation was undertaken. The Tibetan version says that the translation was made at *rin chen sbas pa'i kun dga' ra bar* which Naudou (p. 210) translates as Ratnaguptārāma. The expression *kun dga' ra ba* most commonly means a park or pleasant walled area used by monks for debate and discourse, called *chos ra* in modern Tibetan. It is also used to refer to a temple housing representations of enlightened body, speech and mind.

[2]Ibid., pp.208-09, says, "In Kaśmīr the two most important Buddhist centers are named '*khor-lo 'jin* and *grong khyer dpe med*. The city designated under the names of *grong khyer chen po dpe med* [*anupamamahāpura*], *grong khyer dpe med* [*anupamapura*], *dpe me grong* [*anupamapura*], *kha che'i grong khyer* [*kaśmīrapura*] can then vie in importance, for the work accomplished there, with the large universities of Bengal. ... It is very probable that the city designated under the name of Anupamapura by Cordier, and after him by various authors, is none other than Śrīnagar."

[3]Ibid., p.210, speaks of Sūkṣmajana as the last of a brilliant line. He was the son of Sajjana, who was even more outstanding than his father Mahājana, who collaborated with Marpa. *Tāranātha's History of Buddhism in India*, p. 302, says, "Ratnavajra's son was Mahājana and his son was Sajjana."

[4]Naudou, op.cit., p.169, says that Ratnavajra was born in the second quarter of the tenth century. Until the age of thirty-six he studied in Kashmir and then went to Magadha. He also studied at Vikramaśīla, became a pandit, and although a layman holding layman's vows, gained high regard and status in the university. He later returned to Kashmir and also visted Tibet.

[5]See introduction, page 21.

[6]"The one predicted" refers to Nāgārjuna. The *Fundamental Tantra of Mañjuśrī* (*Mañjuśrīmūlatantra, 'jam dpal gyi rtsa ba'i rgyud*, P162, Vol.6, 259.3.8 ff.) says:

Four hundred years after I,
The Tathāgata, have passed away
A monk called Nāga will arise.
He will have faith and help the teaching.
Attaining the very joyful ground,
He will live for six hundred years.

(Translation by E. Obermiller in *History of Buddhism* by Bu-ston, Part 2, p. 111). The *Descent into Laṅka* (*laṅkāvatārasūtra, lang kar gshegs pa'i mdo*, P775, Vol.29, 74.3.7 ff.) says:

In the south, in the area of Bheda [Vidarbha]
There will be a widely renowned monk, Shriman.

He, called by the name of Nāga,
Will destroy the positions of existence and non-existence.

(Translation by Hopkins and Klein, cited in Napper, *Dependent Arising and Emptiness*, p.250).

[7]Upper Do-kam normally refers to that part of eastern Tibet which extends toward and borders on central Tibet as opposed to that which extends toward China.

[8]Dzay-tang is the largest town in the Hlo-ka (*lho kha*) region, an area south of Lhasa along the banks of the Brahmaputra River.

[9]Drok-ri-wo-che is the mountain Dzong-ka-ba chose as the site for Ganden Monastery. Thurman, *Life and Teachings of Tsong Khapa*, p.27, says, "The main temple and over seventy other buildings were completed within a year ... In the following year, the Year of the Tiger (1410), Tsong Khapa went to Ganden ..." and taught there.

Bibliography of Works Cited

Sūtras and tantras are listed alphabetically by English translation of the title in the first section. Indian and Tibetan treatises are listed alphabetically by author in the second. Other works are listed alphabetically by author in the third section.

The words *ārya* and *mahāyāna* have been deleted from the Sanskrit and Tibetan titles, and many of the English titles have been abbreviated. The fact that the titles of Sanskrit and Tibetan texts have been translated into English does not necessarily imply that the works themselves have been translated.

Abbreviations
P: *Tibetan Tripiṭaka* (Tokyo-Kyoto: Tibetan Tripitaka Research Foundation, 1956)
Toh: *A Complete Catalogue of Tohuku University Collection of Tibetan Works on Buddhism*, ed. Prof. Yensho Kanakura (Sendai, Japan, 1934 and 1953).

I. SŪTRAS AND TANTRAS

Array of Tree Trunks Sūtra
gaṇḍavyūhasūtra
sdong po bkod pa'i mdo
[?]

Brahma Net Sūtra
brahmajālasūtra
tshangs pa'i dra ba'i mdo
P1021, Vol.40

Condensed Perfection of Wisdom Sūtra
sañcayagāthaprajñapāramitāsūtra
shes rab kyi pha rol tu phyin pa sdud pa
P735, Vol.21

Descent into Laṅka Sūtra
laṅkāvatārasūtra
lang kar gshegs pa'i mdo
P775, Vol.29

379

Fundamental Tantra of Mañjuśrī
mañjuśrīmūlatantra
'jam dpal gyi rtsa ba'i rgyud
P162, Vol.6

King of Meditative Stabilizations Sūtra
samādhirajasūtra
ting nge 'dzin rgyal po'i mdo
P795, Vol.31-32

Miraculous Feat of Ascertaining Thorough Pacification Sūtra
praśāntaviniścayaprātihāryasāmadhisūtra
rab tu zhi ba rnam par nges pa cho 'phrul gyi ting nge 'dzin gyi mdo
P797, Vol.32

Nanda Entering the Womb Sūtra
dga' bo mngal 'jug pa'i mdo
see *Topics of Detailed Discipline Sūtra*
P1035, Vol.44, 50.2.3 - 60.5.6

Seal of Engagement in Augmenting the Strength of Faith Sūtra
śraddhābalādhānāvatarāmudrāsūtra
dad pa'i stobs bskyed pa la 'jug pa phyag rgya'i mdo
P867, Vol.34

Sūtra of Advice to Kātyayana
ka tya ya na la gdams pa'i mdo
see *Topics of Detailed Discipline*
P1035, Vol.44, 108.5.6ff.

Sūtra Requested by Gaganagañja
gaganagañjaparipṛcchāsūtra
nam mkha'i mdzod kyis zhus pa'i mdo
P815, Vol.33

Topics of Detailed Discipline
vinayaksudrakavastusūtra
'dul ba phran tshegs kyi gzhi
P1035, Vol.44

Topics of Discipline
vinayavastu
'dul ba gzhi
P1030, Vol.41

II. OTHER SANSKRIT AND TIBETAN SOURCES

Āryadeva
Hundred Syllables
akṣaraśāstra
yi ge brgya pa
P5234, Vol.95

Lamp for the Collection of Deeds
caryāmelāpakapradīpa
spyod pa bsdus pa'i sgron ma
P2668, Vol.61

Compendium of Quintessential Wisdom
jñānasārasamuccaya
ye shes snying po kun las btus pa
P5251, Vol.95

Asaṅga
Bodhisattva Grounds
yogacaryābhūmaubodhisattvabhūmi
rnal 'byor spyod pa'i sa las byang chub sems dpa'i sa
P5538, Vol.110

Compendium of Knowledge
abhidharmasamuccaya
mngon pa kun btus
P5550, Vol.112

Atiśa
Great Compendium of Sūtra
mahāsūtrasamuccaya
mdo kun las btus pa chen po
P5358, Vol.103

Bhāvaviveka
Heart of the Middle Way
madhyamakahṛydayakārikā
dbu ma'i snying po'i tshig le'ur byas pa
P5255, Vol.96

Bö-drül-den-bay-nyi-ma (bod sprul bstan pa'i nyi ma, 1905?-1960?)
Naga King's Ornament for Thought, Explanation of the "Four Hundred on the Middle Way"
dbu ma bzhi brgya pa'i rnam bshad klu dbang dgongs rgyan
(Varanasi: Pleasure of Elegant Sayings Printing Press, 1987)

Bodhibhadra
Explanation of the Compendium of Quintessential Wisdom
jñānasārasamuccayanibandhana
ye shes snying po kun las btus pa'i bshad sbyar
P5252, Vol.95

Candrakīrti
Clear Words, Commentary on (Nāgārjuna's) "Treatise on the Middle Way"
mūlamadhyamakavṛttiprasannapadā
dbu ma rtsa ba'i 'grel pa tshig gsal ba
P5260, Vol.98

Commentary on the "Four Hundred Stanzas on the Yogic Deeds of Bodhisattvas"
bodhisattvayogacaryācatuḥśatakaṭīkā
byang chub sems dpa'i rnal 'byor spyod pa bzhi brgya pa'i rgya cher 'grel pa
P5266, Vol.98

Commentary on (Nāgārjuna's) "Sixty Stanzas of Reasoning"
yuktiṣaṣṭikāvṛtti
rigs pa drug cu pa'i 'grel pa
P5265, Vol.98

Commentary on the "Supplement to the 'Treatise on the Middle Way'"
madhyamakāvatārabāṣya
dbu ma la 'jug pa'i bshad pa
P5263, Vol.98

Supplement to (Nāgārjuna's) "Treatise on the Middle Way"
madhyamakāvatāra
dbu ma la 'jug pa
P5261, P5262, Vol.98

Chim Jam-bay-yang (mchim 'jam pa'i dbyangs, twelfth century)
Ornament for Knowledge, Commentary on the "Treasury of Knowledge"
chos mngon mdzod kyi tshig le'ur byas pa'i 'grel pa mngon pa'i rgyan
(Buxaduor: Nang bstan shes rig 'dzin skyong slob gnyer khang, no date)

Dharmakīrti (seventh century)
Seven Treatises on Valid Cognition
Analysis of Relations
sambandhaparīkṣāvṛtti
'brel pa brtag pa'i rab tu byed pa
P5731, Vol.130

Ascertainment of Valid Cognition
pramāṇaviniścaya
tsad ma rnam par nges pa
P5710, Vol.130

Commentary on the "Compendium of Valid Cognition"
pramāṇavarttikakārikā
tsad ma rnam 'grel gyi tshig le'ur byas pa
P5709, Vol.130

Drop of Reasoning
nyāyabindunāmaprakaraṇa
rigs pa'i thigs pa zhes bya ba'i rab tu byed pa
P5711, Vol.130

Drop of Reasons
hetubindunāmaprakaraṇa
gtan tshigs kyi thigs pa zhes bya ba rab tu byed pa
P5712, Vol.130

Proof of Other Continuums
saṃtānāntarasiddhināmaprakaraṇa
rgyud gzhan grub pa zhes bya ba'i rab tu byed pa
P5716, Vol.130

Reasoning for Debate
vādanyāyananāmaprakaraṇa
rtsod pa'i rigs pa zhes bya ba'i rab tu byed pa
P5715, Vol.130

Dzong-ka-ba (tsong kha pa blo bzang grags pa, 1357-1490)
Golden Rosary of Good Explanation
legs bshad gser gyi phreng ba
P6150, Vol.155

Great Exposition of the Stages of the Path
lam rim chen mo
P6001, Vol.152

Ocean of Reasoning, Explanation of the "Treatise on the Middle Way"
dbu ma rtsa ba'i tshig le'ur byas pa shes rab ces bya ba'i rnam bshad rigs
   pa'i rga mtsho
P6153, Vol.156
[Page nos. in the endnotes refer to the same work, published as
rtsa she ṭik chen rigs pa'i rgya mtsho
(Varanasi: Pleasure of Elegant Sayings Printing Press, 1973).]

Gah-tok Nga-wang-bel-sang (kah thog mkhan po ngag dbang dpal bzang,
   1879-1941)
Sea Spray, Explanation of the "Four Hundred on the Middle Way"
dbu ma bzhi brgya pa'i rnam par bshad pa rgya mtsho'i zeg ma
(Bylakuppe: Nyingmapa Monastery, 1984)

Ge-shay Bo-do-wa (dge bshes po to ba, 1027-1105)

Precious Heap of Analogies for the Teaching
dpe chos rin chen spung pa
(Dharamsala: no further publication data)

Ge-tsang (ke'u tshang sprul sku blo bzang 'jam dbyangs smon lam, late eighteenth century)

Channel for the Sea of the Clear-Minded, Notes on (Dzong-ka-ba's) "Short Exposition of the Stages of the Path to Enlightenment"
byang chub lam gyi rim pa chung ngu'i zin bris blo gsal rgya mtsho'i 'jug ngogs
(Dharamsala: Library of Tibetan Works and Archives, 1984)

Gel-sang-gya-tso, Dalai Lama VII (bskal bzang rgya mtsho, 1708-1757)

Explanation of the Guhyasāmaja Maṇḍala Ritual
gsang 'dus dkyil 'khor cho ga'i rnam bshad
(Delhi: no further publication data)

Gyel-tsap (rgyal tshab dar ma rin chen, 1364-1432)

Commentary on (Nāgārjuna's) "Sixty Stanzas of Reasoning"
rigs pa drug cu pa'i ṭik ka, (rgyal tshab rje'i gsung 'bum, Vol. *ca*)
(Dharamsala: Shes rig par khang, 1981)

Elucidation of the Path to Liberation (in Dharmakīrti's) Commentary on the "Compendium of Valid Cognition"
rnam 'grel thar lam gsal byed
(Varanasi: Pleasure of Elegant Sayings Printing Press, 1974)

Essence of Good Explanations, Explanation of "The Four Hundred"
bzhi brgya pa'i rnam bshad legs bshad snying po
(Varanasi: Pleasure of Elegant Sayings Printing Press, 1971)
and
rgyal tshab rje'i gsung 'bum, Vol. *ka*
(Dharamsala: Shes rig par khang, 1981)

Gateway for Conqueror Children, Explanation of (Śantideva's) "Engaging in the Bodhisattva Deeds"
byang chub sems dpa'i spyod pa la 'jug pa'i rnam bshad rgyal sras 'jug ngogs
(Varanasi: Pleasure of Elegant Sayings Printing Press, 1973)

Jang-gya Rol-bay-dor-jay (lcang skya rol pa'i rdo rje, 1717-1786)

Presentation of Tenets
grub mtha'i rnam bzhag
(Varanasi: Pleasure of Elegant Sayings Printing Press, 1970)

Jay-dzün Chö-gyi-gyel-tsen (rje btsun chos kyi rgyal mtshan, 1469-1546)

General Meaning of the Middle Way
dbu ma'i spyi don
(Buxaduor: Nang bstan shes rig 'dzin skyong slob gnyer khang, 1963)

Ocean of Enjoyment, Clarifying Difficult Points in the Two Explanations of (Maitreya's) "Ornament for Clear Realization" and Its Commentaries
bstan bcos mngon par rtogs pa'i rgyan 'grel pa dang bcas pa'i rnam bshad rnam pa gnyis kyi dka' ba'i gnas gsal bar byed pa legs bshad skal bzang klu dbang gi rol mtsho
(Buxaduor: Nang bstan shes rig 'dzin skyong slob gnyer khang, 1963)

Jik-may-dam-chö-gya-tso ('jigs med dam chos rgya mtsho, 1898-1946)

Gateway to (Dzong-ka-ba's) "Essence of Good Explanations"
drang nges legs bshad snying po'i 'jug ngogs
(Dharamsala: Shes rig par khang, 1988)

Jñānagarbha

Differentiation of the Two Truths
satyadvayavibaṅgakārikā
bden gnyis rnam 'byed
[Not in P], Toh.3881

Maitreya

Ornament for Clear Realization
abhisamayālaṃkāra
mngon par rtogs pa'i rgyan
P5184, Vol.88

Ornament for the Mahāyāna Sūtras
mahāyānasūtralamkārakārikā
theg pa chen po'i mdo sde'i rgyan gyi tshig le'ur byas pa
P5521, Vol.10

Sublime Continuum of the Great Vehicle
mahāyānottaratantraśāstra
theg pa chen po rgyud bla ma'i bstan bcos
P5525, Vol.108

Nāgabodhi

Twenty Rituals of the Guhyasāmaja Maṇḍala
śrīguhyasamājamaṇḍalopāyikāvimśatividhi
dpal gsang ba 'dus pa'i dkyil 'khor gyi cho ga nyi shu pa
P2675, Vol.62

Nāgārjuna (first to second century)

Essay on the Mind of Enlightenment
bodhicittavivaraṇa
byang chub sems kyi 'grel pa
P2665 and 2666, Vol.61

Praise to the Perfection of Wisdom
prajñāpāramitāstotra
shes rab kyi pha rol tu phyin pa'i bstod pa
P2018, Vol.46

Six Collections of Reasoning
Precious Garland of Advice for the King
rājaparikathāratnāvalī
rgyal po la gtam bya ba rin po che'i phreng ba
P5658, Vol.129

Refutation of Objections
vigrahavyāvartanīkārikā
rtsod pa bzlog pa'i tshig le'ur byas pa
P5228, Vol.95

Seventy Stanzas on Emptiness
śūnyatāsaptatikārikā
stong pa nyid bdun cu pa'i tshig le'ur byas pa
P5227, Vol.95

Sixty Stanzas of Reasoning
yuktiṣaṣṭikākārikā
rigs pa drug cu pa'i tshig le'ur byas pa
P5225, Vol.95

Treatise Called "Finely Woven"
vaidalyasūtranāma
zhib mo rnam par 'thag pa zhes byas ba'i mdo
P5226, Vol.95

*Treatise on the Middle Way/Fundamental Treatise on the Middle Way Called
"Wisdom"*
prajñānāmamūlamadhyamakakārikā
dbu ma rtsa ba'i tshig le'ur byas pa shes rab ces bya ba
P5224, Vol.95

Nga-wang-bel-den (ngag dbang dpal ldan, b.1797)
Explanation of the Conventional and Ultimate in the Four Systems of Tenets
grub mtha' bzhi'i lugs kyi kun rdzob dang don dam pa'i don rnam par bshad
pa legs bshad dpyid kyi dpal mo'i glu dbyang
(New Delhi: Guru Deva, 1972)

Pūrṇavardhana
*Following Definitions, Explanation of the Commentary on the "Treasury of Knowl-
edge"*
abhidharmakośaṭīkalakṣaṇānusāriṇī
chos mngon pa'i mdzod kyi 'grel bshad mtshan nyid kyi rjes su 'brang ba
P5594, Vol.117

Ren-da-wa (red mda' ba gzhon nu blo gros, 1349-1412)
Commentary to Āryadeva's "Four Hundred Verses"
dbu ma bzhi brgya pa'i 'grel pa
(Varanasi: Pleasure of Elegant Sayings Printing Press,1974)

Śantideva
Engaging in the Bodhisattva Deeds
bodhisattvacaryāvatāra
byang chub sems dpa'i spyod pa la 'jug pa
P5272, Vol.99

Shen-pen-nang-wa (gzhan dga' gzhan phan chos kyi snang ba, 1871-1927)
Interlinear Commentary on the "Treatise of Four Hundred Stanzas"
bstan bcos bzhi brgya pa zhes bya ba'i tshig le'ur byas pa'i mchan 'grel
(gzhung chen bcu gsum gyi mchan 'grel, Vol. 6)
(Dehra Dun: Nyingmapa Lamas' College, 1978)

Vasubandhu
Explanation of the "Treasury of Knowledge"
abhidharmakoṣabāṣya
chos mngon pa'i mdzod kyi bshad pa
P5591, Vol.115

Science of Exegesis
vyākhyāyukti
rnam par bshad pa'i rigs pa
P5562, Vol.113

Treasury of Knowledge
abhidharmakoṣakārikā
chos mngon pa'i mdzod kyi tshig le'ur byas pa
P5590, Vol.115

III. WORKS IN ENGLISH

Chimpa, Lama and Chattopadhyaya, Alaka, trans. *Tāranātha's History of Buddhism in India.* Calcutta: K.P. Bagchi & Company, rpt.1980.
Gokhale, V.V. *Akṣara-sātakam, The Hundred Letters.* Heidelberg, 1930.
Cowell, E.B., ed. *Buddhist Mahāyāna Texts.* New York: Dover Publication, rpt.1969.
Das, Chandra. *Tibetan-English Dictionary.* Delhi: Motilal Banarsidass, rpt.1976.
Hopkins, Jeffrey. *Emptiness Yoga.* New York: Snow Lion Publications, 1987.
_____. *Meditation on Emptiness.* London: Wisdom Publications, 1983.
_____, trans. Nāgārjuna and the Seventh Dalai Lama, *The Precious Garland and the Song of the Four Mindfulnesses.* New York: Harper and Row, 1975.
Lang, Karen. *Āryadeva's Catuḥśataka.* Copenhagen: Akademisk Forlag, 1986 and Delhi: Motilal Banarsidass.
_____."sPa tshab Nyi ma grags and the Introduction of Prāsaṅgika Madhyamaka into Tibet". In *Reflections on Tibetan Culture: Essays in Memory of Turrell Z. Wylie.* Edited by Lawrence Epstein and Richard Sherburne. Lewiston, New York: Edwin Mellen Press, 1990.
Lati Rinbochay. *Mind in Tibetan Buddhism.* Elizabeth Napper, trans. and ed. Valois, New York: Snow Lion, 1980.

Lopez, Donald. *A Study of Svātantrika*. Ithaca, New York: Snow Lion Publications, 1987.

_____. "On the Relationships of Emptiness and Dependent Arising: Some dGe-lugs-pa Views." *Tibet Journal*, Vol. XIV, No.1. Dharamsala: Library of Tibetan Works and Archives, 1989.

Murti, T.R.V. *The Central Philosophy of Buddhism*. London: Unwin Paperbacks, 1980.

Napper, Elizabeth. *Dependent-Arising and Emptiness*. Boston: Wisdom Publications, 1989.

Naudou, Jean. *Buddhists of Kaśmīr*. Delhi: Agam Kala Prakashan, 1980.

Obermiller, E. *History of Buddhism by Bu-ston*. Heidelberg: Otto Harrassowitz, 1931.

Radhakrishnan. *Indian Philosophy*. Bombay: Blackie & Son, 1977.

Roerich, George N. *The Blue Annals*. Delhi: Motilal Banarsidass, 1976.

Ruegg, David S. "The Jo nan pas: A School of Buddhist Ontologists According to the *Grub mtha' sel gyi me lon*." *Journal of the American Oriental Society* 83 (1963).

Sopa, Geshe Lhundup and Hopkins, Jeffrey. *Practice and Theory of Tibetan Buddhism*. New York: Grove, 1976. Reprinted as *Cutting through Appearances* (Ithaca: Snow Lion, 1989).

Thurman, Robert, ed. *Life and Teachings of Tsong Khapa*. Dharamsala: Library of Tibetan Works and Archives, 1982.

Tucci, Giuseppe. *Pre-Diṅnāga Buddhist Texts on Logic from Chinese Sources*. Madras: Vesta Publications, rpt. 1984.

Index